Practice Your C#

Level 1

First Edition

Plurium™ Programming Practice Series

Practice Your C# Level 1, 1st Edition

by Ayodele M. Agboola

Copyright © 2015 Ayodele M. Agboola. All rights reserved.

Published by **Plurium Press**
        www.pluriumpress.com

First Edition: November, 2015

Edition 1 Revision 1 2015/12

Edition 1 Revision 2 2017/04

ISBN-13: 978-0-9961338-0-7
ISBN-10: 0-9961338-0-1

Downloads & Errata

Errata and downloads for this book are available at www.pluriumpress.com.

To report any errors found in this book, please email the publisher at practiceyourcsharp1@pluriumpress.com.

Sales Information

For bulk purchases, or for customized variants, please contact the publisher at sales@pluriumpress.com.

Trademarks

Microsoft, Windows®, Visual Studio®, .NET, Microsoft Word®, Notepad®, C#, Visual C# are either registered trademarks or trademarks of Microsoft Corporation in the United States and/or other countries.

All other trademarks remain the property of their respective owners.

Disclaimer

All example names and such-like references used in this book are fictitious. Any likeness to any actual bearer of the reference is entirely coincidental.

Care has been taken in the preparation of this book; however, no warranty express or implied of any kind is made for the content thereof or for errors or omissions herein. No liability is assumed by the author, publisher or seller for any damages in connection with or arising out of the use of any of the content of this book.

Rights

All rights reserved. No part of this publication may be reproduced, stored or transmitted in any form without the express written permission of the publisher.

Introduction

Welcome to *Practice Your C# Level 1!* This is a book designed to, through practice, improve the knowledge, skill and confidence of the reader in C# programming. Over 900 carefully designed exercises along with their solutions are presented in this book to help achieve this end.

There are four important objectives that this book is designed to help you achieve. We want to help you *quickly* achieve the following:

(1) Attain a firm understanding of the foundations of this language
(2) Have high retention of the knowledge presented in this book,
thus increasing your (3) skill and (4) confidence in your ability to program in C# at this level and to pursue higher levels of study of this language.

There are two main means by which this book helps achieve these objectives; first by properly ordering the chapters and the contents therein and also, by our unique question structure. We explain these below.

Understanding, Retention, Skill, Confidence by Proper Chapter & Question Order

I have the following saying regarding flying airplanes; "despite the vast number of buttons in the cockpit, an airplane is easy to fly if you just learn things in the right order". When learned and understood in the right order, you will easily remember where each button is and what it does. The same concept holds true for learning C#. Therefore in this book, the presentation of the sub-topics of the language is put in the appropriate order for learning this particular language, thus aiding retention. As the reader proceeds from chapter to chapter, their knowledge and skill in C# is built a methodical fashion.

Understanding, Retention, Skill, Confidence by Optimal Question Structure

It was stated that one of the objectives of this volume is to help aid understanding and also to help aid retention of the material learnt. Before the ubiquity of the internet, a developer had to retain a high degree of knowledge (not just facts) in his head, referring to texts only when necessary. However, now, due to improper learning of and practice in the language at hand, a developer may spend a lot of time online looking for "point solutions" for problems, rather than taking the time to learn the foundation of the language properly.

So how does this volume aid understanding? How does it aid retention? How does it help speed up learning? It aids understanding, retention and speed in learning by the following structure of the exercises:

The reader is often presented one concept/method at a time per exercise

Like when we learnt the alphabet, we learned it letter by letter. Therefore, in this volume, an appropriate number of programming exercises require the use of only a single C# method as the key to the solution of the exercise. This allows the reader to focus on this single method, thus aiding understanding and memorization.

Of course, questions with multiple concepts are presented as well.

The reader is often presented with direct hints for programming questions

This is a very important feature of the exercises in this book. We explain why.

You see, if an exercise is presented on a topic with which a reader is unfamiliar or peripherally familiar, the reader will search (likely on the internet) for possible solutions. This takes time. This wastes time. In fact, for more complex topics, a reader many end up spending so much time reading potential solutions, that when he finally finds a solution he has actually forgotten how he got there and is too fatigued to actually remember the solution! It is better, as done in this volume, to have "hints" which specify the exact C# methods that feature in the solution to the problem so that the reader can spend his time profitably studying the exact methods/language features that pertain to solving the problem at hand and implementing the solution. This focus also aids retention.

Inverse question structure

There are some topics which are somewhat recondite. Instead of requiring that the reader come up with solutions to questions on such topics, completed code is presented as the question, and the reader is asked to analyze the presented solution. The intent of such exercises clearly is to teach the reader the involved topic at hand. Again this saves time and lets the user focus on learning the material instead of spending time searching at length for a solution.

The reader will find this question structure to be most helpful.

The astute reader will actually observe that while indeed this is called a practice volume, the structure of many of the solutions is as one actually teaching the C# topics presented.

Encouragement

The reader is encouraged to not see the number of exercises in this book as overwhelming, but rather as an opportunity to begin to attain mastery of the language. There was a programming book I read many years ago whose preface set my mind at ease by stating, "It isn't difficult". So I'll say this to you: "Please relax! It is actually ok!" A tip for you; if you do get stuck, just go ahead and read the answer; that is what it is there for. Also, as previously stated, a significant number of the exercises have hints which help you to determine the solution quickly and also help your retention of the material.

Target Audience

It is envisaged that this book will fulfill the needs of the beginning to early intermediate C# developer and for those seeking a hands-on review of the topics presented herein. The following usage scenarios are foreseen for this book:

- For the individual without previous experience in C#, this book is intended as a companion text to a C# programming volume to help the reader solidify their understanding, knowledge and skill in C# by way of practice exercises.
- For the returning C# programmer at this level, working through the exercises in this book will suffice as a text, given the depth and extent of the exercises and their solutions.
- The programmer who prefers to learn by practice exercises will find this to be an appropriate volume.
- The classroom instructor, who will be delighted to find that this book is a robust tool for ensuring that their students are well versed in and have a proper foundation in C# programming.

Programming Level

The contents of this volume target the C# beginner up to the early intermediate C# programmer.

Regarding C# 6.0

The latest version of C#, C# 6.0 has been released to the public as of July, 2015. This book contains an appropriate set of exercises which pertain to new features in this version of C#. Given the newness of this version, the C# 6.0 exercises in this book are explicitly noted as being of version 6.0, with the notation "**(6.0)**" appearing before these particular exercises. Also, the index contains a separate section pointing out the addressed C# 6.0 topics/features.

What this book is, what it is not

This book is a book of solved C# exercises targeting the beginning to early intermediate C# programmer. The overarching objective of this book is to ensure that the reader is skilled in the use of C# as a programming language.

All the coding exercises herein are C# console applications. In particular, the book does *not* cover graphical user interface development, the reader of course understanding that proper facility with the language itself is a necessary foundation for being able to implement complete solutions.

Structure of Contents

This book is structured in chapters, with each chapter covering a major topic (or part thereof). Overlap between topics is covered in the appropriate chapter for such.

Chapter Legend/Structure

Exercises are numbered sequentially. The question number column is uniformly on the left-hand side of the pages. The solution to each exercise appears beside or immediately below the exercise.

An *M* appearing in the question column indicates an action which must be performed manually; for example, an instruction to insert a USB stick/drive into the computer.

An *E* followed by a number in the question column indicates that this is an extra unsolved exercise given to you the reader to solve. Where these appear, they are at the end of the chapter.

How To Use This Book

The individual who is fairly new to C# is advised to go through the chapters sequentially.

A classroom instructor or the individual person who is simply refreshing their C# knowledge can go through the individual chapters in an order that best suits their needs.

What You Need To Use This Book

In order to implement the exercises in this book you need to install Microsoft Visual Studio® Express 2012 (or higher), ensuring that you install the C# components. Visual Studio 2015 is required to implement the C# 6.0 exercises. These products are freely available on the Microsoft website.

The user will also need access to the freely available Microsoft MSDN .NET online documentation.

The code for this book is downloadable from the publishers' website.

About The Author

Ayodele "Ayo" Agboola holds a degree in Electrical Engineering from the University of Waterloo in Canada. He has had the pleasure of programming over the course of 30 years, first personally and then professionally. As a professional he has worked globally in many roles, including development, project management and training, implementing software solutions of various scale for telecom service providers.

Acknowledgements

Oluwa ló ṣe èyí; ó sì jẹ́ ohun iyanu lójú wa!

And to all the people whose shared knowledge has contributed to this.

Table of Contents

Chapter 1. For Starters 1

Chapter 2. Console Handling I: Basic Output & Input 5

Chapter 3. Number Handling 9

Chapter 4. Booleans 45

Chapter 5. Strings: Basic Handling 53

Chapter 6. Conditional Processing 67

Chapter 7. Arrays 73

Chapter 8. Iterations/Loops 81

Chapter 9. Console Handling II: More on Input 95

Chapter 10. Console Handling III: Command Line Input 101

Chapter 11. The `Char` Type 105

Chapter 12. Date/Time Handling & Measurement 115

Chapter 13. Collections (Introduction) 127

Chapter 14. Computer Environment & Computer Information 135

Chapter 15. File System I: Path & Directory Handling 141

Chapter 16. File System II: File Handling 149

Chapter 17. Random Numbers 157

Chapter 18. Nullable Types 159

Chapter 19. The StringBuilder Class 165

Chapter 20. The `var` type: implicitly typed variables 171

Chapter 21. Methods (Introduction) 173

Chapter 22. Enumerations 181

Chapter 23. Types, Boxing & Unboxing 185

Chapter 24. Classes 189

Chapter 25. Interfaces (Introduction) 225

Chapter 26. Structures 227

Chapter 27. Tuples 231

Chapter 28. Passing By Reference, Passing By Value 233

Chapter 29. Operator Overloading 239

Chapter 30. Properties 241

Chapter 31. Delegates 247

Chapter 32. Exceptions 253

Chapter 33. Character Encoding 265

Chapter 34. File Streams I	273
Chapter 35. File Streams II: A Finer Look at File I/O	289
Chapter 36. Saving Your Objects to Disk: Serialization & Deserialization (Introduction)	293
Index	297

Chapter 1. For Starters

In this summary chapter, a brief set of exercises pertaining to the basic structure of C# console applications, as well as a cornucopia of basic C# programming topics are presented in order to ensure that the reader is conversant with the basic structure of a C# console application and to refresh the readers' knowledge on the topics presented.

Upon starting a new console application project in Visual C# (we will name our project `PracticeYourCSharp`), the following appears in the code window:

```csharp
using System;
using System.Collections.Generic;
using System.Linq;
using System.Text;
using System.Threading.Tasks;

namespace PracticeYourCSharp
{
  class Program
  {
    static void Main(string[] args)
    {
    }
  }
}
```

1.	With respect to the code block shown above, what do the statements: `using System;`, `using System.Collections.Generic;`, `using System.Linq;`, etc. mean?
	Each of these statements refers to a <u>namespace</u>. A namespace is a grouping of classes as well as other C# types (these other C# types include enumerations, interfaces, etc. which will be seen in later chapters). It is up to the developer of the namespace to group whatever C# types they want into a given namespace.
	A namespace can have *nested namespaces*; nested namespaces are C# type groupings that are deemed logical by the developer to group together within another namespace. That is why you see a statement like `using System.Linq`, where `System.Linq` is a nested namespace within the namespace `System`.
	So, why do you have to inform the compiler that you are `using` particular namespaces in your program? The reason is so that the compiler knows where to find the C# types that you want to use in your program and compile the namespaces containing the types in question along with your program. The namespaces whose content you are using are in effect a part of your program.
	The compiler cannot compile all existing namespaces with your program because (1) there are too many built-in namespaces and thus your compiled program would be bloated and (2) the compiler doesn't know the names of all the namespaces that you want to use because you may have created some and have to inform the compiler of their names.
	You too can create your own namespaces. In fact, it can be seen that the compiler expects that we to intend to create a namespace, giving us by default a namespace that is named the same as the project, namely `PracticeYourCSharp`. We use this namespace `PracticeYourCSharp` for our exercises in this book.
	Another benefit of the `using` statements is that is permits us to avoid having to write the fully resolved name of methods. To wit, we can write:
	`Console.WriteLine("Hello");` *instead of*
	`System.Console.WriteLine("Hello");` which is its fully resolved name (`Console` is a class in the namespace `System`).

		This benefit is afforded because we have stated that we are `using System;`. The C# compiler knows to look for `Console.WriteLine` in all of the included namespaces in order to resolve the full name of the method itself. **In summary**: a namespace is a set of C# types. You must state in your program that you are `using` any namespace whose contents you use in your application. You do so by stating that you are `using <namespace name>;` The namespaces present in the code window by default when you start a new project in Visual C# are the ones that are most commonly used.
2.		In the code block presented at the beginning of the chapter, we see the following statement: `namespace PracticeYourCSharp` What does it mean?
		It means that we are creating our own namespace that we have named `PracticeYourCSharp`. *See the answer to the preceding exercise for the definition of a namespace.*
3.		How many namespaces can there be in a single code file?
		There is no limit.
4.		In the code block presented at the beginning of the chapter, we see the statement `class Program`. What does it mean?
		This indicates that we are creating a class named `Program`. All C# code must be in a class. This is the default class name that is presented when the editor is opened. *(See Chapter 24 for the definition of a class).* We will eventually create and use a number of different classes in this book.
5.		What is the name of the method for which the compiler looks to invoke/execute when you run a program?
		`Main` Every program you want to run must always have a method named `Main` (method names are case-sensitive).
6.		Write out the different possible method declarations that the method `Main` can have.
		`Main` can only be one of the following: 1. `static void Main()` 2. `static void Main(string[] args)` 3. `static int Main()` 4. `static int Main(string[] args)` **Notes:** `Main` can only return either a value of type of `int` or nothing at all (indicated by type `void`). `Main` is always a `static` method.
7.		Apart from the method modifier `static`, what other method modifier can be used for the method `Main`?
		No other. `Main` is <u>always</u> a `static` method. Method modifiers such as `static` are covered in Chapter 24 on Classes.
8.		The code samples below are different, but fully equivalent. Explain why this is the case. ```
using System;

namespace PracticeYourCSharp
{
  class Program
  {
    static void Main(string[] args)
    {
      Console.WriteLine("Hello");
      Console.ReadKey();
    }
  }
}
``` ```
namespace PracticeYourCSharp
{
  class Program
  {
    static void Main(string[] args)
    {
      System.Console.WriteLine("Hello");
      System.Console.ReadKey();
    }
  }
}
``` |
| | | In the code sample on the left, because we have stated that we are using the `System` namespace, we do not have to give the fully resolved name of the methods from that namespace, therefore we can write `Console.WriteLine` and `Console.ReadKey`. In the sample on the right, we did not write that we are using the namespace which |

	contains the class `Console` where the methods `WriteLine` and `ReadKey` appear, and therefore we have to give the fully resolved name of the methods in the classes in the namespace in question; the fully resolved name requires the name of the namespace as the first part of the fully resolved method name.

9.	**(6.0)** The program below is fully equivalent to either of the ones in the preceding question. Explain why.
	``
	using System;
	using static System.Console;
	
	namespace PracticeYourCSharp
	{
	  class Program
	  {
	    static void Main(string[] args)
	    {
	      WriteLine("Hello");
	      ReadKey();
	    }
	  }
	}
	``

	This program uses the `using static` compiler directive, which facilitates the <u>invoking of static methods</u> in the class for which a `using static` directive has been issued without needing to put the class name in front of the name of the static methods in question. In the sample code above, the methods `WriteLine` and `ReadKey` are static methods in the class `Console` which itself is in the namespace `System`. Before the introduction of this feature, the same program would have to be written in the same way as the first sample in the preceding question. What the `using static` feature does is to help cut down on the amount of typing of the class name of static methods.

10.	In the code snippet below, we have the keyword `return`. What does this keyword do?
	``
	static void Main(string[] args)
	{
	  return;
	}
	``

	The `return` keyword, when executed, causes the immediate termination of the method in which it is run and returns control to the calling method. In the case of the method `Main` which is called by the operating system, a `return` statement in `Main` exits the program and returns control to the operating system. In summary, we can say that `return` means "exit the method that you are running now and return control back to whoever called this method".
11.	Explain what the line of code below, when placed in a method, does: ``` return (55); ```
	The code above does the following two things: 1. It passes the value `55` back to whichever method called the method in which the `return (55);` statement appears. 2. The `return` statement causes an immediate exit from the method in which it appears (thus terminating the execution of the method that it appears in), returning control back to the method which called it.
Comments	
12.	What does the string sequence `//` mean when it appears on a line in a program?
	This double forward slash indicates that whatever text comes after it on the same line is a comment, therefore the compiler should ignore it.

13.	What is the output of the following code fragment?
	``
	/*
	  Console.WriteLine("Hello");
	  Console.ReadKey();
	*/
	``

	Nothing will be output. The reason is because the whole block of code in the fragment is commented, as indicated by the starting comment delimiter `/*` and the ending comment delimiter `*/`.

		The delimited code in the question is an example of a *multi-line comment*.

A brief look at instance members & static members

The objective of the following questions is to refresh the reader on the difference between instance members and static members of a class. This is needful because we meet a number of these before we actually get to the chapter which discusses classes at length.

14.	We have the following class definition:
| | ```
class Man
{
  public static string gender="male";
  public string FirstName;
  public string LastName;
}
```  Indicate which are the static members of the class and which are the instance members. |
| | The only static member of this class is the string `gender`. This is discernible by the method modifier `static` in its definition.
The string fields `FirstName` and `LastName` are the instance members of the class. |
| 15. | Show the instantiation(creation) of an object of class man named **man01** in the method `Main`. After this, set the `FirstName` field of **man01** to "Adam", then print out the field man01.FirstName. |
| | ```
using System;

namespace PracticeYourCSharp
{
  class Man
  { // Our earlier created class Man. We put it in the same namespace as the class Program
    public static string gender="male";
    public string FirstName;
    public string LastName;
  }

  class Program
  {
    static void Main(string[] args)
    {
      Man man01 = new Man(); // We have now created an object named man01 of the class Man.
      man01.FirstName = "Adam"; // FirstName is a "public" field so we can set it in any method
      Console.WriteLine("{0}", man01.FirstName);
      Console.ReadKey();
    }
  }
}
``` |
| 16. | What is the difference between a static class member and an instance member? |
| | A static class member is a member which "belongs" to the class, whereas an instance member "belongs" to the individual instances of the class.
A static class member is invoked relative to the class, whereas an instance member is invoked relative to an instantiated object. We can see this by the following example 4-line code fragment that uses the earlier defined class `Man`: |

Code	Commentary
`Man man01 = new Man();`	instantiation of an object named man01 of class Man
`man01.FirstName = "John";`	observe that the instance field `FirstName` is called relative to an object instance
`man01.LastName = "Doe";`	same observation as above applies to this instance field too
`Console.Write(Man.gender);`	observe how the `static string gender` is accessed; it is accessed relative to the class name (Man in this case), NOT relative to an object name. It is <u>NOT</u> accessible as `man01.gender` (you can try it in order to see the result), it is always accessed relative to the class. Whatever is in the static members of a class applies to all of the instances of the class.

Chapter 2. Console Handling I: Basic Output & Input

A significant number of non-graphical programs receive user input from the command line. In this chapter, exercises are presented with which the reader can practice and sharpen their skills in basic console input and output, in particular using the `Console.WriteLine`, `Console.ReadLine` and `Console.ReadKey` methods. Basic use of `string` variables and string output is also covered in this chapter, including the use of certain special characters. Basic composite formatting is also covered.

The key classes utilized in this chapter are `Console` and `String`.

(Note that Chapter 9 has further exercises on this topic; however knowledge of the topics in the intervening chapters is a prerequisite for the exercises in Chapter 9).

1.	What is the difference in output between the `Console.Write` statement and the `Console.WriteLine` statement?
	`Console.Write` outputs the data passed to it to the standard output stream (which by default is the console) and does <u>not</u> output a line terminator afterwards, whereas `Console.WriteLine` outputs both the data passed to it as well as the current line terminator.
2.	What is the character sequence that causes the program to place a new-line in the output of a string?
	`\n`
3.	What is the character sequence that causes the program to place a tab in the output of a string?
	`\t`
4.	What is the function of the method `Console.ReadKey`?
	`Console.ReadKey` pauses execution of the program that is being run in order to wait for a single key-press from the user (the keypress must be of a character key or a function key). Upon receipt of the keypress, program execution continues. To be more precise, if you are running a multi-threaded program (not in the scope of this book), `Console.ReadKey` pauses execution of the program thread in which it is invoked in order to receive the keypress. If the single keypress is actually to be captured for use, `Console.ReadKey` can copy the keypress to an object instance of type `ConsoleKeyInfo`, where the key that is entered is stored in the variable `<ConsoleKeyInfo>.KeyChar`. **Note:** *Throughout all of the programs in this book, ensure that you add the statement* `Console.ReadKey();` *to the end of the program so that you can observe your output in the console window and close it when you choose, otherwise, when the program has run to completion it will automatically close the console window without giving you enough time to observe its contents.*
5.	Write a program which outputs to the console the text *"Hello World"* followed by a newline character. Add the line of code `Console.ReadKey();` to the end of the program to ensure that the program waits for a keystroke before it closes the console window.

	<pre>using System;
	namespace PracticeYourCSharp
	{
	  class Program
	  {
	    static void Main(string[] args)
	    {
	      Console.WriteLine("Hello World");
	      Console.ReadKey();
	    }
	  }
	}</pre> -or- <pre>using System;
	namespace PracticeYourCSharp
	{
	  class Program
	  {
	    static void Main(string[] args)
	    {
	      Console.Write("Hello World\n");
	      Console.ReadKey();
	    }
	  }
	}</pre>

	\multicolumn{2}{l	}{**Note:** You see that a `Console.WriteLine` automatically adds a line terminator to the output. If you choose to use `Console.Write`, then you yourself have to add the newline character '\n' to the data being output in order to get the same output as `Console.WriteLine`.}
6.	Write a program which outputs the text *"Hello World"*, inclusive of the double quotes, to the console. *Hint: use the \ escape sequence.*	```using System;

namespace PracticeYourCSharp
{
  class Program
  {
    static void Main(string[] args)
    {
      Console.Write("\"Hello World\"");
      Console.ReadKey();
    }
  }
}``` **Note:** See the *escaping* of each double quote using the \ in each instance. |
| 7. | Write a program which outputs the exact phrase "*Hello World\n*" inclusive of the double quotes and the "\n". *Hint: use the @ escape character.* | ```using System;

namespace PracticeYourCSharp
{
  class Program
  {
    static void Main(string[] args)
    {
      Console.WriteLine(@"Hello World\n");
      Console.ReadKey();
    }
  }
}``` |
| \multicolumn{3}{|l|}{**Outputting from a variable**} |
| 8. | I have two hardcoded `string` variables defined as follows: `string firstName = "John";` `string lastName  = "Doe";` Write a program which will output these two `string` variables to the console on the same line with a single space in-between them. | ```using System;

namespace PracticeYourCSharp
{
  class Program
  {
    static void Main(string[] args)
    {
      string firstName = "John";
      string lastName = "Doe";

      Console.WriteLine(firstName + " " + lastName);
      Console.ReadKey();
    }
  }
}``` |
| 9. | Redo the exercise above, using *composite formatting* to achieve the same output. | ```using System;

namespace PracticeYourCSharp
{
  class Program
  {
    static void Main(string[] args)
    {
      string firstName = "John";
      string lastName = "Doe";

      Console.WriteLine("{0} {1}", firstName, lastName);
      Console.ReadKey();
    }
  }
}``` |

		Note: We will generally use composite formatting in this book.
| 10. | **(6.0)** Redo the exercise above, using *string interpolation* to achieve the same output. | ```csharp
using System;

namespace PracticeYourCSharp
{
  class Program
  {
    static void Main(string[] args)
    {
      string firstName = "John";
      string lastName = "Doe";

      Console.WriteLine($"{firstName} {lastName}");
      Console.ReadKey();
    }
  }
}
``` |
| 11. | I have two string variables defined as follows:<br>`string firstName = "John";`<br>`string lastName = "Doe";`<br>Concatenate these strings, with a space in-between them, putting the resulting concatenation into a single `string` variable named `fullName` and output the concatenated string to the console. | ```csharp
using System;

namespace PracticeYourCSharp
{
  class Program
  {
    static void Main(string[] args)
    {
      string firstName = "John";
      string lastName = "Doe";

      string fullName = firstName + " " + lastName;
      Console.WriteLine(fullName);
      Console.ReadKey();
    }
  }
}
``` |
Console Input		
12.	What is the function of the method `Console.ReadLine`?	
	It waits for keyboard input from the user. When the user hits the return key (thus signifying the end of the input), whatever the user has typed so far is returned to the program for use as desired. For example, if we have the line of code `string s1 = Console.ReadLine();` in our program, then whatever string that the user types in will be put into the `string` variable `s1`. Contrast this with the method `Console.ReadKey` which only takes a single keypress, does not require a return key press and stores its received data in a different kind of object.	
| 13. | Ask the user for their first name and then output to the console the following string:<br>*Your first name is <entered string>* | ```csharp
using System;

namespace PracticeYourCSharp
{
  class Program
  {
    static void Main(string[] args)
    {
      // Declare a string variable that will receive the value
      // that is entered from the console
      string firstName = "";

      Console.Write("What is your first name? ");
      firstName = Console.ReadLine();

      Console.WriteLine("Your first name is " + firstName);
      //alternate output lines using composite formatting and
      //string interpolation are shown commented out below.
      //Console.WriteLine("Your first name is {0}", firstName);
      //Console.WriteLine($"Your first name is {firstName}");
      Console.ReadKey();
``` |
```

		`      }`
		`   }`
		`}`
| 14. | Ask the user for their first name and then for their last name. Using this input, output the following statement to the console:<br><br>*Your full name is &lt;first name&gt; &lt;last name&gt;.* | ```
using System;

namespace PracticeYourCSharp
{
   class Program
   {
      static void Main(string[] args)
      {
         // Declare string variables that will receive the values
         string firstName = "";
         string lastName = "";

         Console.Write("What is your first name please? ");
         firstName = Console.ReadLine();
         Console.Write("What is your last name please? ");
         lastName = Console.ReadLine();

         Console.WriteLine("Your full name is {0} {1}.",
                           firstName, lastName);
         Console.ReadKey();
      }
   }
}
``` |
| 15. | Name the three different methods of forming output strings in C# as of this version (6.0). Show an example of each. | |
| | The three different methods respectively are:<br>1. String concatenation<br>2. Composite formatting<br>3. String interpolation (newly introduced in C# 6.0)<br><br>These can be seen by the following example: If we want to output the following statement, *"Your name is `<firstName> <lastName>`"*, where `firstName` and `lastName` are string variables, then we get the following line of code for each output mechanism method respectively:<br><br>```
Console.WriteLine("Your name is " + firstName + " " + lastName);
Console.WriteLine("Your name is {0} {1}", firstName, lastName);
Console.WriteLine($"Your name is {firstName} {lastName}");
``` | |

Chapter 3. Number Handling

This chapter offers extensive coverage of the topic of number handling in C#. Your knowledge of numerical types in C# and operations thereon is exercised and enhanced by the wide-ranging set of exercises that are presented in this chapter.

Key topics on which exercises are presented in this chapter include knowledge of various built-in numerical types, appropriate selection of numerical types as well as computation exercises with built-in numerical operators as well as the numerical methods of the class Math.

Beyond the topics noted above, exercises on the usage of constants, the numerical classes BigInteger and Complex, overflow conditions, the checked keyword, infinity handling, hexadecimal numbers, number base conversion, logical and bitwise operations, increment, decrement and shorthand numerical operators are also included. A robust set of exercises on the formatting of numerical output is also presented.

1.	List the different integer types available in C#.	The different integer types are byte, sbyte, short, ushort, int, uint, long, ulong and BigInteger.
int		
2.	What is the minimum value supported by the C# **int** type?	-2,147,483,648
3.	What is the maximum value supported by the C# **int** type?	2,147,483,647
4.	How many bytes are used to represent an **int** in C#?	4 bytes
5.	Write a line of code to show the declaration and initialization of an **int** variable named firstInteger with the value 5.	int firstInteger = 5;
6.	Using the operator **default**, write a program which initializes an **int** variable named integerDefault to the default value for integers and prints the value of this variable out to the console.	

	``
	using System;
	
	namespace PracticeYourCSharp
	{
	  class Program
	  {
	    static void Main(string[] args)
	    {
	      int integerDefault = default(int); // Note the use of the operator default
	      Console.WriteLine("The default value of an int is {0}.", integerDefault);
	      // In C# 6.0 you can write the above line as follows (using string interpolation)
	      // Console.WriteLine($"The default value of an int is {integerDefault}.");
	      Console.ReadKey();
	    }
	  }
	}
	``	

unsigned integer		
7.	State the range of values that the type unsigned integer (**uint**) supports.	minimum = 0 maximum = $2^{32} - 1$ = 4,294,967,295 *Observe that it only represents non-negative integers.*
8.	How many bytes are used to represent a **uint**?	4 bytes Note that this is the same number of bytes as an **int**, it is just that it is used to represent a different range of values.
9.	Write a line of code showing the declaration and initialization of a **uint** variable named firstUInt with the	uint firstUInt = 5001;

		value 5001.
10.	What is the name of the operator that can be used to determine the default value that C# sets value types to?	
	`default` (this operator has been used earlier).	
11.	Write a program which initializes a `uint` variable named `uintDefault` to the default value for unsigned integers. Print out the value of the variable to the console.	
| | ```
using System;

namespace PracticeYourCSharp
{
  class Program
  {
    static void Main(string[] args)
    {
      uint uintDefault = default(uint); // Note again the use of the operator default
      Console.WriteLine("The default value of a uint is {0}.", uintDefault);
      // In C# 6.0 you can write the above line as follows (using string interpolation)
      // Console.WriteLine($"The default value of a uint is {uintDefault}.");
      Console.ReadKey();
    }
  }
}
``` | |
byte		
12.	Describe the C# **byte** type. In particular, describe the number of bytes required to contain a `byte` and the range of supported values for a `byte`.	
	The `byte` type in C# is represented by a single byte(i.e. eight bits). Eight bits can represent a range of $2^8 = 256$ numbers. The range of values that the `byte` type in C# represents is 0 to 255.	
13.	Write a program which declares and initializes a `byte` variable named `firstByte` to the value 122 and then prints out the value of `firstByte` to the console.	
| | ```
using System;

namespace PracticeYourCSharp
{
  class Program
  {
    static void Main(string[] args)
    {
      byte firstByte = 122;
      Console.WriteLine("The value of firstByte is {0}.", firstByte);
      // In C# 6.0 you can write the above line as follows (using string interpolation)
      // Console.WriteLine($"The value of firstByte is {firstByte}.");
      Console.ReadKey();
    }
  }
}
``` | |
| 14. | Write a program which initializes a `byte` variable named `byteDefault` with the default value of a `byte` and prints out its value to the console. | |
| | ```
using System;

namespace PracticeYourCSharp
{
  class Program
  {
    static void Main(string[] args)
    {
      byte byteDefault = default(byte);
      Console.WriteLine("The default value of a byte is {0}.", byteDefault);
      // In C# 6.0 you can write the above line as follows (using string interpolation)
      // Console.WriteLine($"The default value of a byte is {byteDefault}.");
      Console.ReadKey();
    }
``` | |
```

	`    }` `}`	

	signed byte	
15.	Describe the signed byte(**sbyte**) type. In particular describe the number of bytes required to contain an `sbyte`, as well as the range of values that an `sbyte` can represent in C#.	
	A signed byte (**sbyte**) in C# is an integer type which occupies the same space as a **byte** (8 bits) and thus can represent a range of $2^8 = 256$ numbers; however the range of values that it represents is -128 to 127. An easy way to remember what a signed byte is is to think of it as a **byte** which can support a <u>sign</u> (i.e. + *or* -).	
16.	Write a program which declares and initializes a signed byte variable named `firstSignedByte` to the value -115 and then prints the variable to the console.	
| | ```
using System;

namespace PracticeYourCSharp
{
  class Program
  {
    static void Main(string[] args)
    {
      sbyte firstSignedByte = -115;
      Console.WriteLine("The value of firstSignedByte is {0}.", firstSignedByte);
      Console.ReadKey();
    }
  }
}
``` | |
| 17. | Write a program which initializes a signed byte variable named `sbyteDefault` with the default value of a signed byte and prints the value of this variable out to the console. | |
| | ```
using System;

namespace PracticeYourCSharp
{
  class Program
  {
    static void Main(string[] args)
    {
      sbyte sbyteDefault = default(sbyte);
      Console.WriteLine("The default value of a signed byte is {0}.", sbyteDefault);
      Console.ReadKey();
    }
  }
}
``` | |

	short integer	
18.	State the range of values that the type short integer **(short)** supports.	-32,768 to 32,767 (This is the range -2^{15} *to* $2^{15} - 1$)
19.	How many bytes are used to represent a short?	2 bytes
20.	Write a program which initializes a `short` variable named `firstShort` to the value 10,000 and then prints `firstShort` out to the console.	
| | ```
using System;

namespace PracticeYourCSharp
{
  class Program
  {
    static void Main(string[] args)
    {
      short firstShort = 10000;
      Console.WriteLine("The value of the variable firstShort={0}.", firstShort);
``` | |
```

	``` Console.ReadKey(); } } } ```	
21.	Write a program which initializes a **short** variable named **shortDefault** to the default value for a **short** and prints the variable out to the console.	
	``` using System; namespace PracticeYourCSharp { class Program { static void Main(string[] args) { short shortDefault = default(short); Console.WriteLine("The default value of a short = {0}.", shortDefault); Console.ReadKey(); } } } ```	
ushort		
22.	What is the number range supported by an unsigned short integer (**ushort**)?	0 to 65,535 This is the range 0 to $2^{16} - 1$
23.	How many bytes are used to represent an unsigned short integer (**ushort**)?	2 bytes, just like a **short**, however the 2 bytes represent a different range of numbers to what a **short** represents.
24.	Write a program which initializes a **ushort** variable named **firstUShort** to the value 64,000 and then prints the variable out to the console.	
	``` using System; namespace PracticeYourCSharp { class Program { static void Main(string[] args) { ushort firstUShort = 64000; Console.WriteLine("The value of firstUShort={0}.", firstUShort); Console.ReadKey(); } } } ```	
25.	Write a program which initializes a **ushort** variable named **ushortDefault** to the default value for unsigned short integers and then prints the variable out to the console.	
	``` using System; namespace PracticeYourCSharp { class Program { static void Main(string[] args) { ushort ushortDefault = default(ushort); Console.WriteLine("The default of a ushort={0}.", ushortDefault); Console.ReadKey(); } } } ```	
long		
26.	State the range of values that the type	-9,223,372,036,854,775,808 to 9,223,372,036,854,775,807

	long integer (**long**) supports.	This is the range -2^{63} to $2^{63} - 1$.
27.	How many bytes are used to represent a **long**?	8 bytes
28.	Write a program which initializes a **long** variable named firstLong with the value 7,000,000,000 and then prints the variable out to the console.	
| | ```
using System;

namespace PracticeYourCSharp
{
  class Program
  {
    static void Main(string[] args)
    {
      long firstLong = 7000000000;
      Console.WriteLine("The value of firstLong={0}.", firstLong);
      Console.ReadKey();
    }
  }
}
``` | |
| 29. | Write a program which initializes a **long** variable named longDefault to the default value for long integers and then prints longDefault out to the console. | |
| | ```
using System;

namespace PracticeYourCSharp
{
  class Program
  {
    static void Main(string[] args)
    {
      long longDefault = default(long);
      Console.WriteLine("The default value of a long ={0}.", longDefault);
      Console.ReadKey();
    }
  }
}
``` | |
unsigned long		
30.	State the range of values that the type unsigned long integer (**ulong**) supports.	0 to 18,446,744,073,709,551,615 This is the range 0 to $2^{64} - 1$.
31.	How many bytes are used to represent an unsigned long integer (**ulong**)?	8 bytes
| 32. | Write a program which initializes the **ulong** variable firstULong to the value 11,446,744,073,709,551,113 and prints firstULong out to the console. | ```
using System;

namespace PracticeYourCSharp
{
  class Program
  {
    static void Main(string[] args)
    {
      ulong firstULong = 11446744073709551113;
      Console.WriteLine("firstULong={0}.", firstULong);
      Console.ReadKey();
    }
  }
}
``` |
| 33. | Write a program which initializes the **ulong** variable ulongDefault to the default value for a **ulong** and then prints ulongDefault out to the console. | |
| | using System; | |
```

| | ```
namespace PracticeYourCSharp
{
  class Program
  {
    static void Main(string[] args)
    {
      ulong ulongDefault = default(ulong);
      Console.WriteLine("Default value of ulong={0}.", ulongDefault);
      Console.ReadKey();
    }
  }
}
``` | |
Floating Point Numbers (`float`, `double`, `decimal`)		
34.	What is the range of allowable values for the type `float`?	-3.402823×10^{38} to 3.402823×10^{38}
35.	How many bytes are used to represent a `float`?	4 bytes
36.	What is the precision of a `float`?	7 significant digits.
37.	Why is a `float` also described as a *single*?	`float` really refers to what is called a "single precision floating point number", which is a floating point number format that is designed to occupy only 4 bytes.
38.	Write a program which initializes a single precision floating point variable named `firstFloat` with the value 7.919876542 and prints its value out to the console. Note and explain the difference between the initialized value and the value that is printed out.	
| | ```
using System;

namespace PracticeYourCSharp
{
  class Program
  {
    static void Main(string[] args)
    {
      float firstFloat = 7.919876542F; // Note the F at the end
      Console.WriteLine("firstFloat={0}.", firstFloat);
      Console.ReadKey();
    }
  }
}
```<br>**Observation/Explanation:** The output is `7.919877` not the number `7.919876542` that was input! The reason is that the `float` type only supports 7 significant digits. Also note that the compiler rounded up (not truncated) the value that was input. | |
39.	Why is there a suffix/postfix `F` applied to the value assigned to a `float`?	
	The reason is because C# presumes that any floating point number entered is of type `double` *(double means "double precision floating point number")* unless the number is explicitly indicated to be a single precision number as indicated by the postfix `F`. As an experiment, you can modify the code above by removing the `F` from the number and attempt to recompile the program.	
40.	Write a program that prints out the minimum, maximum and default values of the `float` type. *Hint:* `float.MinValue`, `float.MaxValue` *and the operator* `default`.	
| | ```
using System;

namespace PracticeYourCSharp
{
  class Program
  {
    static void Main(string[] args)
    {
      float floatMin = float.MinValue;
``` | |
```

	``
	float floatMax = **float.MaxValue**;
	float floatDefault = **default(float)**;
	Console.WriteLine("Minimum value of a float={0}.", floatMin);
	Console.WriteLine("Maximum value of a float={0}.", floatMax);
	Console.WriteLine("Default value of a float={0}.", floatDefault);
	Console.ReadKey();
	}
	}
	}
	``
41.	Write a program which prints out the smallest positive **float** that C# supports.
	``
	using System;
	namespace PracticeYourCSharp
	{
	class Program
	{
	static void Main(string[] args)
	{
	float floatSmallest = **Single.Epsilon**; //recall that a float is also called a single
	Console.WriteLine("smallest possible positive float ={0}.", floatSmallest);
	Console.ReadKey();
	}
	}
	}
	``

double

42.	What is the numerical range supported by the type **double**?	$-1.79769313486232 \times 10^{308}$ to $1.79769313486232 \times 10^{308}$
43.	Which constant represents the minimum value of the type **double**?	`Double.MinValue`
44.	Which constant represents the maximum value of the type **double**?	`Double.MaxValue`
45.	How many bytes are used to represent a **double**?	8 bytes
46.	What is the precision of a **double**?	15 significant digits. (contrast this with the precision of a **float**/**single**).
47.	Write a line of code that shows the declaration and initialization of a double precision floating point variable named `firstDouble` with the value $5.4857990943 \times 10^{-4}$.	`double firstDouble = 5.4857990943E-4;`
48.	Write a program which prints out the minimum, maximum and default values of a **double**.	
	``	
	using System;	
	namespace PracticeYourCSharp	
	{	
	class Program	
	{	
	static void Main(string[] args)	
	{	
	double doubleMin = Double.MinValue;	
	double doubleMax = Double.MaxValue;	
	double doubleDefault = default(double);	
	Console.WriteLine("Minimum value of a double={0}.", doubleMin);	
	Console.WriteLine("Maximum value of a double={0}.", doubleMax);	
	Console.WriteLine("Default value of a double={0}.", doubleDefault);	
	Console.ReadKey();	
	}	
	}	
	}	
	``	

decimal

49.	What is the range of the type `decimal`?	-79,228,162,514,264,337,593,543,950,335 to 79,228,162,514,264,337,593,543,950,335 which is approximately -7.9×10^{28} to 7.9×10^{28}
50.	Which constant represents the minimum supported value of the `decimal` type?	`Decimal.MinValue`
51.	Which constant represents the maximum supported value of the type `decimal`?	`Decimal.MaxValue`
52.	How many bytes are used to represent a `decimal`?	16 bytes *(128 bits)*
53.	What is the precision of the type `decimal`?	28 significant digits

54. Write a program which initializes a `decimal` variable named `firstDecimal` with the value `10973731.568527333` and prints the variable out to the console.

```
using System;

namespace PracticeYourCSharp
{
  class Program
  {
    static void Main(string[] args)
    {
      decimal firstDecimal = 10973731.568527333m;
      Console.WriteLine("firstDecimal={0}.", firstDecimal);
      Console.ReadKey();
    }
  }
}
```

Note: Note the postfix **m** applied to the value being assigned to the decimal variable in question. This is necessary when assigning a value to a decimal variable.
(*Tip:* think of **m** as "money" as this type due to its high precision and its internal representation in number base 10 is preferred for representing monetary values).

55. Write a program which prints out the minimum, maximum and default values of the `decimal` type.

```
using System;

namespace PracticeYourCSharp
{
  class Program
  {
    static void Main(string[] args)
    {
      decimal decimalMin = Decimal.MinValue;
      decimal decimalMax = Decimal.MaxValue;
      decimal decimalDefault = default(Decimal);
      Console.WriteLine("Minimum value of a decimal={0}.", decimalMin);
      Console.WriteLine("Maximum value of a decimal={0}.", decimalMax);
      Console.WriteLine("Default value of a decimal={0}.", decimalDefault);
      Console.ReadKey();
    }
  }
}
```

56. Why is the type `decimal` advised for financial calculations?

For at least the following two reasons:
1. It has a higher number of significant digits than other number types.
2. It is internally represented in number base 10 *(very important)* and thus is not subject to rounding errors that might occur when a number is first converted by the computer to number base 2 for computation purposes and then back to base 10 for utilization by the end-user as with other number types.

57. Why is a `decimal` number slower for the computer to process than an equivalent integer?

The computer processes numbers of type `decimal` slower than it would process an equivalent integer because the natural number base of computers is base 2 and the integer types are represented internally in that base, whereas

	numbers of type decimal are stored and processed in a different base (base 10 in this case) which is not natural to the computer.	
58.	Write the different signed numerical integer types in order of size, from smallest to largest.	`sbyte`, `short`, `int`, `long`
Numerical suffixes		
59.	What are the suffixes to apply to numerical values to indicate what type they are? In particular list the suffixes for each of `uint`, `long`, `ulong`, `float`, `double` and `decimal`.	`uint` U `long` L `ulong` UL `float` (also known as single) F `double` D `decimal` M **Note:** These suffixes are case insensitive.
Decide which number type best represents the kind of number indicated in the question.		
60.	Which type would be best to represent the salary of an individual?	The type `decimal`. The reasons are: Monetary values are always best represented by variables of type `decimal` because `decimal` is represented internally in number base 10, rather than the number base 2 of most other number types and thus it is not subject to errors that may happen due to conversion from the natural number base 10 of the entered number to base 2 for computation and then back to base 10 for presentation to the user. Also, `decimal` is a high precision type (28 significant places) that is appropriate for computations involving monetary values.
61.	Which type would be best to represent the aggregate salary over 20 years of the salaries of a company which has 50,000 employees?	The type `decimal` would be best because we are representing a monetary value and also because it has high precision (28 significant places).
62.	Which type is sufficient to handle the age of a person?	The type `byte` is sufficient (unless you are interested in fractions of years as well). The reasons for this are: 1. The age of a person never goes below 0. 2. An unsigned byte has a maximum value of 255; that is a reasonable upper limit for lifetimes these days. Note though that while indeed an unsigned byte is sufficient in this case, in practical usage the `int` type is often used for any integer value that is smaller than a `long`.
63.	The population of the world is currently ~7.2 billion people. Which type should be used to represent this?	The type `ulong` is an appropriate type in this case. The reasons for this are: 1. Human beings are integral units. 2. The count of human being is always non-negative. 3. This is the closest type that can contain at least that number of people.
64.	The area of a country is best represented by which type?	The type `decimal`. The base 10 precision afforded by the type `decimal` is appropriate for such an important matter as the area of a country and also, the range of the `decimal` type can support the value in question.
65.	To count the number of siblings you have, which type would be the most likely candidate?	A `byte` will do. The reasons for this are: 1. Human beings are integral units. 2. Chances are no one has up to 255 siblings!
66.	Which type is best to represent the Planck constant which is $6.626\,068\,9633 \times 10^{-34}$?	The type `double` because this number has 11 significant digits and `double` supports up to 15 significant digits.
67.	The speed of light is precisely defined as	A `uint`, or even an `int`, because this number is an integer

	299 792 458 m/s. Which type would be sufficient to represent it?	of approximately ~300 million which is less than the ~2.1 billion that an `int` supports.
68.	The Rydberg constant has a value of 1.0973731568539 x 10^7. Propose which type is best to represent it.	A `double` because this number has 14 significant digits and `double` supports up to 15 significant digits.
69.	The electron magnetic moment to Bohr magneton ratio has a value of -1.001 159 652 1859. Which type best represents it?	A `double` suffices because this number has 14 significant digits and `double` supports up to 15 significant digits.
70.	The electron g factor is -2.002 319 304 3718. Which type best represents it?	A `double` suffices because this number has 14 significant digits and `double` supports up to 15 significant digits.
71.	Electron g factor uncertainty is 0.000 000 000 0075. Which type best represents it?	A `double` suffices because this has 13 significant digits and `double` supports up to 15 significant digits.
72.	The value of Coulomb's constant is 8.9875517873681764×10^9. Which type best represents it?	A `decimal`. This number has 17 significant digits and only `decimal` has enough significant digits (28) to support such a value.

Casting

73.	Explain the concept of *casting*.

Casting is a language feature wherewith you can force the compiler to take a copy of the contents of a variable and convert the copy to the format of another type.

For example, I can do the following:
```
int a = 50;
short b = (short)a;
```
Which means, *give me a copy of* a *that has been converted into the internal format and space of a short (note that* a *itself is not changed)*.

We elucidate further using `short` and `int`; a `short` is represented in 2 bytes and an `int` in 4 bytes. It is reasonable to say that any `int` value which is less than or equal to the width of a short (i.e. an `int` whose actual value is between -32,768 and 32,767) can legally fit into a `short`. However, we have to explicitly inform the compiler that we do indeed want to copy the contents of the `int` in question into a `short`.

Note that you can actually still cast a higher width type whose contents are greater than the width of a lower width type into the lower width type; for example you can cast an `int` whose value is greater than 32,767 into a `short`; while indeed the value in question cannot fit into the space of a `short`, the compiler will cast the value, however the value will be distorted, i.e. wrong, since you cannot fit something of a higher actual width into a smaller space properly.

Casting also pertains to objects; you can cast an object of a given class into a variable of any of its ancestor classes. This ability is facilitated by the concept of polymorphism. We see examples of this in the chapter on classes.

The concepts of *boxing* and *unboxing* can be seen as a special type of casting. We address the topic of boxing and unboxing in a later chapter.

74.	Why would you want to cast variables?

You would want to cast variables in scenarios where you want the contents of a cast*ed* variable to be put into a variable of a different type.

For example, if I have an integer `a=10` and given how small it is, I want to put it into a variable of type `byte` (which supports values from 0 to 255), I would cast it as follows:
```
byte c=(byte)a;
```
This line is saying *take a copy of the contents of* `int` a *and stuff them into* the format of a `byte` *as best as you can*.

If for example I have to add an `int` and a `long` and want the resultant value to be put into a `int`, due to the fact that the output variable has a smaller width than at least one of the input variables, the input variables that are larger than the output variable have to be cast to the width of the output variable. See the following example:

```
    long a=10; int b=50;
    int result = (int)a + b;
```

Some casts are more dramatic. For example, the `char` type (which represents characters) can be cast into an integer representation. For example:

```
char letter = 'A';
int integerEquivalent = (int)letter;
```

With this cast, you are now able to facilitate the sorting of characters because they have an explicit numerical representation, which lends itself to ordering by magnitude.

You can also cast objects. For example, if I have the following object of a class named `Road`:

```
Road x = new Road();
```

If I desire, I can for example cast it to an object of the ultimate object ancestor class `object` as follows:

```
object y = (object)x;
```

(The casting of an object to any of its ancestor classes is made feasible by the concept of polymorphism)

I can cast `y` back to an object of class `Road` as follows:

```
Road z = (Road)y;
```

Note that you *will* lose data in casting if you try to cast a variable which contains a higher value than what the type of the target variable can support. For example if we have the following scenario:

```
int var01 = 75000;
short var02 = (short)var01;
```

Because the value of the variable `var01` exceeds the maximum for a `short`, `var02` definitely will not contain 75,000, but rather a distorted value.

---

75. What is <u>implicit casting</u>?

Implicit casting is a scenario where, given the operation at hand, the compiler sees it fit to silently cast the contents of a variable of a given type to a more appropriate type that it is safe to cast the given type to.

For example, if I wanted to add an `int` to a `long` and put the result into a `long`, the code would look like the following:

```
long a=10; int b = 50;
long result = a + b;
```

In order to perform this computation, the compiler has to make the contents of both `a` and `b` the same type; in this case the compiler will simply silently cast `b` to the wider type `long` (note that it doesn't change `b` itself it just takes a *casted* value of b) and adds it to `a` to obtain `result`.

There would not be any ill-effects since an `int` is of smaller range than the target output variable (a `long` in this case).

Now, if I had the following scenario where `result` is an `int`:

```
long a=10; int b=50;
int result = a + b;
```

The compiler will not implicitly cast the variable `a` to an `int`. Why not? Because casting a given type (`long` in this case) to a smaller type can potentially result in the loss of data. Therefore, in this case, the compiler will insist that you do the casting of the variable `a` yourself if that is what you really want, requiring you to explicitly write the following:

```
int result = (int)a + b;
```

---

76. What is the problem with this program?

```
using System;

namespace PracticeYourCSharp
{
    class Program
    {
```

It will *not* compile. The reason for the non-compilation is that when adding `short` or `int` values, C# converts the values being added to `int`, thus resulting in an `int` result. This conversion by C# is necessary because C# does not define the mathematical operators for any number type smaller than an `int`.

| | ```
    static void Main(string[] args)
    {
      short a = 5;
      short b = 2;
      short result;

      result = a + b;

      Console.WriteLine("Result = {0}.",
                        result);
      Console.ReadKey();
    }
  }
}
``` | To get this to compile, you have to do either of the following:<br><br>(1) result should be declared as an int<br>*or*<br>(2) result = (short)(a+b); that is, you have to cast the result of the computation to the desired type (in this case, a short). |
| 77. | Write a program to multiply the following two ushort values (i=250; j=3). Put the result into a ushort and print the result out to the console. | |
| | ```
using System;

namespace PracticeYourCSharp
{
  class Program
  {
    static void Main(string[] args)
    {
      ushort i = 20; ushort j = 3;
      ushort z; // We will use this variable for output

      z = (ushort)(i * j); // Cast for the same reason as the preceding question
      Console.WriteLine("The value is: {0}.", z);
    }
  }
}
``` | |
| 78. | Write a program which multiplies the following two ushort values (i=250; j=300), puts the result into a ushort and prints the result out to the console. | |
| | ```
using System;

namespace PracticeYourCSharp
{
  class Program
  {
    static void Main(string[] args)
    {
      ushort i = 250; ushort j = 300;

      ushort result = (ushort)(i * j);
      Console.WriteLine("The value is: {0}", result);
      Console.ReadKey();
    }
  }
}
``` | |
| | **Note:** This will print out a value of **9464** instead of **75000**! The reason is because the resultant value is greater than **ushort.Max** (which = 65535) and thus the result of casting a 4 byte integer value of **75000** to a ushort (which has a width of 2 bytes) yields **9464** which is not want we want at all. We have two options to avoid such behavior. These are:
  1. Always use the appropriately sized type for your calculations.
    or
  2. Use the **checked** keyword to ensure that an exception is triggered when a computation goes out of bounds. | |
| 79. | Write a program to multiply the following two ushort variables (i=250; j=300). Put the result into an int and print the result out to the console. | |
```

Chapter 3: Number Handling

```
using System;
namespace PracticeYourCSharp
{
  class Program
  {
    static void Main(string[] args)
    {
      ushort i = 250; ushort j = 300;

      int z = i * j;
      Console.WriteLine("The value is: {0}", z);
      Console.ReadKey();
    }
  }
}
```

Note: The result here could be stored successfully in a different type (`int` in this case) without any negative impact because the target type for the result is an `int` and as previously stated, in C#, computations done with respect to a `short` or an `int` result in an `int`.

Constants

80. What is a constant (`const`) in C#?

A constant is a variable with a hardcoded and immutable value. For example, in the class `Math`, there are the constants `PI` and `E`.

You define constants inside their respective classes as follows:

```
class <class name>
{
  <access level> const <field type> <field name> = <value>;
}
```

In the class `Math` for example, the constants `PI` and `E` are declared as:

```
class Math
{
  public const double PI = 3.14159265358979323846; // See the use of the keyword const
  public const double E =  2.7182818284590452354;
}
```

Note: Note that constants are relative to a given class. Therefore, you access `PI` in the class `Math` as **Math.PI** in your code.

81. Write a program to print out the value of the built-in mathematical constant **PI**.
Hint: `Math.PI`

```
using System;
namespace PracticeYourCSharp
{
  class Program
  {
    static void Main(string[] args)
    {
      Console.WriteLine(Math.PI);
      Console.ReadKey();
    }
  }
}
```

82. Write a program to print out the value of the built-in mathematical constant *e*.

```
using System;
namespace PracticeYourCSharp
{
  class Program
  {
    static void Main(string[] args)
    {
      Console.WriteLine(Math.E);
      Console.ReadKey();
```

		`      }`
		`    }`
		`}`

83.	Write a line of code each to show the implementation of Coulomb's constant and the Rydberg constant as public constants.	`public const decimal coulombs = 8.9875517873681764e9m;` `public const double rydberg = 1.0973731568539e7;`
Built-in mathematical methods, integer overflow, BigMul		
84.	Write a program which adds the following two integers, i=5; j=9; and prints the result out to the console.	```using System;

namespace PracticeYourCSharp
{
  class Program
  {
    static void Main(string[] args)
    {
      int i = 5; int j = 9;
      int result = i + j;
      Console.WriteLine("The sum is: {0}.", result);
    }
  }
}``` |
| 85. | Given two integers i=5; j=9; write a program which subtracts the latter from the former and prints the result out to the console. | ```using System;

namespace PracticeYourCSharp
{
  class Program
  {
    static void Main(string[] args)
    {
      int i = 5; int j = 9;
      int result = i - j;
      Console.WriteLine("Result = {0}.", result);
    }
  }
}``` |
| 86. | Write a program to calculate and print out the remainder of 55 divided by 22.

Hint: Use the % operator | ```using System;

namespace PracticeYourCSharp
{
  class Program
  {
    static void Main(string[] args)
    {
      int rem = 55 % 22;
      Console.WriteLine("The remainder is {0}.", rem);
    }
  }
}``` |
| 87. | Write a program to calculate and print out the square root of 81.39. | |
| | ```using System;

namespace PracticeYourCSharp
{
  class Program
  {
    static void Main(string[] args)
    {
      float x = 81.39f;
      double result;``` | |

	`` result = Math.Sqrt(x);
Console.WriteLine("The square root of {0} = {1}.", x, result);
}
}
}```
88.	Write a program to calculate and print out the cosine of 180°. *Hint: Use the built-in constant* `Math.PI` *and the method* `Math.Cos`.
|    | ```csharp
using System;

namespace PracticeYourCSharp
{
    class Program
    {
        static void Main(string[] args)
        {
            double degrees = 180;
            //convert to radians as the C# trigonometric methods work on radians, not on degrees.
            double radians = (degrees * (Math.PI)) / 180;
            double result;

            result = Math.Cos(radians) ;
            Console.WriteLine("The cosine of {0} degrees is {1}", degrees, result);
        }
    }
}
``` |
| 89. | Write a program to calculate and print out the tangent of 30°. |
|    | ```csharp
using System;

namespace PracticeYourCSharp
{
    class Program
    {
        static void Main(string[] args)
        {
            double degrees = 30;
            //1st convert to radians as the C# trigonometric methods work on radians, not on degrees.
            double degreesInRadians = (degrees * (Math.PI)) / 180;
            double result;

            result = Math.Tan(degreesInRadians);
            Console.WriteLine("The tangent of {0} degrees is {1}", degrees, result);
        }
    }
}
``` |
| 90. | Write a program to calculate and print out the tangent of 60°. |
|    | ```csharp
using System;

namespace PracticeYourCSharp
{
    class Program
    {
        static void Main(string[] args)
        {
            double degrees = 60;
            double degreesInRadians = (degrees * (Math.PI)) / 180;
            double result;

            result = Math.Tan(degreesInRadians);
            Console.WriteLine("The tangent of {0} degrees is {1}", degrees, result);
        }
    }
}
``` |
```

91.	Write a program to calculate and print out the sine of 75°.
| | ```
using System;

namespace PracticeYourCSharp
{
  class Program
  {
    static void Main(string[] args)
    {
      double degrees = 75;
      double degreesInRadians = (degrees * (Math.PI)) / 180;
      double result;
      result = Math.Sin(degreesInRadians);
      Console.WriteLine("The tangent of {0} degrees is {1}", degrees, result);
    }
  }
}
``` |
| 92. | The sine of a given angle is .8660254037. Write a program to calculate and print out in degrees *and* in radians the angle that this value corresponds to. |
| | ```
using System;

namespace PracticeYourCSharp
{
  class Program
  {
    static void Main(string[] args)
    {
      double sine = .8660254037;
      double degrees, radians;

      radians = Math.Asin(sine);
      degrees = (radians * 180) / Math.PI;
      Console.WriteLine("{0} is the sine of {1} degrees (or {2} radians).", sine, degrees,
                        radians);
    }
  }
}
``` |
| 93. | The cosine of a given angle is .8660254037. Write a program to calculate and print out in degrees and in radians the angle that this value corresponds to. |
| | ```
using System;

namespace PracticeYourCSharp
{
  class Program
  {
    static void Main(string[] args)
    {
      double cosine = .8660254037;
      double degrees, radians;

      radians = Math.Acos(cosine);
      degrees = (radians * 180) / Math.PI;
      Console.WriteLine("{0} is the cosine of {1} degrees (or {2} radians)",
                        cosine, degrees, radians);
    }
  }
}
``` |
| 94. | The tangent of a given angle is .8660254037. Write a program to calculate and print out in degrees and in radians the angle that this value corresponds to. |
| | ```
using System;

namespace PracticeYourCSharp
{
``` |

```
        class Program
        {
            static void Main(string[] args)
            {
                double tangent = .8660254037;
                double degrees, radians;

                radians = Math.Atan(tangent);
                degrees = (radians * 180) / Math.PI;
                Console.WriteLine("{0} is the tangent of {1} degrees (or {2} radians)",
                        tangent, degrees, radians);
            }
        }
    }
```

| 95. | Calculate the logarithm to base 10 of 7 and the logarithm to base 10 of 22. Add the resulting values, putting the sum thereof into a variable x. Then compute and print out the value of 10^x. | ```using System;

namespace PracticeYourCSharp
{
    class Program
    {
        static void Main(string[] args)
        {
            double d01 = 7;
            double d02 = 22;

            double logOfd01 = Math.Log10(d01);
            double logOfd02 = Math.Log10(d02);

            double x = logOfd01 + logOfd02;

            double result = Math.Pow(10, x); // This is 10^x
            Console.WriteLine("The result is {0}", result);
            Console.ReadKey();
        }
    }
}``` |
|---|---|---|
| 96. | Calculate the logarithm to base e of 7 and the logarithm to base e of 22. Add the resulting values, putting the sum thereof into a variable x. Then compute and print out the value of e^x. | ```using System;

namespace PracticeYourCSharp
{
    class Program
    {
        static void Main(string[] args)
        {
            double d01 = 7;
            double d02 = 22;

            double logOfd01 = Math.Log(d01);
            double logOfd02 = Math.Log(d02);

            double x = logOfd01 + logOfd02;

            double result = Math.Exp(x); // This is e^x
            Console.WriteLine("The result is {0}", result);
        }
    }
}``` |
| 97. | Calculate the logarithm to base *12* of 7 and the logarithm to base *12* of 22. Add the resulting values, putting the sum thereof into a variable x. Then compute and print out the | ```using System;

namespace PracticeYourCSharp
{
    class Program
    {
        static void Main(string[] args)
        {
            double d01 = 7;``` |

| | value of $12^x$. | ```
        double d02 = 22;

        double logOfd01 = Math.Log(d01, 12);
        double logOfd02 = Math.Log(d02, 12);

        double d03 = logOfd01 + logOfd02;

        double result = Math.Pow(12, d03); // This is 12^d03
        Console.WriteLine("The result is {0}", result);
        Console.ReadKey();
      }
    }
}
``` |
| 98. | Pythagoras' theorem states that for a given right-angled triangle with sides $a$, $b$ and $c$ where $c$ is the hypotenuse, if you have the values $a$ and $b$, the value for $c$ can be determined as follows: $c = \sqrt{(a^2 + b^2)}$. So given a triangle where $a=4$ and $b=3$, write a program to calculate c and print it out. *Hint: Math.Pow, Math.Sqrt* | ```
using System;

namespace PracticeYourCSharp
{
    class Program
    {
        static void Main(string[] args)
        {
            float a = 3;
            float b = 4;
            double c; // this will be the hypotenuse

            c = Math.Pow(a, 2) + Math.Pow(b, 2); // = a² + b²
            c = Math.Sqrt(c);                    // This is sqrt(a² + b²)

            Console.WriteLine("hypotenuse length = {0}", c);
            Console.ReadKey();
        }
    }
}
``` |
| 99. | Given two numbers, 55 and 70, write a program to determine and print out which is the larger of the two. | ```
using System;

namespace PracticeYourCSharp
{
    class Program
    {
        static void Main(string[] args)
        {
            int bigger = Math.Max(55, 70);
            Console.WriteLine("The larger is {0}.", bigger);
        }
    }
}
``` |
| 100. | Given two numbers 320 and -2.95 of type `double`, write a program to determine and print out which is the smaller of the two numbers. | ```
using System;

namespace PracticeYourCSharp
{
    class Program
    {
        static void Main(string[] args)
        {
            Double smaller = Math.Min((Double)(-2.95), (Double)320);
            Console.WriteLine("The smaller is {0}.", smaller);
        }
    }
}
```
**Note:** to do comparisons using `Math.Min` or `Math.Max` the numbers being compared must be of the same type. |
| 101. | Given the `decimal` number 12777.899, write a program to determine and print out | ```
using System;

namespace PracticeYourCSharp
{
``` |
```

| | the *whole number* portion of this number. | ```
class Program
{
    static void Main(string[] args)
    {
        Decimal x = 12777.899m;
        Decimal whole = Math.Truncate(x);
        Console.WriteLine("The whole number portion is {0}.",whole);
        Console.ReadKey();
    }
}
``` |
| 102. | Given the `decimal` number 12777.899, write a program to determine and print out the fractional portion of this number. | ```
using System;
namespace PracticeYourCSharp
{
    class Program
    {
        static void Main(string[] args)
        {
            Decimal x = 12777.899m;
            Decimal remainder = x - Math.Truncate(x);
            Console.WriteLine("The remainder is {0}.", remainder);
        }
    }
}
``` |
| 103. | Round the `decimal` number 12777.899 to the nearest integer and print the result out.<br>*Hint: Math.Round* | ```
using System;
namespace PracticeYourCSharp
{
    class Program
    {
        static void Main(string[] args)
        {
            Decimal x = 12777.899M;
            Decimal integerPart = (Decimal)Math.Round(x);
            Console.WriteLine("The rounded number is {0}.", integerPart);
        }
    }
}
``` |
| 104. | Write a program to print out the <u>floor</u> of 5.799 and 583.6 respectively. | ```
using System;
namespace PracticeYourCSharp
{
    class Program
    {
        static void Main(string[] args)
        {
            double x = 5.799;
            double y = 583.6;

            double floor_x = Math.Floor(x);
            double floor_y = Math.Floor(y);
            Console.WriteLine("The floor values respectively
                              are: {0}, {1}",floor_x, floor_y);
            Console.ReadKey();
        }
    }
}
``` |
| 105. | Write a program to print out the <u>ceiling</u> of 5.799 and 583.6 respectively. | ```
using System;
namespace PracticeYourCSharp
{
    class Program
    {
``` |
```

| | | ```csharp
      static void Main(string[] args)
      {
         double x = 5.799;
         double y = 583.6;

         double ceil_x = Math.Ceiling(x);
         double ceil_y = Math.Ceiling(y);
         Console.WriteLine("The ceiling values respectively
                        are: {0}, {1}.", ceil_x, ceil_y);
         Console.ReadKey();
      }
   }
}
``` |
| 106. | Write a program to round the following number off to 4 decimal places; 576.3345812283. Print the result out. | ```csharp
using System;

namespace PracticeYourCSharp
{
   class Program
   {
      static void Main(string[] args)
      {
         double x = 576.3345812283;

         double round_x = Math.Round(x, 4);

         Console.WriteLine("Result = {0}.", round_x);
         Console.ReadKey();
      }
   }
}
``` |
| 107. | I have the following variables:<br><br>`int x1 = 5;`<br>`double x2 = 12777.899M`<br>`string s1, s2;`<br><br>Write a program which stores x1 and x2 in the string variables s1 and s2 respectively.<br><br>*Hint: ToString method.* | ```csharp
using System;

namespace PracticeYourCSharp
{
   class Program
   {
      static void Main(string[] args)
      {
         int x1 = 5; double x2 = 12777.899;
         string s1 = x1.ToString();
         string s2 = x2.ToString();
         Console.ReadKey();
      }
   }
}
```<br><br>**Note:** This conversion to a **string** has been happening implicitly when we have used the **Console.WriteLine** method to output numerical values.<br>Also note that no visible output is expected from this program. However, you can see the results in the Locals debug window. |
| 108. | Print out the result of the division of the following calculation: **a/b**, where **a** and **b** are both integers with values 1 and 4 respectively. Put the result into a **float**.
Explain the result. | |
| | An initial attempt at writing the code might yield the following:<br><br>```csharp
using System;

namespace PracticeYourCSharp
{
   class Program
   {
      static void Main(string[] args)
      {
         int a = 1, b = 4;
``` | |

```
            float result = a/b;
            Console.WriteLine("{0}/{1}={2}", a, b, result);
            Console.ReadKey();
        }
    }
}
```

Explanation: The result of this code is 0! The issue here is that on seeing integer values (1 and 4 in this case), C# automatically performs an integer calculation (irrespective of the type of the target output variable). If you want the correct results, then ensure that you cast the input variables appropriately. In this case we would write the following calculation for `result`:
```
            float result = (float)a/(float)b;
```

109.	Describe the concept of integer overflow.
	The concept of integer overflow can be described as follows. Using the type `int` as our example, imagine that all its values are represented <u>on a wheel</u>, starting from the lowest integer to the highest integer. Now, say we have `int x=Int32.MaxValue` (largest integer) . if we add the value of 1 to `x`, i.e. `x=x+1`, then interestingly what happens is simply that `x` is moved to the next point on the wheel, which is `Int32.MinValue`! If I added 2 to the value of `x`, then `x` would be moved to the position `Int32.MinValue - 1`. This is how integer overflow occurs in C#. Integer overflow should be assumed to be a risk for any integer computation. Note: Even though we used the `int` type as an example, this concept applies to any integer type.
110.	Describe the concept of integer underflow.
	Integer underflow happens when the result of an integer computation results in a value that is less than (i.e. closer to -∞) the minimum value that the integer type in question can contain. Continuing with the previous analogy of `int` values on a wheel, imagine we have `x=Int32.MinValue`. If we subtract the value of 1 from `x`, i.e. `x=x-1`, we are moving backwards on the wheel and the result is `x=Int32.MaxValue`, which is clearly incorrect!
111.	How do I guard against the integer overflow/underflow issue?
	Apply the **checked** operator to the integer computation at hand.
112.	I have two integers, `a` and `b`, the addition of which has a risk of overflowing and I want to catch this overflow. Write a sample program to show how this would be done.
| | ```
using System;

namespace PracticeYourCSharp
{
    class Program
    {
        static void Main(string[] args)
        {
            int a = int.MaxValue; //just a value for the purposes of this program
            int b = int.MaxValue; //as above
            int total;

            checked
            {
                total = a + b;
            }
            Console.ReadKey();
        }
    }
}
```<br>**Note(s):**<br>1. Running this code for the choice of numbers herein will result in an overflow, which causes the throwing of the <u>exception</u> `System.OverflowException`. Exceptions are discussed in a later chapter.<br>2. Note that if you did not used the `checked` keyword, the result would overflow anyway but <u>not</u> inform you.<br>3. The same exception occurs for integer underflow conditions. |
```

113.	Explain the use of the `unchecked` keyword.	
	The unchecked keyword is used to ensure that the compiler does not perform overflow checking for the integer computation at hand.	
114.	When would you use the `unchecked` keyword?	
	You would use the `unchecked` keyword in the scenario where you have turned on the compiler switch that ensures that all integer computations are `checked` by default and you desire that checking not be done for the computation to which you are applying the `unchecked` keyword.	
115.	Explain the function of the method `Math.BigMul`.	
	Given that for computations involving large integers there is a clear risk of overflow, in C# the provided method `Math.BigMul` is used for the multiplication of integer values and returns a `long` as the result.	
116.	I have two variables of type `int`: `a=Int32.MaxValue` and `b=2` that I want multiplied. Multiply them using `Math.BigMul` and then also without using `Math.BigMul`. Print out the results of each case.	
| | ```csharp
using System;

namespace PracticeYourCSharp
{
  class Program
  {
    static void Main(string[] args)
    {
      int a = Int32.MaxValue;
      int b = 2;
      long result = Math.BigMul(a, b);
      Console.WriteLine("result with BigMul = {0}", result);
      Console.WriteLine("result without BigMul = {0}", a * b);
      Console.ReadKey();
    }
  }
}
``` | |
| 117. | What is the expected output of this code fragment?<br>```csharp
int a = 5;
int b = 0;
Console.WriteLine("{0}/{1}={2}", a, b, (a/b));
Console.ReadKey();
``` | The program will stop running and it will throw the exception `'System.DivideByZeroException'`.<br><br>Chapter 32 on Exceptions shows how to handle the situation of program stoppage due to exception generation. |

Infinity/-Infinity/NaN

| 118. | Write a program which determines and prints out the result of the following computations given the noted variable values:<br>`float a=0, b=0, c=-1, d=1;`<br>1. a/b<br>2. c/a<br>3. d/a | ```csharp
using System;

namespace PracticeYourCSharp
{
  class Program
  {
    static void Main(string[] args)
    {
      float a = 0, b = 0, c = -1, d = 1;

      Console.WriteLine("{0}/{1}={2}", a, b, a / b);
      Console.WriteLine("{0}/{1}={2}", c, a, c / a);
      Console.WriteLine("{0}/{1}={2}", d, a, d / a);
    }
  }
}
```<br>**Results**<br>1. 0/0 = NaN (which means Not a Number)<br>2. -1/0 = -Infinity<br>3. 1/0 = Infinity |
| 119. | Write a program which determines and prints out the result of each of the following calculations: | ```csharp
using System;

namespace PracticeYourCSharp
{
``` |

| | 1. -∞ + ∞<br>2. ∞ / ∞<br>3. -∞ / ∞<br>4. ∞ / 0<br>5. -∞ / 0<br><br>*Hint: The constants*<br>*float.PositiveInifinity,*<br>*float.NegativeInfinity* | ```
class Program
{
  static void Main(string[] args)
  {
    float a = float.PositiveInfinity;
    float b = float.NegativeInfinity;
    Console.WriteLine("{0}+{1}={2}", b, a, b + a);
    Console.WriteLine("{0}/{1}={2}", b, a, b / a);
    Console.WriteLine("{0}/{1}={2}", b, b, b / b);
    Console.WriteLine("{0}/{1}={2}", a, 0, a / 0);
    Console.WriteLine("{0}/{1}={2}", b, 0, b / 0);
    Console.ReadKey();
  }
}
```<br><br>**Results**<br>```
1. -Infinity +  Infinity    = NaN
2. -Infinity /  Infinity    = NaN
3. -Infinity / -Infinity    = NaN
4.  Infinity /  0           =  Infinity
5. -Infinity /  0           = -Infinity
``` |
| **Complex Numbers** | | |
| 120. | I have the following complex numbers:<br><br>a = 10 + 5i<br>b = 24 + 8i<br><br>Write a program which does the following:<br>1. Assigns the complex numbers indicated above to the variables a & b respectively.<br>2. Prints a and b out individually.<br>3. Prints the phase and magnitude of a.<br>4. Prints out the sum of a and b.<br>5. Prints out the result of a/b.<br><br>*Hint: class Complex*<br><br>**Note:** you might have to ensure that the assembly reference System.Numerics is included in your assembly references list in order to do this exercise. This is achieved in both Microsoft Visual Studio 2015 and 2013 through the menu option:<br>PROJECT → Add Reference | ```
using System;
using System.Numerics; //class Complex is in here

namespace PracticeYourCSharp
{
  class Program
  {
    static void Main(string[] args)
    {
      Complex a, b, c, d;

      a = new Complex(10, 5);
      b = new Complex(24, 8);
      Console.WriteLine("a={0}", a);
      Console.WriteLine("b={0}", b);
      Console.WriteLine("The phase of a={0} radians", a.Phase);
      Console.WriteLine("The magnitude of a={0}", a.Magnitude);

      c = new Complex();
      // Now add them as per the question
      c = a + b; // Overloaded operator + (we discuss
                 // operator overloading in a later chapter)
      d = a / b;
      Console.WriteLine("a + b = {0}", c);
      Console.WriteLine("a / b = {0}", d);
      Console.ReadKey();
    }
  }
}
``` |
Increment, decrement and shorthand operators		

121.	Given the following initialized variable:
	`int i=2;`
	State what its value is after the statement:
	`i++;`
		3
		
		The increment operator(++) simply means that the value of the variable in question should be incremented by **1**.

122.	Given the following variable:
	`double i=8.46;`
	State what its value is after the statement:
	`i++;`
		9.46
		
		The increment operator also works on floating point numbers, incrementing the value of the variable in question by **1**.

```

123.	Given the following variable: `int i=26;` State what its value is after the statement: `i--;`	25 The decrement operator(`--`) simply means that the value of the variable in question should be decremented by **1**.

124.	Given the following variable: `int i=23;`
	State what the values of `j` and `i` are after the following statement:
	`int j=++i;`
		This statement is saying `j = incremented value of i`
		Thus `i` is incremented first *before* assigning the incremented value of `i` to `j`. Thus the result is:
		`j=24`
		`i=24`

125.	Given the following variable:
	`int i=23;`
	State what the values of `j` and `i` are after the following statement:
	`int j=i++;`
		`j=23`
		`i=24`
		The statement `j=i++;` means the following:
		assign `i` to `j` and then afterwards increment `i`
		Thus `j` is assigned the current value of `i`, that is `23` and then `i` is incremented to `24`.

126.	Given the following code snippet:
	`int i=5; j=27;`
	`int result = i++ + --j;`
	1. What is the expected value of i?
	2. What is the expected value of j?
	3. What is the expected value of result?
		1. i = 6
		2. j = 26
		3. result = 5+26 = 31
		In words we can say that the line of code means the following:
		`result=`
		`(i, (then increment i), PLUS (decremented value of j))`

127.	Given the following code snippet:
	`int i=5; j=27;`
	`result = --i - --j;`
	1. What is the expected value of i?
	2. What is the expected value of j?
	3. What is the expected value of result?
		1. i=4
		2. j=26
		3. result= 4-26 = -22
		In words we can say:
		`result = (decrement i MINUS decrement j)`

Shorthand operators		
128.	Given the following variable: `int i=26,` state the value of `i` after the statement `i/=2;`	i=13 The given statement is a shorthand way of saying: `i = i/2` (i.e. *divide i by 2*)
129.	Given the following variable: `int j=9,` state the value of `j` after the statement `j*=6;`	j=54 The given statement is a shorthand way of saying: `j = j*6` (i.e. *multiply j by 6*)
130.	Given the following variable: `float x=5.2f,` state the value of `x` after the following statement: `x-=2;`	3.2 The given statement is a shorthand way of saying: `x = x-2` (i.e. *decrement x by 2*)

131.	What is the difference between the following two statements?
	`i+=1;`
	`i++;`
		There is no difference; both mean the same thing, which is *increment i by 1*.

132.	Given two numerical variables `g` and `y`, what does the following statement mean? `g+=y;`	This means *increment g by y*, in short, `g = g+y;`
133.	Given two numerical variables `g` and `y`, what does the following statement mean? `g*=y;`	This means *multiply g by y*, in short it means exactly the same thing as: `g = g*y;`
134.	Given two numerical variables `g` and `y`, what does the following statement mean? `g/=y;`	This means *divide g by y*, in short, `g = g/y;`
135.	Given two numerical variables `g` and `y`, what does the following statement mean?	This means *decrement g by y*, in short, `g = g-y;`

	g-=y;	
BigInteger		
136.	If you have integers of greater value than the type `ulong` can handle, what number class would you use to represent them and why?	
	You would use the class `BigInteger` of namespace `System.Numerics`. This class can handle <u>arbitrarily long</u> integers.	
| 137. | Add the following two numbers and print out the result:<br><br>40,000,000,000,000,000,001<br>19,446,744,073,709,551,611<br><br>*Hint:* `BigInteger.Parse`<br><br>**Note:** Ensure that the assembly reference `System.Numerics` is included in your assembly references list in order to implement the solution to this exercise. This is achieved in both Microsoft Visual Studio 2015 and 2013 through the menu option: PROJECT → Add Reference | ```
using System;
using System.Numerics;

namespace PracticeYourCSharp
{
  class Program
  {
    static void Main(string[] args)
    {
      string s1 = "40000000000000000001";
      string s2 = "19446744073709551611";

      BigInteger a = BigInteger.Parse(s1);
      BigInteger b = BigInteger.Parse(s2);
      BigInteger c = a + b;
      Console.WriteLine("{0}+{1} = {2}", a, b, c);
    }
  }
}
```<br>**Note:** In this example, we converted the input numbers from `string` objects to objects of class `BigInteger`. |
138.	Multiply the two numbers from the preceding exercise and output the result.	Add the following lines to the program above:
		`BigInteger d = a * b;`
		`Console.WriteLine("{0} * {1} = {2}", a, b, d);`

139.	Divide the first number in the preceding exercise by the second and output the result.	Add the following lines the program above:
		`BigInteger e = a/b;`
		`Console.WriteLine("{0} / {1} = {2}", a, b, e);`
		Note: You will observe that `e = 2`, rather than the correct floating point result. This is because `BigInteger` only operates on integers.

140.	Print out the greatest common divisor *(GCD)* of the following numbers: 50000000000000001000 and 18446744073709551615	
| | ```
using System;
using System.Numerics;

namespace PracticeYourCSharp
{
  class Program
  {
    static void Main(string[] args)
    {
      string s1 = "50000000000000001000";
      string s2 = "18446744073709551615";
      BigInteger a = BigInteger.Parse(s1);
      BigInteger b = BigInteger.Parse(s2);
      BigInteger gcd = BigInteger.GreatestCommonDivisor(a, b);

      Console.WriteLine("GCD of {0} & {1} = {2}", a, b, gcd);
      Console.ReadKey();
    }
  }
}
``` | |

Hexadecimal numbers

141. Write a program which assigns the hexadecimal value `FFF0` to an `int` variable named `i01`.
Print out the equivalent base 10 number.

```csharp
using System;

namespace PracticeYourCSharp
{
  class Program
  {
    static void Main(string[] args)
    {
      int i01 = 0xFFF0;
      Console.WriteLine(i01);
    }
  }
}
```

142. Write a program which adds the hexadecimal values `1EC05` and `F238C`.
Print out the resulting base 10 number.

```csharp
using System;

namespace PracticeYourCSharp
{
  class Program
  {
    static void Main(string[] args)
    {
      int i01 = 0x1EC05;
      int i02 = 0xF238C;
      int result = i01 + i02;
      Console.WriteLine(result);
      Console.ReadKey();
    }
  }
}
```

Note: *later we'll see how to print out the result in hexadecimal.*

Formatting of Numerical Output

In our usage up until now of composite formatting for output you have used the index (`{<index>}`) of each element within the output string in conjunction with the parameter list given to `Console.WriteLine`. We now move on to exercises in which you practice more refined output using composite formatting.

143. Explain the components of the following composite formatting field formatting template:

   `{<index>[,<->fieldWidth][:formatString]}`

index is the position of the argument in the argument list to the formatting string.

,<->fieldWidth is an optional argument which indicates by the **minus** sign whether the argument is to be left(`-`) aligned or right aligned (no sign required). **fieldWidth** indicates the width of the field in which the value being output is.

:formatString is an optional argument indicating the *field type specific formatting* that you want applied to this argument. For example, the format string can cause numbers to be displayed as currency, as hexadecimal or with specific numbers of decimal places. Also the different format options possible for the different components of a date can be specified here. Note that each data type in C# has its own formatting strings.

Note that the braces ([and]) in the formatting template are not part of the formatting string and are only there to demarcate the different components of a composite formatting string for the purposes of this explanation.

Formatting: Justification

144. Print the numbers 15, 155 and 1555 on separate lines, *left-justified*, in a 10 character width field. This 10 character width field should be bounded on the left & right by the character '|'.

```csharp
using System;

namespace PracticeYourCSharp
{
  class Program
  {
    static void Main(string[] args)
    {
      int a = 15, b = 155, c = 1555;
      Console.WriteLine("|{0,-10}|", a);
```

		`Console.WriteLine("|{0,-10}|", b);`
		`Console.WriteLine("|{0,-10}|", c);`
		`Console.ReadKey();`
		`        }`
		`    }`
		`}`

145.	Reprint the same numbers as above, *right-justified*, however.	`using System;`
		`namespace PracticeYourCSharp`
		`{`
		`    class Program`
		`    {`
		`        static void Main(string[] args)`
		`        {`
		`            int a = 15, b = 155, c = 1555;`
		`            Console.WriteLine("|{0,10}|", a);`
		`            Console.WriteLine("|{0,10}|", b);`
		`            Console.WriteLine("|{0,10}|", c);`
		`            Console.ReadKey();`
		`        }`
		`    }`
		`}`

146.	**(6.0)** Redo the preceding exercise, this time using string interpolation to output the results.	`using System;`
		`namespace PracticeYourCSharp`
		`{`
		`    class Program`
		`    {`
		`        static void Main(string[] args)`
		`        {`
		`            int a = 15, b = 155, c = 1555;`
		`            Console.WriteLine($"|{a,10}|");`
		`            Console.WriteLine($"|{b,10}|");`
		`            Console.WriteLine($"|{c,10}|");`
		`            Console.ReadKey();`
		`        }`
		`    }`
		`}`

147.	Print the numbers 15.01, 155.1 and 1555 on separate lines, *right-justified*, in a 10 character width field. This 10 character width field should be bounded on the left & right by the character '|'.	`using System;`
		`namespace PracticeYourCSharp`
		`{`
		`    class Program`
		`    {`
		`        static void Main(string[] args)`
		`        {`
		`            double a = 15.01, b = 155.1, c = 1555;`
		`            Console.WriteLine("|{0,10}|", a);`
		`            Console.WriteLine("|{0,10}|", b);`
		`            Console.WriteLine("|{0,10}|", c);`
		`            Console.ReadKey();`
		`        }`
		`    }`
		`}`
		
		Comments: The output is:
		`|     15.01|`
		`|     155.1|`
		`|      1555|`

148.	Note the output of the preceding exercise. Now modify the code from the exercise above to output the same data in the	`using System;`
		`namespace PracticeYourCSharp`
		`{`
		`    class Program`

| | following format:<br><br>\|      15.01\|<br>\|     155.10\|<br>\|    1555.00\|<br><br>*Hint: ensure that all the numbers have 2 points after the decimal.* | ```
{
  static void Main(string[] args)
  {
    double a = 15.01, b = 155.1, c = 1555;
    Console.WriteLine("|{0,10:0.00}|", a);
    Console.WriteLine("|{0,10:0.00}|", b);
    Console.WriteLine("|{0,10:0.00}|", c);
    Console.ReadKey();
  }
 }
}
``` |
| **Formatting: Precision** | | |
| 149. | Write a program which prints out the numbers 477.8763 and 25.3 with a precision of two decimal places. | ```
using System;

namespace PracticeYourCSharp
{
  class Program
  {
    static void Main(string[] args)
    {
      double a = 477.8763, b = 25.3;
      Console.WriteLine("{0:0.00}", a);
      Console.WriteLine("{0:0.00}", b);
      Console.ReadKey();
    }
  }
}
```<br><br>**Output**<br>477.88 This shows you that the number is rounded on output.<br>25.30 Note that the formatting caused 25.3 to have two decimal places. |
| 150. | Write a program which prints out the following numbers, with a maximum of two decimal places: 477.8763 and 25.3.<br><br>Contrast the results with those obtained for the preceding exercise. | ```
using System;

namespace PracticeYourCSharp
{
  class Program
  {
    static void Main(string[] args)
    {
      double a = 477.8763, b = 25.3;
      Console.WriteLine("{0:0.##}", a);
      Console.WriteLine("{0:0.##}", b);
      Console.ReadKey();
    }
  }
}
```<br><br>**Output**<br>477.88<br>25.3 |
| 151. | Write a program to print the following numbers with a *mininum of 1 decimal place* and a *maximum of two decimal places* if so needed:<br>477.8763, 25.3 and the int 43. | ```
using System;

namespace PracticeYourCSharp
{
  class Program
  {
    static void Main(string[] args)
    {
      double a = 477.8763, b = 25.3; int c = 43;
      Console.WriteLine("{0:0.0#}", a);
      Console.WriteLine("{0:0.0#}", b);
      Console.WriteLine("{0:0.0#}", c);
      Console.ReadKey();
    }
``` |

		`}` `}` **Output** 477.88, 25.3 and 43.0 respectively.
Formatting: Currency, Integer format specifier, Scientific Notation		
| 152. | Write a program to output the values 553.89 and -553.891 formatted as currency. | ```
using System;

namespace PracticeYourCSharp
{
  class Program
  {
    static void Main(string[] args)
    {
      decimal a = 553.89m, b = -553.891m;
      Console.WriteLine("{0:C}", a);
      Console.WriteLine("{0:C}", b);
      Console.ReadKey();
    }
  }
}
```<br>**Output**<br>$553.89<br>($553.89)<br>It should be understood that the output style is dependent on what "Culture" is applied to the output (otherwise the default Culture is applied). The topic of Culture is not addressed in this book. |
| 153. | Write a program to output the integer values 553 and -686 with the integer format specifier "D". | ```
using System;

namespace PracticeYourCSharp
{
  class Program
  {
    static void Main(string[] args)
    {
      int a = 553, b = -686;
      Console.WriteLine("{0:D}", a);
      Console.WriteLine("{0:D}", b);
      Console.ReadKey();
    }
  }
}
```<br>**Output**<br>553   *(In countries with Culture = en-US)*<br>-686  *(In countries with Culture = en-US)* |
| 154. | Output the following numbers in scientific notation: 1.03, 17.89, 200.779, 299792458. | ```
using System;

namespace PracticeYourCSharp
{
  class Program
  {
    static void Main(string[] args)
    {
      float a = 1.03f, b = 17.89f, c = 200.779f, d = 299792458f;
      Console.WriteLine("{0:E}", a);
      Console.WriteLine("{0:E}", b);
      Console.WriteLine("{0:E}", c);
      Console.WriteLine("{0:E}", d);
      Console.ReadKey();
    }
  }
}
``` |
```

		} **Output** 1.030000E+000 1.789000E+001 1.007790E+002 2.997925E+008 Note that the exact style of the output is Culture dependant.
| 155. | Modify the code from the answer to the exercise above so that the output has a precision of 4 decimal places. | ```csharp
using System;

namespace PracticeYourCSharp
{
   class Program
   {
      static void Main(string[] args)
      {
         float a = 1.03f, b = 17.89f,
             c = 200.779f, d = 299792458f;
         Console.WriteLine("{0:E4}", a);
         Console.WriteLine("{0:E4}", b);
         Console.WriteLine("{0:E4}", c);
         Console.WriteLine("{0:E4}", d);
         Console.ReadKey();
      }
   }
}
``` |
| 156. | Modify the code from the answer to the exercise above so that the output has a precision of 4 decimal places and does not have the excess zeros after the E. | ```csharp
using System;

namespace PracticeYourCSharp
{
   class Program
   {
      static void Main(string[] args)
      {
         double a = 1.03, b = 17.89, c = 200.779,
             d = 299792458;
         Console.WriteLine("{0:#.0000e+0}", a);
         Console.WriteLine("{0:#.0000e+0}", b);
         Console.WriteLine("{0:#.0000e+0}", c);
         Console.WriteLine("{0:#.0000e+0}", d);
         Console.ReadKey();
      }
   }
}
```<br>**Output**: 1.0300e+0, 1.7890e+1, 2.0078e+2 and 2.9979e+8 respectively. |
| 157. | Modify the answer to the preceding exercise to ensure the following output:<br>1. The exponent is represented by an uppercase 'E' rather than lowercase<br>*and*<br>2. There is no plus sign in the exponent. | ```csharp
using System;

namespace PracticeYourCSharp
{
   class Program
   {
      static void Main(string[] args)
      {
         double a = 1.03, b = 17.89, c = 200.779,
             d = 299792458;
         Console.WriteLine("{0:#.0000E0}", a);
         Console.WriteLine("{0:#.0000E0}", b);
         Console.WriteLine("{0:#.0000E0}", c);
         Console.WriteLine("{0:#.0000E0}", d);
      }
   }
}
``` |
| 158. | Modify the answer to the | using System; |
```

| | preceding exercise to ensure that the exponent in the output is represented by a lowercase 'e'. | ```
namespace PracticeYourCSharp
{
  class Program
  {
    static void Main(string[] args)
    {
      double a = 1.03, b = 17.89, c = 200.779,
             d = 299792458;
      Console.WriteLine("{0:e4}", a);
      Console.WriteLine("{0:e4}", b);
      Console.WriteLine("{0:e4}", c);
      Console.WriteLine("{0:e4}", d);
    }
  }
}
``` |
|---|---|---|
| 159. | Print out the values 1.03, 17.89, 200.779, 299792458, 2.99792458e8 and 3.3e15 in whichever is more compact of fixed-point or scientific notation. | ```
using System;

namespace PracticeYourCSharp
{
  class Program
  {
    static void Main(string[] args)
    {
      double a = 1.03, b = 17.89, c = 200.779,
             d = 299792458, e = 2.99792458e8, f = 3.3e15;
      Console.WriteLine("{0:G}", a);
      Console.WriteLine("{0:G}", b);
      Console.WriteLine("{0:G}", c);
      Console.WriteLine("{0:G}", d);
      Console.WriteLine("{0:G}", e);
      Console.WriteLine("{0:G}", f);
    }
  }
}
```
**Output**: 1.03, 17.89, 200.779, 299792458, 299792458 and 3.3E+15 respectively. |
| 160. | Reprint the numbers from the preceding exercise, this time using the number format "N". Analyze and comment on the difference between this ouput and the output when using the number format "G". | |

```
using System;

namespace PracticeYourCSharp
{
  class Program
  {
    static void Main(string[] args)
    {
      double a = 1.03, b = 17.89, c = 200.779, d = 299792458, e = 2.99792458e8, f = 3.3e15;
      Console.WriteLine("{0:N}", a);
      Console.WriteLine("{0:N}", b);
      Console.WriteLine("{0:N}", c);
      Console.WriteLine("{0:N}", d);
      Console.WriteLine("{0:N}", e);
      Console.WriteLine("{0:N}", f);
    }
  }
}
```

Output: 1.03 17.89 200.779 299,792,458.00 299,792,458.00 and 3,300,000,000,000,000.00 respectively. The main difference between the **G** format and the **N** format is that the G format adds Culture specific separators to the numbers and the G format also by default ensures that each number has two decimal places (try using the G format with an integer to observe this for integers as well).

161.	Explain what the number format "P" is for and how it functions.	The **P** number format is used to express percentages. It takes the value given, multiplies it by 100 and prints the resulting number with the percentage sign appended. For example, if I want to output the string *83.5%*, then I have to print the value .835 with the **P** identifier.
| 162. | Using the "P" number format, print out the values 200.43%, 77.89% and 1.5% | ```csharp
using System;

namespace PracticeYourCSharp
{
    class Program
    {
        static void Main(string[] args)
        {
            double a = 2.0043, b = .7789, c = 0.015;
            Console.WriteLine("{0:P}", a);
            Console.WriteLine("{0:P}", b);
            Console.WriteLine("{0:P}", c);
        }
    }
}
``` |
| 163. | Using the same numbers from the preceding exercise, print out the same percentages to just one decimal point of precision. | ```csharp
using System;

namespace PracticeYourCSharp
{
    class Program
    {
        static void Main(string[] args)
        {
            double a = 2.0043, b = .7789, c = 0.015;
            Console.WriteLine("{0:P1}", a);
            Console.WriteLine("{0:P1}", b);
            Console.WriteLine("{0:P1}", c);

            Console.ReadKey();
        }
    }
}
``` |

Formatting: Hexadecimal Output

| 164. | Print the following integers out in hexadecimal: 2000, 350 and 65536. | ```csharp
using System;

namespace PracticeYourCSharp
{
    class Program
    {
        static void Main(string[] args)
        {
            int a = 2000, b = 350, c = 65536;
            Console.WriteLine("{0:X}", a);
            Console.WriteLine("{0:X}", b);
            Console.WriteLine("{0:X}", c);
        }
    }
}
``` |
| 165. | Reprint the numbers from the preceding exercise, in hexadecimal, this time ensuring that they are output *right-justified* in an 8-character width field. | ```csharp
using System;

namespace PracticeYourCSharp
{
    class Program
    {
        static void Main(string[] args)
        {
            int a = 2000, b = 350, c = 65536;
            Console.WriteLine("{0,8:X}", a);
``` |

| | | ```csharp
Console.WriteLine("{0,8:X}", b);
Console.WriteLine("{0,8:X}", c);
Console.ReadKey();
      }
   }
}
``` |
|---|---|---|
| 166. | Reprint the numbers from the preceding exercise, in hexadecimal, ensuring that their output is *at least* 8 characters in width; for those numbers which are less than 8 characters in width, ensure that they are prepended with 0's. | ```csharp
using System;

namespace PracticeYourCSharp
{
   class Program
   {
      static void Main(string[] args)
      {
         int a = 2000, b = 350, c = 65536;
         Console.WriteLine("{0:X8}", a);
         Console.WriteLine("{0:X8}", b);
         Console.WriteLine("{0:X8}", c);
         Console.ReadKey();
      }
   }
}
``` |
| 167. | Attempt to output the `double` number 65.4 as hexadecimal. Explain why the program will throw an exception when run. | ```csharp
using System;

namespace PracticeYourCSharp
{
   class Program
   {
      static void Main(string[] args)
      {
         double a = 65.4;
         Console.WriteLine("{0:X}", a);
         Console.ReadKey();
      }
   }
}
```
**Output**: While indeed program will compile, when you attempt to run it *it will throw the exception* `System.FormatException`! The reason is because the **X** format is only usable for integer types. |
| 168. | Write a program which adds and prints out in hexadecimal the result of the addition of the hexadecimal numbers 1EC05 and F238C. | ```csharp
using System;

namespace PracticeYourCSharp
{
   class Program
   {
      static void Main(string[] args)
      {
         int result = 0x1EC05 + 0xF238C;
         Console.WriteLine("{0:X}", result);
         Console.ReadKey();
      }
   }
}
``` |

169.	*Number base conversion* Write a program to convert the value 64 to the number bases 2, 8, and 16. Print the converted numbers out. *Hint*: `Convert.ToString(number, base);`
| | ```csharp
using System;

namespace PracticeYourCSharp
{
``` |
```

```csharp
    class Program
    {
      static void Main(string[] args)
      {
        int x = 64; // The number to convert
        int baseA = 2, baseB = 8, baseC = 16;

        string result;

        baseA = 2;
        result = Convert.ToString(x, baseA);
        Console.WriteLine("{0} in numberBase {1} = {2}", x, baseA, result);
        baseB = 8;
        result = Convert.ToString(x, baseB);
        Console.WriteLine("{0} in numberBase {1} = {2}", x, baseB, result);
        baseC = 16;
        result = Convert.ToString(x, baseC);
        Console.WriteLine("{0} in numberBase {1} = {2}", x, baseC, result);

        Console.ReadKey();
      }
    }
}
```

logical & bitwise operators

170. Write a program to output the logical AND of the values 5 and 2.

```csharp
using System;

namespace PracticeYourCSharp
{
  class Program
  {
    static void Main(string[] args)
    {
      uint a = 5; uint b = 2; uint result;

      result = a & b;
      Console.WriteLine("Logical AND of {0},{1} = {2}", a, b, result);
      Console.ReadKey();
    }
  }
}
```

171. Write a program to output the logical OR of the values 5 and 3.

```csharp
using System;

namespace PracticeYourCSharp
{
  class Program
  {
    static void Main(string[] args)
    {
      uint a = 5; uint b = 3; uint result;

      result = a | b;
      Console.WriteLine("Logical OR of {0},{1} = {2}", a, b, result);
      Console.ReadKey();
    }
  }
}
```

172. Write a program to output the logical XOR of the values 5 and 3.

```csharp
using System;

namespace PracticeYourCSharp
{
```

|     | ```
    class Program
    {
        static void Main(string[] args)
        {
            uint a = 5; uint b = 2; uint result;

            result = a ^ b;
            Console.WriteLine("Logical XOR of {0},{1} = {2}", a, b, result);
            Console.ReadKey();
        }
    }
}
``` |
| 173. | Write a program to output the <u>one's complement</u> of 26. |
|     | ```
using System;

namespace PracticeYourCSharp
{
    class Program
    {
        static void Main(string[] args)
        {
            uint a = 26; uint result;

            result = ~a;
            Console.WriteLine("One's Complement of {0} = {1}", a, result); ;
            Console.ReadKey();
        }
    }
}
``` |
| 174. | Write a program which will *left-shift* by four places the value 38. Print the result to the console. |
|     | ```
using System;

namespace PracticeYourCSharp
{
    class Program
    {
        static void Main(string[] args)
        {
            int a = 38; int b = 4; int result;

            result = a << b;
            Console.WriteLine("Left-shifting of {0} by {1} places = {2}", a, b, result);
            Console.ReadKey();
        }
    }
}
``` |
| 175. | What is the difference between
`int a=38;`
`result = a*2*2*2*2;`
and
`int a=38;`
`result = a << 4;`
And why is the result what it is? | There is no difference in the result.
The reason for the equivalence is because computers represent data in base 2, therefore left shifting is the equivalent of multiplying by 2; and thus left shifting by 4 means multiplying by 2^4.

Think about it this way: normally we operate in base 10. Left shifting in base 10, would mean multiplying by 10. Left shifting 4 times in base 10 would mean multiplying the number by 10^4. |
| 176. | Write a program which will *right-shift* by two places the value 38.
Explain the result. |
|     | ```
using System;

namespace PracticeYourCSharp
{
    class Program
``` |

```
        {
            static void Main(string[] args)
            {
                int a = 38; int b = 2; int result;

                result = a >> b;
                Console.WriteLine("Logical right-shifting of {0} by {1} places = {2}", a, b, result);
                Console.ReadKey();
            }
        }
    }
```

Explanation

Right shifting is equivalent to doing an integer division by 2 and returning the quotient of the result. Therefore right-shifting 2 times means, divide by 2 (integer division, ignoring the remainder), then divide the result (the quotient of the earlier computation) by 2 which yields the following computation and result:

```
38 >> 1 = 19
19 >> 1 =  9
```

E1	**(6.0)** Redo all of the programming questions in this chapter using the `using static` compiler directive and the string interpolation feature.

Chapter 4. Booleans

This chapter presents exercises that enable you to practice your knowledge of the boolean (**bool**) type and its associated operators. Exercises on compound boolean expressions are also presented.

1.	Describe the C# boolean (**bool**) type.	The boolean is a type which represents logical *true* or logical *false*.
2.	What is the range of values that the C# type **bool** can support?	Either of the following two distinct values: true *or* false *(case sensitive)*.
3.	Write a line of code to declare a boolean variable named **b01** and assign it a value of **true**.	bool b01 = true; *or* Boolean b01 = true;
Boolean Testing		
4.	I have an **int** variable **x** with a value of **5** and an **int** variable **y** with a value of **7**. Write a program which tests whether *x is equal to y*, putting the result of this test into a **bool** variable named **result**. Print your findings to the console, in a string stating the following: *"The result of whether 5 is equal to 7 is <result>"*	
| | ```
using System;

namespace PracticeYourCSharp
{
  class Program
  {
    static void Main(string[] args)
    {
      bool result;
      int x = 5;
      int y = 7;

      result = x == y;

      Console.WriteLine("The result of whether {0} is equal to {1} is {2}", x, y, result);
      Console.ReadKey();
    }
  }
}
``` | |
| | **Notes**
Think about the statement **result = x==y;** in the following way:
result = *(is x equal to y, true or false?)*
Also note that **result = x==y;** can also be written as **result = (x==y);** that is, with brackets, if it makes the statement easier to understand. | |
| 5. | I have an **int x** with a value of **5** and an **int y** with a value of **7**. Write a program which tests whether *x is greater than y*, putting the result of this test into a **bool** variable named **result**. Print your findings out to the console. | |
| | ```
using System;

namespace PracticeYourCSharp
{
  class Program
  {
    static void Main(string[] args)
    {
      bool result;
      int x = 5; int y = 7;

      result = x > y;

      Console.WriteLine("The result of whether {0} > {1} is {2}", x, y, result);
``` | |

	`          Console.ReadKey();`
	`        }`
	`      }`
	`    }`

6.	I have an **int** **x** with a value of **5** and an **int** **y** with a value of **7**. Write a program which tests whether *x is less than or equal to y*, putting the result of this test into a **bool** variable named **result**. Print your findings out to the console.

	`using System;`
	
	`namespace PracticeYourCSharp`
	`{`
	`  class Program`
	`  {`
	`    static void Main(string[] args)`
	`    {`
	`      bool result;`
	`      int x = 5; int y = 7;`
	
	`      result = x <= y;`
	
	`      Console.WriteLine("The result of whether {0} <= {1} is {2}", x, y, result);`
	`      Console.ReadKey();`
	`    }`
	`  }`
	`}`

7.	I have an **int** **x** with a value of **5** and an **int** **y** with a value of **7**. Write a program which tests whether *x is greater than or equal to y*, putting the result of this test into a **bool** variable named **result**. Print your findings out to the console.

	`using System;`
	
	`namespace PracticeYourCSharp`
	`{`
	`  class Program`
	`  {`
	`    static void Main(string[] args)`
	`    {`
	`      bool result;`
	`      int x = 5; int y = 7;`
	
	`      result = x >= y;`
	
	`      Console.WriteLine("The result of whether {0} >= {1} is {2}", x, y, result);`
	`      Console.ReadKey();`
	`    }`
	`  }`
	`}`

8.	I have an **int** **x** with a value of **5** and an **int** **y** with a value of **7**. Write a program which tests whether *x is less than y*, putting the boolean result of this test into a **bool** variable named **result**. Print your findings out to the console.

	`using System;`
	
	`namespace PracticeYourCSharp`
	`{`
	`  class Program`
	`  {`
	`    static void Main(string[] args)`
	`    {`
	`      bool result;`
	`      int x = 5; int y = 7;`
	
	`      result = x < y;`
	
	`      Console.WriteLine("The result of whether {0} < {1} is {2}", x, y, result);`

|   | ```
      Console.ReadKey();
    }
  }
}
``` |
| 9. | I have an int x with a value of 5 and an int y with a value of 7. Write a program which tests whether *x is not equal to y*. Put the boolean result of this test into a bool variable named result and print your findings out to the console. |
|   | ```
using System;
namespace PracticeYourCSharp
{
  class Program
  {
    static void Main(string[] args)
    {
      bool result;
      int x = 5; int y = 7;

      result = (x != y);

      Console.WriteLine("The result of whether {0} is not equal to {1} is {2}", x, y, result);
      Console.ReadKey();
    }
  }
}
``` |
| 10. | I have an int x with a value of 5 and an int y with a value of 7. Write a program which tests whether *x is not greater than y*. Put the boolean result of this test into a bool named result and print your findings out to the console. |
| | ```
using System;
namespace PracticeYourCSharp
{
  class Program
  {
    static void Main(string[] args)
    {
      bool result;
      int x = 5, y = 7;

      result = !(x > y);

      Console.WriteLine("The result of whether {0} is not > {1} is {2}", x, y, result);
      Console.ReadKey();
    }
  }
}
```
**Note:** There is no not greater than operator. Therefore putting the symbol for not (!) outside the bracket where the > is used has the desired effect of not greater than. |
| 11. | Write a program which tests whether x is greater than 5 *and* y is greater than 7.<br>Test the program with the following combinations of x and y respectively and print the result out after each test: (1,1), (6,7) and (15,15). |
```

	Solution #1
	``csharp
	using System;
	
	namespace PracticeYourCSharp
	{
	  class Program
	  {
	    static void Main(string[] args)
	    {
	      bool result;
	      int x, y;
	
	      x = 1; y = 1; result = ((x > 5) && (y > 7)); Console.WriteLine(result);
	      x = 6; y = 7; result = ((x > 5) && (y > 7)); Console.WriteLine(result);
	      x = 15; y = 15; result = ((x > 5) && (y > 7)); Console.WriteLine(result);
	      Console.ReadKey();
	    }
	  }
	}
	``
	
	Solution #2
	``csharp
	using System;
	
	namespace PracticeYourCSharp
	{
	  class Program
	  {
	    static void Main(string[] args)
	    {
	      bool result;
	      int x, y;
	
	      x = 1; y = 1; result = ((x > 5) & (y > 7)); Console.WriteLine(result);
	      x = 6; y = 7; result = ((x > 5) & (y > 7)); Console.WriteLine(result);
	      x = 15; y = 15; result = ((x > 5) & (y > 7)); Console.WriteLine(result);
	      Console.ReadKey();
	    }
	  }
	}
	``

12.	What is the difference between the two solutions presented to the preceding exercise?
	The first solution is written using a "short-circuiting" logical operator, whereas the second one is not.
13.	What is the difference between short-circuiting logical operators and the regular logical operators?
	The short-circuiting logical operators stop testing as soon as they realize that the whole test can be deemed to have failed as soon as the failure of a sub-test of the test under assessment can be determined as causing the failure of the whole test; therefore there would be no point in continuing/completing the evaluation. Using the first test in the solution to exercise 11 above as an example, there is no point in bothering to check whether y > 7 when you already know that x is less than 5 and that both parts of the test are required to be true. The regular logical operators however will evaluate the whole conditional statement instead of stopping at a failed sub-test. The result of this difference is that the short-circuiting logical operator can potentially perform faster than the regular logical operators.
14.	Write a program which tests whether x is greater than 5 and y is less than 7. (Note: x, y and any other variables in this and subsequent exercises in this chapter are of type int; however you can use any other numerical type if you prefer). Test the program with the following combinations of x and y respectively and print the result out after each test: (1,1), (6,5) and (4,5).

	``csharp
	using System;
	namespace PracticeYourCSharp
	{
	  class Program
	``

```
    {
      static void Main(string[] args)
      {
        bool result;
        int x, y;

        x = 1; y = 1;  result = ((x > 5) && (y < 7)); Console.WriteLine(result);
        x = 6; y = 5;  result = ((x > 5) && (y < 7)); Console.WriteLine(result);
        x = 4; y = 5;  result = ((x > 5) && (y < 7)); Console.WriteLine(result);
        Console.ReadKey();
      }
    }
}
```

15. Write a program which tests whether x is greater than 5 or y is less than 7.
Test the program with the following combinations of x and y respectively and print the result out after each test: (1,1), (6,5) and (4,15).

```
using System;
namespace PracticeYourCSharp
{
  class Program
  {
    static void Main(string[] args)
    {
      bool result;
      int x, y;

      x = 1; y = 1;   result = ((x > 5) || (y < 7)); Console.WriteLine(result);
      x = 6; y = 5;   result = ((x > 5) || (y < 7)); Console.WriteLine(result);
      x = 4; y = 15;  result = ((x > 5) || (y < 7)); Console.WriteLine(result);
      Console.ReadKey();
    }
  }
}
```

16. Write a program which tests whether x is greater than or equal to 5 and y is equal to 0.
Test the program with the following combinations of x and y respectively and print the result out after each test: (6,0), (5,0) and (4,1).

```
using System;
namespace PracticeYourCSharp
{
  class Program
  {
    static void Main(string[] args)
    {
      bool result;
      int x, y;

      x = 6; y = 0; result = ((x >= 5) && (y == 0)); Console.WriteLine(result);
      x = 5; y = 0; result = ((x >= 5) && (y == 0)); Console.WriteLine(result);
      x = 4; y = 1; result = ((x >= 5) && (y == 0)); Console.WriteLine(result);
      Console.ReadKey();
    }
  }
}
```

17. Write a program which tests whether x is greater than or equal to 5 and y is *not* equal to 0.
Test the program with the following combinations of x and y respectively and print the result out after each test: (6,0), (5,0), (4,1) and (7,2).

```
using System;
namespace PracticeYourCSharp
{
  class Program
  {
```

```csharp
    static void Main(string[] args)
    {
      bool result;
      int x, y;

      x = 6; y = 0; result = ((x >= 5) && (y != 0)); Console.WriteLine(result);
      x = 5; y = 0; result = ((x >= 5) && (y != 0)); Console.WriteLine(result);
      x = 4; y = 1; result = ((x >= 5) && (y != 0)); Console.WriteLine(result);
      x = 7; y = 2; result = ((x >= 5) && (y != 0)); Console.WriteLine(result);
      Console.ReadKey();
    }
  }
}
```

18. Write a program which tests whether *only one of* x or y is greater than 5.
Test the program with the following combinations of x, y respectively and print the result out after each test: (5,5), (6,6), (3,3), (1,10) and (10,1).

```csharp
using System;
namespace PracticeYourCSharp
{
  class Program
  {
    static void Main(string[] args)
    {
      bool result;
      int x, y;

      x = 5;  y = 5;   result = ((x > 5) ^ (y > 5)); Console.WriteLine(result);
      x = 6;  y = 6;   result = ((x > 5) ^ (y > 5)); Console.WriteLine(result);
      x = 3;  y = 3;   result = ((x > 5) ^ (y > 5)); Console.WriteLine(result);
      x = 1;  y = 10;  result = ((x > 5) ^ (y > 5)); Console.WriteLine(result);
      x = 10; y = 1;   result = ((x > 5) ^ (y > 5)); Console.WriteLine(result);
      Console.ReadKey();
    }
  }
}
```

19. Write a program which tests whether x is greater than 5 or y is greater than 15 or z is less than or equal to 25.
Test the program with the following combinations of x, y and z respectively and print the result out after each test: (5, 16, 25), (5, 16, 24), (5, 15, 24) and (4, 5, 30).

```csharp
using System;
namespace PracticeYourCSharp
{
  class Program
  {
    static void Main(string[] args)
    {
      bool result;
      int x, y, z;

      x=5; y=16; z=25; result = ((x > 5) || (y > 15) || (z <= 25)); Console.WriteLine(result);
      x=5; y=16; z=24; result = ((x > 5) || (y > 15) || (z <= 25)); Console.WriteLine(result);
      x=5; y=15; z=24; result = ((x > 5) || (y > 15) || (z <= 25)); Console.WriteLine(result);
      x=4; y=5;  z=30; result = ((x > 5) || (y > 10) || (z <= 25)); Console.WriteLine(result);
      Console.ReadKey();
    }
  }
}
```

20. Write a program which tests whether x is greater than or equal to 5 and either of y or z are less than 15.
Test the program with the following combinations of x, y and z respectively and print the result out after each test: (5,14,20), (5,15,13), (5,10,10) and (4,5,30).

```csharp
using System;
```

```
namespace PracticeYourCSharp
{
  class Program
  {
    static void Main(string[] args)
    {
      bool result;
      int x, y, z;

      x=5; y=14; z=20; result = ((x >= 5) && ((y < 15) || (z < 15))); Console.WriteLine(result);
      x=5; y=15; z=13; result = ((x >= 5) && ((y < 15) || (z < 15))); Console.WriteLine(result);
      x=5; y=10; z=10; result = ((x >= 5) && ((y < 15) || (z < 15))); Console.WriteLine(result);
      x=4; y=5;  z=30; result = ((x >= 5) && ((y < 15) || (z < 15))); Console.WriteLine(result);
      Console.ReadKey();
    }
  }
}
```

If desired, the individual sub-conditions can be broken down in the following manner:
```
bool subResult01 = x >= 5;
bool subResult02 = ((y < 15) || (z < 15));
bool result = (subResult01 && subResult02);
```

21. Write a program which tests whether x is greater than or equal to 5 or either y or z are less than 15. Test the program with the following combinations of x, y and z respectively and print the result out after each test: (5,14,20), (5,15,13), (5,10,10), (4,5,30), (1,20,7) and (1,20,20).

```
using System;
namespace PracticeYourCSharp
{
  class Program
  {
    static void Main(string[] args)
    {
      bool result;
      int x, y, z;

      x=5;y=14;z=20; result = ((x >= 5) || ((y < 15) || (z < 15))); Console.WriteLine(result);
      x=5;y=15;z=13; result = ((x >= 5) || ((y < 15) || (z < 15))); Console.WriteLine(result);
      x=5;y=10;z=10; result = ((x >= 5) || ((y < 15) || (z < 15))); Console.WriteLine(result);
      x=4;y=5;z=30;  result = ((x >= 5) || ((y < 15) || (z < 15))); Console.WriteLine(result);
      x=1;y=20;z=7;  result = ((x >= 5) || ((y < 15) || (z < 15))); Console.WriteLine(result);
      x=1;y=20;z=20; result = ((x >= 5) || ((y < 15) || (z < 15))); Console.WriteLine(result);
      Console.ReadKey();
    }
  }
}
```

22. Write a program which tests whether x is greater than or equal to 5 or only one of y or z are less than 15. Test the program with the following combinations of x, y and z respectively and print the result out after each test: (5,14,14), (5,20,13), (6,5,30) and (6,20,20).

```
using System;
namespace PracticeYourCSharp
{
  class Program
  {
    static void Main(string[] args)
    {
      bool result;
      int x, y, z;

      x=5;y=14;z=14; result = ((x >= 5) || ((y < 15) ^ (z < 15))); Console.WriteLine(result);
      x=5;y=20;z=13; result = ((x >= 5) || ((y < 15) ^ (z < 15))); Console.WriteLine(result);
      x=6;y=5;z=30;  result = ((x >= 5) || ((y < 15) ^ (z < 15))); Console.WriteLine(result);
      x=6;y=20;z=20; result = ((x >= 5) || ((y < 15) ^ (z < 15))); Console.WriteLine(result);
```

	``` Console.ReadKey(); } } }```
23.	Write a program which tests whether x is greater than or equal to 5 and only one of y or z are less than 15. Test the program with the following combinations of x, y and z respectively and print the result out after each test: (5,14,14), (5,15,13) and (5,10,10).
	```using System; namespace PracticeYourCSharp { class Program { static void Main(string[] args) { bool result; int x, y, z; x=5;y=14;z=14; result = ((x >= 5) && ((y < 15) ^ (z < 15))); Console.WriteLine(result); x=5;y=15;z=13; result = ((x >= 5) && ((y < 15) ^ (z < 15))); Console.WriteLine(result); x=5;y=10;z=10; result = ((x >= 5) && ((y < 15) ^ (z < 15))); Console.WriteLine(result); Console.ReadKey(); } } }```

24.	Given the following values and boolean statements, state at which point the value of the result is determined and the processing moves on to the next command.
	  1. x=7;y=14;z=14; result = ((x >= 5) || ((y < 15) ^ (z < 15)));
	  2. x=5;y=20;z=13; result = ((x >= 5) | ((y < 15) ^ (z < 15)));
	  3. x=6; y=0; result = ((x >= 5) && (y == 0));
	  4. x=4; y=0; result = ((x >= 5) && (y == 0));
	  5. x=4; y=0; result = ((x >= 5) & (y == 0));

	1. The processing can stop right after determining that x >= 5 is true. The reason for this is because the statement to be evaluated has two parts; and given that they are bound by an OR statement, as soon as one part of it whole statement is true, then the overall statement is true. Therefore, because there is a short-circuiting OR operator, the evaluation can stop as early as possible. 2. The processing will evaluate right to the end of the statement. The reason is because we use a regular OR operator, rather than a short-circuiting one. 3. The statement must be fully evaluated, because even though it uses a short-circuiting boolean operator, the fact that it is an AND operator mandates that all parts have to be true, therefore all parts have to be evaluated until either of 1) a subpart being evaluated is determined to be false or 2) the end of the statement. 4. Evaluation is completed as soon as it is determined that x is less than 5, given that we have a short-circuiting operator. 5. The whole statement is evaluated, even after it is determined that the first part has failed (and thus in this case the whole statement has failed) because we are not using a short-circuiting operator.

In the chapter on *Conditional Processing*, we will use the return values from boolean operations to make decisions on which parts (branches) of our code to run.

Chapter 5. Strings: Basic Handling

The objective of this chapter is to ensure that you are conversant with strings in C#, given the fact that string manipulation is a key feature of any programming language. Among the string exercises presented in this chapter are exercises on string variable declaration, concatenation, case modification, equality testing, substring manipulation as well as formatting of strings for output. Your understanding of the immutability of string objects is also exercised.

The key class on which exercises are presented in this chapter is the class String.

Note: Due to the intertwining of the topic of string handling with other topics yet to be discussed, we will deal with strings as far as possible in this chapter and address other aspects of strings again in the chapters on StringBuffer, the Char type and arrays and also to different degrees in other chapters as appropriate.

1.	In C#, what is the difference between the type String and the type string?	There is no difference. string is a built-in alias for System.String. A general usage convention however is that when declaring a string object we use string, but when refering to string methods we use String.<method name>.
2.	Write a program which declares a string variable named firstName and sets its value to the word *"John"*.	```using System;

namespace PracticeYourCSharp
{
    class Program
    {
        static void Main(string[] args)
        {
            string firstName = "John";
            Console.ReadKey();
        }
    }
}``` |
| 3. | *(string concatenation)*
I have the string variables s1 and s2 with values as indicated:
s1 = "John";
s2 = "Leavings";
Using the overloaded addition (+) operator, put into a third string variable s3 the concatenation of these two strings, ensuring that you put a space in-between them. Print s3 out to the console. | ```using System;

namespace PracticeYourCSharp
{
    class Program
    {
        static void Main(string[] args)
        {
            string s1 = "John";
            string s2 = "Leavings";

            string s3 = s1 + " " + s2;
            Console.WriteLine(s3);
            Console.ReadKey();
        }
    }
}``` |
| 4. | Repeat the preceding exercise, using the Concat method of the class String. | ```using System;

namespace PracticeYourCSharp
{
    class Program
    {
        static void Main(string[] args)
        {
            string s1 = "John";
            string s2 = "Leavings";``` |

|   |   | ```
string s3 = String.Concat(s1, " ", s2);
        Console.WriteLine(s3);
        Console.ReadKey();
      }
    }
}
``` |
| 5. | Determine and print out the length of the string contained in the string variable firstName of exercise 2 above. *Hint: Use the Length property of the String class.* | |
| | ```
using System;

namespace PracticeYourCSharp
{
  class Program
  {
    static void Main(string[] args)
    {
      string firstName = "John";
      int stringLength = 0;   // We will use this variable for the length.
      stringLength = firstName.Length;
      Console.WriteLine("The length of the first name is {0}", stringLength);
      Console.ReadKey();
    }
  }
}
```
**Note:** We could, without having declared the variable stringLength have printed the length of the string directly in the Console.WriteLine statement as shown below:
`Console.WriteLine("The length of the first name is {0}", firstName.Length);` | |
| 6. | Print out the value of the variable firstName from the preceding exercise in uppercase. *Hint: Use the String method ToUpper().* | |
|   | ```
using System;

namespace PracticeYourCSharp
{
  class Program
  {
    static void Main(string[] args)
    {
      string firstName = "John";
      Console.WriteLine("firstName as all uppercase is {0}", firstName.ToUpper());
      Console.ReadKey();
    }
  }
}
``` | |
| 7. | Print out the value of the variable firstName from the preceding exercise in lowercase. | |
| | ```
using System;

namespace PracticeYourCSharp
{
  class Program
  {
    static void Main(string[] args)
    {
      string firstName = "John";
      string firstNameLowerCase =
             firstName.ToLower();
      Console.WriteLine("First name
          as all lowercase is {0}",
          firstNameLowerCase);
      Console.ReadKey();
    }
  }
``` **OR** ```
using System;

namespace PracticeYourCSharp
{
  class Program
  {
    static void Main(string[] args)
    {
      string firstName = "John";
      Console.WriteLine("First name as all
          lowercase is {0}", firstName.ToLower());
      Console.ReadKey();
    }
  }
}
```
**Note:** Here we just executed the desired method within the |
```

	}	parameter field of the method `Console.WriteLine`.
8.	Ask the user for their first name and then for their last name and respond with a statement stating *"Your full name is <last name (in uppercase)>, <first name (in uppercase)>"*. For example, if the user enters a first name of *"Jay"* and a last name of *"Doe"*, print *"Your full name is DOE, JAY"*.	

```
using System;

namespace PracticeYourCSharp
{
  class Program
  {
    static void Main(string[] args)
    {
      string firstName = ""; // declare a string that will receive the value
      string lastName = "";  // declare a string that will receive the value

      Console.Write("What is your first name please? ");
      firstName = Console.ReadLine();
      Console.Write("What is your last name please? ");
      lastName = Console.ReadLine();
      Console.WriteLine("Your full name is {0}, {1}", lastName.ToUpper(), firstName.ToUpper());
      Console.ReadKey();
    }
  }
}
```

9.	What does the statement *a string is immutable* mean?

What it means is that once a value is assigned to a string, C# does not actually allow the value contained in the string to be changed. However, this bears explanation since, in a sense, we can change the contents of a `string` as shown below:

```
string s1 = "Hello.";
s1 = s1 + " How are you?";
```

When we add the string *"How are you?"* to `s1`, what really happens is that the first `s1` string reference is destroyed and a whole brand new string (the contents that is) and string reference is created and assigned to the variable `s1` in the background! (Strings are *reference types*; the concept of reference types will be looked at later in this book).

Why is this knowledge of the immutability of objects of the `string` class important to know? It is important to know for a number of reasons, including (1) the fact that modifying a `string` (which we now know causes the string reference to be destroyed and recreated) is relatively expensive timewise. Therefore, for situations where we have to manipulate a string often, it is best that the class **StringBuilder** which is mutable be used rather than the class **String** and (2) if the particular memory reference to which a given `string` variable pertains is important to you then you should know that it will be changed when you modify the contents of the given `string` variable.

Really strings can be referred to as *immutable reference* types. They have unique behaviour, in particular the following:
  1. (Previously stated) They cannot be changed once created. If you modify a `string` (appending, trimming, etc.), the original string reference is thrown away in the background and a new one is created and presented to the program in which it was changed, *with the same variable name*, giving you the appearance that the contents of the `string` variable in hand were changed (As stated earlier, in a sense it is changed by C# creating a new string and making the variable `s1` point to the location in memory of the new string). For many programs, this fact has no negative impact on the construction of the program as this throwing away and re-creation is hidden from the programmer who requested the modification.
  2. Even though they are reference types, due to their immutability, if you pass a `string` to another method which then tries to modify its contents, unlike other reference types the contents of the original `string` in the calling method will not be modified.
  3. `string` equality functionality is treated like equality for value types rather than equality for reference types.

	Some of these points will be observed in exercises in Chapter 28. Passing By Reference, Passing By Value. **Note:** Despite the extensive explanation above, for general intents and purposes, consider that you *can* change the contents of a string.	
10.	I have a string object reference `s1`, initialized as follows: `string s1 = null;` What does this initialization to the value `null` mean?	
	The initialization to the value `null` is saying in effect that "this string object reference `s1` is not pointing to any object". The value `null` does not only apply to string variables; it can be used for any object reference variable When any object reference has the value of `null`, it is saying that the object reference in question is not pointing to any object. The value `null` is the default value of reference type variables.	
String Equality		

11.	*(comparison of string type with the == operator despite string being a reference type)*
	I have the following two initialized `string` variables:
	  `string s1= "Hello";`
	  `string s2= "Hello";`
	State the result of the following: `bool x = (s1==s2);`	

	Result: True **Explanation:** Yes, while the `string` type is a reference type, the equality operator works for them the same way as for value types. This is because the equality operator has been "overloaded" by the class `String`. We do exercises on <u>reference types</u> and <u>operator overloading</u> later in this book.	

12.	Given two strings `s1` & `s2`, using the `<string>.Equals` *instance method*, write a line of code to test whether `s1` & `s2` are equal and put the result into a `bool` variable `x`.	`bool x = s1.Equals(s2));`
		OR
		`bool x = s2.Equals(s1));`

13.	Given two strings `s1` & `s2`, using the static class method `String.Equals`, write a line of code to test whether `s1` & `s2` are equal and put the result into a `bool` variable `x`.	`bool x = String.Equals(s1,s2);` **Note:** Compare this answer to the code from the exercise above.
Substrings		
14.	What is the index of the first character in a string in C#?	
	The index of the first character in a C# string is 0. Therefore if for example we have 10 characters in a string, the indexes of the individual characters therein from the 1st to the 10th will be from 0 to 9 in order.	
15.	Given the string *"Mary had a little lamb"*, manually determine the position of the character 'h' in the string.	The character is at position 5. This is because character position enumeration in C# for strings starts from 0. Therefore the positions in this string would be; M 0 a 1 r 2 y 3 4 h 5 a 6 d 7
16.	Given the string *"Mary had a little lamb"*, write a program to determine the position of the letter 'i' in this string. Print this position out to the console stating: *The position of letter 'i' is : <position>*. *Hint:* `String` method `<string>.IndexOf`	
	Solution #1	

```
using System;

namespace PracticeYourCSharp
{
  class Program
  {
    static void Main(string[] args)
    {
      string rhymeLine = "Mary had a little lamb";
      int letterPosition = rhymeLine.IndexOf('i'); // note single quotes for the single letter

      Console.WriteLine("The position of the letter \'i\' is: {0}.", letterPosition);
      Console.ReadKey();
    }
  }
}
```

Note: a single character literal is referred to using single quotes, not double quotes; as seen in this example when we look for the index of `'i'` using the `IndexOf` method.

Solution #2

```
using System;

namespace PracticeYourCSharp
{
  class Program
  {
    static void Main(string[] args)
    {
      string rhymeLine = "Mary had a little lamb";
      Console.WriteLine("The position of the letter \"i\" is {0}", rhymeLine.IndexOf('i'));
      Console.ReadKey();
    }
  }
}
```

Note: In this variant of the answer, we simply call the `IndexOf` method directly within the parameter section of the `Console.WriteLine` method.

Solution #3

```
using System;

namespace PracticeYourCSharp
{
  class Program
  {
    static void Main(string[] args)
    {
      int letterPosition = "Mary had a little lamb".IndexOf('i');
      Console.WriteLine("The position of the letter \"i\" is {0}", letterPosition);
      Console.ReadKey();
    }
  }
}
```

Note: Note carefully how in this solution we show how we can apply a string method *directly to the literal string without declaring a variable to hold the string itself*.

Solution #4

```
using System;

namespace PracticeYourCSharp
{
  class Program
  {
    static void Main(string[] args)
    {
```

	``csharp
            Console.WriteLine("The position of the letter \"i\" is {0}",
                        "Mary had a little lamb".IndexOf('i'));
            Console.ReadKey();
        }
    }
}
```
**Note(s):** In this variant of the answer, note how no variables are declared at all; we just apply the `IndexOf` method directly to the string in the parameter section of the `Console.WriteLine` method. |
| 17. | Given the string *"Mary had a little lamb"*, what is the position of the 2nd letter '**a**' in this string?<br>*Hint: the overloaded `String.IndexOf()` method.* |
|   | ```csharp
using System;

namespace PracticeYourCSharp
{
    class Program
    {
        static void Main(string[] args)
        {
            string rhymeLine = "Mary had a little lamb";
            int positionOfFirstOccurrence = rhymeLine.IndexOf('a');
            // Now, that we have the position of the 1st letter 'a' we start looking for
            // the very next letter 'a' after that.
            int positionOfSecondOccurrence = rhymeLine.IndexOf('a',(positionOfFirstOccurrence + 1));
            Console.WriteLine("The position of the 2nd letter \"a\" is {0}",
                        positionOfSecondOccurrence);
            Console.ReadKey();
        }
    }
}
``` |
| 18. | Given the string *"Mary had a little lamb, little lamb, little lamb, Mary had a little lamb that was as white as snow"*, write a program which will determine and output to the console the position of the 2nd occurrence of the word *"little"* in the string. |
|   | ```csharp
using System;

namespace PracticeYourCSharp
{
    class Program
    {
        static void Main(string[] args)
        {
            string rhymeLine = "Mary had a little lamb, little lamb, little lamb, Mary had a little
                        lamb that was as white as snow";
            // So what we have to do is first look for the 1st occurrence of the word "little",
            // and then start searching after that 1st occurrence.
            int iFirstAppearancePosition = rhymeLine.IndexOf("little");
            int iSearchStartPosition = iFirstAppearancePosition + "little".Length;
            // See that we start searching at the end of the 1st instance of the word "little"
            int iSecondAppearancePosition = rhymeLine.IndexOf("little", iSearchStartPosition);
            Console.Write("The 2nd occurrence of \"little\" is at position: {0}",
                        iSecondAppearancePosition);

            Console.ReadKey();
        }
    }
}
``` |
| 19. | Given the string *"Mary had a little lamb,\n little lamb,\n little lamb,\n Mary had a little lamb that was as white as snow"*, write a program to determine and print out the position of the *last* occurrence of the word *"little"* in the string. |
|   | ```csharp
using System;

namespace PracticeYourCSharp
``` |

```csharp
        {
            class Program
            {
                static void Main(string[] args)
                {
                    String rhymeLine = "Mary had a little lamb,\n little lamb,\n little lamb,\n Mary had
                                        a little lamb that was as white as snow";
                    int wordPosition = rhymeLine.LastIndexOf("little");
                    Console.WriteLine("The position of the word \"little\" is {0}", wordPosition);

                    Console.ReadKey();
                }
            }
        }
```

20.	Given the string *"Mary had a little lamb,\n little lamb,\n little lamb,\n Mary had a little lamb that was as white as snow"*, write a program to determine and print out the position of the *last* occurrence of the letter '*w*'. *Hint:* String method `LastIndexOf(char)`
| | ```csharp
using System;

namespace PracticeYourCSharp
{
    class Program
    {
        static void Main(string[] args)
        {
            string rhymeLine = "Mary had a little lamb,\n little lamb,\n little lamb,\n Mary had
                                a little lamb that was as white as snow";
            int letterPosition = rhymeLine.LastIndexOf('w');
            Console.WriteLine("The last position of the letter 'w' is {0}", letterPosition);

            Console.ReadKey();
        }
    }
}
``` |
| 21. | I have the following string, *"Basketball!"*. Print out its length, without declaring any variables. |
| | ```csharp
using System;

namespace PracticeYourCSharp
{
    class Program
    {
        static void Main(string[] args)
        {
            Console.WriteLine("The length is {0}", "Basketball!".Length);
        }
    }
}
``` |
| 22. | Given a C# string that contains the rhyme *"Mary had a little lamb,\nlittle lamb,\nlittle lamb,\nMary had a little lamb that was as white as snow"*, write code to replace the word *"little"* with the phrase *"big big"* (to keep the rhyme ☺) everywhere the word *"little"* appears. Print out the modified string.
 Hint: String method `Replace` |
| | ```csharp
using System;

namespace PracticeYourCSharp
{
    class Program
    {
        static void Main(string[] args)
        {
            string rhymeLine = "Mary had a little lamb,\nlittle lamb,\nlittle lamb,\nMary had
                                a little lamb that was as white as snow";
            String newRhymeLine = rhymeLine.Replace("little", "big big");
``` |
```

|   | ```
        Console.WriteLine("The new rhyme is:\n{0}", newRhymeLine);
        Console.ReadKey();
      }
    }
}
``` |
| 23. | Given the rhyme *"Mary had a little lamb,\n little lamb,\n little lamb,\n Mary had a little lamb that was as white as snow"*, write a program which *removes* the word *"little"* wherever it appears in the rhyme. Print out the resulting string. |
|   | ```
using System;
namespace PracticeYourCSharp
{
  class Program
  {
    static void Main(string[] args)
    {
      string rhymeLine = "Mary had a little lamb,\nlittle lamb,\nlittle lamb,\nMary had
                          a little lamb that was as white as snow";
      string newRhymeLine = rhymeLine.Replace("little", "");
      // "little" is replaced with a blank string. The double-quotes with nothing
      // in-between is a blank string.
      Console.WriteLine("The new rhyme is\n{0}", newRhymeLine);
      Console.ReadKey();
    }
  }
}
``` |
| 24. | We have a phone number given as the string 111-222-3333, of which the first 3 digits are the area code. Extract and print out the area code. |
|   | ```
using System;
namespace PracticeYourCSharp
{
  class Program
  {
    static void Main(string[] args)
    {
      string phoneNumber = "111-222-3333";
      int startPosition = 0; // We are starting at the beginning of the string
      int numberOfCharacters = 3;
      string areaCode = phoneNumber.Substring(startPosition, numberOfCharacters);
      Console.Write("The area code is :{0}.", areaCode);

      Console.ReadKey();
    }
  }
}
``` |
| 25. | We have a phone number given as the string 111-222-3333, of which the last 7 digits are the subscriber number. Extract the subscriber number, that is, the substring 222-3333. |
|   | ```
using System;

namespace PracticeYourCSharp
{
  class Program
  {
    static void Main(string[] args)
    {
      string phoneNumber = "111-222-3333";
      int startPosition = 4;
      // We are starting after the first dash. Remember start counting at 0.
      string SubscriberNum = phoneNumber.Substring(startPosition);
      // Extracts to the end of the string
      Console.Write("The subscriber number is : {0} ", SubscriberNum);
``` |

	``` Console.ReadKey(); } } } ```	
26.	We have a phone number, 111-222-3333, of which the first 3 characters are the area code. The next 3 numbers are the "Central Office number". Extract this number and print it out to the console.	
	``` using System; namespace PracticeYourCSharp { class Program { static void Main(string[] args) { string phoneNumber = "111-222-3333"; int startPosition = 4; // We are starting after the first dash int NumberOfCharsToExtract = 3; string CONumberStr = phoneNumber.Substring(4, NumberOfCharsToExtract); // Extracts to the end of the string Console.Write("The Central Office number is : {0}", CONumberStr); Console.ReadKey(); } } } ```	
27.	We have a phone number given as the string 111-222-3333, of which the first 3 characters are the area code. Find and print out the *last* position of the number **1** within the area code.	
	``` using System; namespace PracticeYourCSharp { class Program { static void Main(string[] args) { string phoneNumber = "111-222-3333"; int lastSearchPosition = 2; int foundPosition = phoneNumber.LastIndexOf('1', lastSearchPosition); Console.Write("Last position of the number 1 in the area code is : {0}",foundPosition); Console.ReadKey(); } } } ```	
28.	I have the following string: " *how are you?* " Write a program which gets rid of both the leading and trailing spaces and print the result out. Confirm that you have erased the trailing spaces by printing out the letter 'X' right behind the trimmed string.	``` using System; namespace PracticeYourCSharp { class Program { static void Main(string[] args) { string s1 = " how are you? "; string ending = "X"; string s2 = s1.Trim(); Console.WriteLine("{0}{1}", s2, ending); Console.ReadKey(); } } } ```
29.	Continuing with the string in the exercise above, write a program	``` using System; namespace PracticeYourCSharp ```

|  | to trim *just the trailing spaces*, but not the leading spaces. Print the trimmed statement out. Confirm that you have erased the trailing spaces by printing out the letter 'X' right behind the trimmed string. | ```
{
  class Program
  {
    static void Main(string[] args)
    {
      string s1 = "    how are you?    ";
      string ending = "X";
      string s2 = s1.TrimEnd();
      Console.WriteLine("{0}{1}", s2, ending);
      Console.ReadKey();
    }
  }
}
``` |
| 30. | Continuing with the string in the exercise above, write code to trim *just the leading spaces*, but not the trailing spaces. Print the trimmed statement out. Confirm that you have erased only the leading spaces by printing out the letter 'X' right behind the trimmed string. | ```
using System;
namespace PracticeYourCSharp
{
  class Program
  {
    static void Main(string[] args)
    {
      string s1 = "    how are you?    ";
      string ending = "X";
      string s2 = s1.TrimStart();
      Console.WriteLine("{0}{1}", s2, ending);
      Console.ReadKey();
    }
  }
}
``` |
| 31. | The string *"Mary had a little lamb,\nlittle lamb,\nlittle lamb,\nMary had a little lamb that was as white as snow"* prints out as:

Mary had a little lamb,
little lamb,
little lamb,
Mary had a little lamb that was as white as snow

Write a program which determines the position relative to the start of the 2nd line of the rhyme of the word *"lamb"*.

Hint: String method IndexOf(startpos, endpos) | |
|  | Code logic<br>We need to find the starting position of the 2$^{nd}$ line; that is determined as the 1$^{st}$ position after the first new line in the rhyme.<br>We then need to find the ending position of the 2$^{nd}$ line; that is determined as the 1$^{st}$ newline that appears <u>after</u> the very first new line found earlier.<br>Then we look for the word *"lamb"*.<br><br>```
using System;
namespace PracticeYourCSharp
{
  class Program
  {
    static void Main(string[] args)
    {
      string rhymeLine = "Mary had a little lamb,\nlittle lamb,\n little lamb,\n Mary had a little lamb that was as white as snow";
      int startPos = rhymeLine.IndexOf('\n') + 1;
      // 1st position after the newline gets us to line 2
      int endPos = rhymeLine.IndexOf('\n', startPos);
      int wordPos = rhymeLine.IndexOf("lamb", startPos, endPos);
      // Now we have the starting and ending positions
``` | |
```

|   | ```
        Console.WriteLine("The last position of the word \"lamb\" in line 2 : {0}",
                        (wordPos - startPos));
        Console.ReadKey();
      }
    }
}
``` |
| **Formatting String Output** ||
| 32. | I have the following `string` objects: `s1="Hello"` and `s2="Jonathan"`, where the shorter string is always in `s1`. Write a program which will print such a pair of strings, each of them out on successive lines, `s1` first, right aligned as follows:

   Hello
Jonathan

Hint: `String.PadLeft` |
|   | ```
using System;

namespace PracticeYourCSharp
{
  class Program
  {
    static void Main(string[] args)
    {
      string s1 = "Hello", s2 = "Jonathan";
      s1 = s1.PadLeft(s1.Length + (s2.Length - s1.Length));// Now s1 is as long as s2
      Console.WriteLine(s1);
      Console.WriteLine(s2);
      Console.ReadKey();
    }
  }
}
```<br><br>**Note:** Here you see the use of the `<string>.PadLeft` method which pads the string in question on the left, bringing it up to the desired length. |
| 33. | Modify the answer to the exercise above, pre-padding the shorter string with the character `'o'` rather than with spaces. |
|   | ```
using System;

namespace PracticeYourCSharp
{
  class Program
  {
    static void Main(string[] args)
    {
      string s1 = "Hello", s2 = "Jonathan";
      s1 = s1.PadLeft(s1.Length + (s2.Length - s1.Length), 'o');
      Console.WriteLine(s1);
      Console.WriteLine(s2);
      Console.ReadKey();
    }
  }
}
``` |
| 34. | I have the following `string` objects: `s1="Hello"` and `s2="Jonathan"`, where the shorter string is always in `s1`. Write a program which will print such a pair of strings, each of them on successive lines, *left aligned*, however, pad the shorter line with as many periods (full-stops) as necessary for it to be the length of the longer string.

The result from this exercise should be:

Hello...
Jonathan |
|   | ```
using System;

namespace PracticeYourCSharp
``` |

| | ```
    {
      class Program
      {
        static void Main(string[] args)
        {
          string s1 = "Hello", s2 = "Jonathan";
          s1 = s1.PadRight(s1.Length + (s2.Length - s1.Length), '.');
          Console.WriteLine(s1);
          Console.WriteLine(s2);
          Console.ReadKey();
        }
      }
    }
``` |
| 35. | I have the following string variables; s1="Mary", s2="had", s3="a", s4="little" and s5="lamb". Print each of them out, , in a field that is of width 10 characters. |
| | ```
using System;

namespace PracticeYourCSharp
{
  class Program
  {
    static void Main(string[] args)
    {
      string s1 = "Mary", s2 = "had", s3 = "a", s4 = "little", s5 = "lamb";
      Console.WriteLine("{0,10}", s1);
      Console.WriteLine("{0,10}", s2);
      Console.WriteLine("{0,10}", s3);
      Console.WriteLine("{0,10}", s4);
      Console.WriteLine("{0,10}", s5);

      Console.ReadKey();
    }
  }
}
``` |
| 36. | Repeat the preceding exercise, however with the output *left-justified*. Also, bound each individual justified string with the character '|' on both the left & right. |
| | ```
using System;

namespace PracticeYourCSharp
{
  class Program
  {
    static void Main(string[] args)
    {
      string s1 = "Mary", s2 = "had", s3 = "a", s4 = "little", s5 = "lamb";
      Console.WriteLine("|{0,-10}|", s1);
      Console.WriteLine("|{0,-10}|", s2);
      Console.WriteLine("|{0,-10}|", s3);
      Console.WriteLine("|{0,-10}|", s4);
      Console.WriteLine("|{0,-10}|", s5);

      Console.ReadKey();
    }
  }
}
``` |
| 37. | What is the output of the following code? |
| | ```
using System;

namespace PracticeYourCSharp
{
  class Program
  {
    static void Main(string[] args)
``` |

|   | ```
        {
            int x = 10;
            string s1 = "hello";
            string formatString01 = "{0," + x + "}";
            Console.WriteLine(formatString01, s1);
            Console.ReadKey();
        }
    }
}
``` |
| | The output of the code is a right justified `string s1` within a 10 character field.

The objective of this particular exercise is to ensure that you are familiar with the fact that the formatting portion of a `Console.Write/WriteLine` composite formatted statement is itself just a `string` (expressed in the variable `formatString01` in this example) and therefore can be prepared separately instead of needing to be hardcoded within the `Console.Write/WriteLine` statement. Therefore, if you need programmatically to modify field widths and anything else within the formatting statement you can.

In this example, if we had hardcoded the formatting string, we would have had to write the following code:

`Console.WriteLine("{0,10}", s01);`

The `{0,10}` is the very string that we created in code and put into the variable `formatString01`. |
| 38. | What is the use of the `String.Format` method? |
| | The `String.Format` method is a method whose behavior is essentially like the `Console.Write/WriteLine` methods, however, its output is put into a string, rather than written to the console.

This method is useful when at given points in your code you produce intermediate output and prefer to append the intermediate output to a string with the intent to put the final string out at a given point later in your processing. |
```

Chapter 6. Conditional Processing

A key part of any computer language is the ability to direct the execution *(or not)* of specific sections/blocks of code based on the result of boolean conditions. This chapter exercises your skill in using conditional processing to direct the execution of specific blocks of code by using the conditional processing statements `if`, `if/else`, `else` as well as the `switch` and `goto` statements.

Conditional Operators: **if** *and* **if/else**
1.	I have two integer variables, x and y, with values 5 and 7 respectively. Compare the two values and on comparison print a statement that states which is greater. Use only `if` conditions to do the comparisons.

<table>
<tr><td>

```
using System;

class Program
{
  static void Main(string[] args)
  {
    bool b01;
    bool b02;
    int x = 5;
    int y = 7;

    b01 = x > y;
    b02 = x < y;

    if (b01 == true)
    {
      Console.WriteLine("{0} is greater
                        than {1}", x, y);
    }
    if (b02 == true)
    {
      Console.WriteLine("{0} is greater
                        than {1}", y, x);
    }
    Console.ReadKey();
  }
}
```

</td><td>**OR**</td><td>

```
using System;

class Program
{
  static void Main(string[] args)
  {
    int x=5;
    int y=7;

    if (x > y)
    {
      Console.WriteLine("{0} is greater
                        than {1}",x, y);
    }
    if (y > x)
    {
      Console.WriteLine("{0} is greater
                        than {1}", y, x);
    }
    Console.ReadKey();
  }
}
```

</td></tr>
</table>

Notes: On comparing the two solutions, it should be observed that the boolean variables `b01` and `b02` are not required, as the statement **(x > y)** or the statement **(y > x)** is a self-contained statement that returns a boolean result of `true` or `false`. The statement `if(<whatever>)` really means **"if(<whatever is in this bracket is true>)**, then run the commands in the braces following the `if`".

2.	I have two floating point variables, x and y, with values 5.77 and 7.83 respectively. Compare the two values and if they are equal state so, otherwise state that they are not equal. Use an `if/else` construct.

```
using System;

namespace PracticeYourCSharp
{
  class Program
  {
    static void Main(string[] args)
    {
      float x = 5.77f;
      float y = 7.83f;

      if (x == y)
      {
```

	``
            Console.WriteLine("The numbers are equal");
        }
        else
        {
            Console.WriteLine("The numbers are not equal");
        }
        Console.ReadKey();
      }
   }
}
```
**Explanation**: the `else` condition can be described as follows:
Whatever is false about the `if` condition is handled by the `else` condition. Recall from the earlier example that `if(<whatever>)` means `if(<whatever is in this bracket is true>)`. The `else` then handles whatever failed the `if` question. |
| 3. | I have two integer variables, x and y. Write a program which compares them and on comparison prints which is greater, otherwise if they are equal then the program should state that they are equal. Hardcode the values 5 and 7 for x and y to test your program. |
|   | <table><tr><td>

```
using System;

namespace PracticeYourCSharp
{
   class Program
   {
      static void Main(string[] args)
      {
         int x = 5;
         int y = 7;

         if (x > y)
         {
            Console.WriteLine("{0} is > {1}",
                              x, y);
         }
         if (y > x)
         {
            Console.WriteLine("{0} is > {1}",
                              y, x);
         }
         if (x == y)
         {
            Console.WriteLine("{0} is eq. {1}",
                              x, y);
         }
         Console.ReadKey();
      }
   }
}
```

</td><td>OR</td><td>

```
using System;

namespace PracticeYourCSharp
{
   class Program
   {
      static void Main(string[] args)
      {
         int x = 5;
         int y = 7;

         if (x > y)
         {
            Console.WriteLine("{0} is > {1}",
                              x, y);
         }
         else if (y > x)
         {
            Console.WriteLine("{0} is > {1}",
                              y, x);
         }
         else if (x == y)
         {
            Console.WriteLine("{0} is eq. {1}",
                              x, y);
         }
         Console.ReadKey();
      }
   }
}
```

</td></tr></table> |
4.	What is the difference between the two solutions shown for the preceding exercise?
	The 1st solution goes through and evaluates each of the conditions in the respective `if(<condition>)` statements. However there is no real need to test subsequent related conditions if a preceding condition has been evaluated to be true (for example in this particular exercise since we already know that x > y then there is no point in checking whether y > x , or whether x==y). Therefore, the 2nd solution which uses the `else if` conditions which are not evaluated if a preceding condition is true is more efficient.
5.	Write a program, which based on a value given for the temperature gives the following output: 1. If the temperature < 60 then output *"Cold enough to wear a coat"* 2. If the temperature > 60 but < 68 then output *"Cold enough to wear a jacket"* 3. Otherwise simply output *"No outerwear required!"*
```

Chapter 6: Conditional Processing

	Hardcode the temperature value into the program.
| | ```csharp
using System;

namespace PracticeYourCSharp
{
  class Program
  {
    static void Main(string[] args)
    {
      int temperature = 0;
      // Set it to an initial value for our code. We can change it and recompile
      // in order to test the code for different temperatures.
      if (temperature < 60)
      {
        Console.WriteLine("Cold enough to wear a coat");
      }
      else if (temperature < 68)
      {
        //We've already handled whatever is less than 60
        Console.WriteLine("Cold enough to wear a jacket");
      }
      else
      {
        Console.WriteLine("No outerwear required!");
      }
      Console.ReadKey();
    }
  }
}
``` |

	Combining multiple conditions	
| 6. | Given two numerical variables x and y, explain what the following code means:<br>```csharp
if ((x > 5) && (y > 20))
{
  // Perform action...
}
``` | The code means, if x is greater than 5 **AND** y is greater than 20 then perform the actions in the braces. |
| 7. | Given two numerical variables x and y, explain what the following code means:<br>```csharp
if ((x > 5) || (y < 20))
{
  // Perform action...
}
``` | The code means, if x greater than 5 **OR** y is less than 20 then perform the actions in the braces. |
| 8. | Given three numerical variables x, y and z, give an explanation of what the following code means:<br>```csharp
if ((x > 5) || (y > 20) || (z == 0))
{
  // Perform action...
}
``` | The code means, if x is greater than 5 **OR** y is greater than 20 **OR** z equals 0 then perform the actions in the braces. |
| 9. | Given three integers x, y and z, give an explanation of what the following code means (pay close attention to the placement of the braces):<br>```csharp
if ((x > 5) && ((y > 20) && (z == 0)))
{
``` | The code is first evaluating two different sets of conditions separately, namely:<br>(x > 5)<br>**AND**<br>((y > 20) && (z == 0))<br>The && condition is stating that "if both of the separate |

69
```

`    // Perform action...` `}`	conditions are true", then perform the actions in the braces.

10. Rewrite this code fragment using the <u>ternary operator</u>:

```
int x = 50, y = 0;
if (x > 10)
   y = 5;
else
   y = 27;
Console.WriteLine(y);
```

```
int x = 50, y = 0;
y = x > 10 ? 5 : 27;
Console.WriteLine(y);
```

Note: You can think about the ternary operator in the following way:
`value = question(the result is either true or false)? value if true: value if false;`

11. Ask the user to enter a phone number in the format xxx-yyy-zzzz. Then print out to the console the last position of number **1** within the subscriber number (the *yyy-zzzz* portion). If the number 1 does not appear in the subscriber number then print that fact out.

```
using System;

namespace PracticeYourCSharp
{
  class Program
  {
    static void Main(string[] args)
    {
      Console.WriteLine("Please enter a phone number in the format xxx-yyy-zzzz");
      string phoneNumber = Console.ReadLine();
      int iStartIndex = phoneNumber.IndexOf("-") + 1; // Starting after the 1st dash

      int foundPosition = phoneNumber.LastIndexOf("1", phoneNumber.Length - 1, iStartIndex);
      // This returns the position relative to the beginning of the string
      foundPosition = foundPosition - iStartIndex;
      // Position relative to the subscriber num.
      if (foundPosition >= 0)
      {
        Console.WriteLine("Last position of the number 1 in the subscriber number is {0}: ",
                          foundPosition);
      }
      else
      {
        Console.WriteLine("The number 1 does not appear in the subscriber number\n");
      }
      Console.ReadKey();
    }
  }
}
```

The switch statement

12. Explain your understanding of how the `switch` statement works. Give an example that uses a `switch` statement.

A `switch` statement is a conditional processing construct which, based on the value of a variable under assessment, will execute specific blocks of code called *cases* according to the value of the variable. A `switch` construct uses the keywords `switch`, `case`, `break` and `default` to determine, bound and exit particular blocks of code within the switch construct that we would like to be processed. Each *case* is bounded by the keywords `case` and `break` (break is not required when a `goto` statement is used at the end of a case block). Any condition for which we do not have a `case`/`break` block can be handled by a `default` statement at the end of the `switch` block.

For example, see the following code block:

```csharp
      int zz=10;
      switch(zz)
      {
        case 5:
         Console.WriteLine("zz is equal to 5");
         break; // means end of this particular block. You exit the case (& thus the switch block)
                // at break statements.
        case 6:
        case 7:
         Console.WriteLine("zz is equal to 6 or 7");
         // See that we can combine multiple cases in one block.
         break;
        case 8:case 9:case 10:
         Console.WriteLine("zz is equal to 8, 9 or 10!");
         break;
        default:
         Console.WriteLine("Default covers anything not covered by a case!");
         break;
      }
```

13. Have the user enter the first three letters of the month, then print out to the user how many days the month in question has. Implement this using a `switch` statement.

```csharp
using System;

namespace PracticeYourCSharp
{
  class Program
  {
    static void Main(string[] args)
    {
      Console.Write("Enter the month for which you want to know the number of days: ");
      string month = Console.ReadLine();
      if (month.Length < 3)
      {
        Console.WriteLine("The length of the month should be at least 3 characters");
        Console.WriteLine("exiting...");
        return;
      }
      month = month.ToLower(); // For uniform processing

      month = month.Substring(0, 3); // 3-leftmost characters
      switch (month)
      {
        case "jan": case "mar": case "may": case "jul": case "aug": case "oct": case "dec":
          Console.WriteLine("This month has 31 days");
          break;
        case "apr": case "jun": case "sep": case "nov":
          Console.WriteLine("This month has 30 days");
          break;
        case "feb":
          Console.WriteLine("This month has 28 days");
          break;
        default:
          Console.WriteLine("Invalid month. Enter at least the first 3 letters of a month");
          break;
      }
      Console.ReadKey();
    }
  }
}
```

14. At our hotel, we have a reward card for frequent guests. There are three card levels, namely gold, silver and bronze, with bronze being the lowest level.

The benefits of each of the levels is as follows:

- all levels get a room
- bronze = adds free parking + newspaper
- silver = bronze level features + breakfast
- gold = silver level features + dinner for one

Write a program which takes as input a string indicating which level the guest is at and then using the `switch` & `goto` commands, print out in detail all the benefits of each level. Ensure that you do not replicate code.

Hint: Within a `switch` block you can jump from one `case` to another, using the `goto` statement.

```csharp
using System;

namespace PracticeYourCSharp
{
  class Program
  {
    static void Main(string[] args)
    {
      Console.Write("What is the customer reward level: ");
      string customerLevel = Console.ReadLine();
      customerLevel = customerLevel.ToLower(); //for uniformity in processing
      if((customerLevel.Equals("bronze")==false)&&
         (customerLevel.Equals("silver")==false)&&
         (customerLevel.Equals("gold")==false))
      {
        Console.WriteLine("Guest level must be one of Bronze, Silver or Gold. Exiting");
        return;
      }
      Console.WriteLine("Your benefits are:");
      switch (customerLevel)
      {
        case "bronze":
          Console.WriteLine("\t room");
          Console.WriteLine("\t free parking");
          Console.WriteLine("\t included newspaper");
          break;
        case "silver":
          Console.WriteLine("\t included breakfast");
          goto case "bronze";
          // see the use of goto within a switch statement
          // also notice that we do not have to add a break statement at the end of
          // a case statement where a goto is the last statement therein.
        case "gold":
          Console.WriteLine("\t included dinner for 1");
          goto case "silver";
      }
      Console.ReadKey();
    }
  }
}
```

Note(s): You are encouraged to step through the solution with the debugger to trace the way in which the `goto` statement moves through the cases, especially in the case of `case "gold"` where it jumps to `case "silver"` which itself jumps to `case "bronze"`.

Also note that this particular problem is not best solved by a `switch` block as it does not present the most elegant possible solution, given the "jumping around" that that `goto` statement facilitates. The use of the `goto` statement is generally discouraged in code; its usage in this example is to show you how a `goto` statement can be used within a switch block.

Chapter 7. Arrays

Arrays are a convenient and necessary part of any computing language, as they facilitate the grouping of data items together as an single indexed unit. In this chapter, you get an opportunity to exercise and enhance your skills with arrays in C#. Among the exercises presented in this chapter are exercises on array declaration, creation, initialization, assignment, access, copying, rank determination, reversal, subset manipulation, sorting and element searches. Exercises on multi-dimensional arrays are also presented.

The key class utilized in this chapter is the class `Array`.

1.	In C#, what is an *array*?	An array is a data element that has an indexed list of items. This index is an integer index.
2.	What is the base class from which all arrays inherit?	The abstract class `Array`. All arrays have the behavior (methods, properties, etc.) of this class. Do have a look at the definition of this class in order to get a good understanding of the functionality that arrays support in C#.
3.	I have an array of integers defined as follows: `int[] intArray = new int[3];` Explain in words what each part of this declaration statement means. 1. `int[]` is the type of what we are going to define, which in this case is an array of integers. In a variable declaration, `[]` after the name of a type indicates that it is an array of the type at hand (`int` in this case). 2. `intArray` is the variable name we've chosen to give to this array of integers. 3. `new int[3]` means that we are asking the system to allocate space for an array of 3 integers. 4. `=` This is saying that the newly allocated array of integers is going to be known by the variable name `intArray` which appears on the left-hand side of the equals sign.	
4.	What is the 1st index of an array?	**0**. Arrays in C# always start at index 0.
5.	Write a line of code which will instantiate an `int` array named `intArray` with a capacity for 20 integers.	`int[] intArray = new int[20];`
6.	Assign the value 2 to the 1st index of the array defined above.	`intArray[0] = 2; // Remember that the 1`st` index is 0`
7.	Assign the value 800 to the 1st index of the array above.	`intArray[0] = 800;` **Note:** This simply overwrites what was previously set therein.
8.	Assign the value 17 to the 3rd index of the array `intArray` defined earlier.	`intArray[2] = 17;`
9.	Write a program which instantiates an integer array named `intArray01` that can hold 50 integers. Print out the length of the array using the `Length` property of the class `Array`.	
| | ```
using System;

namespace PracticeYourCSharp
{
  class Program
  {
    static void Main(string[] args)
    {
      int[] intArray01 = new int[50];

      int ArrayLength = intArray01.Length; // The length of the array
      Console.WriteLine("The length of the array is {0}", ArrayLength);

      Console.ReadKey();
``` | |
```

|  | ```
        }
    }
}
``` | |
| 10. | What is the difference between the following two initialization methods for an array?<br><br>```
int[] intArray01 = new int[5];
intArray01[0] = 10;
intArray01[1] = 11;
intArray01[2] = 12;
intArray01[3] = 13;
intArray01[4] = 14;
```<br><br>*versus*<br><br>```
int[] intArray01 = new int[] { 10, 11, 12, 13, 14 };
``` | |
| | In this example, there is no difference at all. The second method is quite convenient when you are hardcoding arrays into a program and also want the length of the array to match the number of elements that you are initializing it with. In this case (the second case), the compiler infers the desired number of elements of the array by counting the number of comma separated items in the braces.

The benefit of the first initialization method however is that we can declare the array to be of a size greater than the number of elements that we plan to initialize it with, as opposed to the second method where the compiler only allocates as many spaces to the array as the number of elements specified at instantiation.

Nonetheless, irrespective of whichever method is chosen, C# provides the ability to modify the number of allocated spaces in an already existing array. | |
| 11. | We have an `int` array named `intArray01` that has 5 elements as follows:<br><br>    [0] - 10<br>    [1] - 11<br>    [2] - 12<br>    [3] - 13<br>    [4] - 14<br><br>Write a program to reverse the contents of the array. The result is that the array contents should now be:<br><br>    [0] - 14<br>    [1] - 13<br>    [2] - 12<br>    [3] - 11<br>    [4] - 10<br><br>Print out the reversed array.<br><br>*Hint: method* `Array.Reverse` | ```
using System;

namespace PracticeYourCSharp
{
    class Program
    {
        static void Main(string[] args)
        {
            int[] intArray01 = new int[5];

            intArray01[0] = 10;
            intArray01[1] = 11;
            intArray01[2] = 12;
            intArray01[3] = 13;
            intArray01[4] = 14;

            Array.Reverse(intArray01);

            Console.WriteLine("intArray01's contents are now
                              {0},{1},{2},{3},{4}",
                              intArray01[0], intArray01[1],
                              intArray01[2], intArray01[3],
                              intArray01[4]);
            Console.ReadKey();
        }
    }
}
``` |
| 12. | *Reversing a subset of an array*<br><br>We have an integer array `intArray01` that has 5 elements as follows:<br><br>    [0] - 10<br>    [1] - 11<br>    [2] - 12<br>    [3] - 13<br>    [4] - 14 | ```
using System;

namespace PracticeYourCSharp
{
    class Program
    {
        static void Main(string[] args)
        {
            int[] intArray01 = new int[] {10,11,12,13,14};

            int startIndex = 1;
            int numElements = 3;
``` |
```

| | Write a program to reverse elements [1] to [3] of the array so that the array contents are now as follows:<br><br>[0] - 10<br>[1] - 13<br>[2] - 12<br>[3] - 11<br>[4] - 14 | ```
        Array.Reverse(intArray01, startIndex, numElements);
        Console.WriteLine("intArray01's contents are now
                         {0},{1},{2},{3},{4}",
                         intArray01[0], intArray01[1],
                         intArray01[2], intArray01[3],
                         intArray01[4]);
        Console.ReadKey();
    }
  }
}
``` |
| 13. | *Copying part of an array to another*<br><br>We have an integer array `intArray01` that has 5 elements as follows:<br><br>[0] -     55<br>[1] -    747<br>[2] -  15000<br>[3] -     89<br>[4] -   2333<br><br>Copy the 1st three elements of `intArray01` into an array `intArray02` which is an integer array of 5 elements. Print array `intArray02` out. | ```
using System;
namespace PracticeYourCSharp
{
  class Program
  {
    static void Main(string[] args)
    {
      int[] intArray01 = new int[] {500,747,15000,89,2333};
      int[] intArray02 = new int[5];

      Console.WriteLine("intArray02's contents are currently
                       {0},{1},{2},{3},{4}", intArray02[0],
                       intArray02[1], intArray02[2],
                       intArray02[3], intArray02[4]);

      // Now the 1st 3 elements of intArray01 to intArray02
      Array.Copy(intArray01, intArray02, 3);

      Console.WriteLine("intArray02's contents are
                       {0},{1},{2},{3},{4} ", intArray02[0],
                       intArray02[1], intArray02[2],
                       intArray02[3], intArray02[4]);
      Console.ReadKey();
    }
  }
}
``` |
| 14. | We have an integer array `intArray01` which has 5 elements with the following content:<br><br>[0] -     55<br>[1] -    747<br>[2] -  15000<br>[3] -     89<br>[4] -   2333<br><br>Copy the *2nd to the 4th* elements of `intArray01` into the *3rd to 5th* position of `intArray02` which also is an int array of 5 elements. Print the contents of `intArray02` out before and after the copy operation. | ```
using System;
namespace PracticeYourCSharp
{
  class Program
  {
    static void Main(string[] args)
    {
      int[] intArray01 = new int[] {55,747,15000,89,2333};
      int[] intArray02 = new int[5];

      Console.WriteLine("intArray02's contents are
                       {0},{1},{2},{3},{4}", intArray02[0],
                       intArray02[1], intArray02[2],
                       intArray02[3], intArray02[4]);

      Array.Copy(intArray01, 1, intArray02, 2, 3);
      // The 2nd element in intArray01 is position [1],
      // the 3rd element in intArray02 is position [2].
      // and we are copying 3 elements.

      Console.WriteLine("intArray02's contents are now
                       {0},{1},{2},{3},{4}", intArray02[0],
                       intArray02[1], intArray02[2],
                       intArray02[3], intArray02[4]);
      Console.ReadKey();
``` |
```

| | ```
      }
    }
}
``` |
| 15. Write a program to determine and print out the rank *(total number of columns)* of the following array:
`int[] intArray01 = new int[50];` | |
| ```
using System;

namespace PracticeYourCSharp
{
    class Program
    {
        static void Main(string[] args)
        {
            int[] intArray01 = new int[50];
            int iArrayRank = intArray01.Rank;
            Console.WriteLine("The rank of the array is {0}.", iArrayRank);
            Console.ReadKey();
        }
    }
}
``` | |
| 16. We have an array of `int` named `intArray01` which has 5 elements, namely {10,11,12,13,14}. Write a program that determines which array element contains the value 13.
Hint: use the method `Array.IndexOf` | |
| ```
using System;

namespace PracticeYourCSharp
{
    class Program
    {
        static void Main(string[] args)
        {
            int[] intArray01 = new int[] { 10, 11, 12, 13, 14 };

            int soughtValueIndex = -1;
            int soughtValue = 13;

            soughtValueIndex = Array.IndexOf(intArray01, soughtValue);

            Console.WriteLine("The array index of the value 13 is {0}", soughtValueIndex);
            Console.ReadKey();
        }
    }
}
``` | |

| 17. We have an integer array `intArray01` that has 6 elements with the following content:<br><br>[0] - 44<br>[1] - 2<br>[2] - 43<br>[3] - 44<br>[4] - 3<br>[5] - 44<br>[6] - 7<br><br>Determine and print out what the last array index that contains the number 44 is.<br><br>*Hint: use the method* `Array.LastIndexOf` | ```
using System;

namespace PracticeYourCSharp
{
    class Program
    {
        static void Main(string[] args)
        {
            int[] intArray01 = new int[] { 44, 2, 43, 44, 3, 44, 7 };

            int index = -1;
            int soughtValue = 44;

            index = Array.LastIndexOf(intArray01, soughtValue);

            Console.WriteLine("The last index of the value 44 is {0}",
                                 index);
            Console.ReadKey();
        }
    }
}
``` |

| 18. | We have an integer array intArray01 which has 6 elements with the following content:<br><br>    [0] - 109<br>    [1] - 44<br>    [2] - 43<br>    [3] - 44<br>    [4] - 44<br>    [5] - 17<br><br>Find where, looking only in the range of elements 1 to element 3, the last array index that contains the number 44. | ```csharp
using System;
namespace PracticeYourCSharp
{
  class Program
  {
    static void Main(string[] args)
    {
      int[] intArray01 = new int[] { 109, 44, 43, 44, 44, 17 };
      int index = -1;

      index = Array.LastIndexOf(intArray01, 44, 3, 3);
      // Starting at element [3] and looking backwards, 3
      // elements, that is, [3],[2],[1]

      Console.WriteLine("Looking strictly at array elements 1 to
                3, the last index of the value 44 is
                {0}", index);
      Console.ReadKey();
    }
  }
}
```<br>**Note:** This overload of `Array.LastIndexOf` does a *backwards* search. |
|---|---|

19. We have an array named `intArray01` which has 8 elements, namely 1.4×10^9, 1.39×10^9, 42, 43.8, 8, 23.64, 18 and 200. Sort the array and print its contents out.

Hint: `Array.Sort`

```csharp
using System;
namespace PracticeYourCSharp
{
  class Program
  {
    static void Main(string[] args)
    {
      double[] Array01 = new double[] { 1.4E9, 1.39E9, 42, 43.8, 8, 23.64, 18, 200 };
      Array.Sort(Array01);
      Console.WriteLine("Array01's contents are now  {0},{1},{2},{3},{4},{5},{6},{7}",
                Array01[0], Array01[1], Array01[2], Array01[3], Array01[4],
                Array01[5], Array01[6], Array01[7]);
      Console.ReadKey();
    }
  }
}
```

20. We have an integer array named `intArray01` initialized with the following 5 elements: {17,42,43,8,23}. Write a program which appends two more elements, namely the values 57 and 84 to the end of the array.

Hint: make the array bigger by using the `Array.Resize` *method and then add these new values to the array.*

```csharp
using System;
namespace PracticeYourCSharp
{
  class Program
  {
    static void Main(string[] args)
    {
      int[] intArray01 = new int[] { 17, 42, 43, 8, 23 };

      Array.Resize<int>(ref intArray01, 7);
      // The components of this line are explained as follows:
      // 1. <int> that it is going to resize an integer array
      // 2. ref : This keyword this will be looked at closer in a later chapter.
      //    It is a keyword that indicates that allows Array.Resize to modify
      //    the variable intArray01 that appears in our method Main.
```
```

```
            //   3. intArray01 is the name of the array that is to be resized
            //   4. 7 is the target new size of the array being resized
            intArray01[5] = 57;
            intArray01[6] = 84;

            Console.WriteLine("intArray01[5]={0} & intArray01[6]={1}",intArray01[5],intArray01[6]);
            Console.ReadKey();
        }
    }
}
```

	Arrays & Strings	
21.	Write a line of code which declares a string array named sArray01.	`string[] sArray01;`
22.	Write a line of code that initializes the string array of the preceding exercise to have a capacity for 10 elements.	`string[] sArray01 = new string[10];`

23.	Initialize the contents of the `string` array in the preceding exercise with each of the following words in the succeeding indexes of the array:
	"Mary", "had", "a", "little", "lamb".
		`string[] sArray01 = new string[10];`
		`sArray01[0]= "Mary";`
		`sArray01[1]="had";`
		`sArray01[2]="a";`
		`sArray01[3]="little";`
		`sArray01[4]="lamb";`

24. Write a program which will print out the length of the array from the preceding exercise.

```
using System;

namespace PracticeYourCSharp
{
    class Program
    {
        static void Main(string[] args)
        {
            string[] sArray01 = new string[10];
            sArray01[0] = "Mary";   sArray01[1] = "had"; sArray01[2] = "a";
            sArray01[3] = "little"; sArray01[4] = "lamb";
            Console.WriteLine("Array length = {0}", sArray01.Length);
        }
    }
}
```

Note: As seen from the answer above, the `Length` of the array is the number of allocated spaces in the array, not the number of occupied spaces.

25. Write a program that joins the words in the array in the preceding exercise into a string, separating each of the words with a space. Print the resulting string out.
Hint: method `String.Join`

```
using System;

namespace PracticeYourCSharp
{
    class Program
    {
        static void Main(string[] args)
        {
            string[] sArray01 = new string[10];
            sArray01[0] = "Mary";   sArray01[1] = "had"; sArray01[2] = "a";
            sArray01[3] = "little"; sArray01[4] = "lamb";
            string rhyme = String.Join(" ", sArray01);
            Console.WriteLine(rhyme);
        }
    }
}
```

26.	*Matrices/Multi-dimensional arrays* Write a line of code to declare a 2-dimensional integer array/matrix named `matrixA`.	`int[,] matrixA;` `[,]` is what tells the compiler that we are defining a 2-dimensional array/matrix.
27.	Write a line of code to instantiate a 2-dimensional integer matrix named `matrixA` of dimensions 2 x 3.	`int[,] matrixA = new int[2,3];`
28.	Write the appropriate line of code to declare a 5-dimensional integer array/matrix variable named `matrixB`.	`int[,,,,] matrixB;`
29.	Write a line of code that shows the instantiation of a 5-dimensional integer matrix named `matrixB` of dimensions 10 x 4 x 3 x 5 x 12.	`int[,,,,] matrixB = new int[10,4,3,5,12];`

30.	Instantiate two *2 x 3* integer matrices, with variable names `matrix1` and `matrix2` respectively and initialize them as follows:
	
	matrix1
	1 2 3
	4 5 6
	
	matrix2
	5 5 8
	3 1 3
		`using System;`
		`namespace PracticeYourCSharp`
		`{`
		`  class Program`
		`  {`
		`    static void Main(string[] args)`
		`    {`
		`      int[,] matrix1 = new int[,] { { 1, 2, 3 }, { 4, 5, 6 } };`
		`      int[,] matrix2 = new int[,] { { 5, 5, 8 }, { 3, 1, 3 } };`
		`      Console.ReadKey();`
		`    }`
		`  }`
		`}`

31.	With respect to the earlier defined `matrix1`, state what the following code will return: `matrix1.Length;`	6 Reason: `Length` returns the multiplication of all the dimensions of the matrix, which in this case = 2 x 3 = 6.
32.	With respect to `matrix1` above, write a line of code which will print out how many dimensions `matrix1` has.	The pertinent line of code is as follows: `Console.WriteLine(matrix1.Rank);`
33.	Looking specifically at the earlier defined `matrix1`, write code to print out *(1)* the number of its dimensions and *(2)* the length of each dimension.		
| | ```
using System;
namespace PracticeYourCSharp
{
  class Program
  {
    static void Main(string[] args)
    {
      int[,] matrix1 = new int[,] { { 1, 2, 3 }, { 4, 5, 6 } };
      Console.WriteLine("# of dimensions = {0}",matrix1.Rank);
      Console.WriteLine("Length of the 1st dimension is {0} ",matrix1.GetLength(0));
      Console.WriteLine("Length of the 2nd dimension is {0}", matrix1.GetLength(1));
      Console.ReadKey();
    }
  }
}
``` |||
```

Chapter 8. Iterations/Loops

The facility in a programming language to iterate easily through a set of items (for example the individual elements of an array) and perform common actions on each element is a key enabler of compact code. This chapter contains exercises on different loop mechanisms within C#, such as the `while`, `do/while`, `for` and `foreach` loops. Exercises which require the use of the loop jump keywords `continue`, `break` and `goto` are also presented, as well as exercises on nested loops and infinite loops.

while loop

1. We have an integer array `intArray01` which has 5 elements with the following content in the noted positions in the array:

```
[0] - 18
[1] - 42
[2] - 26
[3] - 44
[4] - 55
```

Using a `while` loop, print out the values contained in this array, in the following format:

`intArray01[<index>] = <value>`

```csharp
using System;

namespace PracticeYourCSharp
{
  class Program
  {
    static void Main(string[] args)
    {
      int[] intArray01 = new int[] { 18, 42, 26, 44, 55 };
      int loopCounter = 0; // We are starting at element 0
      int arrayLength = intArray01.Length; // upper limit
      while (loopCounter < arrayLength)
      {
        Console.WriteLine("intArray01[{0}] = {1} ", loopCounter,
                                      intArray01[loopCounter]);
        loopCounter = loopCounter + 1;
      }
      Console.ReadKey();
    }
  }
}
```

2. Print out the contents of the array in the preceding exercise *backwards*, in the same output format, using a `while` loop.

```csharp
using System;

namespace PracticeYourCSharp
{
  class Program
  {
    static void Main(string[] args)
    {
      int[] intArray01 = new int[] { 18, 42, 26, 44, 55 };
      int loopCounter = intArray01.Length - 1; // We are starting at the last element
      while (loopCounter >= 0)
      {
        Console.WriteLine("intArray01[{0}] = {1} ", loopCounter, intArray01[loopCounter]);
        loopCounter = loopCounter - 1;
      }
      Console.ReadKey();
    }
  }
}
```

for loop	

3.	Explain the components and the functioning of a `for` loop, using the sample code below:
	``
	int loopCounter;
	for(loopCounter=3; loopCounter < 10; locpCounter++)
	{
	   // do action
	}
	``

	The control section of a `for` loop consists of the following elements:
	1. The keyword `for`, which brackets the other control elements of the loop.
	2. The other control elements which are semi-colon separated within the brackets.
	
	In the brackets we have, in order, the following:
	1. A statement indicating the name of the control variable for the `for` loop, with its initial value specified. In our example above, we state that our loop counting variable named `loopCounter` has an initial value of 3.
	Note that the initialization of the control variable does not have to be done inside the control section of the `for` loop; in such a case, the initialization section of the `for` loop will be left blank.
	2. A conditional statement that states the condition <u>which while true</u> permits the `for` loop to continue running. In our example we are saying "keep performing this loop *while* the value of the variable `loopCounter` is less than 10".
	3. Finally, an increment statement, which indicates the incremental value to add to the loop counter after each iteration of the actions that are supposed to be performed in the statements governed by the `for` loop are performed. In our example here, we indicate that the loop counter `loopCounter` should be incremented by 1.
	
	The body of the `for` loop is shown in this example as:
	``
	{
	   // do action
	}
	``
	These braces that immediately follow the `for` loop surround the code that is to be run on each iteration of the `for` loop.
	
	A `for` loop is, in a sense, a repackaged `while` loop in C#. This can be said because its conditional statement is saying *"while this condition is true* continue looping".
	
	Note that if you only have one line that you want to be performed for each iteration of a `for` loop, there is no need to put braces around the single line to be run. For example we would write;
	``
	int loopCounter;
	for(loopCounter=3; loopCounter < 10; loopCounter++)
	   single line of action.
	``
	Another point to note is that it is acceptable for any (or all) of the loop control components to be missing! Only the two semicolons in the control statement are mandatory.

4.	We have the following array definition: `int[] intArray01 = new int[]{18,42,26,44,55};` Using a `for` loop, print out the values contained in this array, in the following format: `intArray01[<index>] = <value>`

	``
	using System;
	
	namespace PracticeYourCSharp
	{
	  class Program
	  {
	    static void Main(string[] args)
	    {
	      int[] intArray01 = new int[] { 18, 42, 26, 44, 55 };
	      int loopCounter;
	      for (loopCounter = 0; loopCounter < intArray01.Length; loopCounter = loopCounter + 1)
	      {
	``

	``csharp
          Console.WriteLine("intArray01[{0}] = {1}", loopCounter, intArray01[loopCounter]);
        }
      }
    }
  }
```
**Notes/Explanation of the for loop in C#**
Really, in C#, the for loop can be thought of as a while loop of the following structure (using the answer above as an example):
```csharp
  loopCounter=0; // initial condition
  while(loopCounter < intArray01.Length) // the termination condition
  {
    Console.WriteLine("intArray01[{0}] ={1}",loopCounter,intArray01[loopCounter]);
    loopCounter=loopCounter+1; // the increment of the counter as specified
  }
```
If you are having trouble with formulating for loops, you can first formulate its while loop counterpart. |
| 5. | Write the same array in the preceding exercise *backwards*, with the same output format, using a for loop. |
|   | ```csharp
using System;

namespace PracticeYourCSharp
{
  class Program
  {
    static void Main(string[] args)
    {
      int[] intArray01 = new int[] { 18, 42, 26, 44, 55 };
      int loopCounter;
      for (loopCounter = intArray01.Length - 1; loopCounter >= 0; loopCounter-=1)
      {
        Console.WriteLine("intArray01[{0}] = {1}", loopCounter, intArray01[loopCounter]);
      }
    }
  }
}
``` |
| 6. | What is the difference between the following two for loop code samples? |
| | ```csharp
int i;
for (i=0; i<10; i++)
{
  Console.WriteLine(i);
}
```   vs.   ```csharp
for (int i=0; i<10; i++)
{
  Console.WriteLine(i);
}
``` |
| | The difference between the loops is that in the second code snippet the loop control variable is defined within the control structure of the for loop. Otherwise the loops are entirely similar. Also note that in the second code sample, the lifetime of the loop variable expires at the end of the for loop since it was defined within the control structure of the loop. |
| 7. | Predict and explain the output of the following code snippet:<br>```csharp
int i;
for (i=0; i < 3; i++)
Console.WriteLine(i);
Console.WriteLine("hello");
``` | The output is:<br>0<br>1<br>2<br>hello<br>**Explanation**<br>If there are no braces around lines of code following a for loop, only the first line of code immediately following the for loop is considered to be the body of the loop. |
```

Practice Your C# Level 1

foreach loop		
| 8. | We have an integer array `intArray01` which has 5 elements with the following content in the noted positions:<br><br>    `[0] - 18`<br>    `[1] - 42`<br>    `[2] - 26`<br>    `[3] - 44`<br>    `[4] - 55`<br><br>Using a `foreach` loop, print out the contents of the array *(don't print out the index in this example, just print the values)*. | ```csharp
using System;

namespace PracticeYourCSharp
{
  class Program
  {
    static void Main(string[] args)
    {
      int[] intArray01 = new int[] { 18, 42, 26, 44, 55 };
      foreach (int item in intArray01)
      {
        Console.WriteLine("{0}", item);
      }
      Console.ReadKey();
    }
  }
}
```<br><br>**Note:** The `foreach` loop is more useful when you have to perform an action on each and every element in the array under consideration.<br>Unlike the `for` and `while` loops, the `foreach` loop does not have an index. |
| 9. | Using the same loop as in the exercise above, use a `foreach` loop to print out the values contained in this array, in the following manner:

        `intArray01[<index>] = <value>` | |
| | ```csharp
using System;

namespace PracticeYourCSharp
{
  class Program
  {
    static void Main(string[] args)
    {
      int[] intArray01 = new int[] { 18, 42, 26, 44, 55 };

      int index = 0;
      foreach (int item in intArray01)
      {
        Console.WriteLine("intArray01[{0}] ={1}", index, item);
        index = index + 1;
      }
      Console.ReadKey();
    }
  }
}
```<br><br>**Notes/Explanation:** The `foreach` loop does not have an index; rather, in each iteration it gets the next item in the sequence/array under assessment into the variable that is present in its declaration statement (in this exercise for example, it sequentially puts the content that is in the array `intArray01`, element by element into the variable `item`). Therefore, we have to create our own index if we want to print an index out. | |
| 10. | Using a `foreach` loop, print the values in the array of the preceding exercise *in reverse*, with the same output formatting as the above. | |
| | ```csharp
using System;

namespace PracticeYourCSharp
{
  class Program
  {
    static void Main(string[] args)
    {
      int[] intArray01 = new int[] { 18, 42, 26, 44, 55 };
``` | |
```

```
          int index = 0;
          Array.Reverse(intArray01);
          foreach (int arrayValue in intArray01)
          {
            Console.WriteLine("intArray01[{0}] ={1}", index, arrayValue);
            index = index + 1;
          }
          Console.ReadKey();
        }
      }
    }
```

Note/Explanation: There is no "reverse" equivalent of a `foreach` loop. To wit, you have to reverse the target array and apply the `foreach` to the reversed array (really you should copy the array to a new variable and reverse the copy of the array rather than reversing the original array).

11. With respect to the array in the exercise above, use a `foreach` loop to print out every *2nd value* contained in this array, in the following format:

    intArray01[<index>] = <value>

    (This will print out information for array elements 0, 2, 4 only)

```
using System;
namespace PracticeYourCSharp
{
  class Program
  {
    static void Main(string[] args)
    {
      int[] intArray01 = new int[] { 18, 42, 26, 44, 55 };
      int index = 0;
      foreach (int arrayItem in intArray01)
      {
        if (index % 2 == 0) // if index is an even number (that's how we get every 2nd one)
        {
          Console.WriteLine("intArray01[{0}] ={1}", index, arrayItem);
        }
        index = index + 1;
      }
      Console.ReadKey();
    }
  }
}
```

Explanation: Again, due to the nature of the `foreach` statement, it does not lend itself as smoothly as using any of the other loop constructs for this same scenario.

12. Repeat the preceding exercise, this time using a `for` loop.

```
using System;
namespace PracticeYourCSharp
{
  class Program
  {
    static void Main(string[] args)
    {
      int[] intArray01 = new int[] { 18, 42, 26, 44, 55 };

      for (int j = 0; j < intArray01.Length; j+=2)
        Console.WriteLine("intArray01[{0}] ={1}", j, intArray01[j]);
      Console.ReadKey();
    }
  }
}
```

	Note: Note how the loop index was incremented by 2 to achieve the specified output effect of printing every 2nd entry.
13.	Repeat the preceding exercise using a `while` loop.
| | ``` 
using System;

namespace PracticeYourCSharp
{
  class Program
  {
    static void Main(string[] args)
    {
      int[] intArray01 = new int[] { 18, 42, 26, 44, 55 };

      int counter = 0; // We will be starting at the 0th index.
      int arrayLength = intArray01.Length;

      while (counter < intArray01.Length)
      {
        Console.WriteLine("intArray01[{0}]={1} ", counter, intArray01[counter]);
        counter = counter + 2;
      }
      Console.ReadKey();
    }
  }
}
``` |

do/while loop

14.	Under what circumstances is a `do/while` loop a good candidate to use?
	When you have something that must run at least once before loop conditions are checked. Think of this loop as: *you have to <u>do first</u> and then check conditions for potential subsequent actions.*
15.	Using a `do/while` loop, calculate and print out the factorial of 10.
| | ```
using System;

namespace PracticeYourCSharp
{
  class Program
  {
    static void Main(string[] args)
    {
      double iNumToCalculateFactorial = 10;

      long result = 1;
      int index = 1;
      do
      {
        result = result * index;
        index++;
      } while (index <= iNumToCalculateFactorial);

      Console.WriteLine("{0}! = {1}", iNumToCalculateFactorial, result);
      Console.ReadKey();
    }
  }
}
``` |
| 16. | Using an *infinite* `while` loop, print the following string out indefinitely:<br><br>*"Hello!"* | ```
using System;

namespace PracticeYourCSharp
{
  class Program
  {
    static void Main(string[] args)
    {
      while (true)
      {
``` |
```

		`          Console.WriteLine("Hello!");`
		`        }`
		`      }`
		`    }`
		`}`

17.	Repeat the preceding exercise using an infinite **for** loop.	`using System;`
		`namespace PracticeYourCSharp`
		`{`
		`  class Program`
		`  {`
		`    static void Main(string[] args)`
		`    {`
		`      for ( ; ; )`
		`      {`
		`        Console.WriteLine("Hello!");`
		`      }`
		`    }`
		`  }`
		`}`

18.	What is the output of the following code?
	
	`using System;`
	`namespace PracticeYourCSharp`
	`{`
	`  class Program`
	`  {`
	`    static void Main(string[] args)`
	`    {`
	`      int j, k;`
	`      for (j = 1; j < 5; j++)`
	`      {`
	`        for (k = 1; k < 5; k++)`
	`        {`
	`          Console.Write("({0},{1}) ", j, k);`
	`        }`
	`        Console.WriteLine();`
	`      }`
	`      Console.ReadKey();`
	`    }`
	`  }`
	`}`	

	Output: (1,1) (1,2) (1,3) (1,4) (2,1) (2,2) (2,3) (2,4) (3,1) (3,2) (3,3) (3,4) (4,1) (4,2) (4,3) (4,4) **Note:** The objective of this exercise was to show the application of **nested for loops** in outputting matrices.	
19.	Write a program which will output the following pattern: (A,1) (A,2) (A,3) (A,4) (B,1) (B,2) (B,3) (B,4) (C,1) (C,2) (C,3) (C,4) (D,1) (D,2) (D,3) (D,4) (E,1) (E,2) (E,3) (E,4)	

`using System;`
`namespace PracticeYourCSharp`
`{`
`  class Program`
`  {`
	`using System;`
	`namespace PracticeYourCSharp`
	`{`
	`  class Program`
	`  {`

	``
static void Main(string[] args)
{
  int j, k;

  String[] letters =
   new String[] {"A","B","C","D","E"};

  for (j = 0; j < letters.Length; j++)
  {
    for (k = 1; k < 5; k++)
    {
      Console.Write("({0},{1}) ",
                    letters[j], k);
    }
    Console.WriteLine();
  }
  Console.ReadKey();
}
}
```

**Note:** A `char[]` (we have not looked at the `char` type yet) instead of a `String[]` would work as well in this exercise. | OR | ```
static void Main(string[] args)
{
  int j, k;
  int start = (int)'A';

  for (j = start; j < (start + 5); j++)
  {
    for (k = 1; k < 5; k++)
    {
      Console.Write("({0},{1}) ",
                    (char)j, k);
    }
    Console.WriteLine();
  }
  Console.ReadKey();
}
}
```

Note: While indeed we have not yet formally studied the type `char` and its relationship to the unsigned integer type, we do present this solution as well. |

The continue, break, goto and label keywords		
| 20. | Write a `for` loop that can print out the values 1 to 1000 in sequence; however, using a `break` statement halt the running of the loop when the value of the loop counter is 10. | ```
using System;

namespace PracticeYourCSharp
{
  class Program
  {
    static void Main(string[] args)
    {
      for (int i = 1; i <= 1000; i++)
      {
        if (i == 10) break;
        Console.WriteLine(i);
      }
      Console.ReadKey();
    }
  }
}
``` |
| 21. | What does the `continue` operator do? | The `continue` operator is an operator which when present in a loop causes the code to immediately go back to the start of the loop. |
| 22. | Write a `for` loop which loops from 1 to 50, printing out each value; however, using a `continue` statement, skip every value that is divisible by 5. | ```
using System;

namespace PracticeYourCSharp
{
  class Program
  {
    static void Main(string[] args)
    {
      for (int i = 0; i <= 50; i++)
      {
        if (i % 5 == 0) continue;
        Console.WriteLine(i);
      }
      Console.ReadKey();
    }
  }
}
``` |
| 23. | What is a <u>label</u> in C# and how is it used? | |

	A label is a *named point* within a piece of code which a goto statement can jump to. goto means "go to somewhere" and that somewhere is a label. Therefore when you use goto, the usage of the goto statement is: goto \<label\>: The label is always terminated with a colon. The naming convention for a label is simply any valid identifier (i.e. any name that is valid for a variable). Note that you can put labels in code even if there is no goto that jumps to the label in question.
24.	Describe the functioning of the goto statement.
| | The goto statement is a statement that allows you to transfer control from a given point in code to other *labeled points* in the code. The usage of the goto statement is as follows:<br>    goto \<label\>;<br>The goto statement has the benefit of allowing you to move around in code in a non-sequential manner if so desired. The goto statement even gives you the ability to jump out of loops.<br>Note though that proper programming practice tries to discourage the use of the goto statement as much as possible.<br>Also note that the goto statement is not exclusively used in loops, but can be used in any other code.<br>The example below can be run in order to observe the functioning of the goto statement.<br><br>```csharp
using System;

namespace PracticeYourCSharp
{
  class Program
  {
    static void Main(string[] args)
    {
      Console.WriteLine("1");
      goto POINT_A;
      Console.WriteLine("2");
      POINT_A: Console.WriteLine("3");
      Console.ReadKey();
    }
  }
}
```<br><br>As can be seen when this code is run, the output is as follows:<br><br>1<br>3<br><br>That is, the goto statement jumped to the point in code labelled **POINT_A**, thus skipping the line which was supposed to print out the string "2". |
| 25. | I want to output the following pattern:

A1 A2 A3 A4 A5 A6 A7 A8 A9 A10
B1 B2 B3 B4 B5 B6 B7 B8 B9 B10
C1 C2 C3 C4

Write a program to print the pattern out using a nested for loop and a goto that breaks out of the loop to a label named my_breakout_point. At my_breakout_point, print out "*\nJust saw a C5*". |
| | ```csharp
using System;

namespace PracticeYourCSharp
{
  class Program
  {
    static void Main(string[] args)
    {
      char[] cArray01 = { 'A', 'B', 'C' };
      for (int i = 0; i < cArray01.Length; i++)
      {
``` |

|  | ```
            for (int j = 1; j <= 10; j++)
            {
               string sf01 = String.Format("{0}{1}", cArray01[i], j);
               if (sf01.Equals("C5") == true) goto my_breakout_point;
               Console.Write(sf01); Console.Write(" ");
            }
            Console.WriteLine();
         }
         my_breakout_point: Console.WriteLine("\nJust saw a C5");
         Console.ReadKey();
      }
   }
}
``` |
26.	Describe the purpose of the **break** statement within the context of a loop.
	The **break** statement within the context of a loop causes the loop to end processing immediately and for control to go to the statement immediately after the loop.
27.	I want to output the following pattern: A1 A2 A3 A4 A5 A6 A7 A8 A9 A10 B1 B2 B3 B4 B5 B6 B7 B8 B9 B10 C1 C2 C3 C4 D1 D2 D3 D4 D5 D6 D7 D8 D9 D10 E1 E2 E3 E4 E5 E6 E7 E8 E9 E10 Write a nested **for** loop to implement this. *Hint: Use a **break** statement within the inner loop when **C5** is seen.*
|  | ```
using System;

namespace PracticeYourCSharp
{
   class Program
   {
      static void Main(string[] args)
      {
         char[] cArray01 = { 'A', 'B', 'C', 'D', 'E' };
         for (int i = 0; i < cArray01.Length; i++)
         {
            for (int j = 1; j <= 10; j++)
            {
               string sf01 = String.Format("{0}{1}", cArray01[i], j);
               if (sf01.Equals("C5") == true) break;
               Console.Write(sf01); Console.Write(" ");
            }
            Console.WriteLine();  // that break statement jumps to this line
         }
         Console.ReadKey();
      }
   }
}
``` |
| 28. | Given a matrix **M** of an unknown number of dimensions, write a code fragment with which to determine and print out the length of each dimension thereof.
Note: A matrix is just a multi-dimensional array. |
|  | ```
Console.WriteLine("# of dimensions = {0}", M.Rank);
for(int j=0; j < M.Rank; j++)
{
   Console.WriteLine("The length of dimension {0} = {1} ", j, M.GetLength(j));
}
``` |
| 29. | Enhance/modify the code above, testing it against the following 2 x 3 integer matrix named **matrix1**:

  matrix1
 1   2   3
 4   5   6 |
```

```
using System;
namespace PracticeYourCSharp
{
  class Program
  {
    static void Main(string[] args)
    {
      int[,] matrix1 = new int[,] { { 1, 2, 3 }, { 4, 5, 6 } };
      int rank = matrix1.Rank;
      for (int k = 0; k < rank; k++)
      {
        int length = matrix1.GetLength(k);
        Console.WriteLine("Length of dimension {0}={1}", k, matrix1.GetLength(k));
      }
      Console.ReadKey();
    }
  }
}
```

30. Write a program to print `matrix1` from the preceding exercise out in the tabular form in which it appears in the question.

```
using System;
namespace PracticeYourCSharp
{
  class Program
  {
    static void Main(string[] args)
    {
      int[,] matrix1 = new int[,] { { 1, 2, 3 }, { 4, 5, 6 } };
      int a, b;   // These will be our loop counters

      // Now we are going to print these out row by row
      for (a = 0; a < matrix1.GetLength(0); a++)
      {
        for (b = 0; b < matrix1.GetLength(1); b++)
        {
          Console.Write(" {0} ", matrix1[a, b]);
        }
        Console.WriteLine();
        // We are writing row by row. This line moves us to the next line.
      }
      Console.ReadKey();
    }
  }
}
```

31. Write a program which adds the following two 2×3 matrixes and prints out the resulting matrix in the same 2×3 format.

```
1   2   3
4   5   6
      +
5   5   8
3   1   3
```

```
using System;
namespace PracticeYourCSharp
{
  class Program
  {
    static void Main(string[] args)
    {
      int[,] matrix1 = new int[,] { { 1, 2, 3 }, { 4, 5, 6 } };
      int[,] matrix2 = new int[,] { { 5, 5, 8 }, { 3, 1, 3 } };
      int[,] resultMatrix = new int[2, 3];

      for (int a = 0; a < matrix1.GetLength(0); a++)
      {
        for (int b = 0; b < matrix1.GetLength(1); b++)
        {
          resultMatrix[a, b] = matrix1[a, b] + matrix2[a, b];
```

|   | ```
            Console.Write(" {0} ", resultMatrix[a, b]);
          }
          Console.WriteLine();
        }
        Console.ReadKey();
      }
    }
}
``` |
| 32. | Using a **string** array with the following elements: Draw the following pattern:

o
oo
ooo
oooo
ooooo
oooooo
ooooooo
oooooooo

                    o   o
                   oo   oo
                 ooo   ooo
                oooo oooo
               ooooo ooooo
              oooooo oooooo
             ooooooo ooooooo
            oooooooooooooooo
             ooooooo ooooooo
              oooooo oooooo
               ooooo ooooo
                oooo oooo
                 ooo   ooo
                  oo   oo
                   o   o |
|   | ```
using System;

namespace PracticeYourCSharp
{
  class Program
  {
    static void Main(string[] args)
    {
      string[] patternArray = new string[] { "o", "oo", "ooo", "oooo", "ooooo", "oooooo",
                              "ooooooo", "oooooooo" };

      int maxLength = 0;
      foreach (string s in patternArray)
      {
        if (s.Length > maxLength) maxLength = s.Length;
      }

      int fieldWidth = maxLength;

      for (int i = 0; i < patternArray.Length; i++)
      {
        string formatStr = "{0,-" + fieldWidth + "}" + "{0," + fieldWidth + "}";
        string outputStr = String.Format(formatStr, patternArray[i]);
        Console.WriteLine(outputStr);
      }
      // Now the lower part of the pattern
      for (int i = (patternArray.Length - 2); i >= 0; i--)
      {
        string formatStr = "{0,-" + fieldWidth + "}" + "{0," + fieldWidth + "}";
        string outputStr = String.Format(formatStr, patternArray[i]);
        Console.WriteLine(outputStr);
      }
      Console.ReadKey();
    }
  }
}
``` |

E1	Using the same source pattern as the preceding exercise, write code to output the following pattern:
	`o         o`
	`oo        oo`
	`ooo       ooo`
	`oooo      oooo`
	`ooooo     ooooo`
	`oooooo    oooooo`
	`ooooooo   ooooooo`
	`oooooooo  oooooooo`

E2	Using the same source pattern as above, write code to output the following pattern:
	`o         oooooooo`
	`oo        ooooooo`
	`ooo       oooooo`
	`oooo      ooooo`
	`ooooo     oooo`
	`oooooo    ooo`
	`ooooooo   oo`
	`oooooooo  o`

E3	Write a program which adds two 3-dimensional matrices of the same dimensions.
E4	Write a program to add two $n \times m$ matrices of the same dimensions.
E5	I have an array of strings, each string therein of undetermined length. Write out the array of strings, with the same width for each, bounding the strings left & right with the '|' character. *Hint: determine the length of the longest string. That will be your field width. Then use a* `FormatString` *to output each line as appropriate.*

Chapter 9. Console Handling II: More on Input

There are times when console applications programs require user interaction, this via keyboard input. This necessitates our proper understanding of how to request and interpret data that is input at the keyboard. The data read at the keyboard is always received by the computer as a string of characters (whether the data is numeric or not) and thus it is necessary to know how to convert non-string input -numbers in particular- to their proper type for use. The `TryParse` method that is present in many numerical classes as well as the methods in class `Parse` provide means with which to implement this conversion. Building on the exercises in Chapter 2, the exercises in this chapter address this topic of proper interpretation of console input.

The exercises in this chapter also leverage and further your skills in conditional processing, strings and numbers.

Note: Exercises in this chapter use the `out` keyword which allows a called method (`TryParse` in this case) to in effect set the value of variables in the calling method. The `out` keyword is more fully explored in Chapter 28. Passing By Reference, Passing By Value.

1.	What do the variables `status` and `int01` contain after running the following program?
	
	``csharp
	using System;
	
	namespace PracticeYourCSharp
	{
	  class Program
	  {
	    static void Main(string[] args)
	    {
	      string s1 = "123";
	      int int01;
	      bool status = false;
	      status = Int32.TryParse(s1, out int01);
	    }
	  }
	}
	``

	Result: `status = true, int01 = 123` The method **Int32.TryParse** looks at the string passed to it, and if it is an integer value that is in string form, it converts it to an integer and puts the value into the integer variable passed to it (note the use of the keyword `out`; this keyword is addressed directly in a later chapter. For now, it suffices to understand that it allows the called method to modify the value of a variable passed to it.).
2.	Ask the user for two integers, then add them and print out the sum. If the entered data are not integers the calculation cannot be done, therefore in such a case output a statement indicating which number/numbers is/are in error and then exit the program *(Hint use the Int32.TryParse method to convert the numbers entered at the console to integers)*.

	``csharp
	using System;
	
	namespace PracticeYourCSharp
	{
	  class Program
	  {
	    static void Main(string[] args)
	    {
	      string sInt01; // To hold the string representation of the 1st entered integer
	      string sInt02; // To hold the string representation of the 2nd entered integer
	
	      int iInt01; // To hold the int value as converted from the string representation
	      int iInt02; // To hold the int value as converted from the string representation
	      int iTotal; // will be used to hold the sum of both integers
	``

```csharp
      bool bSuccessfulConversion01 = false;
      bool bSuccessfulConversion02 = false;

      Console.Write("Please enter the 1st integer: ");
      sInt01 = Console.ReadLine();
      Console.Write("Please enter the 2nd integer: ");
      sInt02 = Console.ReadLine();

      // Now see whether the strings entered were indeed integers or not

      bSuccessfulConversion01 = Int32.TryParse(sInt01, out iInt01);
      bSuccessfulConversion02 = Int32.TryParse(sInt02, out iInt02);
      // If indeed the entered strings were integers, using the out keyword the method
      // TryParse puts their integer equivalents into the variables iInt01 & iInt02 respectively.

      // Alright, let us see if we have to avoid doing the calculation
      if ((bSuccessfulConversion01 == false) || (bSuccessfulConversion02 == false))
      {
        if (bSuccessfulConversion01 == false)
        {
          Console.WriteLine("The first entry is not an integer");
        }
        if (bSuccessfulConversion01 == false)
        {
          Console.WriteLine("The second entry is not an integer");
        }
        Console.WriteLine("Cannot do the calculation for the reason(s) noted above");
      }
      else
      {
        iTotal = iInt01 + iInt02;
        Console.WriteLine("Both are integers. The sum is {0}", iTotal);
      }
      Console.ReadKey();
    }
  }
}
```

3. Refine the solution from the preceding exercise as follows:
   On error have the code write whichever *one* is appropriate out of the following error statements:
   1. *"The first entry is not an integer but the second is."*
   2. *"The second entry is not an integer but the first is."*
   3. *"Neither entry is an integer."*

   If both entries are integers, then state so, add them and print out their sum.

```csharp
using System;

namespace PracticeYourCSharp
{
  class Program
  {
    static void Main(string[] args)
    {
      string sInt01, sInt02;      // As with exercise above.
      int iInt01, iInt02, iTotal; // As with exercise above.
      bool bSuccessfulConversion01 = false;
      bool bSuccessfulConversion02 = false;

      Console.Write("Please enter the 1st integer: ");
      sInt01 = Console.ReadLine();
      Console.Write("Please enter the 2nd integer: ");
      sInt02 = Console.ReadLine();

      // Now see whether the strings entered were indeed integers or not
      bSuccessfulConversion01 = Int32.TryParse(sInt01, out iInt01);
      bSuccessfulConversion02 = Int32.TryParse(sInt02, out iInt02);
```

|   | ```csharp
      // Alright, let us see if we have to quit
      if ((bSuccessfulConversion01 == false) && (bSuccessfulConversion02 == false))
        Console.WriteLine("Both entries are not integers");
      else if ((bSuccessfulConversion01 == false) && (bSuccessfulConversion02 == true))
        Console.WriteLine("The first entry is not an integer but the second is");
      else if ((bSuccessfulConversion01 == true) && (bSuccessfulConversion02 == false))
        Console.WriteLine("The second number is not an integer but the first is");
      else
      {
        iTotal = iInt01 + iInt02;
        Console.WriteLine("Both are integers. The sum is {0}", iTotal);
      }
      Console.ReadKey();
    }
  }
}
``` |   |
| 4. | After the `if` and `else if` statements in the answer above, there were no braces around the statements that should run after the `if` and the `else if` conditions, but there were braces bounding the two statements after the `else`. Why? | |
| | When there is only one single program statement that should run when a conditional statement is determined to be true, it does not need braces around it. However, if there is more than one statement (for example see the section of the code controlled by the `else` condition in the answer above), then there must be braces around them. | |
| 5. | Request a first and then a second string from the user. If the strings are the same, output the statement *"The strings are the same!"*, otherwise output the statement *"The strings are different!"*.<br><br>Hint: use the static method `String.Equals`. | ```csharp
using System;

namespace PracticeYourCSharp
{
  class Program
  {
    static void Main(string[] args)
    {
      string s01, s02;
      bool bComparisonValue;

      Console.Write("Please enter the first string: ");
      s01 = Console.ReadLine();

      Console.Write("Please enter the second string: ");
      s02 = Console.ReadLine();

      bComparisonValue = String.Equals(s01, s02);

      if (bComparisonValue == true)
        Console.Write("The strings are the same!");
      else
        Console.Write("The strings are different!");
    }
  }
}
``` |
6.	Redo the preceding exercise using the instance method `<string>.Equals`.	

	Simply replace the line:
	
	  `bComparisonValue = String.Equals(s01, s02);`
	
	from the code above with the following line:
	
	  `bComparisonValue = s01.Equals(s02);`
	
	The difference between this solution and the one in the earlier exercise is that when using `String.Equals(s01,s02)`, we are asking "are these strings equal?". When using `s01.Equals(s02);` we are saying "I'm s01, are you s02 equal to me?"	

7.	Have the user enter a first and then a second string. Print out which appears first alphabetically. If they are both the same string, then inform the user as to that fact. Ignore the case of the strings.	

Hint: use the static method `String.Compare`

```csharp
using System;

namespace PracticeYourCSharp
{
  class Program
  {
    static void Main(string[] args)
    {
      string s01, s02;
      int result;
      bool ignorecase = true;

      Console.Write("Please enter the first string: ");
      s01 = Console.ReadLine();

      Console.Write("Please enter the second string: ");
      s02 = Console.ReadLine();

      result = String.Compare(s01, s02, ignorecase);

      if (result < 0)
        Console.Write("{0} comes before {1} alphabetically", s01, s02);
      else if (result > 0)
        Console.Write("{0} comes before {1} alphabetically", s02, s01);
      else
        Console.Write("{0} and {1} are the same string", s02, s01);

      Console.ReadKey();
    }
  }
}
```

8. We would like to convert a user entered temperature from Celsius to Fahrenheit or vice-versa. Ask the user to enter a temperature in the format <temperature><F|C>, then convert the entered value to the other temperature scale and print it out. For example, if the user enters 20C, detect that it is in Celsius and convert it to its equivalent in Fahrenheit, stating *"Equivalent temp = 68F"*.

```csharp
using System;

namespace PracticeYourCSharp
{
  class Program
  {
    static void Main(string[] args)
    {
      Console.Write("enter temperature: ");
      string sInput = Console.ReadLine();
      string tempScale;
      sInput = sInput.ToLower();//make the input one uniform case

      if (sInput.Contains("f"))
        tempScale = "f";
      else if (sInput.Contains("c"))
        tempScale = "c";
      else
      {
        Console.WriteLine("You have to specify C or F");
        Console.ReadKey();
        return;
      }
      sInput = sInput.Replace("f", "");
      sInput = sInput.Replace("c", "");
      // Now we should only have a number in sInput. Parse it out as a double
      double d01;
      if (!(Double.TryParse(sInput, out d01)))
```

|   | ```
      {
        Console.WriteLine("what you entered was not a valid number");
        Console.ReadKey();
        return;
      }
      // Okay, now do the conversion
      if (tempScale.Equals("f"))
      {
        Console.WriteLine("Equivalent temp = {0}C", (d01 - 32) * ((float)5 / (float)9));
      }
      else
        Console.WriteLine("Equivalent temp = {0}F", (d01 * (float)9 / (float)5) + 32);
      Console.ReadKey();
    }
  }
}
``` |
| 9. | Using an infinite loop, repeatedly ask the user to enter any of the following data types: boolean, short integer, integer, long integer, float, double, decimal, big integer or string.
Determine what type the data is and print the type out. When the user types *"quit"*, exit the program.
Hint: use the `<class name>.TryParse` *methods.* |
|   | ```
using System;
using System.Numerics;

namespace PracticeYourCSharp
{
  class Program
  {
    static void Main(string[] args)
    {
      bool inputBool;
      short inputInt16;
      int inputInt32;
      long inputInt64;
      float inputFloat; // This is also known as single
      double inputDouble;
      decimal inputDecimal;
      BigInteger inputBigInt;

      while (true)
      {
        Console.Write("Enter any integer, float, double, BigInt,
                            boolean or string item: ");
        string sInput = Console.ReadLine();

        if (Boolean.TryParse(sInput, out inputBool))
          Console.WriteLine("You entered a boolean");
        else if (Int16.TryParse(sInput, out inputInt16))
          Console.WriteLine("You entered a short integer ");
        else if (Int32.TryParse(sInput, out inputInt32))
          Console.WriteLine("You entered an integer (4 bytes)");
        else if (long.TryParse(sInput, out inputInt64))
          Console.WriteLine("You entered a long integer ");
        else if (BigInteger.TryParse(sInput, out inputBigInt))
          Console.WriteLine("You entered a Big Integer ");
        else if (float.TryParse(sInput, out inputFloat))
          Console.WriteLine("You entered a float");
        else if (double.TryParse(sInput, out inputDouble))
          Console.WriteLine("You entered a double ");
        else if (Decimal.TryParse(sInput, out inputDecimal))
          Console.WriteLine("You entered a decimal ");
        else
          Console.WriteLine("the type you entered is a string");
``` |

```
                if (sInput.Equals("quit")) break;
            }
            Console.ReadKey();
        }
    }
}
```

Note: Note that the numerical comparisons in the code are written in a particular order; from smallest to largest. The reason is, for example, if we checked for a `float` using `double.TryParse` before we did a `float.TryParse`, it would return `true` for what was really just a `float`! This logic also applies to the string/string-like types; we have to check whether the entered data is a boolean before checking whether it is a string, because an entered string of "true" or "false" looks like a string.

Chapter 10. Console Handling III: Command Line Input

There are a significant number of programs in existence which are run directly from the command line or are invoked by other programs without any direct user input. A number of these programs require that parameters be passed to them on the command line (or by their calling program) at the time of their invocation. This chapter presents exercises which ensure understanding of how a program receives and processes command line input that is passed to it on invocation.

Given that we are running our programs from within the Visual Studio environment and not the actual command line, we will use the facility provided by Visual Studio to provide command line arguments to programs that are being run from within it.

How to pass command line arguments to your program from within Visual Studio

(the instructions below pertain to both Visual Studio 2015 and 2013):

1. In **Solution Explorer** (select this from the View menu option if Solution Explorer is not already visible in your workspace), right-click on the *Properties* option and choose the option *Open*.
2. Look at the list of options on the left and note the option *Debug*. Select it.
3. A text box should appear on the right-side of the window entitled *Command Line Arguments*. This is where you enter the command line arguments.

We now proceed to the exercises.

1.	What does the information in the brackets in the following method declaration mean?
	`static void Main(string[] args)`
	It means that this method is expecting to be passed an array of strings. This being the method `Main` which in effect is invoked by the operating system, it means that this method is expecting that an array of type `string` will be passed to it by the operating system (or by whatever program invokes this program directly). It is acceptable that an empty array is passed to it, in which case the `Length` property of the string array `args` will be 0.
2.	What is the type that command line input is interpreted as?
	Command line input is always interpreted as a `string`. This implies that if we are expecting numerical input, we have to use the `TryParse` methods to convert the strings in question to numbers.
3.	Write and test a program which can take any number of command line arguments, then prints out the number of command line arguments received and also prints each argument value out in the following format: *argument[<x>] = <argument value>*
	``using System;

namespace PracticeYourCSharp
{
  class Program
  {
    static void Main(string[] args)
    {
      Console.WriteLine("Number of args={0}", args.Length);
      for (int i = 0; i < args.Length; i++)
      {
        Console.WriteLine("argument[{0}] = {1}", i, args[i]);
      }
      Console.ReadKey();
``` |
```

	``
	    }
	  }
	}
	``

4.	Write a program which receives the first name and last name of a person on the command line. Print these out to the console in the format *<last name>, <first name>* If anything other than two arguments are entered, output the statement *"Please pass exactly 2 arguments."* and then exit the program.
|   | ```csharp
using System;

namespace PracticeYourCSharp
{
  class Program
  {
    static void Main(string[] args)
    {
      if (args.Length != 2)
      {
        Console.WriteLine("Please pass exactly 2 arguments.");
        Console.ReadKey();
        return;
      }
      Console.WriteLine("{0}, {1}", args[1], args[0]);
      Console.ReadKey();
    }
  }
}
``` |
| 5. | Write a program which takes an unlimited number of integers from the command line and does the following:
1. Adds them up and prints out the summation of the integers presented on the command line.
2. Prints out how many integers were passed on the command line.
3. Prints out how many arguments were presented on the command line. |
|   | ```csharp
using System;

namespace PracticeYourCSharp
{
  class Program
  {
    static void Main(string[] args)
    {
      long sum = 0;
      int numOfIntegers = 0;

      if (args.Length < 1)
      {
        Console.WriteLine("No arguments passed. Exiting");
        return;
      }
      for (int i = 0; i < args.Length; i++)
      {
        long potentialInteger;

        if (long.TryParse(args[i], out potentialInteger) == true)
        {
          // We have to use TryParse to check whether the input data is a valid integer.
          // any non-integer is ignored since it won't pass the if condition.
          sum = sum + potentialInteger;
          numOfIntegers++; // we are keeping a running total of the number of integers.
        }
      }
      Console.WriteLine("Total = {0}", sum);
      Console.WriteLine("Number of integers={0}", numOfIntegers);
      Console.WriteLine("Number of args={0}", args.Length);
      Console.ReadKey();
    }
``` |

| | ```
    }
  }
}
``` |
| 6. | Modify the code in the preceding solution to handle any integer or floating point number up to a `double`. |
| | ```csharp
using System;

namespace PracticeYourCSharp
{
  class Program
  {
    static void Main(string[] args)
    {
      double sum = 0;
      int numberCount = 0;

      if (args.Length < 1)
      {
        Console.WriteLine("No arguments put in. Exiting");
        return;
      }
      for (int i = 0; i < args.Length; i++)
      {
        double potentialNum;
        if (double.TryParse(args[i], out potentialNum) == true)
        {
          sum = sum + potentialNum;
          numberCount++; // running count of the number of numbers used.
        }
      }
      Console.WriteLine("Total = {0}", sum);
      Console.WriteLine("Number of numbers={0}", numberCount);
      Console.WriteLine("Number of args={0}", args.Length);
      Console.ReadKey();
    }
  }
}
``` |

Chapter 11. The Char Type

The C# language presents the ability to manipulate single characters, whether they are of type `char`, or individual characters in a `string`. This chapter presents exercises pertaining to various aspects of the `char` type. Also exercises on the relationship between the `char` type and integers and individual elements of strings are presented.

The main classes utilized in this chapter are the classes `Char` and `ConsoleKeyInfo`.

1.	What is Unicode?
	Unicode is a convention by which characters from various languages are assigned a particular positive numerical value. The Unicode character range exceeds one million, however, most of the characters that are in use are in the range *0000(hex) to FFFF(hex)* (0 to 65535 in number base 10), a range which can be represented in 2 bytes.
2.	What is the `char` type?
	The `char` type is a C# type that is used to represent Unicode characters.
3.	What is the default Unicode encoding used for characters in C#?
	The particular Unicode encoding known as UTF-16. It uses either 2 or 4 bytes to represent characters. (There are different ways that Unicode encodes characters; these include UTF-8, UTF-16 and UTF-32).
4.	How many bytes are used to represent a `char` in C#?
	2 bytes, which represents a range of 65536 numbers. Given that the `char` type is represented by positive integer values, the range of the numbers that these 2 bytes represent is 0 to 65535, which corresponds to the range of an unsigned short. Note however though, that there are certain Unicode characters that require 4 bytes for representation; these characters are represented in C# by 2 chars.
5.	What numerical type corresponds most directly to the numerical range that a `char` will fit into?
	An unsigned short integer, which has a range of 0…65535.

6.	Write a line of code which will initialize the `char` variable `FirstChar` to the value `'x'`.	`char FirstChar = 'x';`
		Or
		`Char FirstChar = 'x';`
		Note: The first declaration style is the usual way to initialize a `char`.

7.	Run the following program and explain its output. ```\nusing System;\nnamespace PracticeYourCSharp\n{\n class Program\n {\n static void Main(string[] args)\n {\n char char01 = (char)100;\n Console.WriteLine(char01);\n Console.ReadKey();\n }\n }\n}\n```
	Output: The program will output the following: d
	The reason why we can cast an integer to a `char` is because every character has been mapped to a numerical equivalent in Unicode and its various encoding schemes. In this example, we see that the value `100` maps to the character d.
	The reader is urged to review the Unicode UTF-16 character encodings for the first 127 characters and to compare these values to the 127 values of an ASCII table.
8.	Run the following program and explain its output.

```
using System;

namespace PracticeYourCSharp
{
  class Program
  {
    static void Main(string[] args)
    {
      char char01 = 'A';
      uint num = char01; //built-in implicit conversion from char to integer
      Console.WriteLine(num);
      Console.ReadKey();
    }
  }
}
```

Output: The code will output the following value: 65

The reason for this is because the Unicode UTF-16 mapping of the character 'A' is the numeric value 65.

This exercise and the preceding one are here to show the relationship between the char type and integer values, moving in-between them using the required cast.

9.	Using a for loop, print out the equivalent characters of the number range 65 to 150.

```
using System;

namespace PracticeYourCSharp
{
  class Program
  {
    static void Main(string[] args)
    {
      for (int j = 65; j <= 150; j++)
        Console.WriteLine("{0} is equivalent to {1}", j, (char)j);

      Console.ReadKey();
    }
  }
}
```

Notes: You will note that above a certain integer value the console window will show a question mark for each character. This does not mean that each of those values necessarily represents the question mark, but rather that the console cannot display those characters (they can be displayed properly in a GUI) due to the way in which the console displays items. The reader should study the concept of *Windows Code Pages* if more understanding on the topic is desired.

10.	Given the following array of char (see below), print out the numerical value of each char in the array. `char charArray01[] = { '?', '1', '2', '3', '4', '5', '6', '7', '8', '9', '0', 'A', 'a' };`

```
using System;

namespace PracticeYourCSharp
{
  class Program
  {
    static void Main(string[] args)
    {
      char[] charArray01 = new char[] { '?', '1', '2', '3', '4', '5', '6', '7', '8',
                                        '9', '0', 'A', 'a' };
      for (int j = 0; j < charArray01.Length; j++)
        Console.WriteLine("{0} is equivalent to {1}", charArray01[j], (int)charArray01[j]);
    }
  }
}
```

11.	*Char & Hexadecimal* Write a program which assigns the hexadecimal value 2A to a char variable. Print the variable out.

```
using System;
```

|  | ```
namespace PracticeYourCSharp
{
  class Program
  {
    static void Main(string[] args)
    {
      char c01 = '\x002A';   // or it can be written as '\u002A';
      Console.WriteLine(c01);
      Console.ReadKey();
    }
  }
}
``` |
| 12. | Write a program which requests a single character from a user and then prints the received character out. |
|  | ```
using System;

namespace PracticeYourCSharp
{
  class Program
  {
    static void Main(string[] args)
    {
      char FirstChar;

      ConsoleKeyInfo cki;
      Console.Write("Enter a char please: ");
      cki = Console.ReadKey();
      FirstChar = cki.KeyChar;

      Console.WriteLine("\nThe character you entered is {0}.", FirstChar);
    }
  }
}
``` |
| 13. | Write a program which requests a single character from a user. Analyze the character and state whether it is a letter or not.
Hint: Use the `Char.IsLetter` *method.* |
|  | ```
using System;

namespace PracticeYourCSharp
{
  class Program
  {
    static void Main(string[] args)
    {
      char FirstChar;
      bool bIsLetter = false;

      Console.WriteLine("Enter a char please: ");

      FirstChar = Console.ReadKey().KeyChar;
      // This style of appending methods is called "method chaining"

      bIsLetter = Char.IsLetter(FirstChar);

      if (bIsLetter == true)
        Console.WriteLine("The character you entered is indeed an alphabetic character");
      else
        Console.WriteLine("The character you entered is not an alphabetic character");
    }
  }
}
``` |
| 14. | Have the user enter an alphabetic character. Determine and print out the case of the character and then print out the character in the opposite case to which it was originally entered. For example if an uppercase character is entered, print out the following: *"It is uppercase. Its lowercase equivalent is <lower case equivalent>."* |
```

```
using System;
namespace PracticeYourCSharp
{
  class Program
  {
    static void Main(string[] args)
    {
      char char01;
      Console.WriteLine("Enter a char please: ");

      char01 = Console.ReadKey().KeyChar;

      if (!Char.IsLetter(char01))
      {
        Console.WriteLine("\nThe character you entered is not an alphabetic character");
        return;
      }
      Console.WriteLine("\nThe character you entered is indeed an alphabetic character");
      // Okay now check for case.
      if (Char.IsUpper(char01))
      {
        Console.WriteLine("It is uppercase. Its lowercase equivalent is {0}.",
                          Char.ToLower(char01));
      }
      if (Char.IsLower(char01))
      {
        Console.WriteLine("It is lowercase. Its uppercase equivalent is {0}.",
                          Char.ToUpper(char01));
      }
      Console.ReadKey();
    }
  }
}
```

15. Write a program which requests a character from a user. Analyze it and state to the user as to whether or not it is a numerical character.
    Hint: Use the `Char.IsDigit` *method.*

```
using System;
namespace PracticeYourCSharp
{
  class Program
  {
    static void Main(string[] args)
    {
      char FirstChar;
      bool bIsDigit = false;

      Console.WriteLine("Enter a char please: ");

      FirstChar = Console.ReadKey().KeyChar;

      bIsDigit = Char.IsDigit(FirstChar);

      if (bIsDigit == true)
        Console.WriteLine("\nThe character you entered is indeed a digit");
      else
        Console.WriteLine("\nThe character you entered is not a digit");
    }
  }
}
```

16. Write a program which requests a character from a user. Analyze the character and inform the user as to whether or not it is an alphanumeric character.
    Hint: Use the `Char.IsLetterOrDigit` *method.*

```
using System;

namespace PracticeYourCSharp
{
  class Program
  {
    static void Main(string[] args)
    {
      char char01;
      bool bIsAlphaNumeric = false;

      Console.WriteLine("Enter a char please: ");

      char01 = Console.ReadKey().KeyChar;

      bIsAlphaNumeric = Char.IsLetterOrDigit(char01);

      if (bIsAlphaNumeric == true)
        Console.WriteLine("\nThe character you entered is indeed alphanumeric");
      else
        Console.WriteLine("\nThe character you entered is not alphanumeric");

      Console.ReadKey();
    }
  }
}
```

17.	Write a program which requests a character from a user. Analyze the character and inform the user as to whether or not it is a punctuation character. *Hint: Use the `Char.IsPunctuation` method.*

```
using System;

namespace PracticeYourCSharp
{
  class Program
  {
    static void Main(string[] args)
    {
      char char01;
      bool bIsPunctuation = false;

      Console.Write("Enter a char please: ");

      char01 = Console.ReadKey().KeyChar;

      bIsPunctuation = Char.IsPunctuation(char01);

      if (bIsPunctuation == true)
        Console.WriteLine("\nThe character you entered is indeed a punctuation character");
      else
        Console.WriteLine("\nThe character you entered is not a punctuation character");

      Console.ReadKey();
    }
  }
}
```

18.	Write a program which requests a character from a user. Analyze the character and inform the user as to whether or not it is a whitespace character. *Hint: Use the `Char.IsWhiteSpace` method.*

```
using System;

namespace PracticeYourCSharp
{
  class Program
  {
    static void Main(string[] args)
    {
```

| | ```
    char char01;
    bool bIsWhiteSpace = false;

    Console.Write("Enter a char please: ");

    char01 = Console.ReadKey().KeyChar;

    bIsWhiteSpace = Char.IsWhiteSpace(char01);

    if (bIsWhiteSpace == true)
      Console.WriteLine("\nThe character you entered is indeed a whitespace character");
    else
      Console.WriteLine("\nThe character you entered is not a whitespace character");

    Console.ReadKey();
  }
 }
}
``` |
| 19. | I have two `char` variables, `c01` and `c02` (for testing purposes hardcode values for them). Write a program which determines if they contain the same value and print out your findings as to whether or not they are equal. |
| | ```
using System;

namespace PracticeYourCSharp
{
  class Program
  {
    static void Main(string[] args)
    {
      char c01 = 'x';
      char c02 = 'x';

      if (c01 == c02)
        Console.WriteLine("They are equal!");
      else
        Console.WriteLine("They are not equal!");
    }
  }
}
```
**Notes:** Alternatively, to check for equality you can also use the `<char>.Equals` method and write:
       `if(c01.Equals (c02))` instead of `if(c01==c02)` |

## String/Char relationship

| | | |
|---|---|---|
| 20. | What is the relationship between the `char` type and the type `string`? | |
| | A `string` is a datatype that *has the appearance* of being a sequence/array of `char`, however the relationship is not so. Nonetheless, due to the clear natural relationship of `char` to `string`, the individual elements of a `string` can be accessed as if they are elements of type `char` in a contiguous sequence.

Restating the above we are saying the following: a `char[]` is not equal to a `string`. There are however methods which convert between both types. | |
| 21. | State what the difference between "x" and 'x' is. | |
| | `"x"` refers to a string object.<br>`'x'` refers to a char. | |
| 22. | Write a program which converts the char `'x'` to a `string` which you should then print out. | ```
using System;

namespace PracticeYourCSharp
{
  class Program
  {
    static void Main(string[] args)
    {
      char c01 = 'x';
      string s01 = c01.ToString();
      Console.WriteLine(s01);
``` |
```

		``
      }
    }
}
```
**Note:** A single character, for example *x* is referred to in code as `'x'`, whereas a string of that same single character *x* is referred to in code as `"x"`. |
| 23. | Write a program which converts the string *"Xavier"* to an array of type `char`.<br>Loop through the resulting `char` array and write out each character one after the other. | ```
using System;
namespace PracticeYourCSharp
{
  class Program
  {
    static void Main(string[] args)
    {
      char[] cArray01;
      string s01 = "Xavier";
      cArray01 = s01.ToCharArray();
      for (int j = 0; j < cArray01.Length; j++)
        Console.Write(cArray01[j]);

      Console.ReadKey();
    }
  }
}
``` |
| 24. | I have the following `string`: s1="Xavier". Copy the 2<sup>nd</sup> character in s1 to the `char` variable `c01` and print `c01` out to the console.<br>*(This exercise shows how to access a string as if it is an array of char)* | ```
using System;
namespace PracticeYourCSharp
{
  class Program
  {
    static void Main(string[] args)
    {
      char c01;
      string s01 = "Xavier";

      c01 = s01[1]; // The 2nd character.
      // Accessing a string as if it is an array of char.
      Console.WriteLine(c01);
      Console.ReadKey();
    }
  }
}
``` |
| 25. | I have a `string` variable which contains the following: *"Hello how are you?"*
Write a program which *reverses* this string and print out the result.
Hint: One way in which this can be done is to first convert the string to an array of char. Then loop through the array of char backwards, adding each character to the new string that represents the reversed string (you add a char to a string by first converting the char to a string using the ToString method of char). Another way is to use the Array.Reverse method. | |
| | **Solution #1**<br>```
using System;

namespace PracticeYourCSharp
{
  class Program
  {
    static void Main(string[] args)
    {
      string original = "Hello how are you?";
      string reversed = null;
      char[] cArray01 = original.ToCharArray();

      for (int index = cArray01.Length - 1; index >= 0; index--)
``` | |

```
            {
                reversed += cArray01[index].ToString();
            }
            Console.WriteLine(reversed);
            Console.ReadKey();
        }
    }
}
//The above solution can be written more efficiently, but this suffices.
```

Solution #2
```
using System;

namespace PracticeYourCSharp
{
    class Program
    {
        static void Main(string[] args)
        {
            string original = "Hello how are you?";
            string reversed = null;
            char[] cArray01 = original.ToCharArray();
            Array.Reverse(cArray01);
            reversed = new string(cArray01);
            Console.WriteLine(reversed);
            Console.ReadKey();
        }
    }
}
```

26. Write a program to do the following: Have the user enter a string and then, loop through the string, indicating for each character therein what type of character it is, whether a number, letter, punctuation, white space or separator character. For any other type of character simply indicate that it is an unspecified character.
Write the output as follows: <index# (*starting from 1*)>. <character> <character type>

```
using System;

namespace PracticeYourCSharp
{
    class Program
    {
        static void Main(string[] args)
        {
            Console.Write("Enter the string you want analyzed: ");

            string s01 = Console.ReadLine();
            if (s01.Length < 1)
            {
                Console.WriteLine("Nothing entered. Bye bye.");
                Console.ReadKey();
                return;
            }

            for (int index = 0; index < s01.Length; index++)
            {
                if (Char.IsLetter(s01, index))
                    Console.WriteLine("{0}. {1} is a letter", index + 1, s01[index]);
                else if (Char.IsNumber(s01, index))
                    Console.WriteLine("{0}. {1} is a number", index + 1, s01[index]);
                else if (Char.IsPunctuation(s01, index))
                    Console.WriteLine("{0}. {1} is punctuation", index + 1, s01[index]);
                else if (Char.IsWhiteSpace(s01, index))
                    Console.WriteLine("{0}. {1} is white space", index + 1, s01[index]);
                else if (Char.IsSeparator(s01, index))
                    Console.WriteLine("{0}. {1} is a separator", index + 1, s01[index]);
                else
```

| | | ```
            Console.WriteLine("{0}. {1} is unspecified", index + 1, s01[index]);
        }
        Console.ReadKey();
    }
  }
}
``` |
| 27. | We have the following string:<br><br>`">>>>>>How are you<<<<<<"`<br><br>Using the `Trim` method of class `String`, erase the extraneous characters bounding the phrase *"How are you"*. Print the trimmed string out. | ```csharp
using System;

namespace PracticeYourCSharp
{
  class Program
  {
    static void Main(string[] args)
    {
      string s1 = ">>>>>>>how are you<<<<<<<<";
      char[] chaff = new char[] { '>', '<' };

      string s2 = s1.Trim(chaff);
      Console.WriteLine(s2);
      Console.ReadKey();
    }
  }
}
``` |

The reader is urged to work through Chapter 33. Character Encoding in order to get an even deeper understanding of characters and their interaction with the char type in C#.

Chapter 12. Date/Time Handling & Measurement

An important part of any computer language is the ability to determine and measure time, including determination of the current date and time (and sub-elements thereof such as year, month, day, hour, minute, second), past or future dates and times, timezones, measurement of date and time differences, as well as the formatting of date/time output. This chapter presents exercises on each of these topics. Also, introductory exercises on the measurement of the running time of code segments are presented.

Key classes utilized in this chapter include: `DateTime`, `TimeSpan`, `TimeZone` and `Stopwatch`.

1.	Write a program which prints out the current date & time in the default format.
|    | ```csharp
using System;

namespace PracticeYourCSharp
{
  class Program
  {
    static void Main(string[] args)
    {
      DateTime currentDateTime = DateTime.Now;
      Console.WriteLine("The current date & time is {0}", currentDateTime);
      Console.ReadKey();
    }
  }
}
``` |
| 2. | Write a program which prints out the current UTC date & time in the default format. |
|    | ```csharp
using System;

namespace PracticeYourCSharp
{
  class Program
  {
    static void Main(string[] args)
    {
      DateTime currentDateTimeUTC = DateTime.UtcNow;
      Console.WriteLine("The current date & time in UTC is {0}", currentDateTimeUTC);

      Console.ReadKey();
    }
  }
}
``` |
| 3. | Write a program which:
  1. determines and prints out the difference in hours and minutes between your current time zone and UTC.
  2. states whether your current time zone is UTC, behind UTC or ahead of UTC.
Hint: use the `DateTime.Subtract` method which returns a `TimeSpan` object. |
|    | ```csharp
using System;

namespace PracticeYourCSharp
{
  class Program
  {
    static void Main(string[] args)
    {
      DateTime currentDateTime = DateTime.Now;
      DateTime currentDateTimeUTC = DateTime.UtcNow;

      // Now we've gotten those 2 values, now find the difference
      TimeSpan timeDiff = currentDateTime.Subtract(currentDateTimeUTC);
``` |
```

|   | ```csharp
        Console.WriteLine("The difference in time is is {0} hrs {1} mins", timeDiff.Hours,
                                                                           timeDiff.Minutes);
        // Alright we want to state whether we are behind or ahead of UTC;
        // this can be easily determined by noting the sign of the returned TimeSpan
        if ((Math.Sign(timeDiff.Hours) == -1) || (Math.Sign(timeDiff.Minutes) == -1))
        {
          Console.WriteLine("My current timezone is behind UTC");
        }
        else if (((timeDiff.Hours) == 0) && (timeDiff.Minutes == 0))
        {
          Console.WriteLine("My current timezone is UTC");
        }
        else
        {
          Console.WriteLine("My current timezone is ahead of UTC");
        }
        Console.ReadKey();
      }
    }
}
``` |
| 4. | *Printing the components of a DateTime object*
Determine the current date and time and then print out the following components thereof:
year, month, day, day of week, hour, minute, second, milliseconds. |
|   | ```csharp
using System;
namespace PracticeYourCSharp
{
  class Program
  {
    static void Main(string[] args)
    {
      DateTime currentDateTime = DateTime.Now;

      int currentYear = currentDateTime.Year;
      int currentMonth = currentDateTime.Month;
      int currentDay = currentDateTime.Day;
      string currentDayOfWeek = currentDateTime.DayOfWeek.ToString();
      int currentHour = currentDateTime.Hour;
      int currentMin = currentDateTime.Minute;
      int currentSec = currentDateTime.Second;
      int currentMillisecs = currentDateTime.Millisecond;

      Console.WriteLine("The year is {0}", currentYear);
      Console.WriteLine("The month is {0}", currentMonth);
      Console.WriteLine("The day is {0}", currentDay);
      Console.WriteLine("The day of the week is {0}", currentDayOfWeek);
      Console.WriteLine("The hour is {0}", currentHour);
      Console.WriteLine("The minutes are {0}", currentMin);
      Console.WriteLine("The seconds are {0}", currentSec);
      Console.WriteLine("The milliseconds are {0}", currentMillisecs);

      Console.ReadKey();
    }
  }
}
``` |
| 5. | Determine the current date and print out which day of the year it is. |

```
using System;
namespace PracticeYourCSharp
{
  class Program
  {
    static void Main(string[] args)
    {
      DateTime currentDateTime = DateTime.Now;

      int dayOfYear = DateTime.Now.DayOfYear;
      Console.WriteLine("Today is day {0} of the year.", dayOfYear);

      Console.ReadKey();
    }
  }
}
```

6.	What will the date & time be exactly one month from now?
	Hint: `<DateTime>.AddMonths`
| | ```
using System;
namespace PracticeYourCSharp
{
  class Program
  {
    static void Main(string[] args)
    {
      DateTime currentDateTime = DateTime.Now;

      DateTime oneMonthFromNow = currentDateTime.AddMonths(1);
      Console.WriteLine("The date and time one month from now is {0}", oneMonthFromNow);

      Console.ReadKey();
    }
  }
}
``` |
| 7. | What was the date & time exactly 2 months ago? |
| | ```
using System;
namespace PracticeYourCSharp
{
  class Program
  {
    static void Main(string[] args)
    {
      DateTime currentDateTime = DateTime.Now;

      DateTime twoMonthsAgo = currentDateTime.AddMonths(-2);
      Console.WriteLine("The date and time two months ago was: {0}", twoMonthsAgo);
      Console.ReadKey();
    }
  }
}
``` |
| 8. | What will the date & time be exactly 1 year from now? |
| | ```
using System;
namespace PracticeYourCSharp
{
  class Program
  {
    static void Main(string[] args)
    {
      DateTime currentDateTime = DateTime.Now;
``` |
```

|   | ```
      DateTime oneYearFromNow = currentDateTime.AddYears(1);
      Console.WriteLine("One year from now is {0}", oneYearFromNow);

      Console.ReadKey();
    }
  }
}
``` |
| 9. | What will the time (not date) be exactly 2 hours from now? |
|   | ```
using System;

namespace PracticeYourCSharp
{
  class Program
  {
    static void Main(string[] args)
    {
      DateTime currentDateTime = DateTime.Now;

      DateTime twoHoursFromNow = currentDateTime.AddHours(2);
      Console.WriteLine("In 2 hours the time will be {0} hrs {1} mins {2} seconds",
                        twoHoursFromNow.Hour, twoHoursFromNow.Minute, twoHoursFromNow.Second);
      Console.ReadKey();
    }
  }
}
``` |
| 10. | What will the time (not date) be exactly 25 minutes from now? |
|   | ```
using System;

namespace PracticeYourCSharp
{
  class Program
  {
    static void Main(string[] args)
    {
      DateTime currentDateTime = DateTime.Now;

      DateTime timeFromNow = currentDateTime.AddMinutes(25);
      Console.WriteLine("In 25 minutes the time will be {0} hrs {1} mins {2} seconds",
                        timeFromNow.Hour, timeFromNow.Minute, timeFromNow.Second);
      Console.ReadKey();
    }
  }
}
``` |
| 11. | Initialize a `DateTime` object to your birthday. |
|   | ```
using System;

namespace PracticeYourCSharp
{
  class Program
  {
    static void Main(string[] args)
    {
      DateTime birthday = new DateTime(1970, 1, 1); // For one born on 1st Jan. 1970

      Console.ReadKey();
    }
  }
}
``` |
| 12. | Express your age in days.
*Hint: Use a **TimeSpan** object.* |
|   | ```
using System;

namespace PracticeYourCSharp
``` |
```

```csharp
        {
          class Program
          {
            static void Main(string[] args)
            {
              DateTime birthday = new DateTime(1970, 1, 1); // For one born on 1st Jan. 1970
              DateTime currentDateTime = DateTime.Now;
              TimeSpan age = currentDateTime.Subtract(birthday);

              double ageInDays = age.TotalDays;
              Console.WriteLine("My age is {0} days", ageInDays);

              Console.ReadKey();
            }
          }
        }
```

13.	Express your age in hours.

```csharp
using System;

namespace PracticeYourCSharp
{
  class Program
  {
    static void Main(string[] args)
    {
      DateTime birthday = new DateTime(1970, 1, 1); // For one born on 1st Jan. 1970
      DateTime currentDateTime = DateTime.Now;
      TimeSpan age = currentDateTime.Subtract(birthday);

      double ageInHours = age.TotalHours;
      Console.WriteLine("My age is {0} hours", ageInHours);

      Console.ReadKey();
    }
  }
}
```

14.	Calculate how many days there are to your next birthday.

```csharp
using System;

namespace PracticeYourCSharp
{
  class Program
  {
    static void Main(string[] args)
    {
      DateTime birthday = new DateTime(1970, 1, 1); // E.g. one born on 1st Jan. 1970
      DateTime nextBirthDay = new DateTime(DateTime.Today.Year, birthday.Month, birthday.Day);
      // This is my birthday this year. Let us see whether it has passed or not

      TimeSpan timeToNextBirthday = nextBirthDay.Subtract(DateTime.Today);
      int numberOfDays = timeToNextBirthday.Days;

      if (numberOfDays < 0)
      {
        nextBirthDay = nextBirthDay.AddYears(1);
        timeToNextBirthday = nextBirthDay.Subtract(DateTime.Today);
        numberOfDays = timeToNextBirthday.Days;
      }
      Console.WriteLine("Number of days to next birthday is {0}", numberOfDays);
      Console.ReadKey();
    }
  }
}
```

15.	Write a program that determines whether your birthdate is before, after or on March 15, 1985.

Hint: `DateTime.Compare`

```csharp
using System;

namespace PracticeYourCSharp
{
  class Program
  {
    static void Main(string[] args)
    {
      DateTime birthdate = new DateTime(1970, 1, 1, 0, 0, 0); // birthdate = 1st Jan. 1970
      DateTime otherDate = new DateTime(1985, 3, 15, 0, 0, 0); // March 15th 1985

      int earlier = DateTime.Compare(birthdate, otherDate);
      if (earlier == -1) Console.WriteLine("My birthdate is earlier than March 15, 1985");
      else if (earlier == 1) Console.WriteLine("My birthdate is later than March 15, 1985");
      else Console.WriteLine("My birthdate is actually March 15, 1985");

      Console.ReadKey();
    }
  }
}
```

16. How many days were there in the month of February 2008?
    Hint: static method `DateTime.DaysInMonth`

```csharp
using System;

namespace PracticeYourCSharp
{
  class Program
  {
    static void Main(string[] args)
    {
      int daysInFeb2008 = DateTime.DaysInMonth(2008, 2);

      Console.WriteLine("The number of days in Feb 2008 = {0} days", daysInFeb2008);
      Console.ReadKey();
    }
  }
}
```

17. Write a program which determines whether the year 2032 is a leap year. If it is, state so, otherwise state that it is not a leap year.

```csharp
using System;

namespace PracticeYourCSharp
{
  class Program
  {
    static void Main(string[] args)
    {
      bool is2032LeapYear = DateTime.IsLeapYear(2032);
      if (is2032LeapYear == true)
        Console.WriteLine("2032 is indeed a leap year");
      else
        Console.WriteLine("2032 is not a leap year");

      Console.ReadKey();
    }
  }
}
```

18. Print out the latest possible date that can be represented in C#.

```csharp
using System;

namespace PracticeYourCSharp
{
  class Program
  {
    static void Main(string[] args)
```

|     | ```
        {
            DateTime maxDateTime = DateTime.MaxValue;
            Console.WriteLine("The maximum date supported is: {0}", maxDateTime);

            Console.ReadKey();
        }
    }
}
``` |
| 19. | Print out the earliest possible date that can be represented in C#. |
|     | ```
using System;

namespace PracticeYourCSharp
{
    class Program
    {
        static void Main(string[] args)
        {
            DateTime minDateTime = DateTime.MinValue;
            Console.WriteLine("The minimum date supported is: {0}", minDateTime);

            Console.ReadKey();
        }
    }
}
``` |
| 20. | Print out your current timezone. |
|     | ```
using System;

namespace PracticeYourCSharp
{
    class Program
    {
        static void Main(string[] args)
        {
            TimeZone myTimeZone = TimeZone.CurrentTimeZone;
            string timeZoneName = myTimeZone.StandardName;
            Console.WriteLine("My current timezone is: {0}", myTimeZone.StandardName);
            Console.ReadKey();
        }
    }
}
``` |
| 21. | Determine whether you are currently in Daylight Savings Time. |
|     | ***Solution #1***<br>```
using System;

namespace PracticeYourCSharp
{
    class Program
    {
        static void Main(string[] args)
        {
            DateTime now = DateTime.Now;
            bool inDST = now.IsDaylightSavingTime();
            if (inDST == true) Console.WriteLine("Yes we are currently in DST");
            else Console.WriteLine("We are not in DST");
        }
    }
}
```<br>***Solution #2***<br>```
using System;

namespace PracticeYourCSharp
{
``` |
```

Practice Your C# Level 1

```
        class Program
        {
          static void Main(string[] args)
          {
            TimeZone tz = TimeZone.CurrentTimeZone;
            bool inDST = tz.IsDaylightSavingTime(DateTime.Now);
            if (inDST == true) Console.WriteLine("Yes we are currently in DST");
            else Console.WriteLine("We are not in DST");
          }
        }
}
```

22.	What is the Daylight Savings Time timezone name for the timezone that you are currently in? If your timezone doesn't support the concept of Daylight Savings Time, print this fact out.

```
using System;

namespace PracticeYourCSharp
{
  class Program
  {
    static void Main(string[] args)
    {
      TimeZone myTimeZone = TimeZone.CurrentTimeZone;
      string DSTName = myTimeZone.DaylightName;

      if (DSTName.Equals("") == false)
      {
        Console.WriteLine("The DST Name of my current timezone = {0}", DSTName);
      }
      else Console.WriteLine("This timezone doesn't have daylight savings time");

      Console.ReadKey();
    }
  }
}
```

Date/Time Formatting

23.	In utilizing composite formatting so far in our exercises you have used {<index>} to print out the desired data. Explain the components of the following composite formatting template. `{<index>[,<+/->fieldWidth][:formatString]}`
	`{<index>[,<->fieldWidth][:formatString]}` **index** is the position of the argument in the argument list to the formatting string. **,<+/->fieldWidth** is an optional argument which indicates by the +/- whether the argument is to be left(-) aligned or right aligned (no sign required). **fieldWidth** indicates the width of the field in which the value in question is. **:formatString** is an optional argument indicating the field type specific formatting that you want applied to this argument. For example, numbers can be displayed as currency, hexadecimal or decimal place specific. Another set of examples <u>are the different format options possible for the different components of a date</u>. Note that the braces ([and]) in the formatting template are not part of the formatting string and are only there to demarcate the different components of a composite formatting string for the purposes of this explanation.
24.	I have the following DateTime object: `DateTime dt01 = new DateTime(2015, 2, 1, 17, 6, 4, 512);` Write a program to output all of the different ways in which each of the components of this object can be written with the <u>custom</u> DateTime format specifiers.

```
using System;

namespace PracticeYourCSharp
{
  class Program
  {
    static void Main(string[] args)
    {
      DateTime dt01 = new DateTime(2015, 2, 1, 17, 6, 4, 512);
```

122

```
            Console.WriteLine("{0:y } {0:yy}", dt01); //year one or 2 digit formats
            Console.WriteLine("{0:yyyy } {0:yyyyy}", dt01); //year 4 or 5 digit format
            Console.WriteLine("{0:M } {0:MM}", dt01); //month formats, numerical
            Console.WriteLine("{0:MMM } {0:MMMM}", dt01); //month formats (text)
            Console.WriteLine("{0:d } {0:dd}", dt01);    //Day of month
            Console.WriteLine("{0:ddd } {0:dddd}", dt01);    //Day of week

            Console.WriteLine("{0:g } {0:gg}", dt01); //period A.D, B.C.
            Console.WriteLine("{0:h } {0:hh}", dt01); //hour in 12 hour formats
            Console.WriteLine("{0:H } {0:HH}", dt01); //hour in 24 hour formats
            Console.WriteLine("{0:t } {0:tt}", dt01); //a.m. p.m. formats
            Console.WriteLine("{0:m } {0:mm}", dt01); //minute
            Console.WriteLine("{0:s } {0:ss}", dt01); //seconds
            Console.WriteLine("{0:f } {0:ff} {0:fff} {0:ffff} {0:fffff} {0:ffffff} {0:fffffff}", dt01);
            //10ths,100ths,1000ths, 10000ths,100000ths, millionths of seconds

            Console.WriteLine("{0:z } {0:zz}", dt01); //hours offset from UTC
            Console.WriteLine("{0:zzz }", dt01); //hours & minutes offset from UTC
            Console.ReadKey();
        }
    }
}
```

25.	Write a program which prints out the date 1st March, 2019, 2:15:07am in the following formats:
	1. 2019/3/1 02:15:07
	2. 20190301 02:15:07
		`using System;`
		
		`namespace PracticeYourCSharp`
		`{`
		`  class Program`
		`  {`
		`    static void Main(string[] args)`
		`    {`
		`      DateTime dt01 = new DateTime(2019, 3, 1, 2, 15, 7);`
		`      Console.WriteLine("{0:yyyy/M/d hh:mm:ss}", dt01);`
		`      Console.WriteLine("{0:yyyyMMdd hh:mm:ss}", dt01);`
		
		`      Console.ReadKey();`
		`    }`
		`  }`
		`}`

26.	I have a date of 1st February, 2015, with a time component of 12hrs, 30mins, 23.5 seconds. Write this full date, its date component and its time component out in all of the standard date/time formats provided in C#.	

```
using System;

namespace PracticeYourCSharp
{
  class Program
  {
    static void Main(string[] args)
    {
      DateTime dt01 = new DateTime(2015, 2, 1, 15, 6, 4, 500);
      Console.WriteLine("{0:d}", dt01); // "2/1/2015"           ShortDate (locale specific)
      Console.WriteLine("{0:D}", dt01); // "Sunday, February 01, 2015"   LongDate
      Console.WriteLine("{0:f}", dt01); // "Sunday, February 01, 2015 3:06 PM"
                                        // LongDate+ShortTime
      Console.WriteLine("{0:F}", dt01); // "Sunday, February 01, 2015 3:06:04 PM"
                                        // FullDateTime
      Console.WriteLine("{0:g}", dt01); // "2/1/2015 4:06 PM"  ShortDate+ShortTime
      Console.WriteLine("{0:G}", dt01); // "2/1/2015 4:06:04 PM"  ShortDate+LongTime
      Console.WriteLine("{0:m}", dt01); // "February 1"            MonthDay
      Console.WriteLine("{0:y}", dt01); // "February 2015"         YearMonth
      Console.WriteLine("{0:r}", dt01); // "Sun, 01 Feb 2015 15:06:04 GMT"   RFC1123 date/time
      Console.WriteLine("{0:s}", dt01); // "2015-02-01T15:06:04"   SortableDateTime
      Console.WriteLine("{0:u}", dt01); // "2015-02-01 15:06:04Z"  UniversalSortableDateTime
      Console.WriteLine("{0:t}", dt01); // "3:06 PM"               ShortTime
      Console.WriteLine("{0:T}", dt01); // "3:06:04 PM"            LongTime
```

	`    }`
	`  }`
	`}`	
| 27. | Write generic code which prints out dates in the following format:<br><br><date><*suffix*> <month>, <year><br><br>for example, 1st March, 2019, 2:15:07am as:<br><br>*Friday 1st March, 2019*<br><br>*Hint: There is no built-in method that provides that provides the day suffix, so you have to write your own code to do it.* | ```
using System;
namespace PracticeYourCSharp
{
  class Program
  {
    static void Main(string[] args)
    {
      DateTime dt01 = new DateTime(2019, 3, 1, 2, 15, 7);
      int iDay = dt01.Day;
      string suffix;
      switch (iDay)
      {
        case 1:
        case 21:
        case 31:
          suffix = "st";
          break;
        case 2:
        case 22:
          suffix = "nd";
          break;
        case 3:
        case 23:
          suffix = "rd";
          break;
        default:
          suffix = "th";
          break;
      }
      Console.WriteLine("{0:dddd} {1}{2} {0:MMMM}, {0:yyyy}",
                        dt01, dt01.Day, suffix);
      Console.ReadKey();
    }
  }
}
``` |
| 28. | Write the date from the preceding exercise in the following format: 2:15am on the 1st of March, 2019. | |
|  | Here is the relevant code fragment:<br><br>```
DateTime dt01 = new DateTime(2019, 3, 1, 2, 15, 0);
string sAMorPM = String.Format("{0:tt}",dt01);
sAMorPM = sAMorPM.ToLower();
  // Add suffix code from preceding solution here
Console.WriteLine("{0:hh}:{0:mm}{1} on the {2}{3} of {0:MMMM}, {0:yyyy}", dt01, sAMorPM,
                  dt01.Day, suffix);
```<br><br>**Notes:** The way in which the built-in direct date formats output data is based on the "culture" in which you are working. If you want to display the dates for specific cultures, you can either change the culture that you are working in for the program, or print out the date, specifying the desired culture. |  |

| 29. | Write a program which does the following:<br>1. Gets the current time<br>2. Sleeps for 10 seconds<br>3. Rereads the time<br>4. Prints the difference between the 1st time reading and the 2nd time | ```
using System;
using System.Threading;
namespace PracticeYourCSharp
{
  class Program
  {
    static void Main(string[] args)
    {
      Console.WriteLine("Testing waiting in a program");
``` |
```

| | reading<br><br>*Hint:* `DateTime, Thread.Sleep` | ```
            Console.WriteLine("Will sleep for 10secs (10000msecs)");
            DateTime dtA = DateTime.Now;
            Thread.Sleep(10000);
            DateTime dtB = DateTime.Now;
            Console.WriteLine("Done. Elapsed Time={0}",
                                  dtB.Subtract(dtA));
            Console.ReadKey();
        }
    }
}
``` |
| 30. | Rewrite the solution to the preceding exercise using the `Stopwatch` class instead of the class `DateTime`. | |
| | ```csharp
using System;
using System.Threading;    // For Thread.Sleep
using System.Diagnostics; // For Stopwatch

namespace PracticeYourCSharp
{
  class Program
  {
    static void Main(string[] args)
    {
      Stopwatch swatch01 = new Stopwatch();
      swatch01.Reset();
      Console.WriteLine("Sleeping for 10secs (10000 millisecs)");
      swatch01.Start();
      Thread.Sleep(10000);
      swatch01.Stop ();
      Console.WriteLine("Done. Elapsed Time={0}", swatch01.Elapsed);
      Console.ReadKey();
    }
  }
}
``` | |
| E1 | Write a program to calculate and print out how old you are in years, months and days (for example, "35 years, 11 months and 3 days old"). | |

Chapter 13. Collections (Introduction)

Collections are built-in classes which represent well-known data structures such as lists, stacks, queues and dictionaries among others.

The exercises in this chapter largely pertain to the `List`, `Dictionary` and `SortedDictionary` classes.

1.	Which would be the best out of (1) a `Stack`, (2) a `Queue` or (3) a `List` to represent each of the following scenarios: a) You put 5 books on top of each other into a box b) People lining up to pay for groceries at a single checkout counter c) Books on a bookshelf	a) A `Stack`. The reason is because a stack is a last-in first-out structure and clearly, the last book you put into the box is the first that you will bring out. b) A `Queue`. A queue is generally a first-in first-out structure and the first person on the queue is the one that is generally next to be served. c) A `List`. A bookshelf has no specific order in which you must take books out or put them in.
2.	*True or False*: A `List` is a built-in data structure that can be used for different types of data.	True The `List` class is a child class of the class `Collection` which has generic support, that is, it can handle any type of element (strings, numbers, user defined objects and structures) that you desire to put into a list.
3.	What is the concept of Generics in C#?	
	The concept of Generics in C# is the means within C# to create classes that can apply to any type. For example, the `List` class in C# can be a `List` of `int`, `List` of `string` or a `List` of whatever type we want. When talking about the `List` class, because it can handle any data type, it is spoken of/written as `List<T>`, the placeholder `T` being replaced by whichever specific type the `List` instance at hand is handling. The placeholder `T` is referred to as a "generic type parameter".	
4.	Explain what is meant by the following declaration: `List<int> firstList = new List<int>();`	We are telling the compiler that we want to instantiate a `List` object that will contain objects of type `int`. As noted in the answer to the preceding exercise, the `List` class is a class that supports the use of a generic type parameter that lets the user specify what kind of type they want each given instance of a `List` to contain.
5.	Instantiate a `List<string>` variable named `stringList01`.	`List<string> stringList01 = new List<string>();`
6.	Instantiate a `List<char>` variable named `charList01`.	`List<char> charList01 = new List<char>();`
7.	Instantiate a `List<object>` variable named `objList01`.	`List<object> objList01 = new List<object>();`
8.	Write a program to instantiate a `List<int>` variable. Put the values 10, 20, 30 and 40 into it, using the `List<T>.Add` method.	```using System;
using System.Collections.Generic;
namespace PracticeYourCSharp
{
class Program
{
static void Main(string[] args)
{
List<int> intList01 = new List<int>();```

| | | ```
            intList01.Add(10);
            intList01.Add(20);
            intList01.Add(30);
            intList01.Add(40);
            Console.ReadKey();
        }
    }
}
``` |
| 9. | Rewrite the solution to the preceding exercise, this time however, initialize the List<int> at the same time that it is instantiated. | ```
using System;
using System.Collections.Generic;

namespace PracticeYourCSharp
{
    class Program
    {
        static void Main(string[] args)
        {
            List<int> intList01 = new List<int>(){10,20,30,40};

            Console.ReadKey();
        }
    }
}
``` |
| 10. | Write a program to instantiate a List<string> and put the following list of words into it:<br><br>Mary<br>had<br>a<br>little<br>lamb<br>little<br>lamb<br>little<br>lamb | ```
using System;
using System.Collections.Generic;

namespace PracticeYourCSharp
{
    class Program
    {
        static void Main(string[] args)
        {
            List<string> stringList01 = new List<string>();

            stringList01.Add("Mary");
            stringList01.Add("had");
            stringList01.Add("a");
            stringList01.Add("little");
            stringList01.Add("lamb");
            stringList01.Add("little");
            stringList01.Add("lamb");
            stringList01.Add("little");
            stringList01.Add("lamb");

            Console.ReadKey();
        }
    }
}
``` |
| 11. | Extend the solution to the preceding exercise to determine and print out how many elements are in the List<string>. | ```
using System;
using System.Collections.Generic;

namespace PracticeYourCSharp
{
    class Program
    {
        static void Main(string[] args)
        {
            List<string> stringList01 = new List<string>();

            stringList01.Add("Mary");   stringList01.Add("had");
            stringList01.Add("a");      stringList01.Add("little");
            stringList01.Add("lamb");   stringList01.Add("little");
            stringList01.Add("lamb");   stringList01.Add("little");
``` |

|   |   | ```
                        stringList01.Add("lamb");
                        int listLength = stringList01.Count;
                        Console.WriteLine("There are {0} items in the list",
                                                listLength);
                        Console.ReadKey();
                    }
                }
            }
``` |
| 12. | Print out the 4th element in the List<string> in the preceding solution. | |
|   | ```
using System;
using System.Collections.Generic;

namespace PracticeYourCSharp
{
    class Program
    {
        static void Main(string[] args)
        {
            List<string> stringList01 = new List<string>();

            stringList01.Add("Mary");   stringList01.Add("had");
            stringList01.Add("a");      stringList01.Add("little");
            stringList01.Add("lamb");   stringList01.Add("little");
            stringList01.Add("lamb");   stringList01.Add("little");
            stringList01.Add("lamb");

            Console.WriteLine("The 4th item is: {0}", stringList01[3]);

            Console.ReadKey();
        }
    }
}
``` | |
| 13. | What is the current capacity of the List<string> in the preceding exercise? Print it out to the console. | |
|   | ```
using System;
using System.Collections.Generic;

namespace PracticeYourCSharp
{
    class Program
    {
        static void Main(string[] args)
        {
            List<string> stringList01 = new List<string>();

            stringList01.Add("Mary ");   stringList01.Add("had ");
            stringList01.Add("a ");      stringList01.Add("little ");
            stringList01.Add("lamb ");   stringList01.Add("little ");
            stringList01.Add("lamb ");   stringList01.Add("little ");
            stringList01.Add("lamb ");

            int listCapacity = stringList01.Capacity; //Capacity is a property of a List<T>

            Console.WriteLine("The list capacity is {0}", listCapacity);
            Console.ReadKey();
        }
    }
}
``` | |
| | **Note:** From this exercise we observe that a List<T> is assigned a default capacity. When you add enough items to exceed the capacity of the list, the capacity of the list will be automatically increased. | |
| 14. | Print the elements of the List<string> from the | *Add the following code to the exercise above:*
`for (int i = 0; i < stringList01.Count; i++)` |
```

| | preceding exercise out, using a for loop. | ```
{
    Console.WriteLine(stringList01[i]);
}
``` |
| 15. | Copy the contents of the List<string> in exercise 10 to an array of string named stringArray01 and print the array out, stating *Array item <x> = <value>*
Hint: Use the <List>.CopyTo *method* | |
| | ```
using System;
using System.Collections.Generic;

namespace PracticeYourCSharp
{
  class Program
  {
    static void Main(string[] args)
    {
      List<string> stringList01 = new List<string>();
      int listLength;

      stringList01.Add("Mary"); stringList01.Add("had"); stringList01.Add("a");
      stringList01.Add("little"); stringList01.Add("lamb"); stringList01.Add("little ");
      stringList01.Add("lamb"); stringList01.Add("little"); stringList01.Add("lamb");

      listLength = stringList01.Count;

      // Now create the string array
      string[] stringArray01 = new string[listLength];
      // See the length given to the string array; we've matched the lengths
      // of the list & the array;

      // Now copy the list over to the array
      stringList01.CopyTo(stringArray01);

      for (int i = 0; i < stringArray01.Length; i++)
        Console.WriteLine("Array item {0} = {1}", i, stringList01[i]);

      Console.ReadKey();
    }
  }
}
``` | |
| 16. | Prepare a List<string> whose individual entries are the individual words in the phrase *"Mary had a little lamb"*.<br>Now using List<T> methods, modify this List<string> to do the following:<br>1. Put the word *didn't* after the word *Mary*<br>2. Change the word *had* to the word *have*<br>The end result should be: *Mary didn't have a little lamb.*<br>Print out the list. | ```
using System;
using System.Collections.Generic;

namespace PracticeYourCSharp
{
  class Program
  {
    static void Main(string[] args)
    {
      List<string> stringList01
        = new List<string>(){"Mary","had","a","little","lamb"};

      // Now put the word didn't after Mary
      stringList01.Insert(1, "didn't");
      // Pushes everything below it down
      stringList01.RemoveAt(2); // We've removed the "had" now
      stringList01.Insert(2, "have");

      // Now print out its value to the console the list
      foreach (string item in stringList01)
        Console.WriteLine("{0} ", item);
      Console.ReadKey();
    }
  }
}
``` |
| 17. | Prepare a List<string> whose | using System; |
```

	individual entries are the individual words in the phrase *"Mary had a little lamb"*.
	
	Sort the `List<string>` using the `Sort` method of class `List` and print out each of the elements of the sorted list in order.
		``csharp
		using System.Collections.Generic;
		namespace PracticeYourCSharp
		{
		  class Program
		  {
		    static void Main(string[] args)
		    {
		      List<string> stringList01 = new List<string>();
		
		      stringList01.Add("Mary"); stringList01.Add("had");
		      stringList01.Add("a"); stringList01.Add("little");
		      stringList01.Add("lamb ");
		      stringList01.Sort();
		      // Now print out the list
		      foreach (string item in stringList01)
		        Console.WriteLine("{0} ", item);
		
		      Console.ReadKey();
		    }
		  }
		}
		``

18.	We've noted earlier that a `List<T>` can be used to support any kind of data. How then does the `List` class know how to sort the different types of data types that it might be assigned, as ordering is a function of the type of item (`int`, `string`, user defined type, etc.) in the `List`?	
	The `List<T>` class is able to sort (which involves knowing the relative order of the items it contains) the different types it supports because the type in question has "implemented" the **interface IComparable**. An introduction to the concept of interfaces is made later in this book.	
19.	**Dictionary** The list of continents, along with their sizes (in square kilometres) expressed in exponential form is as follows: (Europe, 1.018×10^8), (North America, 2.449×10^8), (Africa, 3.037×10^8), (Asia, 4.382×10^8), (Australia, 9.0085×10^7), (South America, 1.7840×10^8) and (Antarctica, 1.372×10^8). Write a program which will first create an object of class `Dictionary` named `continents` and afterwards put each of these pairs of data (with the continent name as the key) into the object. Following this insertion, use a `foreach` loop to print out the name of each continent and its size as entered into the `Dictionary` object.	

	``csharp
	using System;
	using System.Collections.Generic;
	
	namespace PracticeYourCSharp
	{
	  class Program
	  {
	    static void Main(string[] args)
	    {
	      Dictionary<string, double> continents = new Dictionary<string, double>();
	      continents["Europe"] = 1.018E8;
	      continents["North America"] = 2.449E8;
	      continents["Africa"] = 3.037E8;
	      continents["Asia"] = 4.382E8;
	      continents["Australia"] = 9.0085E7;
	      continents["South America"] = 1.7840E8;
	      continents["Antarctica"] = 1.372E8;
	      foreach (KeyValuePair<string, double> x in continents)
	      {
	        Console.WriteLine("{0}: {1} million square km.", x.Key, x.Value);
	      }
	    }
	  }
	}
	``	

20.	**(6.0)** Rewrite the solution to the preceding exercise, this time however, initialize the `Dictionary` object at the	

time of instantiation. Also, rewrite the output line in the `foreach` loop to use string interpolation. Also use `using static` to ensure that you avoid having to write `Console.WriteLine` in the code.

```
using System;
using static System.Console;
using System.Collections.Generic;

namespace PracticeYourCSharp
{
  class Program
  {
    static void Main(string[] args)
    {
      Dictionary<string, double> continents = new Dictionary<string, double>()
      {
        {"Europe",1.018E8 },
        {"North America",2.449E8 },
        {"Africa",3.037E8 },
        {"Antarctica",1.372E8},
        {"Asia",4.382E8 },
        {"Australia",9.0085E7 },
        {"South America",1.7840E8 }
      };
      foreach (KeyValuePair<string, double> x in continents)
      {
        WriteLine($"{x.Key}: {x.Value} million square km.");
      }
    }
  }
}
```

21. Extend the solution to question 19 above by adding to it a `SortedDictionary` object named `scontinents` which should be directly initialized using the previously defined `Dictionary` object. Print out the contents of the `SortedDictionary` object to confirm that indeed the output has been sorted according to its keys.

Add the following code to the solution in question:

```
SortedDictionary<string, double> scontinents = new SortedDictionary<string, double>(continents);
foreach (KeyValuePair<string, double> x in scontinents)
{
  Console.WriteLine("{0}: {1} million square km.", x.Key, x.Value);
}
```

22. Write a program which, using a `SortedDictionary`, will print the continents out in ascending order of size. *(Hint: use the size of the continents as the key).*

```
using System;
using System.Collections.Generic;

namespace PracticeYourCSharp
{
  class Program
  {
    static void Main(string[] args)
    {
      SortedDictionary<double, string> continentsBySize = new SortedDictionary<double, string>();
      continentsBySize[1.018E8] = "Europe";
      continentsBySize[2.449E8] = "North America";
      continentsBySize[3.037E8] = "Africa";
      continentsBySize[4.382E8] = "Asia";
      continentsBySize[9.0085E7] = "Australia";
      continentsBySize[1.7840E8] = "South America";
      continentsBySize[1.372E8] = "Antarctica";

      foreach (KeyValuePair<double, string> x in continentsBySize)
      {
        Console.WriteLine("{0,-14}: {1,12} million square km.", x.Value, x.Key);
```

```
            }
          }
        }
      }
```

23. Given the following line: *"Mary had a little lamb little lamb little lamb Mary had a little lamb that was as white as snow"*, using an object of class `Dictonary` do the following:
    1. Count how many times each word occurs.
    2. Give a total of how many words are in the `Dictionary` object
    3. Print out how many times each individual word occurs.

    Hint: Break the string up using the `String.Split` *method then use a* `Dictionary<string, int>` *to do the counting. You will need a* `KeyValuePair<string,int>` *to extract the values from the* `Dictionary` *for counting.*

```
using System;
using System.Collections.Generic;
using System.Linq;

namespace PracticeYourCSharp
{
  class Program
  {
    static void Main(string[] args)
    {
      string sRhyme = "Mary had a little lamb little lamb little lamb Mary had a little lamb
                       that was as white as snow";
      string[] rhymeArray = sRhyme.Split(' '); // Splits at the spaces
      Dictionary<string, int> rhymeDictionary = new Dictionary<string, int>();

      bool isFound = false;
      int iWordCount;

      for (int count = 0; count < rhymeArray.Length; count++)
      {
        isFound = rhymeDictionary.ContainsKey(rhymeArray[count]);
        if (isFound == true)
        {
          // Means its already in there, so just increment its count
          iWordCount = rhymeDictionary[rhymeArray[count]];
          iWordCount++; // increment it, then we will put it back
          rhymeDictionary[rhymeArray[count]] = iWordCount;
        }
        else
        {
          // It is a new word. Put it in the dictionary and assign it a count of 1.
          rhymeDictionary.Add(rhymeArray[count], 1);
        }
      }

      // Alright, now lets print out the words, along with their frequency
      Console.WriteLine("The number of elements in the dictionary = {0}",
                        rhymeDictionary.Count);
      for (int count = 0; count < rhymeDictionary.Count; count++)
      {
        KeyValuePair<string, int> item = rhymeDictionary.ElementAt(count);
        Console.WriteLine("word={0}, frequency={1}", item.Key, item.Value);
      }

      Console.ReadKey();
    }
  }
}
```

E1	Write a program which requests a string from the user. The program should then, using a `Dictionary`, determine the frequency of each unique character in the string. The unique characters and their respective frequencies should be printed out in alphabetical order. Put this code into an infinite loop which requests successive strings from the user (which you then assess as described above) until the user types the CTRL-C sequence to end the program.
E2	Modify the program in exercise 22 to print the continents out in descending order of size.
E3	The reader is encouraged to study the C# class `DataTable` in order to observe the functionality of a built-in multi-column data structure.

Chapter 14. Computer Environment & Computer Information

This chapter presents exercises with which to practice and enhance your knowledge on how to use built-in C# methods to determine information about your computer. Exercises on such topics as the determination of the location of the *Desktop* directory, processor count, drive information, operating system version, computer name, system uptime and other such related topics are presented in this chapter.

The key classes utilized in this chapter include `Environment` and `DriveInfo`.

1.	Write a program which obtains and prints the location of the *Desktop* directory. *Hint*: `Environment.GetFolderPath(Environment.SpecialFolder.Desktop)`

	``
	using System;
	
	namespace PracticeYourCSharp
	{
	  class Program
	  {
	    static void Main(string[] args)
	    {
	      string myDesktop = Environment.GetFolderPath(Environment.SpecialFolder.Desktop);
	      Console.WriteLine(myDesktop);
	      Console.ReadKey();
	    }
	  }
	}
	``

2.	Write a program that determines and prints out the following:
	  1. The total number of drives in this computer
	  2. A list of all the drives in this computer
	Hint: `DriveInfo.GetDrives`

	``
	using System;
	using System.IO;
	
	namespace PracticeYourCSharp
	{
	  class Program
	  {
	    static void Main(string[] args)
	    {
	      DriveInfo[] driveList = DriveInfo.GetDrives();
	      int numberOfDrives = driveList.Length;
	      int index = numberOfDrives;
	
	      Console.WriteLine("The number of drives in this computer = {0}", numberOfDrives);
	
	      while (index > 0)
	      {
	        index--;// We are using this variable as the array index to go through the list.
	        Console.WriteLine("Drive name: {0}", driveList[index].Name);
	      }
	      Console.ReadKey();
	    }
	  }
	}
	``

3.	Write a program which prints out the following information about the drives on this computer: 1. Drive name

2. Volume label
3. Total drive size
4. Available free space
5. Drive format
6. Drive type
7. Root directory of the drive

```csharp
using System;
using System.IO;

namespace PracticeYourCSharp
{
  class Program
  {
    static void Main(string[] args)
    {
      DriveInfo[] driveList = DriveInfo.GetDrives();
      int numberOfDrives = driveList.Length;
      int index = numberOfDrives;

      Console.WriteLine("The number of drives in this computer is={0}\n", numberOfDrives);
      if (index > 0)
      {
        while (index > 0)
        {
          index--;
          Console.WriteLine("Drive name              : {0}", driveList[index].Name);
          if (driveList[index].IsReady)
          {
            Console.WriteLine("\tVolume Label                      : {0}",
                              driveList[index].VolumeLabel);
            Console.WriteLine("\tTotal Drive Size (bytes)          : {0}",
                              driveList[index].TotalSize);
            Console.WriteLine("\tTotal Free Space (bytes)          : {0}",
                              driveList[index].TotalFreeSpace);
            Console.WriteLine("\tAvail. Free Space to current user: {0}",
                              driveList[index].AvailableFreeSpace);
            Console.WriteLine("\tDrive Format                      : {0}",
                              driveList[index].DriveFormat);
            Console.WriteLine("\tDrive Type                        : {0}",
                              driveList[index].DriveType);
            Console.WriteLine("\tRoot Directory                    : {0}",
                              driveList[index].RootDirectory);
          }
          else
            Console.WriteLine("The drive is not ready for reading of its data");
        }
      }
      else
        Console.WriteLine("There are no drives in this computer");
      Console.ReadKey();
    }
  }
}
```

4.	Put a USB stick (thumb drive) into the computer and run the solution to the preceding exercise again. What is the *Drive Type* indicated for a USB stick?	Removable

Environment Class

5.	Print the string which represents the major, minor, build and revision numbers of the .NET CLR that you are running on at present.
	`using System;`

Chapter 14: Computer Environment

```
namespace PracticeYourCSharp
{
  class Program
  {
    static void Main(string[] args)
    {
      string version = Environment.Version.ToString();
      Console.WriteLine("The .NET version is {0}", version);

      Console.ReadKey();
    }
  }
}
```

6. Write a program to print out the command line for this program that you are currently running.

```
using System;

namespace PracticeYourCSharp
{
  class Program
  {
    static void Main(string[] args)
    {
      string commandLine = Environment.CommandLine;
      Console.WriteLine("The command line is\n: {0}", commandLine);

      Console.ReadKey();
    }
  }
}
```

7. Write a program to print out the command line arguments for this program that you are currently running.

```
using System;

namespace PracticeYourCSharp
{
  class Program
  {
    static void Main(string[] args)
    {
      string[] commandLineArgs = Environment.GetCommandLineArgs();
      if (commandLineArgs.Length > 0)
      {
        foreach (string s in commandLineArgs)
        {
          Console.Write("{0} ", s);
        }
        Console.WriteLine("\n");
      }
      else
        Console.WriteLine("There are no command line arguments for this process");

      Console.ReadKey();
    }
  }
}
```

8. Write a program that determines and prints out the operating system version running on this computer.

```
using System;

namespace PracticeYourCSharp
{
  class Program
  {
    static void Main(string[] args)
    {
      Console.WriteLine("The OS version is {0}", Environment.OSVersion);
```

	``` Console.ReadKey(); } } } ```
9.	Determine and print out whether or not you are running on 64-bit Windows.
	``` using System; namespace PracticeYourCSharp { class Program { static void Main(string[] args) { if (Environment.Is64BitOperatingSystem) Console.WriteLine("The OS version is 64-bit"); else Console.WriteLine("The OS version is not 64-bit"); Console.ReadKey(); } } } ```
10.	Determine and print out the name of the computer that you are working on.
	``` using System; namespace PracticeYourCSharp { class Program { static void Main(string[] args) { string computerName = Environment.MachineName; Console.WriteLine("The computer name is: {0}", computerName); Console.ReadKey(); } } } ```
11.	Obtain and print the system uptime in seconds.
	``` using System; namespace PracticeYourCSharp { class Program { static void Main(string[] args) { long uptime = Environment.TickCount; // This is in milliseconds Console.WriteLine("Uptime (in seconds): {0}", (uptime / 1000)); Console.ReadKey(); } } } ```
12.	Write a program which prints out the username with which you logged into the computer.	``` using System; namespace PracticeYourCSharp { class Program { static void Main(string[] args) { string userName = Environment.UserName; Console.WriteLine("The user name is: {0}", userName); ```

		`                Console.ReadKey();`
		`            }`
		`        }`
		`    }`

13.	Write a program that determines and prints out how many processors this computer has.	`using System;`
		`namespace PracticeYourCSharp`
		`{`
		`    class Program`
		`    {`
		`        static void Main(string[] args)`
		`        {`
		`            int iProcessorCount = `**`Environment.ProcessorCount`**`;`
		`            Console.WriteLine("# Processors ={0}", iProcessorCount);`
		`            Console.ReadKey();`
		`        }`
		`    }`
		`}`

14.	Identify and print out the list of all the logical drives on this computer.	

	`using System;`
	
	`namespace PracticeYourCSharp`
	`{`
	`  class Program`
	`  {`
	`    static void Main(string[] args)`
	`    {`
	`      string[] logicalDriveList = Environment.GetLogicalDrives();`
	`      Console.WriteLine("The number of logical drives on this computer={0}",`
	`                        logicalDriveList.Length);`
	
	`      if (logicalDriveList.Length > 0)`
	`      {`
	`        Console.WriteLine("And their names are:");`
	`        for (int j = 0; j < logicalDriveList.Length; j++)`
	`        {`
	`          Console.WriteLine("logical drive[{0}] = {1}", j, logicalDriveList[j]);`
	`        }`
	`      }`
	`      Console.ReadKey();`
	`    }`
	`  }`
	`}`	

E1	Write a program which determines the system uptime in days, hours, minutes and seconds.	

Chapter 15. File System I: Path & Directory Handling

The ability to access and manipulate files and their associated directories is a key skill in any computer language. This chapter is the first of many with which to which ensure your facility with the computer filesystem. Among the exercises in this chapter are exercises on directory path handling, as well as creation and manipulation (moving, renaming, deleting, etc.) of directories.

The reader is advised in this and the subsequent chapter to write their solutions carefully, as improperly written file handling code will result in *exceptions* occuring. We address the concept of *exceptions* later in this book.

The key classes utilized in this chapter are the classes `Directory` and `Environment`.

1.	Write a program that obtains and prints out the path of the current working directory.
	You can use either of the following two ways to retrieve the string that contains the location of the current working directory:

	```Directory.GetCurrentDirectory()```
	or
	```Environment.CurrentDirectory;```

	See both of them used in the solution below.
| | ```csharp
using System;
using System.IO;

namespace PracticeYourCSharp
{
  class Program
  {
    static void Main(string[] args)
    {
      string dir01 = Directory.GetCurrentDirectory();
      string dir02 = Environment.CurrentDirectory;
      Console.WriteLine(dir01);
      Console.WriteLine(dir02);

      Console.ReadKey();
    }
  }
}
``` |
| 2. | Write a program that prints the directory path of the *Desktop* out to the console. |
| | ```csharp
using System;

namespace PracticeYourCSharp
{
  class Program
  {
    static void Main(string[] args)
    {
      string myDesktop = Environment.GetFolderPath(Environment.SpecialFolder.Desktop);
      Console.WriteLine(myDesktop);
      Console.ReadKey();
    }
  }
}
``` |

3.	Set the path of the current working directory to the *Desktop*. Afterwards, print the path of the current working directory out to confirm that it indeed has been modified.
	Hint: `Environment.CurrentDirectory`

```
using System;
using System.IO;

namespace PracticeYourCSharp
{
  class Program
  {
    static void Main(string[] args)
    {
      Environment.CurrentDirectory =
            Environment.GetFolderPath(Environment.SpecialFolder.Desktop);

      // Now print out its value to the console just to confirm...
      string dir02 = Environment.CurrentDirectory;
      Console.WriteLine("the current directory is {0}", dir02);
    }
  }
}
```

4.	Write a program which determines whether a directory named `Dir_A` exists on the *Desktop* and inform the user as to your findings.
	Hint: `Directory.Exists()`

```
using System;
using System.IO;

namespace PracticeYourCSharp
{
  class Program
  {
    static void Main(string[] args)
    {
      bool DoesExist = false;
      string sDirName = "Dir_A";

      Environment.CurrentDirectory =
            Environment.GetFolderPath(Environment.SpecialFolder.Desktop);
      DoesExist = Directory.Exists(sDirName);
      if (DoesExist)
        Console.WriteLine("Yes, the directory exists on the desktop!");
      else
        Console.WriteLine("No, the directory does not exist on the desktop");

      Console.ReadKey();
    }
  }
}
```

5.	Create each of the following directories on the Desktop: `Dir_A`, `Dir_B`, `Dir_C`, `Dir_D` and `Dir_E`, after first confirming that they do not already exist.
	Hint: `Directory.CreateDirectory()`

```
using System;
using System.IO;

namespace PracticeYourCSharp
{
  class Program
  {
    static void Main(string[] args)
    {
      bool DoesExist = false;
      string[] sDirNames = new string[] { "Dir_A", "Dir_B", "Dir_C", "Dir_D", "Dir_E" };
```

|   | ```
            Environment.CurrentDirectory =
                Environment.GetFolderPath(Environment.SpecialFolder.Desktop);
            foreach (string s in sDirNames)
            {
                DoesExist = Directory.Exists(s);
                if (DoesExist == false)
                {
                    Directory.CreateDirectory(s);
                    Console.WriteLine("Directory {0} has been created in {1}", s,
                                            Environment.CurrentDirectory);
                }
                else
                    Console.WriteLine("The directory {0} already exists in {1}", s,
                                            Environment.CurrentDirectory);
            }
            Console.ReadKey();
        }
    }
}
``` |
| 6. | Write a program which will create the subdirectories Dir_A_1, Dir_A_2, Dir_A_3, Dir_A_4 and Dir_A_5 in the earlier created Dir_A. |
|   | ```csharp
using System;
using System.IO;

namespace PracticeYourCSharp
{
    class Program
    {
        static void Main(string[] args)
        {
            bool DoesExist = false;
            string[] sDirNames = new string[] {"Dir_A_1", "Dir_A_2", "Dir_A_3", "Dir_A_4", "Dir_A_5"};

            Environment.CurrentDirectory = Environment.GetFolderPath(Environment.SpecialFolder.Desktop);
            Directory.SetCurrentDirectory("Dir_A"); // So we move to the proper directory.

            //Now create the sub-directories therein
            foreach (string s in sDirNames)
            {
                DoesExist = Directory.Exists(s);
                if (DoesExist == false)
                {
                    Directory.CreateDirectory(s);
                    Console.WriteLine("Directory {0} has been created", s);
                }
                else
                    Console.WriteLine("The directory {0} already exists", s);
            }
            Console.ReadKey();
        }
    }
}
``` |
| 7. | Delete the just created empty subdirectory Dir_A_4.
Hint: Directory.Delete() |
|   | ```csharp
using System;
using System.IO;

namespace PracticeYourCSharp
{
    class Program
    {
``` |
```

```
      static void Main(string[] args)
      {
        bool DoesExist = false;
        string sDirName = "Dir_A_4";

        Environment.CurrentDirectory =
              Environment.GetFolderPath(Environment.SpecialFolder.Desktop);
        Directory.SetCurrentDirectory("Dir_A"); // So we move to the proper directory.

        DoesExist = Directory.Exists(sDirName);
        if (DoesExist == true)
        {
          Directory.Delete(sDirName);
          Console.WriteLine("Directory {0} has been deleted", sDirName);
        }
        else
          Console.WriteLine("The directory {0} was not existent", sDirName);

        Console.ReadKey();
      }
    }
}
```

Note: Using Windows Explorer look at the directory Dir_A and confirm that indeed the subdirectory in question was deleted.

8.	Write a program which deletes the directory Dir_E that was created on the desktop.

```
using System;
using System.IO;

namespace PracticeYourCSharp
{
  class Program
  {
    static void Main(string[] args)
    {
      bool DoesExist = false;
      string sDirName = "Dir_E";

      Environment.CurrentDirectory =
            Environment.GetFolderPath(Environment.SpecialFolder.Desktop);

      DoesExist = Directory.Exists(sDirName);
      if (DoesExist == true)
      {
        Directory.Delete(sDirName);
        Console.WriteLine("Directory {0} has been deleted", sDirName);
      }
      else
        Console.WriteLine("The directory {0} was not existent", sDirName);

      Console.ReadKey();
    }
  }
}
```

9.	Print out the names of all the directories that are on the *Desktop*.
	Hint: `Directory.GetDirectories()`

```
using System;
using System.IO;

namespace PracticeYourCSharp
{
  class Program
  {
    static void Main(string[] args)
```

| | ```csharp
    {
      string[] sDirNames;

      Environment.CurrentDirectory =
            Environment.GetFolderPath(Environment.SpecialFolder.Desktop);

      sDirNames = Directory.GetDirectories(Environment.CurrentDirectory);
      if (sDirNames.Length == 0)
        Console.WriteLine("There are no directories on the desktop");
      else
      {
        Console.WriteLine("Here is the list of directories:");
        foreach (string s in sDirNames)
        {
          Console.WriteLine("\t{0}", s);
        }
      }
      Console.ReadKey();
    }
  }
}
``` |
| 10. | Print out the names of all of the <u>files</u> that are on the *Desktop*.
Hint: `Directory.GetFiles()` |
| | ```csharp
using System;
using System.IO;

namespace PracticeYourCSharp
{
  class Program
  {
    static void Main(string[] args)
    {
      string[] sDirNames;

      Environment.CurrentDirectory =
            Environment.GetFolderPath(Environment.SpecialFolder.Desktop);

      sDirNames = Directory.GetFiles(Environment.CurrentDirectory);
      if (sDirNames.Length == 0)
        Console.WriteLine("There are no files on the desktop");
      else
      {
        Console.WriteLine("Here is the list of files:");
        foreach (string s in sDirNames)
        {
          Console.WriteLine("\t{0}", s);
        }
      }
      Console.ReadKey();
    }
  }
}
``` |
| 11. | List all of the file names on the *Desktop* that have an extension of *.doc*. |
| | **Note:** This code might take a while to run, for its running time depends on the number of subdirectories you have on your *Desktop*.<br><br>```csharp
using System;
using System.IO;

namespace PracticeYourCSharp
{
  class Program
  {
``` |
```

```
        static void Main(string[] args)
        {
          string[] sDirNames;

          Environment.CurrentDirectory =
                Environment.GetFolderPath(Environment.SpecialFolder.Desktop);

          sDirNames = Directory.GetFiles(Environment.CurrentDirectory, "*.doc");
          if (sDirNames.Length == 0)
            Console.WriteLine("There are no files on the desktop");
          else
          {
            Console.WriteLine("Here is the list of files:");
            foreach (string s in sDirNames)
            {
              Console.WriteLine("\t{0}", s);
            }
          }
          Console.ReadKey();
        }
      }
    }
```

12. Print the names of all of the files that are on the *Desktop and in subfolders* thereof *(all subfolders, recursively that is)* that have an extension of *.doc*.

```
using System;
using System.IO;

namespace PracticeYourCSharp
{
  class Program
  {
    static void Main(string[] args)
    {
      string[] sDirNames;

      Environment.CurrentDirectory =
            Environment.GetFolderPath(Environment.SpecialFolder.Desktop);

      sDirNames = Directory.GetFiles(Environment.CurrentDirectory, "*.doc",
                                SearchOption.AllDirectories);
      if (sDirNames.Length == 0)
        Console.WriteLine("There are no files on the desktop");
      else
      {
        Console.WriteLine("Here is the list of files:");
        foreach (string s in sDirNames)
        {
          Console.WriteLine("\t{0}", s);
        }
      }
      Console.ReadKey();
    }
  }
}
```

13. Print out, in local time as well as in UTC, the creation time of the earlier created directory `Dir_A`.
    Hint: `Directory.GetCreationTime()`

```
using System;
using System.IO;

namespace PracticeYourCSharp
{
  class Program
  {
```

```
      static void Main(string[] args)
      {
        string sDirName = "Dir_A";
        DateTime creationDateTime;
        Environment.CurrentDirectory =
              Environment.GetFolderPath(Environment.SpecialFolder.Desktop);

        creationDateTime = Directory.GetCreationTime(sDirName);

        Console.WriteLine("The directory {0} was created on {1}",
                  sDirName, creationDateTime.ToString("MMM ddd d HH:mm yyyy"));
      }
    }
}
```

14. Write a program to modify the creation time of the directory Dir_A to 1st Jan, 2000 00:00:00.

```
using System;
using System.IO;

namespace PracticeYourCSharp
{
    class Program
    {
      static void Main(string[] args)
      {
        string sDirName = "Dir_A";
        DateTime newCreationDateTime = new DateTime(2000, 1, 1, 0, 0, 0);
        Environment.CurrentDirectory =
              Environment.GetFolderPath(Environment.SpecialFolder.Desktop);

        Directory.SetCreationTime(sDirName, newCreationDateTime);
      }
    }
}
```

Note: You can confirm this change of date by manually checking the properties of the file in Windows Explorer.

15. Print out the last time, in local time & also UTC, that directory Dir_A was accessed.

```
using System;
using System.IO;

namespace PracticeYourCSharp
{
    class Program
    {
      static void Main(string[] args)
      {
        string sDirName = "Dir_A";
        DateTime creationDateTime, lastAccessDateTime, lastAccessDateTimeUTC;

        Environment.CurrentDirectory =
              Environment.GetFolderPath(Environment.SpecialFolder.Desktop);
        lastAccessDateTime = Directory.GetLastAccessTime(sDirName);
        lastAccessDateTimeUTC = Directory.GetLastAccessTimeUtc(sDirName);

        Console.WriteLine("The directory {0} was last accessed at\n\t{0}\nand\n\t{1} UTC",
                    lastAccessDateTime.ToString("MMM ddd d HH:mm yyyy"),
                    lastAccessDateTimeUTC.ToString("MMM ddd d HH:mm yyyy"));
      }
    }
}
```

16. Write a program to move the earlier created subdirectory Dir_A_5 to the *Desktop*.

```
using System;
using System.IO;

namespace PracticeYourCSharp
```

```
{
    class Program
    {
        static void Main(string[] args)
        {
            string dir = "Dir_A_5";
            string parentDir = "Dir_A";
            string fullOrigin, fullTarget;
            string separator = Path.DirectorySeparatorChar.ToString(); // Note this.

            fullOrigin = Environment.GetFolderPath(Environment.SpecialFolder.Desktop)
                        + separator + parentDir + separator + dir;
            fullTarget = Environment.GetFolderPath(Environment.SpecialFolder.Desktop)
                        + separator + dir;
            Directory.Move(fullOrigin, fullTarget);
        }
    }
}
```

17. Write a program to rename Dir_A_5 that is on the *Desktop* to the name Dir_E.

```
using System;
using System.IO;

namespace PracticeYourCSharp
{
    class Program
    {
        static void Main(string[] args)
        {
            Environment.CurrentDirectory =
                    Environment.GetFolderPath(Environment.SpecialFolder.Desktop);

            if (Directory.Exists("Dir_E"))
                Console.WriteLine("The directory already exists");
            else
            {
                Directory.Move("Dir_A_5", "Dir_E");
                Console.WriteLine("The directory name has now been changed");
            }
        }
    }
}
```

Chapter 16. File System II: File Handling

As stated in the introduction to the previous chapter, the concept of file handling is a central one to any programming language. By file handling is meant the concept of creating, locating, renaming, deleting, copying/replicating, reading, writing, compressing, decompressing files and such related activities.

This chapter presents exercises which cover these concepts.

The main classes utilized in this chapter are the classes `File`, `FileInfo` and `ZipFile`.

Note: Exercises which cover file reading and writing at a lower and more precise level are covered in Chapters 33 to 35.

M		Using Notepad, create a text file on the *Desktop* and enter any text of your choosing into it. Name the file `sample01` (it will be assigned the actual name `sample01.txt`). Note the time at which you created it.
1.		Write a program to ascertain whether a file named `sample01.txt` exists on the *Desktop*. If it does exist, ascertain whether it is a read-only file or not.
	<td colspan=2>

```
using System;
using System.IO;

namespace PracticeYourCSharp
{
  class Program
  {
    static void Main(string[] args)
    {
      string fileName = "sample01.txt";
      string fullFileName;

      // First get the full path+filename of the file in question
      fullFileName = Environment.GetFolderPath(Environment.SpecialFolder.Desktop) +
                     Path.DirectorySeparatorChar + fileName;

      if (File.Exists(fullFileName) == false)
      {
        Console.WriteLine("File {0} does not exist on the Desktop. Exiting...\n", fileName);
        Console.ReadKey();
        return;
      }
      Console.WriteLine("File {0} exists on the Desktop", fileName);

      FileInfo fi01 = new FileInfo(fullFileName);
      if (fi01.IsReadOnly)
        Console.WriteLine(" It {0} is read-only", fileName);
      else
        Console.WriteLine(" It {0} is NOT read-only", fileName);

      Console.ReadKey();
    }
  }
}
```

</td> |
| | | **Note:** To further test this code, you can set the permissions on the file *sample01.txt* to *read-only* via the Windows interface and re-run the code. |
| 2. | | Determine and print out the extension of the file `sample01.txt`. |
| | <td colspan=2>

```
using System;
using System.IO;

namespace PracticeYourCSharp
{
  class Program
```

</td> |

```
        {
            static void Main(string[] args)
            {
                string fileName = "sample01.txt";
                string fullFileName;

                fullFileName = Environment.GetFolderPath(Environment.SpecialFolder.Desktop) +
                                Path.DirectorySeparatorChar + fileName;
                Console.WriteLine(fullFileName);

                if (File.Exists(fullFileName) == false)
                {
                    Console.WriteLine("The file does not exist. Exiting...\n");
                    Console.ReadKey();
                    return;
                }

                FileInfo fi01 = new FileInfo(fullFileName);
                Console.WriteLine("The extension of the file is: {0}", fi01.Extension);
                Console.ReadKey();
            }
        }
    }
```

3. Determine and print out the time that the file **sample01.txt** was created.

```
using System;
using System.IO;

namespace PracticeYourCSharp
{
    class Program
    {
        static void Main(string[] args)
        {
            string fileName = "sample01.txt";
            string fullFileName;
            DateTime creationDateTime;

            fullFileName = Environment.GetFolderPath(Environment.SpecialFolder.Desktop) +
                            Path.DirectorySeparatorChar + fileName;

            creationDateTime = File.GetCreationTime(fullFileName);

            Console.WriteLine("The file {0} was created on {1:ddd MMM dd HH:mm yyyy}", fileName,
                                creationDateTime);
            Console.ReadKey();
        }
    }
}
```

4. Determine and print out the last time that the file **sample01.txt** was accessed.

```
using System;
using System.IO;

namespace PracticeYourCSharp
{
    class Program
    {
        static void Main(string[] args)
        {
            string fileName = "sample01.txt";
            string fullFileName;
            DateTime accessDateTime;

            fullFileName = Environment.GetFolderPath(Environment.SpecialFolder.Desktop) +
                            Path.DirectorySeparatorChar + fileName;

            accessDateTime = File.GetLastAccessTime(fullFileName);
```

	`            Console.WriteLine("The file {0} was last accessed on {1:ddd MMM dd HH:mm yyyy}",`
	`                                                      fileName, accessDateTime);`
	`            Console.ReadKey();`
	`        }`
	`    }`
	`}`
	
	Note: The method `File.GetLastAccessTime` sometimes returns an inaccurate time.

5.	Set the creation time of the file `sample01.txt` to 1st January 2000.
|   | ```
using System;
using System.IO;

namespace PracticeYourCSharp
{
    class Program
    {
        static void Main(string[] args)
        {
            string fileName = "sample01.txt";
            string fullFileName;

            fullFileName = Environment.GetFolderPath(Environment.SpecialFolder.Desktop) +
                           Path.DirectorySeparatorChar + fileName;
            FileInfo fi01 = new FileInfo(fullFileName);
            DateTime newCreationDateTime = new DateTime(2000, 1, 1, 0, 0, 0);
            fi01.CreationTime = newCreationDateTime;
            Console.ReadKey();
        }
    }
}
```<br><br>**Note:** To confirm the modification of the creation time, check the properties of the file using Windows Explorer. |
| 6. | Print out the full name (path and file name) of `sample01.txt`. |
|   | ```
using System;
using System.IO;

namespace PracticeYourCSharp
{
    class Program
    {
        static void Main(string[] args)
        {
            string fileName = "sample01.txt";
            string fullFileName;

            fullFileName = Environment.GetFolderPath(Environment.SpecialFolder.Desktop) +
                           Path.DirectorySeparatorChar + fileName;
            Console.WriteLine("The full file name is {0}", fullFileName);
            Console.ReadKey();
        }
    }
}
``` |
| 7. | Determine and print out the size of the file `sample01.txt`. |
|   | ```
using System;
using System.IO;

namespace PracticeYourCSharp
{
    class Program
    {
        static void Main(string[] args)
        {
            string fileName = "sample01.txt";
            string fullFileName;
``` |
```

```
            fullFileName = Environment.GetFolderPath(Environment.SpecialFolder.Desktop) +
                           Path.DirectorySeparatorChar + fileName;
            FileInfo fi01 = new FileInfo(fullFileName);

            double fileSize = fi01.Length;
            Console.WriteLine("The size of {0} = {1} bytes", fullFileName, fileSize);
            Console.ReadKey();
        }
    }
}
```

8.	Write a program which copies the text file sample01.txt to a new file on the *Desktop* named sample02.txt, ensuring that the target file does not already exist before attempting to copy it. If it already exists, then exit the program. Hint: *File.Exist*, *File.Copy*

```
using System;
using System.IO;

namespace PracticeYourCSharp
{
    class Program
    {
        static void Main(string[] args)
        {
            string fileName01 = "sample01.txt";
            string fileName02 = "sample02.txt";

            string sTarget, sNewTarget;

            sTarget = Environment.GetFolderPath(Environment.SpecialFolder.Desktop) +
                               Path.DirectorySeparatorChar + fileName01;
            sNewTarget = Environment.GetFolderPath(Environment.SpecialFolder.Desktop) +
                               Path.DirectorySeparatorChar + fileName02;

            if (File.Exists(sNewTarget))
            {
                Console.WriteLine("{0} already exists...quitting", fileName02);
                Console.ReadKey();
                return;
            }
            File.Copy(sTarget, sNewTarget);
            Console.WriteLine("file copied");
            Console.ReadKey();
        }
    }
}
```

9.	Append the following text to the contents of the already existing file sample01.txt; *"Mary did have a little lamb!"*. Put it on a new line in the file.

```
using System;
using System.IO;

namespace PracticeYourCSharp
{
    class Program
    {
        static void Main(string[] args)
        {
            string fileName = "sample01.txt";
            string sAddition = "\r\nMary did have a little lamb!";
            string sTarget;

            sTarget = Environment.GetFolderPath(Environment.SpecialFolder.Desktop) +
                               Path.DirectorySeparatorChar + fileName;

            if (File.Exists(sTarget) == false)
            {
```

|     | ```
                  Console.WriteLine("The target file {0} does not exist on the desktop...exiting", fileName);
                  return;
                }
                File.AppendAllText(sTarget, sAddition);
                Console.WriteLine("Appending done. Have a look at the file");
                Console.ReadKey();
            }
        }
    }
``` |
| | **Note:** Open the file `sample01.txt` and confirm that the extra text has indeed been appended to the file. |
| 10. | *Force* the copying of `sample01.txt` to the already existent file `sample02.txt` |
|     | ```
using System;
using System.IO;

namespace PracticeYourCSharp
{
    class Program
    {
        static void Main(string[] args)
        {
            string fileName01 = "sample01.txt";
            string fileName02 = "sample02.txt";

            string sTarget, sNewTarget;

            sTarget = Environment.GetFolderPath(Environment.SpecialFolder.Desktop) +
                                    Path.DirectorySeparatorChar + fileName01;
            sNewTarget = Environment.GetFolderPath(Environment.SpecialFolder.Desktop) +
                                    Path.DirectorySeparatorChar + fileName02;

            File.Copy(sTarget, sNewTarget, true); // Force the copy by the parameter "true"
            Console.WriteLine("file copied");
            Console.ReadKey();
        }
    }
}
``` |
| M | Manually create a directory `X_1` on the *Desktop*. |
| 11. | Write a program which will move the file `sample01.txt` into the newly created directory `X_1`. |
|     | ```
using System;
using System.IO;

namespace PracticeYourCSharp
{
    class Program
    {
        static void Main(string[] args)
        {
            string fileName01 = "sample01.txt";

            string sSource, sTarget;
            string sTargetDirectory = "X_1";
            sSource = Environment.GetFolderPath(Environment.SpecialFolder.Desktop) +
                                    Path.DirectorySeparatorChar + fileName01;
            sTarget = Environment.GetFolderPath(Environment.SpecialFolder.Desktop) +
                                    Path.DirectorySeparatorChar + sTargetDirectory +
                                    Path.DirectorySeparatorChar + fileName01;

            File.Move(sSource, sTarget);
            Console.WriteLine("file moved");
            Console.ReadKey();
        }
    }
}
``` |
```

12.	Write a program with which to delete the file **sample02.txt** that is on the *Desktop*.
| | ```
using System;
using System.IO;

namespace PracticeYourCSharp
{
  class Program
  {
    static void Main(string[] args)
    {
      string fileName01 = "sample02.txt";
      string sTarget;

      sTarget = Environment.GetFolderPath(Environment.SpecialFolder.Desktop) +
                            Path.DirectorySeparatorChar + fileName01;
      File.Delete(sTarget);
      Console.WriteLine("file {0} has been celeted", sTarget);
      Console.ReadKey();
    }
  }
}
``` |
| *M* | Manually create a directory named **ToZip** on the *Desktop* and put a few files of your choosing into it. |
| 13. | Write a program to <u>compress</u> the directory in question into a .zip file named **zip01.zip**
Note: you might have to ensure that the assembly reference System.IO.Compression.FileSystem is included in your assembly references list *(accessed through View→Solution Explorer→References)* |
| | ```
using System;
using System.IO;
using System.IO.Compression;

namespace PracticeYourCSharp
{
  class Program
  {
    static void Main(string[] args)
    {
      string dirName = "ToZip";
      string zipName = "zip01.zip";

      string fullDirPath = Environment.GetFolderPath(Environment.SpecialFolder.Desktop) +
                                      Path.DirectorySeparatorChar + dirName;
      string fullZipPath = Environment.GetFolderPath(Environment.SpecialFolder.Desktop) +
                                      Path.DirectorySeparatorChar + zipName;
      ZipFile.CreateFromDirectory(fullDirPath, fullZipPath);
      Console.WriteLine("Zip done");
      Console.ReadKey();
    }
  }
}
``` |
| 14. | Write a program to uncompress the previously created zip file **zip01.zip** and put the unzipped content into a directory on the *Desktop* called **Unzipped**. |
| | ```
using System;
using System.IO;
using System.IO.Compression;

namespace PracticeYourCSharp
{
  class Program
  {
    static void Main(string[] args)
    {
      string dirName = "Unzipped";
      string zipName = "zip01.zip";
``` |
```

|   | ```
            string fullTargetPath = Environment.GetFolderPath(Environment.SpecialFolder.Desktop) +
                                    Path.DirectorySeparatorChar + dirName;
            string fullZipPath = Environment.GetFolderPath(Environment.SpecialFolder.Desktop) +
                                    Path.DirectorySeparatorChar + zipName;
            ZipFile.ExtractToDirectory(fullZipPath, fullTargetPath);
            Console.WriteLine("The archive is unzipped");
            Console.ReadKey();
        }
      }
    }
``` |
| **M** | Manually move the file sample01.txt from directory X_1 back to the *Desktop*. |
| 15. | Read the contents of the file sample01.txt and print them out.
If the file is empty state this fact.
Hint: `File.ReadAllLines` |
|   | ```
using System;
using System.IO;

namespace PracticeYourCSharp
{
  class Program
  {
    static void Main(string[] args)
    {
      string fileName = "sample01.txt";

      string sTarget;
      sTarget = Environment.GetFolderPath(Environment.SpecialFolder.Desktop)+
                          Path.DirectorySeparatorChar+fileName;
      // Check for file existence. Always do this.
      if (File.Exists(sTarget) == false)
      {
        Console.WriteLine("The target file does exist on the desktop...exiting");
        Console.ReadKey();
        return;
      }
      string[] contents = File.ReadAllLines(sTarget);
       // the above line reads the file contents into a string array.
      if(contents.Length > 0)
      {
        Console.WriteLine("Here are the file contents:");
        foreach(string s in contents)
          Console.WriteLine(s);
      }
      else
        Console.WriteLine("The file {0} is empty!",fileName);

      Console.ReadKey();
    }
  }
}
``` |
| 16. | In a single operation, create a file on the *Desktop* named sample03.txt and write the line *"Did Mary have a little lamb or not?"* to it. |
|   | ```
using System;
using System.IO;

namespace PracticeYourCSharp
{
  class Program
  {
    static void Main(string[] args)
    {
      string fileName = "sample03.txt";
``` |
```

```
            string newData = "Did Mary have a little lamb or not?";
            string sTarget;
            sTarget = Environment.GetFolderPath(Environment.SpecialFolder.Desktop) +
                                    Path.DirectorySeparatorChar + fileName;
            File.WriteAllText(sTarget, newData);
      }
    }
}
```

Note: You should check for the prior existence of the file so that you don't attempt to recreate an already existing file. Attempting to recreate an already existing file using the method `File.WriteAllText` will result in an *exception*. We deal with exceptions in a later chapter.

17.	Put the whole first verse of the nursery rhyme *"Mary had a little lamb…"* into a `string` array line by line. Then in a single operation create a new text file `sample04.txt` on the *Desktop* and write the string array to the file.
| | ```
using System;
using System.IO;

namespace PracticeYourCSharp
{
  class Program
    {
      static void Main(string[] args)
        {
          string fileName = "sample04.txt";
          string[] fileData = new String[5];
          string sTarget;

          fileData[0] = "Mary had a little lamb";
          fileData[1] = "little lamb";
          fileData[2] = "little lamb";
          fileData[3] = "Mary had a little lamb";
          fileData[4] = "That was as white as snow";

          sTarget = Environment.GetFolderPath(Environment.SpecialFolder.Desktop)+
                                    Path.DirectorySeparatorChar+fileName;
          File.WriteAllLines(sTarget, fileData);
          Console.ReadKey();
        }
    }
}
``` |
E1	Write a program which prints out, recursively, the directories in your computer in the indented format shown below.
	  `<parent>`
	    `<child dir>`
	      `<grand child dir>`
	        `<etc.>`

E2	Write a program which determines the largest file on your computer.
E3	Write a program which creates 50 empty files in a directory of your choice with the naming scheme `JPG0001` to `JPG0050`.
E4	I downloaded some pictures from a camera into a given directory on the *Desktop*. The camera named the files `JPGP0001…JPGP0050`. I then deleted one of the files, thus creating a hole in my numbering scheme. Write a program which shifts the names of the files after the one I deleted up by one, so that there is no longer a hole in the numbering scheme (Thus we will now have files `JPG0001` to `JPG0049`).
```

Chapter 17. Random Numbers

The ability to produce random numbers is an important feature in such scenarios as the generation of random data for statistical purposes, for adding randomness to computer games and particularly for cryptographic applications. This chapter presents exercises that ensure your basic ability to use random number generation in C#.

The key class on which exercises are presented in this chapter is the class **Random**.

1.	*Initialization of the random number generator*
	 What is the difference between the following two initialization methods for the random number generator?
	   1. Using a user supplied seed value
	   2. Using the built-in time-based seed for the generator

	In the first case, you the user supply the seed value. However if you use the same seed value again the random number generator will simply generate the same random value. In the second case, you are entrusting randomness to the built-in seed generator, which indeed uses the time-honored method of using the system clock as one of the inputs in generating the seed.
2.	Using the built-in time-based seed for the random number generator, seed the generator and print out the first 10 numbers returned by the generator.
	`` using System;

namespace PracticeYourCSharp
{
  class Program
  {
    static void Main(string[] args)
    {
      Random random01 = new Random();
      for (int count = 0; count < 10; count++)
      {
        int value = random01.Next(); // This is how to get the next random number
        Console.WriteLine("The next random number is {0}", value);
      }
      Console.ReadKey();
    }
  }
}
``` |
| 3. | Using an integer of your choosing, seed the random number generator with it and then print out the first 10 random numbers returned by the random generator. Take record of the numbers. |
| | ``` using System;

namespace PracticeYourCSharp
{
  class Program
  {
    static void Main(string[] args)
    {
      int seed = 250;

      Random random01 = new Random(seed);

      for (int count = 0; count < 10; count++)
      {
        int value = random01.Next(); // This is how to get the next random number
        Console.WriteLine("The next random number is {0}", value);
      }
      Console.ReadKey();
    }
``` |

157

		`    }` `}`
4.		Run the preceding exercise again with the same seed and compare the output with what was output in the earlier exercise.
		Result: The output is the same, since the seed is the same.
5.		Simulate the throwing of a pair of dice by seeding the generator and then requesting two integer values (request each value one after the other) between 1 and 6 from the random number generator. Print out the returned values.
| | | ```csharp
using System;

namespace PracticeYourCSharp
{
  class Program
  {
    static void Main(string[] args)
    {
      Random random01 = new Random();

      int die01 = random01.Next(1, 6); // min & max values given for the output range
      int die02 = random01.Next(1, 6);

      Console.WriteLine("The value of the 1st die is {0}", die01);
      Console.WriteLine("The value of the 2nd die is {0}", die02);

      Console.ReadKey();
    }
  }
}
``` |
| E1 | | Study the random number generation class `RNGCryptoServiceProvider` which is a more suitable generator for cryptography purposes. |
```

Chapter 18. Nullable Types

We have dealt with number types. However, C# has variants of these named <u>nullable types</u>. This chapter presents exercises which ensure your grasp of this important topic as well as the related null-coalescing operator. After this, exercises on the new C# 6.0 operator, the "null propagating operator" are presented.

1.	What is the result when you try to compile the following program and what is the reason for the given response?
	
	```using System;```
	
	```namespace PracticeYourCSharp```
	```{```
	`  class Program`
	`  {`
	`    static void Main(string[] args)`
	`    {`
	`      int int01 = null;`
	`    }`
	`  }`
	`}`
		It will *not* compile.
		The reason is because you cannot assign the value null to a non-nullable built-in value type.

2.	What is the result when you try to compile the following program and what is the reason for the given response?
	
	```using System;```
	
	```namespace PracticeYourCSharp```
	`{`
	`  class Program`
	`  {`
	`    static void Main(string[] args)`
	`    {`
	`      int? int01 = null;`
	`      Console.ReadKey();`
	`    }`
	`  }`
	`}`
		It *will* compile without any problems.
		Reason: C# has the nullable built-in value type, **int?** *(which is a structure)* and these can legitimately be assigned the value null.

3.	Describe the difference between the following types: **int?** and **int**.	
	int is a regular value type. **int?** is a nullable type, meaning that it is an int that can have the value null assigned to it.	
4.	Why are nullable types useful?	
	A nullable type is useful when you want to have a value for a variable that indicates that the variable is "unassigned".	
5.	Write a program which checks if a given nullable integer named int01? has a value assigned to it. If it has a value assigned to it, print the value out to the console. *Hint: method* **HasValue**	

	```using System;```
	
	```namespace PracticeYourCSharp```
	`{`
	`  class Program`
	`  {`
	`    static void Main(string[] args)`
	`    {`
	`      int? int01 = null;`	

	``
        if (int01.HasValue)
          Console.WriteLine("int01 has a value of {0}", int01);
        // See alternate line to this line above at the bottom of the page
        else
          Console.WriteLine("int01 is currently unassigned");

        Console.ReadKey();
      }
    }
}
```
**Alternate Line**
`Console.WriteLine("int01 has a value of {0}", int01.Value);` |
| 6. | Given the following initialization:<br><br>`int? int01 = null;`<br><br>State what the result is when you try to print out the value of `int01` using each of the following lines of code:<br>• `Console.WriteLine(int01);`<br>• `Console.WriteLine(int01.Value);` |
| | In the 1$^{st}$ case, the program not having anything to print out will not print anything out.<br>In the 2$^{nd}$ case, the program will throw an exception.<br><br>This is an important distinction to note in the handling of the output of nullable types. It is advised that before you use the `Value` field of a nullable type variable you should validate whether or not it has been assigned a value by using its `HasValue` method. |
| 7. | Assign the value of a nullable integer `int01nullable` to a regular integer `int01regular`. |
| | ```
using System;

namespace PracticeYourCSharp
{
  class Program
  {
    static void Main(string[] args)
    {
      int? int01nullable = null;
      int int01regular;

      if (int01nullable.HasValue)
        int01regular = (int)int01nullable; // The cast is mandatory using this logic.
      // an alternate line to the above is: int01regular = int01nullable.Value;

      Console.ReadKey();
    }
  }
}
``` |
| 8. | Assign the value of a regular integer `int01` to a nullable integer `int01nullable`. |
| | ```
using System;

namespace PracticeYourCSharp
{
  class Program
  {
    static void Main(string[] args)
    {
      int? int01nullable = null;
      int int01 = 5;

      int01nullable = int01;
      //Two things to note:
      //  1. No casting is required.
      //  2. An alternate line to the above is: int01nullable = (int?)int01;
``` |
```

| | | ``` 
      Console.ReadKey();
    }
  }
}
``` |
| 9. | Create an array which can support 7 integers and fill it with the following values at the noted indexes:<br><br>    [0] = 27<br>    [2] = 33<br>    [4] = 55<br>    [6] = 11<br><br>Print the whole array out using a for loop. Observe and comment on the values printed out. | ```
using System;
namespace PracticeYourCSharp
{
  class Program
  {
    static void Main(string[] args)
    {
      int[] intArray = new int[7];

      intArray[0] = 27; intArray[2] = 33;
      intArray[4] = 55; intArray[6] = 11;

      for (int i = 0; i < intArray.Length; i++)
        Console.WriteLine("intArray[{0}] = {1}", i,intArray[i]);

      Console.ReadKey();
    }
  }
}
```<br>**Output**<br>```
intArray[0] = 27
intArray[1] = 0
intArray[2] = 33
intArray[3] = 0
intArray[4] = 55
intArray[5] = 0
intArray[6] = 11
```<br>**Notes/Comments:** Note that the array entries that were not assigned any values are reported as having a value of 0, which we never assigned them! Clearly the unassigned entries are automatically assigned the default value for their type. Contrast this answer with the solution to the exercise below using a int? array instead of the int array just used. |
| 10. | Create an array that can support 7 *nullable integers* and fill it with the following values in the indicated indexes:<br><br>    [0] = 27<br>    [2] = 33<br>    [4] = 55<br>    [6] = 11<br><br>*(the same array contents as the int[] in the preceding exercise)*<br>Print the whole array out using a for loop and observe and comment on the values therein, comparing and contrasting the values thereof with the output from the exercise above. | ```
using System;
namespace PracticeYourCSharp
{
  class Program
  {
    static void Main(string[] args)
    {
      int?[] intArray = new int?[7];

      intArray[0] = 27; intArray[2] = 33;
      intArray[4] = 55; intArray[6] = 11;

      for (int i = 0; i < intArray.Length; i++)
        Console.WriteLine("intArray[{0}] = {1}", i, intArray[i]);
      Console.ReadKey();
    }
  }
}
```<br>**Output**<br>```
intArray[0] = 27
intArray[1] =
intArray[2] = 33
intArray[3] =
intArray[4] = 55
intArray[5] =
``` |
```

		intArray[6] = 11 **Notes/Comments:** We see here for an array of nullable integers that no value (or specifically the value *null*) is assigned to the values that we ourselves did not initialize.
11.	Write a line of code showing the initialization of a `List<T>` variable named `intList01` of nullable integers.	`List<int?> intList01 = new List<int?>();`

Null Coalescing Operator

12.	What does the null coalescing operator (`??`) mean/do?	
	It provides a means to safely assign a value from a nullable type (or a reference type) to a non-nullable variable. If the value of the nullable type (or reference type) variable in question is null, then a given default value, specified with the null coalescing operator, is assigned to the variable in question. For example if we have an `int x` and an `int? y` and we want to assign the value of y to x, we know that if y has a value of *null* (as a nullable type can have), then the value of y cannot be assigned to x. The null coalescing operator allows us to specify a default value to assign to x in case y is *null*.	
| 13. | I have a sparsely populated `int?` array of length 7 populated as follows:<br><br>    [0] = 27<br>    [2] = 33<br>    [4] = 55<br>    [6] = 11<br><br>I want to copy these to an array of integers, however, for the null entries in the nullable integer array, I want to set the corresponding position in the integer list to a value of -1. Implement this default assignment using the null coalescing operator.<br><br>Print out the values of the resulting integer array. | ```csharp
using System;

namespace PracticeYourCSharp
{
  class Program
  {
    static void Main(string[] args)
    {
      int?[] intArrayA = new int?[7];
      int[] intArrayB = new int[7];

      intArrayA[0] = 27; intArrayA[2] = 33;
      intArrayA[4] = 55; intArrayA[6] = 11;

      for (int i = 0; i < intArrayA.Length; i++)
      {
        intArrayB[i] = intArrayA[i] ?? -1;
        Console.WriteLine("intArrayB[{0}]= {1}",i,intArrayB[i]);
      }
      Console.ReadKey();
    }
  }
}
```<br><br>**Output**<br>`intArray[0] = 27`<br>`intArray[1] = -1`<br>`intArray[2] = 33`<br>`intArray[3] = -1`<br>`intArray[4] = 55`<br>`intArray[5] = -1`<br>`intArray[6] = 11` |

(6.0) Null Propagating Operator

14.	What is the function of the null propagating operator?
	The null-propagating operator exists to allow for the programmer to attempt to assign a value from a potentially null object reference to another, yielding a value of null if the object reference is indeed null, rather than generating an exception condition.

15.	What is the result of running the following program?
	
	`using System;`
	
	`class Program`
	`{`

```

```
    static void Main(string[] args)
    {
      string s1 = null;
      string s2 = s1.Substring(5, 3);
      Console.WriteLine(s2);

      Console.ReadKey();
    }
}
```

The program stops running, due to the exception System.NullReferenceException that it caused due to trying to access a field of a null object.

16. Modify the program above to use the null propagating operator on the attempt to obtain a substring of s1. Report the output of the program.

```
using System;

class Program
{
    static void Main(string[] args)
    {
      string s1 = null;
      string s2 = s1?.Substring(5, 3);
      Console.WriteLine(s2);
      Console.ReadKey();
    }
}
```

Output: nothing

The output is as expected, since s1 is null. The benefit of the null propagating operator is that it has helped avoid the exception, and does so without requiring try/catch blocks (to be seen in the chapter on exceptions).

17. What is the result of running the following program?

```
using System;

class Program
{
    static void Main(string[] args)
    {
      string s = null;
      int? int01 = s.Length;
      Console.WriteLine("Length={0}.", int01);
    }
}
```

The program stops running, due to the exception System.NullReferenceException that it caused due to trying to access a field of a null object.

18. Using the null propagating operator, assign the length of the string in the preceding exercise to the int? variable int01. What is the resulting output of the program now?

```
using System;

class Program
{
    static void Main(string[] args)
    {
      string s = null;
      int? int01 = s?.Length;
      Console.WriteLine("Length={0}.", int01);
      Console.ReadKey();
    }
}
```

Output: Length=.

This shows that the int? has been assigned a value of null by the null propagating operator.

19. What is the output of this program? Explain why it is so.

```
using System;
class Program
{
  static void Main(string[] args)
  {
    string s = null;
    int int02 = s?.Length ?? 0;
    Console.WriteLine("Length={0}.", int02);
    Console.ReadKey();
  }
}
```

Output: Length=0.

In assigning a value to `int02`, we have used the null propagating operator and the null-coalescing operator together, with the result in this case being that the value 0 is assigned to the int `int02`.

Chapter 19. The StringBuilder Class

This chapter presents exercises pertaining to the `StringBuilder` class, which is the mutable counterpart of the `String` class. Also exercises comparing the `String` class to the `StringBuilder` class are presented.

The key class presented in this chapter is the class `StringBuilder`.

1.	Describe the `StringBuilder` class and how it relates to and differs from the `String` class.
	The `StringBuilder` class is a class that supports the same content as the `String` class, however objects of class `StringBuilder` are mutable, as opposed to the `String` class whose objects are immutable (the immutability of string objects has been discussed in *Chapter 5. Strings: Basic Handling*. Due to this mutability, the `StringBuilder` class manipulates string data faster than the `String` class.
2.	*String to StringBuilder* Convert the following string object to a `StringBuilder` object and print the contents of the resulting `StringBuilder` out to the console. `string s01 = "Mary had a little lamb";`

	``‍
	using System;
	using System.Text; //StringBuilder is in here
	
	namespace PracticeYourCSharp
	{
	  class Program
	    {
	      static void Main(string[] args)
	        {
	          string s01 = "Mary had a little lamb";
	          StringBuilder sb01 = new StringBuilder();
	          sb01 = sb01.Append(s01);
	          Console.WriteLine(sb01);
	          Console.ReadKey();
	        }
	    }
	}
	``
	 Notes: Or you can use another one of the `StringBuilder` constructors which takes a string directly as a parameter as follows:
	 `StringBuilder sb01 = new StringBuilder(s01);`

3.	Write a program which appends the line *"That was as white as snow"*, preceded and followed by a newline to the `StringBuilder` instance in the preceding exercise.

	``‍
	using System;
	using System.Text;
	
	namespace PracticeYourCSharp
	  {
	    class Program
	    {
	      static void Main(string[] args)
	        {
	          string s01 = "Mary had a little lamb";
	          StringBuilder sb01 = new StringBuilder();
	          sb01.AppendLine(s01);
	          sb01.AppendLine("\nThat was as white as snow\n");
	          Console.WriteLine(sb01);
	
	          Console.ReadKey();
	        }
	    }
	``

	`}`
4.	*StringBuilder to String* Convert the following `StringBuilder` object to a `string` and then print the string out: `StringBuilder sb01 = new StringBuilder("Doe a deer, a female deer");`
| | ```
using System;
using System.Text;

namespace PracticeYourCSharp
{
  class Program
  {
    static void Main(string[] args)
    {
      StringBuilder sb01 = new StringBuilder("Doe a deer, a female deer");
      string s01 = sb01.ToString();
      Console.WriteLine(s01);
      Console.ReadKey();
    }
  }
}
``` |
| 5. | I have a `StringBuilder` object, which contains the value *"ACD"*. Insert the letter B after the A.
Print the modified `StringBuilder` out. |
| | ```
using System;
using System.Text;

namespace PracticeYourCSharp
{
  class Program
  {
    static void Main(string[] args)
    {
      StringBuilder sb01 = new StringBuilder("ACD");
      sb01.Insert(1, 'B');
      Console.WriteLine(sb01);

      Console.ReadKey();
    }
  }
}
``` |
| 6. | I have a `StringBuilder` object `sb01`, which contains the phrase *"Mary a little lamb"*. Insert the string *" had"* after the word *"Mary"* in `sb01` and then print `sb01` out to the console. |
| | ```
using System;
using System.Text;

namespace PracticeYourCSharp
{
  class Program
  {
    static void Main(string[] args)
    {
      StringBuilder sb01 = new StringBuilder("Mary a little lamb");
      sb01.Insert(4, " had");
      Console.WriteLine(sb01);

      Console.ReadKey();
    }
  }
}
``` |
| 7. | Given a `StringBuilder` object `sb01` with the value *"Mary had a little lamb"*, empty `sb01` of its contents. |
| | ```
using System;
using System.Text;
``` |

```
namespace PracticeYourCSharp
{
  class Program
  {
    static void Main(string[] args)
    {
      StringBuilder sb01 = new StringBuilder("Mary had little lamb");
      sb01.Clear();
      Console.WriteLine(sb01);

      Console.ReadKey();
    }
  }
}
```

8.	Given a `StringBuilder` object `sb01` with the value "*Mary had a little lamb*". Remove the substring " *had*" from it.

```
using System;
using System.Text;

namespace PracticeYourCSharp
{
  class Program
  {
    static void Main(string[] args)
    {
      StringBuilder sb01 = new StringBuilder("Mary had a little lamb");
      sb01.Remove(4, 4); // Starting at position 5
      Console.WriteLine(sb01);

      Console.ReadKey();
    }
  }
}
```

9.	Rewrite the solution to the preceding code in a generic manner.

Solution: The `StringBuilder` class does not have the equivalent of a `<String>.IndexOf` method. So in order to determine the index of the sought for string in the target string, we have to convert the `StringBuilder` to a string first in order to use the `IndexOf` method of class `String`.

```
using System;
using System.Text;

namespace PracticeYourCSharp
{
  class Program
  {
    static void Main(string[] args)
    {
      StringBuilder sb01 = new StringBuilder("Mary had a little lamb");
      String substring = " had";
      int substringIndex = sb01.ToString().IndexOf(substring);
      if (substringIndex >= 0)
        sb01.Remove(4, substring.Length);
      Console.WriteLine(sb01);

      Console.ReadKey();
    }
  }
}
```

10.	*StringBuilder to Char array*
	Given a `StringBuilder` object `sb01` with the value "*Mary had a little lamb*", copy the first 4 letters in it to the first 4 elements of a `char[]` named `c1`. Print `c1` out.

```
using System;
using System.Text;
```

```
namespace PracticeYourCSharp
{
  class Program
  {
    static void Main(string[] args)
    {
      StringBuilder sb01 = new StringBuilder("Mary had a little lamb");
      char[] c1 = new char[4];
      sb01.CopyTo(0,c1, 0, 4);
      Console.WriteLine(c1);
      Console.ReadKey();
    }
  }
}
```

11. *String vs StringBuilder performance*

    We want to assess the performance of String vs StringBuilder.

    To this end, write a program which does the following:

    1. Creates an object sbTest of class StringBuilder. Using a for loop, the program appends the string *"A"* to it 25,000 times.
    2. Using DateTime objects, measure how long it takes for the code to run and prints this time out to the console.
    3. Creates a string sTest and appends the string *"A"* to it 25,000 times using a for loop.
    4. Measures the running time as with the StringBuilder code and prints out the time out to the console.

    Note the difference in times.

    Next: increase the loop counter to 100,000 and note the difference in time again.

```
using System;
using System.Text;

namespace PracticeYourCSharp
{
  class Program
  {
    static void Main(string[] args)
    {
      // Testing StringBuilder concatenation time
      Console.WriteLine("\nStart: Testing Stringbuilder concatenation time");
      StringBuilder sbTest = new StringBuilder("A");
      DateTime dt01 = DateTime.Now;

      for (int i = 0; i < 50000; i++)
        sbTest.Append("A");

      DateTime dt02 = DateTime.Now;
      Console.WriteLine("End : Testing Stringbuilder concatenation time");
      Console.WriteLine("Time taken = {0}", (dt02 - dt01));
      Console.WriteLine("stringbuilder length = {0}", sbTest.Length);
          // to check what was done.
      Console.WriteLine("Press any key to test string concatenation time");
      Console.ReadKey();

      // Testing string concatenation time
      Console.WriteLine("\nStart: Testing String concatenation time");
      string sTest = "A";
      DateTime dt03 = DateTime.Now;
      for (int i = 0; i < 50000; i++)
        sTest += "A";

      DateTime dt04 = DateTime.Now;
      Console.WriteLine("End : Testing string concatenation time");
      Console.WriteLine("Time taken = {0}", (dt04 - dt03));
```

|   | ```
          Console.WriteLine("string length = {0}", sTest.Length);   // To check what was done.
          Console.ReadKey();
        }
      }
    }
```  |
| | **Notes:** It can be seen clearly that the `StringBuilder` concatenates far faster than the `string`. In scenarios where a limited amount of string manipulation is done, a `string` is an acceptable variable choice.
(One thing though; if the object reference of the object in which you are storing the string data is of importance to you and you want it constant throughout the program, then use a `StringBuilder` object). |
| 12. | Rewrite the `StringBuilder`/`String` performance test program of the preceding exercise, this time however, use a `Stopwatch` object to measure the elapsed time instead of using `DateTime` objects. |
|   | ```
using System;
using System.Text;
using System.Diagnostics; // The class Stopwatch is in here.

namespace PracticeYourCSharp
{
  class Program
  {
    static void Main(string[] args)
    {
      Stopwatch swatch01 = new Stopwatch();

      // Testing StringBuilder concatenation time
      Console.WriteLine("\nStart: Testing Stringbuilder concatenation time");
      StringBuilder sbTest = new StringBuilder("A");

      swatch01.Reset();
      swatch01.Start();
      for (int i = 0; i < 50000; i++)
        sbTest.Append("A");

      swatch01.Stop();
      Console.WriteLine("End : Testing Stringbuilder concatenation time");
      Console.WriteLine("Time taken = {0}", swatch01.Elapsed);
      Console.WriteLine("stringbuilder length = {0}", sbTest.Length);
         // To check what was done.
      Console.WriteLine("Press any key to test string concatenation time");
      Console.ReadKey();

      // Testing string concatenation time
      Console.WriteLine("\nStart: Testing string concatenation time");
      string sTest = "A";
      swatch01.Reset(); // We are going to reuse this stopwatch, so reset it.
      swatch01.Start();
      for (int i = 0; i < 50000; i++)
        sTest += "A";

      swatch01.Stop();
      Console.WriteLine("End : Testing string concatenation time");
      Console.WriteLine("Time taken = {0}", swatch01.Elapsed);
      Console.WriteLine("string length = {0}", sTest.Length);   // To check what was done.
      Console.ReadKey();
    }
  }
}
``` |

Chapter 20. The var type: implicitly typed variables

This chapter helps to ensure your grasp of the var type, which is very useful when there is uncertainty concerning which variable type to use.

1.	What does it mean when a variable is declared to be of type var?	
	When a variable is defined as type var, it means that the compiler should figure out the actual type of the variable <u>from whatever is assigned to it</u>. In short, the variable type is inferred by the compiler from what is assigned to it.	
	For example, if I write:	
	`var x=12;`	
	The compiler will figure out that x is an int and treat it as an int **and compile it as an int**.	

2.	What is the output of the following code snippet?
	`var x=10;`
	`var y=55;`
	`var z=x+y;`
	`Console.WriteLine(z);`
		The output is: 65
		(See explanation of var above).

3.	What is the output of the following code snippet?
	`var x = "Hello ";`
	`var y = 10;`
	`var z = x + y;`
	`Console.WriteLine(z);`
		The output is: `Hello 10`
		The compiler has acted in the following manner:
		`string x="Hello";`
		`int y=10;`
		`string z="Hello " + 10.ToString();`
| 4. | I have a List<int> with the following contents: 1, 27 and 89. Using a var variable in a foreach loop, print each of these items out. | ```
using System;
using System.Collections.Generic;
namespace PracticeYourCSharp
{
  class Program
  {
    static void Main(string[] args)
    {
      List<int> list01 = new List<int>();
      list01.Add(1); list01.Add(27); list01.Add(89);
      foreach (var x in list01)
        Console.WriteLine(x);

      Console.ReadKey();
    }
  }
}
``` |
```

Chapter 21. Methods (Introduction)

So far in this book all of the code written has been within the method `Main()`, although we have been calling built-in methods all along. In this chapter, exercises which require the reader to create methods are presented. The exercises in this chapter cover a number of different concepts that pertain to methods; these concepts include the definition of methods, `ref` and `out` parameters, parameter arrays, named arguments and optional arguments/default values.

Up to this point we have been doing our programming within the confines of the default class `Program` presented by the .NET framework when you first create a console application. The methods that we are going to create in this chapter will still be within this provided class *(see below)*.

```
using System;
namespace PracticeYourCSharp
{
  class Program
  {
    < our methods here >

    static void Main(string[] args)
    {
      ...
    }
  }
}
```

Also, all the methods we create in this chapter will be `static` methods just as `Main` is, that is, methods that are not tied to a particular object but rather to the class (non-static methods will be dealt with later when we deal directly with classes).

Note: Due to the interrelationship between methods and classes, the concept of methods is further enhanced and refined in Chapter 24 which covers Classes.

1.	In C#, what is meant by the term *"method signature"*?
	Method signature in C# means the following: the method name and the types of its input parameters in order. For example, for a `public` method named `addIntegers` which adds two integers passed to it and returns a type of `long`, the method signature is: `addIntegers(int, int);` **Note**: When dealing with delegates, the return type is considered to be part of the signature.
2.	What is meant by the term *"method declaration"*?
	Method declaration means the following: the method name, its access scope (whether `public`, `private`, etc.) the input types and parameter names in the order in which they are sent to the method and the output type of the method. For example, for a `public` method named `addIntegers` which adds two integers `x` and `y` passed to it and returns a type of `long`, the method declaration is: `public long addIntegers(int x, int y);`
3.	What kind of types can be returned by a method?
	Any type can be returned by a method, whether a user defined type or a built-in type.
4.	What is meant by the term *method overloading*?
	This means that for a given method name, there can be different versions of it with different input types and it is up to the C# compiler to call the correct one (the compiler determines which one to invoke by looking at the

types of the parameters that you pass to it).
For example, if I have the following methods which have the same name but different input parameters:

```
addIntegers(int, int );
addIntegers(int, int , int );
```

then if another method invokes **addIntegers** passing three integer values to it, the compiler knows that I mean to call the 2nd version of **addIntegers** indicated above; if I invoke **addIntegers** passing only two integers to it, the compiler knows to invoke the 1st version of **addIntegers** shown above.

Note however, that a method cannot be overloaded only with respect to the return type, for example the following pair cannot jointly appear in the same class:

```
long    addIntegers(int , int);
decimal addIntegers(int , int);
```

The compiler would not know which of the two methods to call since both have the same input parameters.

5. Create a static method named **helloMethod** which does not return anything and does not take any parameters. All it should do is print out the statement *"Hello, how are you?"* and then return to its caller.
Call this method from **Main()**.

```
using System;

namespace PracticeYourCSharp
{
  class Program
  {
    static void helloMethod()
    {
      Console.WriteLine("Hello, how are you?");
    }

    static void Main(string[] args)
    {
      helloMethod(); // OR invoke it as Program.helloMethod();
      Console.ReadKey();
    }
  }
}
```

Note: we called the method **helloMethod()** directly from **Main()**, without prepending it with the name of its class, **Program**. This works because the caller (in this case, **Main**) is in the same class as the called static method. If the caller was in a different class then we would have to use the `<className>.<method name>` to call the static method in question (for example **Math.Cos**). Note though that it is valid to call a static method in a given class from other methods in the same class as `<class>.<method name>` as well, rather than just `<method name>`.

6. **(6.0)** Rewrite the solution from the preceding question using the **using static** directive for **System.Console**, and using an expression-bodied method for **helloMethod()**.

```
using System;
using static System.Console;

namespace PracticeYourCSharp
{
  class Program
  {
    static void helloMethod() => WriteLine("Hello, how are you?");

    static void Main(string[] args)
    {
      helloMethod(); // OR invoke it as Program.helloMethod();
      ReadKey();
    }
  }
}
```

7.	What are the different ways in which you can pass variables *to* a method?	You can pass variables to a method in one of the following two ways: 1. By value 2. By reference
8.	What does the term *passing by value* mean?	
		It means merely passing the value of the variable at hand to the called method. For example, if I have a variable x which has a value of 27 and I pass the variable *by value* to a method, it means I simply passed the value 27 to the method. The method that I am passing the value to doesn't know anything about x itself, just the value of what x contains.
9.	What does the term *passing by reference* mean?	
		It means passing the actual variable to the called method. Continuing with the example of x=27 above, if I pass the variable x by reference, it means I actually pass x itself to the called method, rather than just passing the value 27 to the method. The main feature of passing by reference is that when I pass by reference, the called method can modify the value in the variable I passed to it; whereas in calling by value, in a sense I didn't pass any variable to it, I only passed a value, so there really is no variable to modify.
10.	What are the three ways a method can directly return values to its caller?	1. By the return type indicated in the method declaration 2. By using a **ref** parameter, which is a type of passing by reference 3. By using an **out** parameter, which also is a way of passing by reference
11.	What is the difference between a **ref** parameter and the **out** parameter?	**ref** requires that the <u>calling method</u> initialize the variable in question before it is passed. The called method is free to change the **ref** parameter that is passed to it. **out** mandates that the variable be assigned a value by the *called* method before it is sent back.
12.	Why would you prefer to use call by reference over receiving the returned value via the method declaration?	One reason for this preference is that calling by reference ensures that the variable that is passed by reference is directly modified, rather than the called method returning a value that the calling method then has to assign to a variable. Another reason for passing by reference is that only one value can be passed back directly via the return parameter of a method (unless the returned variable is a data structure of some sort, which has to be explicitly defined (either a class, a structure or tuple)), whereas when you pass variables by reference to a method, there is no limit to the number of variables in the method declaration that can be modified by the called method.
| 13. | Write a **static** method named **addIntegers** with a return type of **void** that adds two integers and returns the resulting integer value in a third integer parameter to the calling method via a **ref** parameter.<br><br>To test the method, pass two integer values of choice from Main to addIntegers and have Main print out the result. | ```
using System;

namespace PracticeYourCSharp
{
   class Program
   {
      static void addIntegers(int a, int b, ref int c)
      {
         c = a + b;
      }
      static void Main(string[] args)
      {
         int total = 0; // Because we are passing using ref,
                        // we have to initialize this first
         addIntegers(5, 2, ref total);
         Console.WriteLine(total);
         Console.ReadKey();
      }
   }
}
``` |
| 14. | Rewrite the preceding exercise, returning the resulting integer via | *Modify the code above as follows:* |
```

| | an out parameter. | ```csharp
static void addIntegers(int a, int b, out int c)
{
    c = a + b;
}

static void Main(string[] args)
{
    int total;
    addIntegers(5, 2, out total);
    Console.WriteLine(total);
    Console.ReadKey();
}
``` |
| 15. | Write a static method named subs that returns the 2nd and 4th substrings of a given string. Test it from Main, with the string *"Mary had a little lamb, little lamb"*. | ```csharp
using System;

namespace PracticeYourCSharp
{
    class Program
    {
        static void subs(string inputStr, out string a, out string b)
        {
            a = String.Empty; // initialize this out parameter
            b = String.Empty; // as above
            string[] inputArray = inputStr.Split(' ');
            if(inputStr.Length>=1) a = inputArray[1];
            if(inputStr.Length>=3) b = inputArray[3];
        }

        static void Main(string[] args)
        {
            string str1 = "Mary had a little lamb, little lamb";
            string str2, str3;
            subs(str1, out str2, out str3);
            Console.WriteLine("2nd str={0}",str2);
            Console.WriteLine("4th str={0}",str3);
            Console.ReadKey();
        }
    }
}
``` |

Parameter arrays		
16.	What is a *parameter array*?	
	A parameter array is a mechanism with which to pass a variable number of arguments of a given type to a method. For example, a method used to calculate and return the sum of a variable number of integers passed to it can receive the set of integers in question as a parameter array. Thus, any method calling this one can put any number of integers in the parameter list that they send to this method. The called method would simply note the number of items in the parameter array and add them up using a loop. A parameter array must be the last parameter in the method declaration. Also, there can only be one parameter array in a method declaration.	
| 17. | Write a static method, that can add *any number of integers* passed to it in a parameter array and returns a long as the result. Call this method from Main, testing it with the following sets of data:<br>1.  1, 2, 3, 4, 5, 6, 7, 8, 9, 10<br>2.  55, 76, 88, 13<br>3.  3, 7<br>4.  An integer array containing the values 1, 5, 15, 19 | ```csharp
using System;

namespace PracticeYourCSharp
{
    class Program
    {
        static long addIntegers(params int[] intArray)
        {
            if (intArray.Length == 0) return (0);
            long total = 0;
            for (int i = 0; i < intArray.Length; i++)
                total += intArray[i];
            return (total);
        }
``` |
```

Chapter 21: Methods (Introduction)

| | ```
        static void Main(string[] args)
        {
            long result1 = 0, result2 = 0, result3 = 0, result4 = 0;
            result1 = addIntegers(1, 2, 3, 4, 5, 6, 7, 8, 9, 10);
            result2 = addIntegers(55, 76, 88, 13);
            result3 = addIntegers(3, 7);
            int[] intArray01 = { 1, 5, 15, 19 };
            result4 = addIntegers(intArray01);
            Console.ReadKey();
        }
    }
}
``` |
| 18. | Using the `String.Concat` method which takes a parameter list, concatenate the elements of the following array: `string[] sArray01 = new string[]{"A", "B", "C", "D", "E", "F"};` |
| | ```csharp
using System;

namespace PracticeYourCSharp
{
    class Program
    {
        static void Main(string[] args)
        {
            string[] sArray01 = new string[] { "A", "B", "C", "D", "E", "F" };

            string s1 = String.Concat(sArray01);
            Console.WriteLine(s1);
            Console.ReadKey();
        }
    }
}
``` |
| **Named Arguments** | |
| 19. | The 1st of Newton's Laws of Motion states: velocity$_{Final}$=velocity$_{Initial}$ + acceleration x time;

Write a static method which computes this. The declaration of the method is shown below.

`public static float velocityF(float velocityI, float time, float acceleration)`

Call it from `Main`, with values `velocityI=100, time=25, acceleration=10`, in the following ways:
1. Simply passing the arguments to the method
2. Naming the arguments and passing them to the method
3. Reverse the order of the named arguments and call the method again

Verify that the results are the same in all three cases. |
| | ```csharp
using System;

namespace PracticeYourCSharp
{
    class Program
    {
        public static float velocityF(float velocityI, float time, float acceleration)
        {
            return (velocityI + (acceleration * time));
        }

        static void Main(string[] args)
        {
            float velocity;
            velocity = velocityF(100, 10, 25);
            Console.WriteLine("The velocity={0}", velocity);

            velocity = velocityF(velocityI: 100, acceleration: 25, time: 10);
            Console.WriteLine("The velocity={0}", velocity);

            velocity = velocityF(time: 10, acceleration: 25, velocityI: 100);
            Console.WriteLine("The velocity={0}", velocity);
``` |
```

	``` Console.ReadKey(); } } } ```
20.	Using the exercise above as a guide, write a static method for Newton's 2nd Law of Motion and test the method, calling it by <u>naming the arguments</u> as done in the preceding exercise. *Newton's Second Law of Motion*: distance = velocity$_{Initial}$*t + 0.5*acceleration*t^2 , *where t=time.*
	``` using System; namespace PracticeYourCSharp { class Program { public static float distance(float velocityI, float time, float acceleration) { return((float)(velocityI*time + 0.5*acceleration*time*time)); } static void Main(string[] args) { float dist; dist = distance(100, 10, 25); Console.WriteLine("The distance={0}", dist); dist = distance(velocityI: 100, acceleration: 25, time: 10); Console.WriteLine("The distance={0}", dist); dist = distance(time: 10, acceleration: 25, velocityI: 100); Console.WriteLine("The distance={0}", dist); Console.ReadKey(); } } } ```
21.	Name the clear benefit(s) of having named arguments.
	One clear benefit of having named arguments is that the calling method does not have to remember the order in which to send arguments to the called method. As the preceding exercises show, it should not matter what the order of calling is, (for it wouldn't matter to a human being who knows the names of the arguments) as long as you pass all the required parameters in.
22.	**(6.0)** Rewrite each of the methods `velocityF` and `distance` of exercises 19 and 20 respectively as expression bodied methods.
	``` public static float velocityF(float velocityI, float time, float acceleration) => (float)(velocityI + (acceleration * time)); public static float distance(float velocityI, float time, float acceleration) => (float)(velocityI * time + 0.5 * acceleration * time * time); ```
23.	**(6.0)** Given the following static class, rewrite its methods as expression-bodied methods. ``` static class DistanceConvert { public static double Km2Miles(float x) { return (x / 1.6);} public static double Miles2Km(float x) { return (x * 1.6);} } ```
	``` static class DistanceConvert { public static double Km2Miles(float x) => (x / 1.6); public static double Miles2Km(float x) => (x * 1.6); } ```

optional arguments/default values

24. Rewrite the method for Newton's 2nd law of motion to support a default value for the acceleration, setting it to the value for the earth's gravitational constant (*9.81* if you're using metric units, or *32.174* if you're using imperial units).
 	
Invoke the method in the following ways, passing values for only time and velocity:
    1. using named arguments
    2. using positional arguments only (the standard way)
 	
Use the following values: time = 10, velocity = 24.
Print out the results.

```csharp
using System;

namespace PracticeYourCSharp
{
  class Program
  {
    public static float distance(float velocityI, float time, float acceleration = 32.174f)
    {
      return((float)(velocityI*time + 0.5*acceleration*time*time));
    }

    static void Main(string[] args)
    {
      float dist;

      dist = distance(time:10, velocityI:100);
      Console.WriteLine("The distance={0}", dist);
      dist = distance(100, 10);
      Console.WriteLine("The distance={0}", dist);
    }
  }
}
```

Chapter 22. Enumerations

This chapter presents exercises on the concept of enumerations in C#.

1.	What is an enumeration (`enum`) and why is it useful?
	An `enum` (short for *enumeration*) is a type that has a *set of string constants* that have each been assigned a unique integral value. You have the choice to either assign values of your choosing to the string constants, or let the compiler do it for you, which it will, starting at the value 0 and incrementing by 1, in order from the first string constant listed in the enumeration to the last. Why is an `enum` useful? It allows the programmer to use meaningful names in code for related items among which numerical ordering is determined to be desirable. Also, by this numerical ordering the writing of code for comparisons is simplified. If for example I have the set of months January to December and I have to write code to do month order comparisons, I can either write an extensive `if/else` block to compare the string values of the month names, or I can create an `enum` that represents each of these months in order as an integer from 1 to 12, an integer comparison clearly being an easier way of doing month order comparisons instead of comparing the strings directly.
2.	What is the default underlying data type used to represent the values of an `enum`?
	A signed integer (`int`).
3.	Is it also possible to specify the underlying type that is used to represent an `enum`?
	Yes.
4.	Which other type can be used as the underlying type for representing an `enum`?
	Any of the integer types can be used.
5.	Create an `enum` named `Gender` that represents *male* and *female*, in the order *male*, then *female*.
	`enum Gender {male, female};`
6.	Write a program which prints out the default value of the `enum Gender` created above.
| | ```csharp
using System;

namespace PracticeYourCSharp
{
  class Program
  {
    enum Gender { male, female };

    static void Main(string[] args)
    {
      Console.WriteLine("{0}", (Gender)0);
    }
  }
}
```<br><br>**Note:** What it prints out is `male`, which is the `Gender` value that is assigned the value `0`. |
| 7. | Write a program which initializes a variable named `gender` that is of type `Gender` and assigns to it the value `male`. |
| | ```csharp
using System;

namespace PracticeYourCSharp
{
  class Program
  {
    enum Gender { male,  female};

    static void Main(string[] args)
    {
       Gender gender = Gender.male;
    }
  }
``` |

	`}`
8.	With respect to the earlier defined `enum Gender`, what is the equivalent integer value of `Gender.male` and `Gender.female` respectively?
	`male=0, female=1` This is because the compiler will assign values to the contents of an `enum` in order, assigning the value `0` to the first entry, `1` to the next and so on.

9.	With regard to the `enum Gender`, what is the output of the following code snippet?
	    `Gender g1;`
	    `Console.WriteLine(g1);`

	The output is `male`, which is the value in the `enum` that corresponds to 0. Why the value that corresponds to 0? Because an `enum` variable (`g1` in this case), being a value type, is by default assigned a value of 0 by C#.
10.	Modify `Gender` to assign an equivalent value of `1` to `male` and `2` to `female`.
	`enum Gender {male=1, female=2};`

11.	Predict the output of the code below.
	
	`using System;`
	
	`namespace PracticeYourCSharp`
	`{`
	  `class Program`
	  `{`
	    `enum Gender { male = 1, female = 2 };`
	
	    `static void Main(string[] args)`
	    `{`
	      `Console.WriteLine("{0}", (Gender)0);`
	    `}`
	  `}`
	`}`

	Observations/Comments: It outputs the value `0`! The reason for this is that if there is no equivalent string in the `enum` in question for the attempted cast, C# will simply return the same value that was attempted in the cast. For example if you write **(Gender)10**, in the output line above C# will simply output the value **10**, since there is no such value defined in the `enum`. **Conclusion:** You should only look for values in the `enum` which correspond to values that have actually been assigned to the `enum` entries.

12.	With regard to the *modified* `enum Gender`, what is the output of the following code snippet?
	    `Gender g1;`
	    `Console.WriteLine(g1);`

	The output is `0`, even though `Gender` does not have any such value defined for it! The reason for this is that an `enum`, being a value type, <u>is by default assigned a value of 0</u>. Even though 0 is not a valid value for this `enum`, C# can actually set an `enum` to any value even if it is not a valid value for the `enum`. **Note:** It is advised that you always ensure that **0** is a valid entry for your `enums`.
13.	With regard to the findings in the preceding exercise, what are the implications of this default setting to 0 for an `enum` which does not have a value of 0 as one of its entries?
	The implication is that when such an `enum` variable is created, the developer should as quickly as reasonable set it to a valid value, otherwise as already noted its contents are invalid by default.
14.	I have permanent employees and contractors. Create an `enum` named `EmploymentType` to represent the employee types *permanent* and *contractor*. Use an underlying type of `ushort` for this `enum`. Add this new `enum` to the solution to exercise 7.

	`using System;`
	
	`namespace PracticeYourCSharp`
	`{`
	  `class Program`
	  `{`
	    `enum Gender { male = 1, female = 2 };`
	    `enum EmploymentType : ushort { permanent, contractor };`

|     | ```
        static void Main(string[] args)
        {
            Gender gender = Gender.male;
        }
    }
}
``` |
| 15. | Extend the solution to the preceding exercise to include a variable called `employmentTerm` of type `EmploymentType`. Assign it a value of `permanent`. |
|     | ```
using System;

namespace PracticeYourCSharp
{
    class Program
    {
        enum Gender { male = 1, female = 2 };
        enum EmploymentType : ushort { permanent, contractor };

        static void Main(string[] args)
        {
            Gender gender = Gender.male;
            EmploymentType employmentTerm = EmploymentType.permanent;
            Console.ReadKey();
        }
    }
}
``` |
| 16. | I have different positions within a company (see below). Put the listed positions along with their noted enum values into an `enum` named `Position`:
   CEO=20,VP=16,Director=10,SeniorManager=9,Manager=7,StaffA=7,StaffB=5,StaffC=3,Staff1=1.
Add this `enum` to the solution to exercise 15. |
|     | ```
  enum Position
  {
      CEO=20, VP=16, Director=12, SeniorManager=10,
      Manager=9, StaffA=7, StaffB=5, StaffC=3, StaffD=1
  };
``` |
17.	Extend the solution to exercise 16 to include a variable named `position` of type `Position`. Assign it a value of CEO.
	Add the following line to the earlier written code: `Position position = Position.CEO;`
18.	Write a program which prints out the *string values* of all the elements of the `enum Position`.
|     | ```
using System;

namespace PracticeYourCSharp
{
    class Program
    {
        enum Position
        {
            CEO = 20, VP = 16, Director = 12, SeniorManager = 10,
            Manager = 9, StaffA = 7, StaffB = 5, StaffC = 3, StaffD = 1
        };

        static void Main(string[] args)
        {
            foreach (string name in Enum.GetNames(typeof(Position)))
                Console.WriteLine(name);

            Console.ReadKey();
        }
    }
}
``` |

19.	Write a program to print out the *numerical values* of all the elements of the `enum Position` defined earlier.	
| | ```csharp
using System;

namespace PracticeYourCSharp
{
  class Program
  {
    enum Position
    {
      CEO = 20, VP = 16, Director = 12, SeniorManager = 10,
      Manager = 9, StaffA = 7, StaffB = 5, StaffC = 3, StaffD = 1
    };

    static void Main(string[] args)
    {
      foreach (int position_value in Enum.GetValues(typeof(Position)))
        Console.WriteLine(position_value.ToString());

      Console.ReadKey();
    }
  }
}
``` | |
20.	With respect to the `enum Position` defined above, what is the value of the following calculation: `int result = 2 * (int)Position.CEO;`	
	40 The reason this code is possible is because the underlying equivalent value of an `enum` can be cast to an integer value.	
21.	Create an enum called `SalaryType` with the entries *salaried* and *hourly*, with equivalent integer values of `0` and `1` respectively.	
	`enum SalaryType {salaried=0,hourly=1};`	
22.	Create an enumeration named `monthsOfTheYear` that starts from a value of `1`, for the months of the year from *January* to *December*, using only the first 3 letters of the months as the entries for the enumeration.	
	`enum monthsOfTheYear {jan=1,feb,mar,apr,may,jun,jul,aug,sep,oct,nov,dec};`	
| 23. | Create a public enum named `VehicleTypes` that supports the following vehicle types: *bicycle, motorbike, car, truck, boat, train, trailer, airplane.* Enumerate the contents thereof starting at a value of `20`, in increments of `10`. | ```csharp
public enum VehicleTypes
{
  bicycle = 20, motorbike = 30,
  car = 40, truck = 50, boat = 60,
  train = 70, trailer = 80,
  airplane = 90
};
``` |
| 24. | Give a clear benefit of choosing the equivalent values for items in your enumeration. | One key benefit is the fact that you do not need to keep the items in the enumeration in order. For example, if for the enumeration `Gender` with contents `{male=1, female=2}` I changed the contents to `{female=2, male=1}`, then there would be no ill-effect on my code. However, if I had the enumeration `{male, female}` and someone changed it to `{female, male}` then the values assigned to the fields, being that they are determined based on position in the `enum`, will change and whatever code was using the `enum` entries would have to be modified. |

Chapter 23. Types, Boxing & Unboxing

The concepts of boxing and unboxing are simple but important topics in C#. Boxing and unboxing take advantage of the unified type system that C# presents and enables the use of features such as mixed lists of value and reference types. To wit, this chapter presents exercises which deal with the definition of types (value types, reference types), the built-in ancestor class `object` and the concepts of boxing and unboxing.

1.	What is a *type*?	A *type* is a specific "template" for whatever data it is appropriate for. For example, the `int` type is appropriate for integer values, the `float` type is appropriate for floating point numbers, the `string` type is appropriate for string values.
		These "templates" are necessary for the compiler to determine many things regarding the data at hand, such as how much memory to use to store the data and what data manipulations/handling are valid for the data in question.
		There are built-in types and there are also user-defined types which are based on the built-in types.

2.	What is a *variable*?	A variable <u>is an instance of a type</u>. For example, if we have the following declarations in our code:
		`  int x01;`
		`  int x02;`
		`  int x03;`
		We have told the compiler that we have three variables that we have named `x01`, `x02` and `x03` and they are of type `int`.

3.	What is a *value type*?	A value type is one whose variable directly contains its data. *(Contrast the value type with the reference type)*
4.	*default values* State the default value of variables of the following types: 1. a reference type 2. a numerical type 3. the `char` type 4. boolean	1. `null` 2. `0` 3. `'\0'` 4. `False`
5.	Give the different categories of value types.	Value types include all numerical types(`int`, `uint`, `long`, `ulong`, `float`, `decimal`, etc.) and their nullable equivalents, `char`, `bool`, `enum` and structures.
6.	Explain what a *reference type* variable is.	
	A reference type variable is one whose value is a reference to the place in memory where the data it refers to is stored; for reference types this data pointed to is always an *object*.	
	To restate the above, we would say that a variable that is a reference type variable is not the actual container of the data of the reference type, but contains the address of where the data that it represents is stored in memory.	
	Stated simply we can say that "a variable that is a reference type contains the address of the data being referred to".	
	Here is an analogy to help explain the concept further. Say I have 10 dollars. If I was a value type I would have the 10 dollars in my pocket. If I was a reference type I wouldn't have the 10 dollars in my pocket, but rather a piece of paper in my pocket that tells you the address of where the 10 dollars is; physically you would then have to go and get the money from the address on the paper in my pocket.	
	Note though, for issues of basic access, when I use the name of a variable, whether value or reference, the C# runtime does the work of fetching the 10 dollars for me, so that in the case of reference types I don't have extra	

work to do; the compiler does it for me. (Think of it as the compiler internally doing two steps to fetch the actual value of a reference type for me; of taking the variable which contains the address of the value we want and then going to get the value from the address in question).

The nature of the type that we are dealing with (reference or value) is of importance when it comes to dealing with questions of equality. For example, for variables `a=2` and `b=4` of any given *value type*, for the question `a==b` (i.e. is the value of `a` equal to the value of `b`), the `==` operator does a direct comparison of the values `2` & `4` and gives the appropriate result (which in this case is `false`).

In the case of reference types, if we have for example reference type variables `x` and `y` and these are assigned as follows: `x=object1` and `y=object1`, then the question `x==y` will yield a value of `false`! This will happen because, to continue the analogy of a reference type variable being a piece of paper on which the address of what it refers to is written, clearly `x` and `y` are different pieces of paper (even though the same thing is written on them). Now, while indeed sometimes you want to "check whether you are talking about the same sheet of paper", very often you really want to compare what is written on the papers, i.e. compare the contents of what `x` and `y` are referring to. Thus you have to use the specific comparer method for the reference type in question to compare the values referred to by reference types.

Special note on strings: Even though strings are reference types, they respond to the equality operator just like value types, therefore for given strings `p="Hello"` and `q="Hello"`, `p==q` will yield the response true. The usage of the equality operator for objects of class `String` is because class `String` has *overloaded* the equality operator.

7.	List the different types of reference types.
	Classes, array types, interfaces, delegate types, strings.
8.	What is meant by the statement "strings are immutable" ?
	This means that once they are created they do not change. If you attempt to modify a string, what actually happens is that a new string is created (i.e., the old is not modified, but rather discarded by the system as and when appropriate). You the programmer do not see the re-creation of the string going on in the background since you reference the string by variable name, not by its memory position which has now been changed. For more detail on this topic, see Chapter 5.
9.	What is an object?
	An object is an instance of a given class.
10.	What is the process of obtaining an instance of a class called?
	Object instantiation.
11.	What does it mean when it is said that C# has a *unified type system*?
	It means that every data type in C#, whether reference type or value type has the same ultimate ancestor; the class `object` (or `System.Object` to be more precise). Due to this unified ancestry and the concept of polymorphism, every type in C#, including value types can be represented as an object of class `System.Object` (aliased as `object`).
12.	What is the concept of *boxing*?
	The concept of boxing is the means by which C# takes a value type and represents it as an object of class `object` which is the ultimate ancestor of all types in C#.
13.	What is the concept of *unboxing*?
	Unboxing is the means by which you explicitly, by means of a cast, convert a boxed type back to a value type.
14.	What does the method `GetType()` of class `object` do?
	This method is used to discern the real/actual type of the object at hand which has been cast into an object of class `object`. It is useful when unboxing objects, so that you can convert the object back to its original type.

15.	Predict the output of this code when it is compiled as part of a program:
	`    float f1 = 79.55F;`
	`    object o1 = f1;`

	This is completely valid code; being able to assign a `float` to a variable of type `object` demonstrates boxing. The boxing is done implicitly.
16.	Write a line of code which shows the unboxing of the float that was boxed in the exercise immediately above.
	This single line of code unboxes the float:

	`float f2 = (float)o1;`
17.	I have the following variables: `int a=2`, `float b=59.77F`; `string c="Hello!"`. Put them all into a single `List<object>` instance.
| | ```
using System;
using System.Collections.Generic;

namespace PracticeYourCSharp
{
  class Program
  {
    static void Main(string[] args)
    {
      int a = 2; float b = 59.77F; string c = "Hello";
      List<object> everything = new List<object>();
      everything.Add(a);
      everything.Add(b);
      everything.Add(c);
    }
  }
}
``` |
| | **Note:** We note that integers, floats and strings (and any other object type actually) go into a `List` of type `object` with no problem. However, in order to do this the `List<object>` had to *box* the value types in order to be able to store them (done implicitly), as the `List<object>` is a list of objects, not a list of value types. |
| 18. | Create one each of `List<int>`, `List<float>` and `List<string>`. Then using a `foreach` loop, go through the `List<object>` in the solution to the preceding exercise and put each item in it into the list `List<T>` that corresponds to its type.
Hint: Use the method `GetType` of the class `object` to determine the class of each object in the `List<object>`. |
| | ```
using System;
using System.Collections.Generic; // List<T> is defined in here

namespace PracticeYourCSharp
{
  class Program
  {
    static void Main(string[] args)
    {
      int a = 2; float b = 59.77F; string c = "Hello";
      List<object> everything = new List<object>();
      everything.Add(a); everything.Add(b); everything.Add(c);

      // now create the individual lists in this question
      List<int>    intList    = new List<int>();
      List<float>  floatList  = new List<float>();
      List<string> stringList = new List<string>();

      foreach (object x in everything)
      {
        string objectClass = x.GetType().Name;
        if (objectClass == "String") stringList.Add((string)x); // note the casting.
        if (objectClass == "Int32")  intList.Add((int)x);
        if (objectClass == "Single") floatList.Add((float)x);
      }
      Console.ReadKey();
    }
  }
}
``` |
19.	Briefly describe the class `ArrayList`.
	`ArrayList` is an older class than `List` that supports a medley of objects; in practice an `ArrayList` is in effect like `List<object>`.
20.	Rewrite the code from the solution to exercise 18 above using an `ArrayList` instead of `List<object>`.

```csharp
using System;
using System.Collections; // ArrayList is defined in here
using System.Collections.Generic;

namespace PracticeYourCSharp
{
  class Program
  {
    static void Main(string[] args)
    {
      int a = 2; Single b = 59.77F; string c = "Hello";
      ArrayList everything = new ArrayList();
      everything.Add(a); everything.Add(b); everything.Add(c);

      List<int> intList = new List<int>();
      List<float> floatList = new List<float>();
      List<string> stringList = new List<string>();

      foreach (object x in everything)
      {
        string objectClass = x.GetType().Name;
        if (objectClass == "String") stringList.Add((string)x);
        if (objectClass == "Int32") intList.Add((int)x);
        if (objectClass == "Single") floatList.Add((float)x);
      }
      Console.ReadKey();
    }
  }
}
```

Chapter 24. Classes

C# is an object-oriented language and thus the concept of classes is foundational to it. This chapter is a very important one as it presents exercises which cover the concepts of classes and types thereof, class instances (objects), class/object member accessibility, inheritance, polymorphism and other key related topics. The operators `as` and `is` as well as the type `dynamic` are also explored in this chapter.

Please note that the exercises in this chapter in particular should be completed in sequential order, as often through this chapter subsequent exercises build their predecessors.

1.	In C#, what is a class?
	A class is a data structure that can combine fields, methods, properties, constants, events, structures, operators, indexers, interfaces, enumerations, delegates as well as other class definitions in a single unit. A class is a "template" for dynamically created **instances** of the class; these instances are called **objects**. Classes support the concept of **inheritance**, a mechanism whereby **derived classes** obtain the functionality of their parent class and can enhance the inherited functionality as desired.
2.	List and define the potential members of a class.
	1. Constants – constant values associated with the class (for example `Math.PI`) 2. Fields – variables of the class or its instances 3. Methods – distinct code blocks that can be performed by the class or its instances 4. Constructors – methods which are invoked on the instantiation of instances of the class or before any instances or members of the class are referenced 5. Destructors – a method that is run automatically at the end of the lifetime of objects of the class 6. Properties – specialized methods with field-like syntax for reading/writing private fields of the class or instances thereof (for example `DateTime.Now`) 7. Indexers – code that supports the indexing of instances of the class in an array-like fashion 8. Events – notifications which can be generated by the class or instances thereof 9. Operators – methods which override the function of built-in operators such as +,-,*,/, etc. for the class in question 10. Types – other classes, structures, interfaces, enumerations or delegates **Note:** Not all of these members are required to be present in a given class at once.
3.	In C#, can a class be defined within another class?
	Yes. (In the solution to exercise 2 above it was stated that a class can have other classes defined within it).
4.	Explain the concept of a "top-level" class.
	A top-level class is simply a class that is *not* defined <u>within</u> another class. (In the solution to exercise 2 above it was stated that a class can have other classes defined within it). All the classes defined in this chapter are top-level classes.

5.	*top-level class access modifiers*
	 Explain the meaning of each of the following top-level class access modifiers:
	   1. `public`
	   2. `internal`

	1. `public` – the class in question can be accessed by any other class 2. `internal` – can only be accessed within the assembly in which it is defined and by friend assemblies (contrast with `public`) *(Discussion on assemblies is beyond the scope of this book)*
6.	Create the outline of a `public` class named `Vehicle`.

| | ```
using System;
namespace PracticeYourCSharp
{
  public class Vehicle
  {
    // This is the new class. It is empty for now.
  }
  class Program
  {
    // This is the previously existing class Program...the new class and this
    // are happily co-existing in the same namespace.
    static void Main(string[] args)
    {

    }
  }
}
```<br>**Note:** Observe that the new class is happily coexisting with other classes (the class `Program` in this example) in the same namespace. |
| 7. | *Class member accessibility modifiers*
There are different possible accessibility modifiers for the members of a class (even if the member(s) in question are classes). Explain what the following accessibility modifiers mean:
1. `public`
2. `protected`
3. `private` |
| | 1. `public` – means that the member to which it is applied can be accessed by callers from anywhere, be it from within the class itself, its child classes, or even unrelated classes
2. `protected` – the member is directly accessible only by members of its class and classes derived therefrom
3. `private` – means that the item to which it is applied can be accessed directly only by members of its class (not even by descendant classes)
Note: Other accessibility levels include `internal` and `protected internal`. These are beyond the scope of this book. |
| 8. | Add the following fields to the class `Vehicle` created earlier:<br>1. A `protected string` named `license`<br>2. A `protected string` named `chassisNumber`<br>3. A `protected enum` named `VehicleType` of type `VehicleTypes`. This enum is defined as follows:<br>```
public enum VehicleTypes
  {
    bicycle = 20, motorbike = 30,
    car = 40, truck = 50, boat = 60,
    train = 70, trailer = 80,
    airplane = 90
  };
```<br>4. A `protected string` named `color`<br>5. A `protected ushort` field named `numberOfWheels` |
| | ```
public class Vehicle
{
  protected string license;
  protected string chassisNumber; // Vehicle identification number
  protected VehicleTypes VehicleType;
  protected string color;
  protected ushort numberOfWheels;
}
``` |
| 9. | What is the title of the special method which when present in any class is automatically invoked on creation of an instance of the class? |
```

		It is called a *constructor*.
10.		What is the function of a constructor method?
		A constructor is used to perform initialization actions on a newly instantiated object. Initialization parameters can be passed to the constructor at the time of instantiation of the object. Beyond initializing the newly instantiated object, a constructor is free to perform any desired actions on any other aspect of the program at the time of object instantiation if so desired; its function is not limited to initializing objects.
11.		At what point in the lifetime of an object is the constructor invoked?
		It is invoked automatically on instantiation of the object.
12.		What is the minimum number of constructors a class can have in C#?
		The minimum number of constructors a class can have is 1, as every class must have at least one constructor. If you the programmer do not define any constructor for the class, the compiler will create one automatically; the compiler created constructor is called the <u>default parameterless constructor</u>, as it is created by default, and takes no parameters.
13.		Can constructors be overloaded?
		Yes constructors can be overloaded like any other method.
14.		For the earlier defined class `Vehicle`, what would be the name of any of its constructor methods?
		The name of the constructor of a class named `Vehicle` is `Vehicle`. Constructor methods <u>always</u> have the same name as the class itself. Constructors are the only methods which have the same name as the class in which they appear.
15.		What is the return type of a constructor?
		Constructors do not have a return type at all (not even `void`).
16.		What is a *parameterless* constructor?

		A parameterless constructor is a constructor that has no parameters passed to it. It is invoked when an object is instantiated without any parameters. For example we can have the following:
		`    Vehicle v01 = new Vehicle(); // Example of instantiation using a parameterless constructor;`
		`                               // No parameters passed in the braces.`
		The programmer can create the parameterless constructor, or leave the construction thereof to the compiler to do implicitly (for our class `Vehicle`, the compiler created the constructor), which the compiler will do only if the programmer has not defined any constructor for the class in question.

17.		Define and describe what an implicit/default parameterless constructor is.
		This is a constructor that is created by the compiler automatically only if the class does not have any programmer defined constructor. Using as example the class `Vehicle` which we created earlier, we did not define any constructor for it and since we didn't define one, the compiler created one for the class implicitly and so we are thus able to instantiate objects of the class `Vehicle`. The characteristics/behavior of the default parameterless constructor are as follows: 1. It does not take any parameters. 2. It has an accessibility level of `public`. 3. This constructor will set the different types in the class to their default values 4. It will invoke the parameterless constructor of its parent class before its own body runs; if the parent class does not have one, the code will not be able to compile. *It should be understood that in C# the creation of an object provokes its constructor to invoke the parameterless constructor of its parent class (unless the constructor of the child class has designated another of the parents' constructors to be called) before its own body runs. The constructor of the parent will in turn invoke a designated constructor in its own parent class (the parameterless constructor is the default), and it a designated constructor in its own parent, etc. to the top of the inheritance hierarchy).* Note that once you yourself define a constructor for a given class, the compiler expects that any object created for the class in question will need to invoke one of the programmer defined constructors. For example if you have only the following constructor defined for the class `Vehicle`: `    public Vehicle(string vehicleColor)`

	``
{
color = vehicleColor;
}
``` Then you *cannot* do the following object instantiation: ```
Vehicle vehicle01 = new Vehicle();
`` The reason why you cannot do this is because once you yourself have defined at least one constructor for a class the compiler will not create a default one (the default parameterless constructor) for you. However you are free to create your own parameterless constructor.	
18.	With respect to the class `Vehicle` created earlier, if you have not defined a constructor for the class, what values would the object fields `numberOfWheels` and `color` of a newly instantiated `Vehicle` instance have?	
	`numberOfWheels` would have a value of `0` `color` is initialized to *null*. The reason for these values is because C# by default initializes the fields in objects to the default value for their respective given type, the default for numerical types being `0` and the default for strings being *null*.	
19.	Write the code for a `public` parameterless constructor for the class `Vehicle`. This code needn't perform any actions.	
| | ```
public Vehicle()
{
}
``` | |
| 20. | What does the keyword `this` mean and how is it used? | |
| | The keyword `this` means "this object with which we are dealing at present". It is used within methods to refer to the object itself. Here are a few scenarios in which `this` would be used: **scenario 1: field/parameter disambiguation** If for example I have a class `Car` that has a field `color` defined as follows: ```
class Car
{
    protected string color;
}
``` If the class has a method `SetColor(string color){...}` whose function it is to set the field `color` of a `Car` object, a problem arises because the parameter name in the method declaration matches the field name in the class itself. You see we can't say: ```
SetColor(string color)
{
    color = color;
    // Our intent is that the 1st color here is the object field color and the 2nd color
    // the parameter passed to the method. The compiler however can't tell which is which.
}
``` Such a statement is confusing to the compiler as it is not sure which field or variable `color` is being referenced on either side of the equation as it has to ask the question *"which one am I dealing with, the field in the object or the parameter in the method declaration?"* Therefore, we use `this` to effect a disambiguation and instead rewrite the method as follows: ```
SetColor(string color)
{
    this.color = color; //says object field color (on the left) = value of passed parameter color
}
``` **scenario 2: passing an object from a method of its own class** Sometimes an instance method needs to pass the very object instance to which it pertains to another method. Recall that the object at hand refers to itself as `this`. The way in which the object passing is effected can be seen in the sample code snippet below: ```
sendMeElsewhere()
``` | |
```

	{
	   sendOff(**this**);
	}

	scenario 3: invoking an overloaded constructor There are scenarios where there is a need to access a constructor of a class from within another constructor of the same class. In such cases `this` comes into play. We will see this concept in a later exercise in this chapter.
21.	Explain the use of an overloaded constructor.

	This is like overloading any method; you would want an overloaded constructor in order to accommodate the different input values and input value types that you choose to initialize your objects with at instantiation time. For example, if I have a class `Person` that has fields named `lastName`, `firstName` and `age`, I can for example have the following constructors:
	
	``
	public Person(string lastName, string firstName);
	public Person(string lastName, int age);
	public Person(string lastName, string firstName, int age);
	``
	
	The first constructor would be used when the code instantiating an object of class `Person` only has values for the fields `lastName` and `firstName` at hand at the time of object creation. In the second case, perhaps only the values for the fields `lastName` and `age` are at hand. In the third case values for all three fields are at hand at the time of object creation.
	
	Note that these reasons are not exhaustive.

22.	Create a constructor to input and set all the fields of the previously defined class `Vehicle`.

	``
	public Vehicle(string license, string chassisNumber, VehicleTypes VehicleType, string color,
	                ushort numOfWheels)
	{
	  this.license = license; //note the use of the keyword this (explained earlier)
	  this.chassisNumber = chassisNumber;
	  this.VehicleType = VehicleType;
	  this.color = color;
	  numberOfWheels = numOfWheels;
	}
	``

23.	Add a `public` method named `SetLicense` to the class `Vehicle`. This method should set the field `license`. The return type of the method should be `void`.

	``
	public class Vehicle
	{
	  // other fields and other code such as the constructor and other methods here...
	  public void SetLicense(string license)
	  {
	    this.license = license;
	  }
	}
	``

24.	Add a `public` method named `SetChassisNumber` to the class `Vehicle`. This method should set the field `chassisNumber`. The return type of the method should be `void`.

	``
	public void SetChassisNumber(string chassisNumber)
	{
	  this.chassisNumber = chassisNumber;
	}
	``

25.	In the parameterless constructor for the `Vehicle` class, add a line that prints *"I am a Vehicle!"*.

	``
	public Vehicle()
	{
	  Console.WriteLine("I am a Vehicle!");
	}
	``

26.	In `Main`, create an instance of the class `Vehicle`, naming it `v01`. Instantiate it using the parameterless constructor. What is the output to the console?

	(only method `Main` shown here):
	
	``
	static void Main(string[] args)
	{
	``

| | ```
    Vehicle v01 = new Vehicle();
    Console.ReadKey();
}
```<br>The output is: *"I am a Vehicle!"*, which is what the parameterless constructor was coded to do. |
27.	What is the title of the special method which if present in a class is invoked at the end of the lifetime of an object of the class in question?
	It is called a *destructor*.
28.	For a class named `Vehicle`, what would be the method declaration of the destructor method?
	`~Vehicle()`
29.	How is the destructor invoked?
	It is not invoked directly by your code, but rather it is invoked by the garbage collector at the end of the lifetime of the object. **Note:** *In this book, we will not be examining the destructor further as the topic is beyond the scope of this book and also, the system naturally takes care of the destruction of objects; we would have a destructor if we had particular actions that we wanted done before the object was destroyed (for example, we might want to log the end of the lifetime of this object to a file).*

30.	In C#, what is the concept of inheritance?
	Inheritance is a feature in C# by which a class can be specified to be a descendant of another class (termed the "parent class"). By virtue of this feature the child class "inherits" all of the components of its parent class. The child class is generally free to modify or override what is not desired of what it inherited and also to add extra functionality.
31.	What is the concept of multiple inheritance?
	Multiple inheritance is a feature in some computer languages by which a given class can have multiple parent classes and thus inherit the components of all the parent classes.
32.	How is multiple inheritance implemented in C#?
	C# <u>DOES NOT</u> support multiple inheritance. It only supports single inheritance, that is, a class can only have one parent class. However, the concept of *interfaces* can seem to have a similar effect as multiple inheritance. We look at the concept of interfaces in a later chapter.
33.	*(child class creation)* Create the outline of a `public` class named `Car` that is a <u>child class</u> of the earlier created class `Vehicle`.
| | ```
public class Car : Vehicle
{
}
``` |
| 34. | Write a program which instantiates an object named `car01` of the class `Car` defined earlier. Observe and explain the output of the code. |
| | *(Put the lines of code below into `Main` (remove any code currently in `Main`) and run it.*<br><br>```
Car car01 = new Car(); // Instantiate an object of class Car.
Console.ReadKey();
```<br><br>**Output**<br>`I am a Vehicle!`<br><br>This output comes from the parameterless constructor of the parent class of class `Car`!<br><br>**Explanation**<br>  As previously explained, whenever an object of any given class is instantiated, the constructor of the class in question will first of all invoke a designated constructor in its parent class *(yes, you can choose which of your parents' constructors you want to invoke)*. If no parent constructor is explicitly designated as the one to invoke, the parameterless constructor of the parent class will be invoked. Also, as previously stated, whichever parent constructor is invoked will invoke a designated constructor in its own parents' class (the parameterless one is the default), which will in turn invoke a designated constructor in its own parents' class and so on recursively to the top of the object hierarchy. |
| 35. | Under what circumstances is the keyword `base` used? |
```

	The keyword **base** is used under the following circumstances:
1. A constructor in a child class can use it to invoke a constructor of choice in its parent class.
2. A method in a child class can use it to invoke a method of the same name in its parent class that it the child class has hidden with the keyword **new** or overridden with the keyword **override**.

Exercises on these will be seen later. |
| 36. | What is the problem with the following code?

```
using System;

namespace PracticeYourCSharp
{
  public class A
    {
      public A(int x)
      {
        return;
        // Here we have defined a constructor which is not parameterless for this class.
      }
    }

    public class B:A
    {
    }

    class Program
    {
      static void Main(string[] args)
      {
        B obj1 = new B();
      }
    }
}
```

(Note first that class A has one constructor which takes arguments and that class B only has as constructor the default parameterless constructor)

Stated succinctly, the problem is that there is no constructor in the parent class A for the constructor of its child class B (B has the compiler created default parameterless constructor) to invoke. A detailed explanation of the problem appears below.

It has been stated previously that once a constructor is defined for a class by the programmer, the compiler no longer takes on the responsibility of providing a parameterless constructor for the class in question. Thus, class A in this example does not have a parameterless constructor. This is not wrong, but in this example, it is a part of the problem. We also know that when an object of a given class is created, the constructor of the object will by default seek to invoke the parameterless constructor of its parent class. In the code sample given above, the problem is that there is no parameterless constructor in class A to be invoked when an object of class B is instantiated. |
| 37. | What is the solution to the non-compilation of the code in the preceding question? |
| | The most direct solution is to create a parameterless constructor in the parent class. |
| 38. | Identify what is wrong with the code below and propose how to fix it.

```
using System;

namespace PracticeYourCSharp
{
  public class A
    {
      public A(int x)
      {
        return;
      }
    }

    public class B:A
``` |

|     | ```
    {
      public B(string y)
      {
        return;
      }
    }
    class Program
    {
      static void Main(string[] args)
      {
        B obj1 = new B("ABCD");
      }
    }
}
``` |
| | The issue is the same as in the preceding exercise; the constructor created for class B is seeking to invoke the parameterless constructor of its parent class, however, the parent class does not have one! (In the previous question it was the default parameterless constructor of class B that had no constructor to call in its parent class, in this question it is a programmer defined constructor that has no constructor to call in the parent class; as stated the problem is the same as in the preceding exercise).

The potential solutions include the following:

Create a parameterless constructor in the parent class
or
Have the constructor in the child class explicitly invoke one of the constructors in its parent class (there is only one constructor in the parent class in this example), by using the keyword **base**, as shown below:

```
    public B(string y):base(77) //specifying which particular constructor to call in the parent...
    {                           //by using the keyword base
      return;
    }
```
Note that in this example the constructor of the parent is expecting an integer (which in this case we know it is not using), so we just passed it any number, **77** in this case. |
| 39. | **Seeing how protected works**
Add the following two lines of code to the method Main (which is of class Program). Attempt to compile and run the program and comment on your observations.
```
    Console.WriteLine("Vehicle type={0}", car01.VehicleType);
    Console.WriteLine("number Of Wheels={0}", car01.numberOfWheels);
``` |
| | The code will NOT compile. The reason is that the class members VehicleType and numberOfWheels are declared as **protected** within their class of origin and therefore can only be accessed directly from a method in their class of origin or descendant classes of their class of origin; the problem here is that we are trying to access them from a method (Main) in a class (Program) that is not the class Vehicle nor a descendant of it!

The solution is to create <u>public methods</u> or properties (to be seen in a later chapter) in either the class Vehicle or the class Car to return the value(s) of interest to us. Another solution is to make the fields in question **public**; this however is not a preferred option as best programming practice prefers that field visibility should be as narrow as possible. |
| 40. | Write individual **public** methods for the class Vehicle to return each of the following fields:

  1. license
  2. chassisNumber
  3. VehicleType
  4. color
  5. numberOfWheels

Add these methods to the class Vehicle. | The methods are as follows:
```
public string GetLicense() {return(license);}
public string GetChassisNumber() {return(chassisNumber);}
public VehicleTypes GetVehicleType() {return (VehicleType);}
public string GetColor() {return (color);}
public ushort GetNumberOfWheels(){return (numberOfWheels);}
``` |
```

41.	For the earlier declared object `car01`, write code in `Main` to print its fields `VehicleType`, `numberOfWheels` and `color` using the methods defined in the preceding exercise.
	Explain the output of the program.
	Add the following lines of code to `Main`:
	``
	Console.WriteLine("Vehicle type={0}",car01.GetVehicleType());
	Console.WriteLine("number Of Wheels={0}",car01.GetNumberOfWheels());
	Console.WriteLine("color={0}",car01.GetColor());
	``
	Output
	``
	I am a Vehicle!
	Vehicle type=0
	numberOfWheels=0
	color=
	``
	Explanation
	The reason for the output is as follows:
	Line 1: This is because the parameterless constructor **of the parent class** is called (This was explained in the solution to exercise 34).
	Line 2: When there is no explicit initialization of fields, the fields are initialized by C# to their default values. `VehicleType` being an `enum`, it is initialized to the element of the enum with the value `0`; and if there is no element defined to be of value `0` the enum variable is initialized to the value `0` (See the chapter on *Enumerations*).
	Line 3: If not explicitly initialized, numerical values are initialized to their default: `0`.
	Line 4: Similarly, if not explicitly initialized, a `string` <u>field</u> is initialized to *null* and thus no value is printed.
	Note(s): Observe that due to inheritance the object of class `Car` has inherited the methods of its parent class and is employing them as its own.
42.	Create a parameterless constructor for the class `Car`. Have it set the `enum` field `VehicleType` to the value `car` and the field `numberOfWheels` to `4`. Then create an instance `car01` of the class `Car` and print out the same fields as in exercise 41.
	Explain the output of the program.
	``
	public class Car : Vehicle
	{
	//... other parts of the class here ...
	public Car() // Constructor
	{
	VehicleType = VehicleTypes.car;
	numberOfWheels = 4;
	}
	}
	``
	`Main` is as in the preceding exercise.
	Output
	``
	I am a Vehicle!
	Vehicle type=car
	numberOfWheels=4
	color=
	``
	Explanation
	The reason for the output is as follows: the parameterless constructor of the class `Car` which we just defined in this exercise (in the preceding exercise since we didn't explicitly create a constructor for `Car`, the compiler did so for us) was invoked.
	A line by line analysis of the output follows below:
	Line 1: Now indeed the parameterless constructor of the class is being called. However, it invoked the parameterless constructor of its parent class *before* it itself ran. The parents' constructor prints out the string *"I am a Vehicle!"*.
	Line 2: We initialized the `VehicleType` to `VehicleTypes.car` in the constructor for the class `Car`.

	Line 3: We initialized the `numberOfWheels` to 4 in our constructor.
Line 4: The string field `color` is initialized to *null*, and thus it has nothing to print.

Do step through this code in the IDE to observe the order in which the code is run; by doing this you will see that when the constructor for the object of class `Car` is called, the constructor will first call the parameterless constructor of its parent class. |
| 43. | *Overloaded constructor*

Create a constructor for the class `Car` which takes as parameters values for the following fields: `chassisNumber`, `license` and `color`. Afterwards, create an instance `car02` of the class `Car` using this new constructor, giving input values of your choice and then, using the methods defined in exercise 40, print out all the fields of object `car02`.

Explain the output of the program.
```
public class Car : Vehicle
{
  // other code...

  public Car(string chassisNumber, string license, string color)
  { // This is the new constructor
    this.chassisNumber = chassisNumber;
    this.license = license;
    this.color = color;
  }
}
```
In Main, we have the following code:
```
Car car02 = new Car("VIN11111232","DRV0123A3432","blue");

Console.WriteLine("Vehicle type={0}",       car02.GetVehicleType());
Console.WriteLine("number Of Wheels={0}",   car02.GetNumberOfWheels());
Console.WriteLine("color={0}",              car02.GetColor());
Console.WriteLine("license={0}",            car02.GetLicense());
Console.WriteLine("chassisNumber={0}",      car02.GetChassisNumber());
```

Output
```
I am a Vehicle!
VehicleType=0       ← the constructor we just used never initialized this
number Of Wheels=0  ← same reason as above
color=blue
license=DRV0123A3432
chassisNumber=VIN111111232
``` |
| 44. | How can you prevent the constructor of the parent class from being invoked when instantiating an object? |
| | It is not possible to block the constructor of the parent class from being invoked. However, here are some potential ways to mitigate the effect of this running/invocation:

1. Ensure that the parent class does not have a functional parameterless constructor, which can be done by giving the parameterless constructor of the parent an empty body.
2. Invoke a different constructor of the parent which has an empty body. When you do this, the compiler says "Well you've called one parent constructor already, so I don't have to call the default one".

    The constructor of choice is called from the child class constructor with the addendum
    `:base(<parameters>)`
    This call is done in the heading line of the child constructor, for example,
    ```
    public Car():base() // Constructor
    {
      // This particular example explicitly calls the parameterless constructor of the parent
      // class; the keyword base in this context refers to the constructor of the parent class
    }
    ```
3. Overwrite all of the functionality of the constructors of your ancestor classes in your own constructors. |
| 45. | *Calling an overloaded constructor from another constructor for the same class* |

Modify the constructor in exercise 43 for the class `Car` to set the fields `VehicleType` and `color` to the values in the earlier created parameterless constructor (see exercise 42). Effect this by calling the parameterless constructor for the class `Car` from the constructor being modified, since we know that the parameterless constructor already sets those particular fields.

Create an instance `car02` of the class `Car` using this new constructor and print out all the fields of `car02`. Explain the output of the program.

Hint: `:this()`

```
public class Car : Vehicle
{
  < other previously written code...>

  public Car(string chassisNumber, string license, string color):this()
  {
    this.chassisNumber = chassisNumber;
    this.license = license;
    this.color = color;
  }
}
```

In Main, we have:

```
Car car02 = new Car("VIN11111232","DRV0123A3432","blue");

Console.WriteLine("Vehicle type={0}", car02.GetVehicleType());
Console.WriteLine("number Of Wheels={0}", car02.GetNumberOfWheels());
Console.WriteLine("color={0}", car02.GetColor());
Console.WriteLine("license={0}",car02.GetLicense());
Console.WriteLine("chassisNumber={0}",car02.GetChassisNumber());
```

Output
```
I am a Vehicle!
VehicleType=car
number Of Wheels=4
color=blue
license=DRV0123A3432
chassisNumber=VIN111111232
```

The output is as expected.

Explanation
Instead of copying the lines of code:

```
    VehicleType = VehicleTypes.car;
    numberOfWheels = 4;
```

which are already present in the parameterless constructor to this constructor, we simply invoked the parameterless constructor which already has this code, from the other constructor by enhancing the constructor with the code

`:this(<constructor parameters>)`.

Do step through the code in the IDE to get a better feeling for the order of how the code is run.
You will see that when this constructor is called, before running its own body, it first calls the other constructor we requested by using `:this(<constructor parameters>)`. Whichever constructor we invoke can be observed to first call the parameterless constructor of the parent class before it itself runs.

46. Create a class `Motorcycle` as a child class of the class `Vehicle`.
Give it a parameterless constructor that sets the field `VehicleType` to the value `motorbike`. The constructor should also set the field `numberOfWheels` to a value of 2.

```
public class Motorcycle : Vehicle
{
  public Motorcycle() // Constructor
  {
    VehicleType = VehicleTypes.motorbike;
```

| | ```
        numberOfWheels = 2;
    }
}
``` |
| 47. | Create a class `Train` as a child class of the class `Vehicle`. Create for it a constructor that sets the field `VehicleType` to the value `train`.<br>```
public class Train : Vehicle
{
    public Train()
    {
        VehicleType = VehicleTypes.train;
    }
}
``` |
| 48. | *class modifiers*
Explain the meaning of each of the following class modifiers:
1. `abstract`
2. `sealed`
3. `static`
4. `partial` |
| | 1. `abstract` – a class which we desire not be instantiable. Its members may or may not be fully defined, however, even the defined members thereof cannot be invoked. Only non-abstract descendant classes of abstract classes can be directly instantiated
2. `sealed` – no other class can be derived from such a class (i.e. it cannot have child classes)
3. `static` – the class in question cannot be instantiated; any members it has are invoked as class members
4. `partial` – indicates that there are parts of the class in question defined in other files
The reader should be aware that class modifiers and class access modifiers (see exercises 5 and 7) are used in tandem. |

static classes	
49.	What is the difference between an *instance member* of a class and a *static member* of a class?
	An *instance member* of a class can only be invoked on an instance (instantiated object) of a class; a *static member* however is invoked relative to the class itself; i.e., a static member operates without reference to any object. Let us take examples from the class `Int32` which has both instance and static methods. The static method `Int32.Parse(String)` is invoked relative to the class, for example as `int int01 = Int32.Parse("5000");` As you can see, the method is invoked relative to the class name `Int32`. On the other hand, the instance method `ToString` of the same class would have to be called for a given object instance as `<instance>.ToString();` that is, this particular method has to be invoked relative to an instance `<instance>` of class `Int32`. For example, to invoke it for the object instance `int01` above, we would have to invoke it as `int01.ToString();`
50.	If I do *not* want a class to be instantiable, but want its members to be usable, what class modifier should I give the class in question?
	Use the class modifier `static`. Look at the definition of the built-in `static` class `Math` as an example of a static class.
51.	Create a `static` class named `Volume`, with the following `static` methods which calculate the volume of their respective namesake geometric object: • `Sphere` which takes the radius of a sphere as parameter. • `Cube` which takes the length of a cube as parameter. • `Cone` which takes the radius and height of a cone as parameters. • `Cylinder` which takes the radius and height of a cylinder as parameters. Each of these should return a value of type `double`.
| | ```
public static class Volume
{
    static public double Sphere(float radius)
    {
``` |
```

|     | ```
      return ((4.0 / 3.0) * Math.PI * Math.Pow(radius, 3));
    }
    static public double Cube(float x)
    {
      return(Math.Pow(x,3));
    }
    static public double Cone(float r, float h)
    {
      return (((float)1/(float)3) * (Math.PI) *r*r*h);
    }
    static public double Cylinder(float r, float h)
    {
      return (Math.PI * r * r * h);
    }
}
``` |
| 52. | Test the above created static class `Volume`, for the following objects:
1. A sphere of radius 40,000
2. A cube of side 2.5
3. A cone of radius 50 and height 50
4. A cylinder of radius 50 and height 25

Print the results out.
(Put the code into the method `Main`.) |
|     | *We show only* `Main` *below.*<br><br>```
static void Main(string[] args)
{
  double sphereVolume = Volume.Sphere(40000);
  double cubeVolume = Volume.Cube(2.5f);
  double coneVolume = Volume.Cone(50, 50);
  double cylinderVolume = Volume.Cylinder(50, 25);

  Console.WriteLine("{0}\n{1}\n{2}\n{3}\n", sphereVolume, cubeVolume, coneVolume,
                                                         cylinderVolume);
  Console.ReadKey();
}
``` |
| 53. | Create a static class named `Circle`, that defines static methods named `Area`, `Diameter` and `Circumference` which calculate their namesake values(area, diameter, circumference) for a given radius. Each of these should return a value of type `double`. |
|     | ```
public static class Circle
{
  public static double Area(double radius)          { return (Math.PI * radius * radius); }
  public static double Diameter(double radius)      { return (2 * radius); }
  public static double Circumference(double radius) { return (2 * Math.PI * radius); }
}
``` |
| 54. | Using the static class created above, print the area, circumference and diameter for circles of radius 2 and 12 to two decimal places. |
|     | ```
using System;

// <put the static class defined above here>

class Program
{
  static void Main(string[] args)
  {
    double r=2;   // The radius
    Console.WriteLine("the area,circumference,diameter of a circle of radius {0} is
                  {1:0.00},{2:0.00},{3:0.00} respectively", r, Circle.Area(r),
                  Circle.Diameter(r), Circle.Circumference(r));
    r=12;   // The second radius
    Console.WriteLine("the area,circumference,diameter of a circle of radius {0} is
                  {1:0.00},{2:0.00},{3:0.00} respectively", r, Circle.Area(r),
``` |

	Circle.Diameter(r), Circle.Circumference(r)); Console.ReadKey(); } }
55.	**(6.0)** Rewrite the code for exercises 51 and 52 above, using expression bodied methods for the class methods and string interpolation for the output in `Main`. Also, use the `using static` statement for `System.Console`.
	``
public static class Volume
{
  static public double Sphere(float radius)   => (4.0/3.0) * Math.PI * Math.Pow(radius, 3);
  static public double Cube(float x)   => Math.Pow(x,3);
  static public double Cone(float r, float h)   => ((float)1/(float)3) * (Math.PI) *r*r*h;
  static public double Cylinder(float r, float h) => Math.PI * r * r * h;
}
```

Ensure to put the following line into the list of using directives:
**using static** System.Console;

Main is shown below.

```
static void Main(string[] args)
{
  double sphereVolume = Volume.Sphere(40000);
  double cubeVolume = Volume.Cube(2.5f);
  double coneVolume = Volume.Cone(50, 50);
  double cylinderVolume = Volume.Cylinder(50, 25);

  WriteLine($"{sphereVolume}\n{cubeVolume}\n{ coneVolume}\n{ cylinderVolume}\n");
  Console.ReadKey();
}
``` |
| 56. | **(6.0)** Rewrite the code for exercises 53 and 54 above, using expression bodied methods for the class methods and string interpolation for the output in `Main`. Use the `using static` statement for `System.Console`. |
|    | ```
using System;
using static System.Console;

public static class Circle
{
  public static double Area(double radius)          => Math.PI * radius * radius;
  public static double Diameter(double radius)      => 2 * radius;
  public static double Circumference(double radius) => 2 * Math.PI * radius;
}

class Program
{
  static void Main(string[] args)
  {
    double r=2;   // The radius
    WriteLine($"the area,circumference,diameter of a circle of radius {r} is
            {Circle.Area(r):0.00}, {Circle.Diameter(r):0.00}, {Circle.Circumference(r):0.00}
            respectively");
    r=12;   // The second radius
    WriteLine($"the area,circumference,diameter of a circle of radius {r} is
            {Circle.Area(r):0.00}, {Circle.Diameter(r):0.00},{ Circle.Circumference(r):0.00}
            respectively");
    Console.ReadKey();
  }
}
``` |
| 57. | Modify the `Circle` class so that it is no longer a static class.
 It should also have the following modifications:
   1. A constructor which saves the passed radius value into a private field of type `double` named `radius`.
   2. It should have a method called `getRadius` which returns the value of `radius`.
   3. It should have a method called `setRadius` which sets the value of `radius`.
   4. Modify the existing methods of the class so that they get the radius from the private field `radius`, rather |

	than that value being passed in the call to the methods of the class.
|    | ```
public class Circle
{
  private double radius;

  public double Area()            {return (Math.PI * radius * radius);}
  public double Diameter()        {return (2 * radius);}
  public double Circumference()   {return (2 * Math.PI * radius);}
  public void   setRadius(double r)  {radius = r; }
  public double getRadius()       {return (radius); }
  public Circle(double r)         {radius = r; }
}
``` |
| 58. | Instantiate an object of the modified class Circle with a radius of 2 and another one with a radius of 4. Print the area, circumference and diameter of these objects to two decimal places. |
|    | ```
using System;

// <put the class definition here>

class Program
{
  static void Main(string[] args)
  {
    Circle circle01 = new Circle(2);
    Circle circle02 = new Circle(4);

    Console.WriteLine("The area,circumference,diameter of a circle of radius {0} is 
            \n{1:0.00}\n{2:0.00}\n{3:0.00} respectively", circle01.getRadius(),
            circle01.Area(), circle01.Diameter(), circle01.Circumference());
    Console.WriteLine("The area,circumference,diameter of a circle of radius {0} is 
            \n{1:0.00}\n{2:0.00}\n{3:0.00} respectively", circle02.getRadius(),
            circle02.Area(), circle02.Diameter(), circle02.Circumference());
    Console.ReadKey();
  }
}
``` |

59.	*Polymorphism* As seen earlier, the class Car is a descendant of the class Vehicle. If we have an object car01 of class Car, explain why is it valid to write the following code: Vehicle v01 = car01;
	The code in question is valid because it is a feature of polymorphism. Polymorphism is a characteristic of object oriented programming. One of the characteristics of polymorphism is that an object of a descendant class can be assigned to a variable that is of the same type as *any* of its ancestor classes.

60.	*Member modifiers* What does each of these member <u>modifier</u> keywords mean? 1. virtual 2. abstract 3. override 4. new 5. sealed 6. static
	1. virtual – a virtual member is one that can be overridden in a descendant class (think of this keyword as saying "you have permission to override this member in descendant classes if you want"). The overriden version of the member is now the one that pertains to the overriding class and its descendant classes. 2. abstract – an abstract member is a member that is unimplemented (for example abstract methods have just a semicolon in the body) and it *must* be overriden in every non-abstract descendant class. 3. override – this is a keyword that is used to override an inherited *virtual, abstract or override* (i.e. you can re-

		override an overriden member down the class hierarchy) member.
	4.	**new** – allows a descendant class to "hide" members that appear in ancestor classes. Another way to explain the function of the modifier **new** is that it facilitates member reuse (for methods we can say that it facilitates method signature reuse) in descendant classes. You see, as far as the ancestor class is concerned, if it didn't label a member as **virtual** it didn't mean for it to be overriden; **new** helps get around that limitation set by the ancestor class. *However*, if we access objects of the descendant class in question with variables of an ancestor class (facilitated by polymorphism, see exercise 59), then the original member of the ancestor class is what is applied to the object of the descendant class. This is different from the handling of virtual members that are overriden by the **override** keyword, in that for overriden members, irrespective of how the object in question is accessed, it is the member which was created with the keyword **override** in the descendant class that will be executed for the object of the descendant class.
	5.	**sealed** – indicates that the member in question cannot be <u>overridden</u> in descendant classes. This keyword can only be applied to an override of an inherited virtual member (implying that both the keywords **sealed** and **override** will appear jointly against the same member). Note though that a sealed member can still be hidden using the keyword **new**.
	6.	**static** – indicates that the member in question belongs to the type itself, and not to the instances. For example `String.Equals(string,string)` exists relative to the class `String` rather than a copy thereof within instances of the class.
	Note: Not all of these modifiers are valid for every potential member type. They are all valid though for methods.	
61.	What is meant when it is said that the keyword **new** applied to a method with the same signature as a method in an ancestor class merely "hides" the method in the ancestor class?	
	The keyword **new** is merely informing the compiler that we are creating a method in the descendant class with the same signature as a method in an ancestor class and that as far as objects of this descendant class and its own descendants are concerned, the version of the method that applies to them is the one that was created with the keyword **new**.	
	However the ancestor class never intended for that method to be overridden otherwise it would have marked the method as **virtual**. The implication of this overriding by using the keyword **new** is that when objects of a descendant class that has hidden ancestor class methods using the keyword **new** are accessed by variables declared as being of the ancestor class (this through the instrumentality of polymorphism, see exercise 59), C# will actually use the version of the method that applies to the ancestor class, not the method created with the keyword **new** in the descendant class. On the other hand, for a virtual method under the same access scenario of an object being accessed by a variable of an ancestor class, C# will ensure that it checks to see if the method has been overridden for the descendant class; it is this overridden version of the method that it will run.	
	The phenomena described herein will be observed in later exercises.	
62.	Given the explanation above, why would you want to use the keyword **new** since it is clear that it doesn't absolutely override the method in a parent class?	
	A reason for why you would use **new** is simply because the method in the parent class was not defined as a **virtual** method when the parent class was designed and you indeed need to use that method signature for functionality that is more appropriate for the descendant class and for various reasons it is not feasible to change the method in the ancestor class to have the modifier **virtual**.	

Abstract classes	
63.	What is an abstract class?
	An abstract class is one of the following:
	A class where some of the expected implementation thereof (methods and such like) are not implemented and thus the class itself and these incomplete components have been explicitly denoted as being **abstract**. Such abstract components are merely placeholders and it is intended that they be completed in a derived class. OR A class which it is desired that it itself not be instantiated at all but that only classes derived from it be instantiable (note that all of the components of the class may be completely implemented however we choose to denote the class as being **abstract**).

	Once *any* component of a class is denoted as **abstract**, then the class itself must be marked **abstract**.
64.	What is the procedure for instantiating an object of an abstract class?
	An abstract class *cannot* be instantiated directly. Only a non-abstract descendant class (which by definition will not have any abstract components) of the abstract class can be instantiated.
65.	Why are abstract classes useful?
	An abstract class is a class which demands that a certain mandatory set of components be defined in its child classes before the child class is usable. By doing this, the abstract class forces a certain minimum implementation for its derived classes. For example, if we have a class named **Shape** and want to derive classes from it representing the shapes square, circle, triangle, pentagon and hexagon and want to ensure that the programmer provided methods for computing the perimeter and area of the derived sub-classes, the act of defining abstract methods in the class **Shape** for computing the perimeter and area compels any non-abstract class that derives from **Shape** to implement the methods that compute perimeter and area.
66.	Write a line of code that defines an abstract method named **square** that takes a **float** for input and returns a **float**.
	`public abstract float square(float x);`
	Note that an abstract method does not have a body like other methods, rather a semi-colon is all that is written after the method declaration.
67.	Define a **public abstract** class named **Shape**. We are going to use it as a parent class for sub-classes that represent equilateral polygons. Ensure that the class has the following features: 1. A **protected** field named **length** of type **double** to store the length/radius of shapes. 2. A **public** method named **GetSideLength** that can return the value of the stored **length** field. 3. A constructor that simply stores a length/radius into the field **length**. 4. A **public** abstract method named **Area** that supports the computation of area. 5. A **public** abstract method named **Perimeter** that supports the computation of the perimeter/circumference.
| | ```
public abstract class Shape
{
   protected double length;
   public abstract double Area();
   public abstract double Perimeter();
   public double GetSideLength(){return(length);}

   public Shape(double length)
   { // constructor
      this.length = length;
   }
}
``` |
| 68. | Define the following non-abstract child classes of the previously created class **Shape** (the formulas for the area and perimeter of each is given for your convenience):
1. **Circle**: (Area = πr^2; Perimeter = $2\pi r$)
2. **Triangle**: (Area of equilateral triangle = $\sqrt{3}/4 *$ length^2; Perimeter = length * 3)
3. **Square**: (Area = length^2; Perimeter = length * 4)
4. **Pentagon**: (Area = 1.720477401* length^2; Perimeter = length * 5)
5. **Hexagon**: (Area = 2.598076211* length^2; Perimeter = length * 6)

The constructors of the respective classes should simply invoke the constructor of their parent class.
*Hint: Use the keyword **override** to override the **Area** and **Perimeter** methods of the parent class.* |
```

	``csharp
public class Circle : Shape
{
  public override double Area()
  {
    return (Math.PI *
        Math.Pow(length, 2));
  }
  public override double Perimeter()
  {
    return(this.Circumference());
  }
  public double Circumference()
  {
    return (2 * Math.PI * length);
  }
  public Circle(double x): base(x){}
}

public class Pentagon : Shape
{
  public override double Area()
  {
     return(1.720477401 *
Math.Pow(length,2));
  }
  public override double Perimeter()
  {
    return (length * 5);
  }
  public Pentagon(double x) : base(x){}
}
``` ```csharp
public class Triangle : Shape
{
  public override double Area()
  {
    return((Math.Sqrt(3)/(float)4) * length*length);
  }
  public override double Perimeter()
  {
      return (length * 3);
  }
  public Triangle(double x): base(x){}
}

public class Square : Shape
{
  public override double Area()
  {
    return (length * length);
  }
  public override double Perimeter()
  {
      return (length * 4);
  }
  public Square(double x): base(x){}
}

public class Hexagon : Shape
{
  public override double Area()
  {
    return(2.598076211 * Math.Pow(length, 2));
  }
  public override double Perimeter()
  {
    return (length * 6);
  }
  public Hexagon(double x) : base(x){}
}
``` |
| 69. | **(6.0)** Where appropriate, rewrite the methods in the classes defined in the preceding exercise using expression bodied methods. |
|    | ```csharp
public class Circle : Shape
{
  public override double Area()         => Math.PI * Math.Pow(length, 2);
  public override double Perimeter()    => this.Circumference();
  public double Circumference()         => 2 * Math.PI * length;
  public Circle(double x): base(x){}
}
public class Triangle : Shape
{
  public override double Area()         => (Math.Sqrt(3)/(float)4) * length*length;
  public override double Perimeter()    => length * 3;
  public Triangle(double x): base(x){}
}
public class Square : Shape
{
  public override double Area()         => length * length;
  public override double Perimeter()    => length * 4;
  public Square(double x): base(x){}
}
public class Pentagon : Shape
``` |
```

| | ```
{
  public override double Area()      => 1.720477401 * Math.Pow(length,2);
  public override double Perimeter() => length * 5;
  public Pentagon(double x) : base(x){}
}
public class Hexagon : Shape
{
  public override double Area()      => 2.598076211 * Math.Pow(length, 2);
  public override double Perimeter() => length * 6;
  public Hexagon(double x) : base(x){}
}
``` |
| 70. | Instantiate an object of each of class Circle, Triangle, Square, Pentagon, Hexagon, each with a side length/radius of 6.2.
Put each of them into a List<Shape> object named shapeList. |
| | ```
using System;
using System.Collections.Generic; // for the List<T> class

namespace PracticeYourCSharp
{
  class Program
  {
    static void Main(string[] args)
    {
      Circle circle01   = new Circle(6.2);
      Triangle triangle01 = new Triangle(6.2);
      Square square01   = new Square(6.2);
      Pentagon pentagon01 = new Pentagon(6.2);
      Hexagon hexagon01   = new Hexagon(6.2);

      List<Shape> shapeList = new List<Shape>();
      shapeList.Add(circle01);   shapeList.Add(triangle01); shapeList.Add(square01);
      shapeList.Add(pentagon01); shapeList.Add(hexagon01);
      Console.ReadKey();
    }
  }
}
```
**Note:** The usage of List<Shape> in this exercise is to show you that you can put an object of a derived class into a collection which has the same type as its ancestor class, without the need to cast the object that you are putting in. |
| 71. | Extending the answer above, using a foreach loop go through the list created and print out the following data about each item in the list:<br>1. The class of the item (Use instance method <object>.GetType())<br>2. Its area *(to two decimal places)*<br>3. Its perimeter *(to two decimal places)* |
| | *Add the following code to* Main:<br><br>```
foreach (Shape z in shapeList)
{
  Console.WriteLine();
  Console.WriteLine("Object class  = {0:0.00}", z.GetType().Name);
  Console.WriteLine("Its area      = {0:0.00}", z.Area());
  Console.WriteLine("Its perimeter = {0:0.00}", z.Perimeter());
}
```<br><br>In C# 6.0 this solution can be written as follows:<br>(Ensure that you have **using static System.Console;** as part of your *using* declarations):<br><br>```
foreach (Shape z in shapeList)
{
  WriteLine();
  WriteLine($"Object class  = {z.GetType().Name:0.00}");
``` |

```
        WriteLine($"Its area      = {z.Area():0.00}");
        WriteLine($"Its perimeter = {z.Perimeter():0.00}");
    }
```

Note: The output shows that the overridden abstract methods of each of the objects are what are being invoked, even though they are in a List<T> of an ancestor class (The class Shape in this example).

This is an example of polymorphism in action.

There are more exercises pertaining to polymorphism later in this chapter.

	Sealing classes and methods
72.	Seal the earlier defined Hexagon class.
	Change the 1st line of the class definition from:
	`public class Hexagon : Shape`
	to
	`public sealed class Hexagon : Shape`
	Note: For practice, you can attempt to derive a class from this sealed class to observe the reaction of the compiler.
73.	What is the result of attempting to compile the following code and why?
	```\nusing System;\n\nnamespace PracticeYourCSharp\n{\n public sealed class A\n {\n public virtual void Hello()\n {\n Console.WriteLine("1");\n }\n }\n public class B:A\n {\n public override void Hello()\n {\n Console.WriteLine("2");\n }\n }\n\n class Program\n {\n static void Main(string[] args)\n {\n\n }\n }\n}\n```
	It will *not* compile because it is not possible to derive from a sealed class as was attempted with class B.
74.	What is the result of attempting to compile the code below and why?
	```\nusing System;\n\nnamespace PracticeYourCSharp\n{\n public class A\n {\n public virtual void Hello()\n {\n Console.WriteLine("1");\n }\n }\n```

|  | ```csharp
      public class B:A
      {
        public sealed override void Hello()
        {
          Console.WriteLine("2");
        }
      }
      public class C : B
      {
        public override void Hello()
        {
          Console.WriteLine("3");
        }
      }

      class Program
      {
        static void Main(string[] args)
        {

        }
      }
    }
``` |
| | The code will *not* compile, because the method `Hello` has been sealed in class `B` and therefore it can no longer be overridden in any further descendant class as was attempted in class `C`. |
| 75. | What is the result of attempting to compile the code below and why?<br><br>```csharp
using System;
namespace PracticeYourCSharp
{
  public class A
  {
    public  virtual void Hello()
    {
      Console.WriteLine("Class A");
    }
  }
  public class B:A
  {
    public sealed override void Hello()
    {
      Console.WriteLine("Class B");
    }
  }
  public class C : B
  {
    public new void Hello()
    {
      Console.WriteLine("Class C");
    }
  }

  class Program
  {
    static void Main(string[] args)
    {

    }
  }
}
``` |
| | The code *will* compile. It is legal to hide a sealed method using the keyword **new**. |

Understanding virtual methods vs non-virtual methods

There are a significant number of exercises presented on this important sub-topic; these exercises focus heavily on the usage of the keywords new, virtual and override as well as other related topics.

Method hiding using the keyword new

76. Predict and explain the output of the program shown below.

```
using System;

namespace PracticeYourCSharp
{
  class A
  {
    public void MyName() { Console.WriteLine("My Name is class A."); }
  }
  class B:A
  {
    public new void MyName() { Console.WriteLine("My Name is class B."); }
  }

  class Program
  {
    static void Main(string[] args)
    {
      B object01 = new B();
      object01.MyName();
      Console.ReadKey();
    }
  }
}
```

Output: My Name is class B.
Explanation: The method MyName in class B <u>hides</u> the inherited method MyName in class A, by virtue of having used the keyword new for MyName in class B.

77. Identify the differences between the program below and the one in the preceding exercise. Predict the output of this program and explain why it is so. Also note and explain the compilation issues that arise when compiling the program.

```
using System;

namespace PracticeYourCSharp
{
  class A
  {
    public void MyName() { Console.WriteLine("My Name is class A."); }
  }
  class B:A
  {
    public void MyName() { Console.WriteLine("My Name is class B."); }
  }

  class Program
  {
    static void Main(string[] args)
    {
      B object01 = new B();
      object01.MyName();
      Console.ReadKey();
    }
  }
}
```

Difference(s): The difference between both programs is that in the program in this question the keyword new is not used in the declaration of method MyName of class B, a method which has the same signature as a method in

	the parent class. **Output:** `My Name is class B.` **Explanation:** The method `MyName` in class `B` hides the inherited method `MyName` of class `A`, exactly the same way as when the keyword `new` in the preceding exercise was used! **Compilation Issues:** The program compiles and runs, however the compiler issues <u>warning</u> `CS0108` which states: `'PracticeYourCSharp.B.MyName()' hides inherited member 'PracticeYourCSharp.A.MyName()'. Use the new keyword if hiding was intended.`
78.	Explain the compiler warning noted for the program in the preceding exercise and its implications for the program.
	The compiler is advising that when it is intended that an inherited method be hidden, the developer should use the keyword `new`. Nonetheless, even if the keyword `new` is not present, it is *not* considered to be an error and **the compiler will act as if you did use the keyword new**.
| 79. | **(Very Important)**<br>Determine the output of this program and explain why it is so.<br><br>```csharp
using System;

namespace PracticeYourCSharp
{
  class A
  {
    public void MyName() { Console.WriteLine("My Name is class A."); }
  }
  class B:A
  {
    public new void MyName() { Console.WriteLine("My Name is class B."); }
  }
  class Program
  {
    static void Main(string[] args)
    {
      A object01 = new B(); // We are using a variable of type class A
                            // to access an object of type class B
      object01.MyName();
      Console.ReadKey();
    }
  }
}
``` |
| | **Output:** `My Name is class A.`

Explanation: It is very important to note that we did create an object of class `B`, but assigned it to a variable of an ancestor class, class `A` (this assignment is possible by virtue of polymorphism).

We observe in the output that the version of method `MyName` that was run was from class `A`, not from class `B`. The reason for this output is that the original method `MyName` in the parent class was <u>not</u> defined to be a virtual method. What happened is that C# looked at the variable `object01`, looked at its class (class `A`) and then looked at which of its methods were defined as `virtual` or not. If the method was defined as `virtual`, C# knows that there is a chance that it might have been overridden and so it would then identify the actual type of the object that is being accessed by a variable of class `A` and identify if indeed the method was overridden for that descendant class; if so it will apply the overridden method to the object. However, if the method is not defined to be `virtual`, it can be said in a sense that it is not expected to be overridden, so C# just uses the method as defined in the class whose variable is under consideration (class `A` in this case).

Summary
1. For non-virtual methods, C# looks at the class of the **variable** <u>under consideration</u> and then uses the non-virtual methods from that class.
2. For virtual methods, C# looks at the class of the **object** <u>under consideration</u> and runs the overridden method (if any) that pertains to the class of the object. |
| 80. | Determine the output of this program and explain why it is so. |
```

```
using System;
namespace PracticeYourCSharp
{
  class A
  {
    public void MyName() { Console.WriteLine("My Name is class A."); }
  }
  class B : A
  {
    public new void MyName() { Console.WriteLine("My Name is class B."); }
  }
  class Program
  {
    static void Main(string[] args)
    {
      A object01 = new B();
      ((B)object01).MyName(); //note the cast
      Console.ReadKey();
    }
  }
}
```

Output: My Name is class B.

Explanation: We have cast the variable `object01` to the type class B, so as far as C# is concerned, in this program line it is accessing a variable of class B and thus will access the methods of class B.

Method overriding using the keywords virtual and override

81. Predict the output of this program and explain why it is so.

```
using System;
namespace PracticeYourCSharp
{
  class A
  {
    public virtual void MyName() { Console.WriteLine("My Name is class A."); }
  }
  class B:A
  {
    public override void MyName() { Console.WriteLine("My Name is class B."); }
  }
  class Program
  {
    static void Main(string[] args)
    {
      B object01 = new B();
      object01.MyName();
      Console.ReadKey();
    }
  }
}
```

Output: My Name is class B.

Explanation: The method `MyName` in class B <u>overrides</u> the inherited **virtual** method `MyName` in class A, by using the keyword **override** for `MyName` in class B.

Do observe the results of the next exercise carefully.

82. Predict the output of this program and explain why it is so.

```
using System;
namespace PracticeYourCSharp
{
```

```csharp
class A
{
  public virtual void MyName() { Console.WriteLine("My Name is class A."); }
}
class B:A
{
  public override void MyName() { Console.WriteLine("My Name is class B."); }
}

class Program
{
  static void Main(string[] args)
  {
    A object01 = new B(); // We are using a variable of type class A
                          // to access an object of type class B
    object01.MyName();
    Console.ReadKey();
  }
}
}
```

Output: `My Name is class B.`
(Contrast this with the results from exercise 79).

Explanation: As previously explained, whenever a method designated as a virtual method is invoked for an object reference variable (`object01` is the variable in this case), the compiler looks at the type of the actual object being referred to (which is an object of class B) and looks for <u>the last overridden version of the method in the inheritance hierarchy of the class in question</u>, up to that determined object class (B in this case) and applies it to the object at hand.

What is meant by the phrase "the last overridden version of the method in the inheritance hierarchy of the class in question" can be explained by the following example: We have the classes W, X, Y and Z in descending order of inheritance. Class X and then class Y override a virtual method that first appeared in W. The version of the method that pertains to Z is the last overridden one, that is, the one in its ancestor Y.

83. Run the program below and explain its output.

```csharp
using System;

namespace PracticeYourCSharp
{
  class A
  {
    public virtual void MyName() { Console.WriteLine("vMethod:My name is class A."); }
    public void ClassNumber()  { Console.WriteLine("1"); } //non-virtual method
  }
  class B : A
  {
    public override void MyName()   { Console.WriteLine("vMethod:My name is class B...
                                    I am overriding the method in A"); }
    public new void ClassNumber() { Console.WriteLine("2"); }
  }
  class C : B
  {
    public new void MyName()   { Console.WriteLine("vMethod:My name is class C...
                                    I am hiding the method in B"); }
    public new void ClassNumber() { Console.WriteLine("3"); }
  }
  class Program
  {
    static void Main(string[] args)
    {
      A obj01 = new C();

      obj01.MyName();
      obj01.ClassNumber();
```

|  | ``` 
      Console.ReadKey();
    }
  }
}
``` |
| | **Output**
vMethod:My name is class B...I am overriding the method in A
1

Explanation
We note that we accessed an object of class **C** with a variable of one of its ancestor classes, **A**, <u>which is not its immediate ancestor class</u>.

The reason for the 1st line of output is as follows: The virtual method **MyName** was overridden in class **B**, but merely hidden in class **C** via use of the keyword **new**. As previously stated, whenever a virtual method is invoked (it is defined as **virtual** in class **A**, which is the class of the variable being used to access the object), the compiler looks at the actual type of the object in hand (which is an object of class **C**) and looks for the last overridden (*overridden*, not hidden by **new**) version in the inheritance hierarchy of the method in question (the last ancestor to override that method was its ancestor class **B**) and applies it to the object at hand.

The reason for the 2nd line of output is as follows: we accessed a non-virtual method. As noted earlier, when a non-virtual method is accessed, C# only looks at the type of the variable in question (therefore it looks at the fact that the variable **obj01** is of type class **A**) to determine which method is the appropriate method; this is method **ClassNumber** of class **A**. |
| 84. | Modify **Main** from the preceding exercise as shown below and predict and explain its output.<br><br>```
static void Main(string[] args)
{
  B obj01 = new C();

  obj01.MyName();
  obj01.ClassNumber();
  Console.ReadKey();
}
``` |
| | **Output**
vMethod:My name is class B...I am overriding the method in A
2

Explanation
We note that we accessed an object of class **C** with a variable of one of its ancestor classes, **B**, in this case.
The reason for the 1st line of output is the same as the reason for the output of the first line in the solution to the preceding exercise.

The reason for the 2nd line of output is as follows: we accessed a non-virtual method. As noted earlier, when a non-virtual method is accessed, C# only looks at the type of the variable with which the method is being accessed (so it looks at the fact that **obj01** is of type class **B**) to determine which is the appropriate method; this corresponded to method **ClassNumber** in class **B**. |
| 85. | What is the output of this program? Explain why.<br><br>```
using System;

namespace PracticeYourCSharp
{
  class A
  {
    public virtual void MyName() { Console.WriteLine("My Name is class A."); }
  }
  class B : A
  {
    public void MyName() { Console.WriteLine("My Name is class B."); }
    //Note, that we didn't use the keyword override
  }
  class Program
``` |
```

|   | ```
    {
      static void Main(string[] args)
      {
        A object01 = new B(); // We are using a variable of type class A to
                              // access an object of type class B
        object01.MyName();
        Console.ReadKey();
      }
    }
}
``` |   |
| | **Output:** My Name is class A.

Explanation: While indeed method `MyName` in class `A` is a `virtual` method (meaning it is "overridable"), we however didn't actually override it in class `B`, we merely hid it; recall that the compiler presumes we mean to hide the method even when we don't explicitly use the keyword `new`). Therefore, the explanation to exercise 79 applies.

It can be seen from this exercise that if you do not explicitly override even a method that has been defined as `virtual`, when you reuse the name of the method in a descendant class, the method is considered to be hidden. | |
| 86. | Create a class named `Road` that represents roads.<br>Create for it the following methods:<br>1. A `virtual` `public` method of return type `void` named `TollPayRequest` which outputs the line *"That will be 1 token please!"*<br>2. A `public` method named `PrintRoadType` of return type `void` that *prints "I am a Road!"*<br>3. A `public` method named `WhichClass` with a return type of `void` that prints out what type of class this is by using the `GetType()` method. | ```
public class Road
{
  public virtual void TollPayRequest()
  {
    Console.WriteLine("That will be 1 token please!");
  }
  public void PrintRoadType()
  {
    Console.WriteLine("I am a Road!");
  }
  public void WhichClass()
  {
    Console.WriteLine("My class using GetType = {0} ",
                            this.GetType().Name);
  }
}
``` |
| 87. | Extending the answer above, create a new child class `TollRoad` of the class `Road`.<br>Override the `TollPayRequest()` method to output *"That will be 3 tokens please!"*<br>Hide the inherited `PrintRoadType()` method (using the keyword `new`) and have the new version print *"I am a TollRoad!"* | ```
public class TollRoad : Road
{
  public override void TollPayRequest()
  {
    Console.WriteLine("That will be 3 tokens please!");
  }
  new public void PrintRoadType()
  {
    Console.WriteLine("I am a TollRoad!");
  }
}
``` |
| 88. | Create another child class of the class `Road` named `Highway`.<br>Override the `TollPayRequest()` method to output *"That will be 5 tokens please!"*<br>Hide the inherited `PrintRoadType()` method and | ```
public class Highway : Road
{
  public override void TollPayRequest()
  {
     Console.WriteLine("That will be 5 tokens please!");
  }
  new public void PrintRoadType()
``` |

| | have the new version print *"I am a Highway!"* | ```
{
    Console.WriteLine("I am a Highway!");
}
}
``` |
| 89. | Create a child class of the class Highway and name the child class SuperHighway.<br>Override the TollPayRequest() method to output *That will be 10 tokens please!*<br>Hide the PrintRoadType() method and have the new version print *I am a Super Highway!* | ```
public class SuperHighway : Highway
{
    public override void TollPayRequest()
    {
        Console.WriteLine("That will be 10 tokens please!");
    }
    new public void PrintRoadType()
    {
        Console.WriteLine("I am a Super Highway!");
    }
}
``` |
| 90. | Write a program to instantiate the following objects: road1, road2 and road3 and road4 of classes Road, TollRoad, Highway and SuperHighway respectively and then for each object invoke the methods WhichClass, PrintRoadType and TollPayRequest.
Study the output, noting especially how the virtual method in the parent class(es) have been overriden. | |
| | *The partial program is shown below.*<br>```
using System;
using System.Collections;
using System.Collections.Generic;

namespace PracticeYourCSharp
{
    <The classes Road etc. go here>

    class Program
    {
        static void Main(string[] args)
        {
            Road road1 = new Road();
            TollRoad road2 = new TollRoad();
            Highway road3 = new Highway();
            SuperHighway road4 = new SuperHighway();

            road1.WhichClass(); road1.PrintRoadType(); road1.TollPayRequest(); Console.WriteLine("");
            road2.WhichClass(); road2.PrintRoadType(); road2.TollPayRequest(); Console.WriteLine("");
            road3.WhichClass(); road3.PrintRoadType(); road3.TollPayRequest(); Console.WriteLine("");
            road4.WhichClass(); road4.PrintRoadType(); road4.TollPayRequest();
            Console.ReadKey();
        }
    }
}
```<br>**Output**<br>```
My class using GetType = Road
I am a Road!
That will be 1 token please!

My class using GetType = TollRoad
I am a TollRoad!
That will be 3 tokens please!

My class using GetType = Highway
I am a Highway!
That will be 5 tokens please!

My class using GetType = SuperHighway
I am a Super Highway!
``` | |

	That will be 10 tokens please!

This shows clearly how the virtual method `TollPayRequest` in the parent class is overridden in each of the child classes. And even for the class two levels down, `SuperHighway`, we see that it has also overridden the method that was originally declared `virtual` at its highest ancestor class. |
| 91. | Predict what the output of the code below is.
Note and explain the difference in output between this program and the ouput from the preceding exercise.

```
using System;
using System.Collections;
using System.Collections.Generic;

namespace PracticeYourCSharp
{
  <The classes Road etc. go here>

  class Program
  {
    static void Main(string[] args)
    {
      Road road1          = new Road();
      TollRoad road2      = new TollRoad();
      Highway road3       = new Highway();
      SuperHighway road4  = new SuperHighway();

      List<Road> roadListA = new List<Road>();
      // Now add each of the objects to the list.
      roadListA.Add(road1); roadListA.Add(road2);
      roadListA.Add(road3); roadListA.Add(road4);

      foreach (Road x in roadListA)
      {
        x.TollPayRequest();
        x.PrintRoadType();
        x.WhichClass();
        Console.WriteLine("");
      }
    }
  }
}
``` |
| | **Output**
```
That will be 1 token please!
I am a Road!
My class using GetType = Road

That will be 3 tokens please!
I am a Road!
My class using GetType = TollRoad

That will be 5 tokens please!
I am a Road!
My class using GetType = Highway

That will be 10 tokens please!
I am a Road!
My class using GetType = SuperHighway
```

Differences
Each one of them is printing out the statement **I am a Road!** That is, each object is running the method `PrintRoadType()` from the class `Road` instead of the method `PrintRoadType()` for their own class.

(Note that this exercise is similar to exercises 83 and 84.)

Explanation |

	This is the result of how non-virtual methods are handled as discussed in exercises 61, 79, *83 and 84*.
92.	Modify the answer to exercise 91 above to, still using a `List<Road>`, first determine what object is in hand by using the method `<object>.GetType.Name` and on determining the object type, run the actual methods that pertain to the class of the object at hand by casting each object to its correct class in the `foreach` loop.
|     | ```
class Program
{
  static void Main(string[] args)
  {
    Road road1          = new Road();
    TollRoad road2      = new TollRoad();
    Highway road3       = new Highway();
    SuperHighway road4 = new SuperHighway();

    List<Road> roadListA = new List<Road>();
    // Now add each of the objects to the list.
    roadListA.Add(road1); roadListA.Add(road2);
    roadListA.Add(road3); roadListA.Add(road4);

    foreach (object item in roadListA)
    {
      string className = item.GetType().Name;
      switch (className)
      {
        case "Road":
          ((Road)item).WhichClass(); ((Road)item).PrintRoadType();
          ((Road)item).TollPayRequest(); Console.WriteLine("");
          break;
        case "TollRoad":
          ((TollRoad)item).WhichClass(); ((TollRoad)item).PrintRoadType();
          ((TollRoad)item).TollPayRequest(); Console.WriteLine("");
          break;
        case "Highway":
          ((Highway)item).WhichClass(); ((Highway)item).PrintRoadType();
          ((Highway)item).TollPayRequest(); Console.WriteLine("");
          break;
        case "SuperHighway":
          ((SuperHighway)item).WhichClass(); ((SuperHighway)item).PrintRoadType();
          ((SuperHighway)item).TollPayRequest(); Console.WriteLine("");
          break;
      }
    }
    Console.ReadKey();
  }
}
``` |
	Note: Instead of using a `List<Road>` feel free to use a `List<object>`
93.	*(For practice with the `ArrayList` class)*
	Modify the answer to the immediately preceding exercise to use an `ArrayList` object instead of a `List<T>`.
|     | ```
class Program
{
  static void Main(string[] args)
  {
    Road road1          = new Road();
    TollRoad road2      = new TollRoad();
    Highway road3       = new Highway();
    SuperHighway road4 = new SuperHighway();

    ArrayList arrayListA = new ArrayList();
    arrayListA.Add(road1); arrayListA.Add(road2);
    arrayListA.Add(road3); arrayListA.Add(road4);

    for (int i = 0; i < arrayListA.Count; i++)
    {
``` |

```
                  string className = arrayListA[i].GetType().Name;
                switch (className)
                {
                  case "Road":
                    ((Road)arrayListA[i]).WhichClass();
                    ((Road)arrayListA[i]).PrintRoadType();
                    ((Road)arrayListA[i]).TollPayRequest();
                    Console.WriteLine("");
                    break;
                  case "TollRoad":
                    ((TollRoad)arrayListA[i]).WhichClass();
                    ((TollRoad)arrayListA[i]).PrintRoadType();
                    ((TollRoad)arrayListA[i]).TollPayRequest();
                    Console.WriteLine("");
                    break;
                  case "Highway":
                    ((Highway)arrayListA[i]).WhichClass();
                    ((Highway)arrayListA[i]).PrintRoadType();
                    ((Highway)arrayListA[i]).TollPayRequest();
                    Console.WriteLine("");
                    break;
                  case "SuperHighway":
                    ((SuperHighway)arrayListA[i]).WhichClass();
                    ((SuperHighway)arrayListA[i]).PrintRoadType();
                    ((SuperHighway)arrayListA[i]).TollPayRequest();
                    Console.WriteLine("");
                    break;
                }
              }
              Console.ReadKey();
          }
        }
```

Notes: The correct results are observed; each object type is properly identified using `GetType.Name()`.

---

94. Reimplement the above solution using the **is** operator rather than `GetType.Name()` to test for the class. Write three solutions, as follows:
- one using `List<Road>`
- one using `List<object>`
- one using an `ArrayList`

Solution using a List<Road>
```
using System;
using System.Collections;
using System.Collections.Generic;

static void Main(string[] args)
{
  Road road1         = new Road();
  TollRoad road2     = new TollRoad();
  Highway road3      = new Highway();
  SuperHighway road4 = new SuperHighway();

  List<Road> roadListA = new List<Road>();
  roadListA.Add(road1); roadListA.Add(road2);
  roadListA.Add(road3); roadListA.Add(road4);

  for (int i = 0; i < roadListA.Count; i++)
  {
   if (roadListA[i] is TollRoad)
   {
     ((TollRoad)roadListA[i]).WhichClass();
     ((TollRoad)roadListA[i]).PrintRoadType();
     ((TollRoad)roadListA[i]).TollPayRequest();
```

Solution using an ArrayList
```
using System;
using System.Collections;
using System.Collections.Generic;

static void Main(string[] args)
{
  Road road1         = new Road();
  TollRoad road2     = new TollRoad();
  Highway road3      = new Highway();
  SuperHighway road4 = new SuperHighway();

  ArrayList arrayListA = new ArrayList();
  arrayListA.Add(road1); arrayListA.Add(road2);
  arrayListA.Add(road3); arrayListA.Add(road4);

  for (int i = 0; i < arrayListA.Count; i++)
  {
   if (arrayListA[i] is TollRoad)
   {
     ((TollRoad)arrayListA[i]).WhichClass();
     ((TollRoad)arrayListA[i]).PrintRoadType();
     ((TollRoad)arrayListA[i]).TollPayRequest();
```

```
          Console.WriteLine("");                          Console.WriteLine("");
      }                                              }
      else if (roadListA[i] is SuperHighway)         else if (arrayListA[i] is SuperHighway)
      {                                              {
       ((SuperHighway)roadListA[i]).WhichClass();      ((SuperHighway)arrayListA[i]).WhichClass();
       ((SuperHighway)roadListA[i]).PrintRoadType();   ((SuperHighway)arrayListA[i]).PrintRoadType();
       ((SuperHighway)roadListA[i]).TollPayRequest(); ((SuperHighway)arrayListA[i]).TollPayRequest();
       Console.WriteLine("");                         Console.WriteLine("");
      }                                              }
      else if (roadListA[i] is Highway)              else if (arrayListA[i] is Highway)
      {                                              {
       ((Highway)roadListA[i]).WhichClass();           ((Highway)arrayListA[i]).WhichClass();
       ((Highway)roadListA[i]).PrintRoadType();        ((Highway)arrayListA[i]).PrintRoadType();
       ((Highway)roadListA[i]).TollPayRequest();       ((Highway)arrayListA[i]).TollPayRequest();
       Console.WriteLine("");                          Console.WriteLine("");
      }                                              }
      else if (roadListA[i] is Road)                 else if(arrayListA[i] is Road)
      {                                              {
       ((Road)roadListA[i]).WhichClass();              ((Road)arrayListA[i]).WhichClass();
       ((Road)roadListA[i]).PrintRoadType();           ((Road)arrayListA[i]).PrintRoadType();
       ((Road)roadListA[i]).TollPayRequest();          ((Road)arrayListA[i]).TollPayRequest();
       Console.WriteLine("");                          Console.WriteLine("");
      }                                              }
    }                                              }
    Console.ReadKey();                             Console.ReadKey();
}                                              }
```

Solution using a List<object>
Same code as for List<Road>, except change this line:
```
List<Road> roadListA = new List<Road>();
```
to
```
List<object> roadListA = new List<object>();
```

95. Using either an ArrayList or a List<object>, rewrite the solution to the preceding exercise using the **as** operator to determine the appropriate class.

```
static void Main(string[] args)
{
  Road road1          = new Road();
  TollRoad road2      = new TollRoad();
  Highway road3       = new Highway();
  SuperHighway road4 = new SuperHighway();

  ArrayList arrayListA = new ArrayList();
  arrayListA.Add(road1); arrayListA.Add(road2);
  arrayListA.Add(road3); arrayListA.Add(road4);

  for (int i = 0; i < arrayListA.Count; i++)
  {
    Road objAsRoad                   = arrayListA[i] as Road;
    TollRoad objAsTollRoad           = arrayListA[i] as TollRoad;
    Highway objAsHighway             = arrayListA[i] as Highway;
    SuperHighway objAsSuperHighway = arrayListA[i] as SuperHighway;

    if (objAsTollRoad != null)
    {
      objAsTollRoad.WhichClass(); objAsTollRoad.PrintRoadType();
      objAsTollRoad.TollPayRequest();
      Console.WriteLine("");
    }
    else if (objAsSuperHighway != null)
    {
      objAsSuperHighway.WhichClass(); objAsSuperHighway.PrintRoadType();
      objAsSuperHighway.TollPayRequest();Console.WriteLine("");
```

	``
      }
      else if (objAsHighway != null)
      {
        objAsHighway.WhichClass(); objAsHighway.PrintRoadType();
        objAsHighway.TollPayRequest(); Console.WriteLine("");
      }
      else if (objAsRoad != null)
      {
        objAsRoad.WhichClass(); objAsRoad.PrintRoadType();
        objAsRoad.TollPayRequest(); Console.WriteLine("");
      }
    }
    Console.ReadKey();
}
```
This exercise will be revisited after we look at the topic of <u>dynamic resolution</u>. |
| 96. | Describe the concept of **dynamic resolution**. |
| | Dynamic resolution is a feature whereby at runtime and <u>not at compile time</u>, the type of the dynamic variable in question is determined, based on the object/value being assigned to it. Again note that this determination is done at run-time, not at compile-time. |
| | This feature is useful when you do not know exactly at compile-time what precise type you will be dealing with at run-time. For example, if I have a `List<object>` of objects being passed to me and I know that all of them support a given method (say `ToString()`), I can do the following with a dynamic variable: |
| | ```
List<object> listA = new List<object>();
foreach (dynamic item in listA)
{
   item.ToString();
}
``` |
	The type of the variable `item` <u>will change dynamically</u> for each object in the `List<T>` to match the type of the object being accessed.
	This kind of code cannot be written with a `var` variable; it will not be able to compile. If we had to use a `var` variable, then we would have to *1)* know in advance the different object types for represented in the `List` and then *2)* cast the statements like `item.ToString()` in the above example to `(objectType)item.ToString;` this casting would need to be hardcoded for each distinct item type in the `List` (as seen earlier exercises).
97.	When using a variable of type `var`, at what point is the actual type of the variable determined?
	At *compile* time.
98.	When using a variable of type `dynamic` at what point is the actual type of the variable determined?
	At *run-time*. Therefore, when the compiler sees a `dynamic` variable, it doesn't determine the type of what is being returned to the dynamic variable; it leaves it to be determined at run-time.
99.	Rewrite the solution to exercise 95 using dynamic run-time resolution to achieve the same result. Use either of an `ArrayList` or `List<object>`.
	ArrayList solution ```
static void Main(string[] args)
{
   //ArrayList variant
   Road road1 = new Road();
   TollRoad road2 = new TollRoad();
   Highway road3 = new Highway();
   SuperHighway road4 = new SuperHighway();

   ArrayList ListA = new ArrayList();
   ListA.Add(road1);
   ListA.Add(road2);
   ListA.Add(road3);
   ListA.Add(road4);

   for (int i = 0;i < ListA.Count;i++)
   {
```  OR **List<Road> solution**<br>For the `List<Road>` variant of the code modify the appropriate lines to the following:<br>```
List<Road> roadListA
            = new List<Road>();
// Now add each of the objects to the list.
roadListA.Add(road1); roadListA.Add(road2);
roadListA.Add(road3); roadListA.Add(road4);

foreach (dynamic x in roadListA)
{
   x.TollPayRequest();
   x.PrintRoadType();
   x.WhichClass();
   Console.WriteLine();
``` |

```csharp
            dynamic x = ListA[i];
            x.WhichClass();
            x.PrintRoadType();
            x.TollPayRequest();
            Console.WriteLine("");
        }
        Console.ReadKey();
    }
```

Notes: It can be seen that dynamic runtime resolution through the usage of the variable type **dynamic** has yielded a solution which is greatly reduced in size from the use of non-dynamic resolution. It should be understood that the type assigned to the dynamic variable at <u>each</u> iteration in the loop is the actual type/class of the object in the list/array and therefore the methods that are accessed are those that are of that class, whether virtual or not (thus obviating the need for the casts that were done in the earlier solutions).

---

100. *Accessing methods in the parent class using the keyword* **base**

What is the output of this program? Explain why.

```csharp
using System;

namespace PracticeYourCSharp
{
    class A
    {
        public void Greeting() { Console.WriteLine("Hello how are you?"); }
    }

    class B : A
    {
        public void Greeting()
        {
            base.Greeting();
            Console.WriteLine("I'll be returning now...");
        }
    }

    class Program
    {
        static void Main(string[] args)
        {
            B object01 = new B();
            object01.Greeting();
            Console.ReadKey();
        }
    }
}
```

Output: Hello how are you?
          I'll be returning now...

The purpose of this exercise is *(1)* to show that the "hidden" method **Greeting** in the parent class can still be invoked by an object of the child class by using the keyword **base** and *(2)* to ensure that you know how to access methods in the parent class using the keyword **base**.

---

101. *Accessing overriden methods in the parent class using the keyword* **base**

What is the output of this program? Explain why.

```csharp
using System;

namespace PracticeYourCSharp
{
    class A
    {
        public virtual void Greeting() { Console.WriteLine("Hello how are you?"); }
    }
```

```
        class B : A
        {
          public override void Greeting()
          {
            base.Greeting();
            Console.WriteLine("I'll be returning now...");
          }
        }
        class Program
        {
          static void Main(string[] args)
          {
            B object01 = new B();
            object01.Greeting();
            Console.ReadKey();
          }
        }
}
```

Output: Hello how are you?
I'll be returning now...

The purpose of this exercise is to show that even though the virtual method `Greeting` in the parent class has been overridden in a child class, it can still be invoked from the child class by using the keyword **base**.

102.	What is a `readonly` variable?
	A `readonly` variable is a constant which you can set at compile time or inside the constructor, after which it cannot be modified again.
103.	What is the difference between a `const` and a `readonly` variable?
	A `const` must be set at compile time and it is unchangeable thereafter, whereas, a `readonly` variable can be set both at compile time and also once at run-time in the constructor.
104.	Create a class named `ObjectUnderGravity`. This class will support the computation of heights fallen under gravity. The class should have the following features: 1. The constructor of this class will take a string *"metric"* or *"imperial"* for us to know what units the user is going to use. 2. The default unit will be *metric*, that is **g** (gravitational constant) = 9.81 m/s^2. 3. Within the class, **g** should be made a `readonly` field, with a default value of 9.81m/s^2. If the user wants to use imperial units then the constructor of this class should set the field **g** to **g** in ft/s^2, which is 32.174 ft/s^2. The constructor, on receiving *"imperial"* as input will set the field **g** appropriately. 4. Also, there should be a `readonly` string field named `units`, which has a default value of *"meters"*, but if the user prefers imperial units, then it should be set to *"feet"* by the constructor. 5. Create a method named `Height` that computes and returns the value of the height fallen, using the formula: $$\text{Height} = V_{\text{Initial}} * t + 0.5 * g * t^2$$ 6. Also create a method named `GetUnits` that returns the field `units`. After creating the class, in `Main` instantiate two objects of the class, the first one named `obj1`, which uses imperial units and has an initial velocity of 30ft/sec. for 5 seconds and the second named `obj2`, which uses metric units and has an initial velocity of 10m/sec. for 5 seconds. Output the height travelled by each, stating, *The object has travelled <x> <metres|feet>*.
| | ```
using System;
namespace PracticeYourCSharp
{
  public class ObjectUnderGravity
  {
    protected readonly string units = "meters";
``` |
```

```
          protected readonly float g = 9.81f; // Default value

       public ObjectUnderGravity(string metricOrImperialSystem)
       {
         if (metricOrImperialSystem == "imperial")
         {
          this.units = "feet";
          this.g = 32.174f;
         }
       }

       public double Height(double vInitial, double time )
       {
        return(vInitial*time + 0.5*g*time*time);
       }

       public string GetUnits()
       {
        return (units);
       }
    }
    class Program
    {
       static void Main(string[] args)
       {
          ObjectUnderGravity obj1 = new ObjectUnderGravity("imperial");
          Console.WriteLine("The object has travelled {0} {1}", obj1.Height(30,5), obj1.GetUnits());
          ObjectUnderGravity obj2 = new ObjectUnderGravity("metric");
          Console.WriteLine("The object has travelled {0} {1}", obj2.Height(10,5), obj2.GetUnits());
          Console.ReadKey();
       }
    }
}
```

105.	We have looked at **readonly** variables. What is a **static readonly** variable?
	A **static readonly** variable is a class variable, whereas a **readonly** variable would belong to an instance of a given class.

Chapter 25. Interfaces (Introduction)

The concept of interfaces is an important one in C#, as it permits the enforcement of certain behaviors on the classes that *implement* the interface. The exercises presented in this chapter are an introduction to this topic.

1.	What is an **interface**?	
	An interface is a "contract" *(which in practice looks like a class)* that defines unimplemented methods that must be implemented by any class or structure that "implements" the interface.	
	An interface can be *implemented* by a class or a structure; in fact, multiple interfaces can be implemented by any given class or structure.	
	The requirement for implementing an interface is that any class or structure that implements the interface in question must implement *all* of the methods of the interface in question.	
	Formally, an interface is said to be a "contract" that the implementing class enters into, mandating the developer of the implementing class to define in the implementing class all of the methods specified in the interface.	
	The interface does not specify how to implement its methods, it only specifies an interface for them.	
	Why interfaces? Interfaces are useful for ensuring that specific functionality is implemented by the classes that implement the interface so that any user of those classes is assured that the functionality specified by the interface is present in the class in question. For example, if a class implements the interface `IComparable` (which specifies a single method that is used to establish ordering among objects of the same kind), then any program that needs to sort a list of elements of the given class is assured that the class itself has provided way of ordering objects of the class.	
	A class is said to *implement* an interface.	
2.	What kind of class is most like an interface?	An interface is most like an abstract class, because the methods in an interface are not implemented and when an interface is implemented **all** of its methods must be implemented.
3.	How many interfaces can a given class/structure implement?	There is no limit.
4.	What benefits do interfaces present over abstract classes?	The main benefit is that a given class can implement multiple interfaces, however it can only inherit from one class at a time, whether that class be abstract or otherwise.
5.	What is the default accessibility level of the members of an interface?	`public`
6.	What is the naming convention for interfaces?	The name must start with uppercase 'I'.
7.	Write the declaration template of the basic syntax of a class that inherits from another and also implements some interfaces.	
	`<accessibility> <class name>:<parent class>,<interface`$_1$`>,…<interface`$_n$`>` The name of the parent class must come before the names of the interfaces.	
8.	At this time, the reader is invited to look at the official class definition of any number of the built-in classes (for example, `String`, `List`, `StringBuffer`, etc.) that have been utilized in this book, look at the interfaces that are associated therewith and do a web search for the definitions of the interfaces in question.	

| 9. | *Implementing an interface*<br>We define a class **Alphabet** as follows:<br>```csharp
public class Alphabet
{
  public char character;
  public Alphabet(char singleCharacter)
  {
    character = singleCharacter;
  }
}
```<br>Create a class named **AlphabetComparer** that implements the **IComparer** interface for this class.<br>*(**IComparer** is a fairly simple interface that only has one method).* | ```csharp
public class AlphabetComparer: IComparer
{
  int IComparer.Compare(object obj1, object obj2)
  {
    Alphabet x = (Alphabet)obj1;
    Alphabet y = (Alphabet)obj2;
    if (x.character < y.character)
      return (-1);
    if (x.character > y.character)
      return (1);
    // implied else condition next…
    return (0); // They are equal
  }
}
``` |
| 10. | Create a number of instances of the class **Alphabet** and put them into an **ArrayList**.
Using the method **Sort(IComparer)** of the **ArrayList** and the class **AlphabetComparer** which implements the interface **IComparer**, sort the contents of the **ArrayList** and print the contents out.
(This method **Sort** takes an instance of a class that implements **IComparer**; in our case an instance of the class **AlphabetComparer**). | |
| | ```csharp
static void Main(string[] args)
{
  Alphabet x01 = new Alphabet('X');
  Alphabet x02 = new Alphabet('A');
  Alphabet x03 = new Alphabet('P');

  ArrayList list01 = new ArrayList();
  list01.Add(x01); list01.Add(x02); list01.Add(x03);

  AlphabetComparer ac01 = new AlphabetComparer();

  list01.Sort(ac01);
  Console.WriteLine(" The list is now sorted using the comparer");
  foreach (object x in list01)
  {
    Alphabet z = (Alphabet)x;
    Console.WriteLine("{0}", z.character);
  }
    Console.ReadKey();
}
``` | |
11.	Can an interface implement another interface?	
	Yes. See for example the definition of the interface **ICollection** which implements the interface **IEnumerable**.	
12.	Write the template of the basic syntax of the declaration of an interface that is implementing another interface.	
| | ```csharp
public interface <interface name>: <name of implemented interface>
```<br>For example **ICollection** implements **IEnumerable**. The declaration of **ICollection** is as follows:<br>```csharp
public interface ICollection : IEnumerable
``` | |
```

Chapter 26. Structures

This chapter presents exercises on C# structures, which are in certain aspects are similar to classes, however with notable differences.

1.	What is a structure(struct)?	A structure is similar to a class in content, however: 1. It is a value type. 2. You cannot inherit from a structure, nor can a structure inherit from another type. 3. While a structure can have a constructor, it cannot have a destructor.
2.	Explain when you might decide to use a struct instead of a class.	

	A struct is useful in the following scenarios:
	1. When you simply need a data element that you want to use to keep related data items together in a single packet. For example the following struct might be useful for a conference attendee:
	    `struct attendee`
	    `{`
	      `public string firstName;`
	      `public string lastName;`
	      `public string registrationNumber;`
	    `}`
	2. When there is no chance that inheritance is going to occur for the new type being considered, then a struct might be a sufficient data structure to use.	

3.	Define a structure named Vehicle, with the following public members: • make (string) • regID (string) • VehicleYear (ushort) In the method Main, create an instance v01 of the structure and print out the values of its fields.	<pre>using System;

namespace practiceYourCSharp
{
  struct Vehicle
  {
    public string make;
    public string regID;// RegistrationID#
    public ushort VehicleYear;
  }
  class Program
  {
    static void Main(string[] args)
    {
      Vehicle v01 = new Vehicle();
      Console.WriteLine("The Vehicle info is: make={0} regID={1}
            year={2}", v01.make, v01.regID, v01.VehicleYear);
      Console.ReadKey();
    }
  }
}</pre>**Notes:** The output should indicate that make = null, regID = null and VehicleYear=0. The reason for this is that when you instantiate a structure, its value type values are initialized to their default values (unless otherwise set in a constructor). |
| 4. | Enhance the solution to the preceding exercise, declaring an instance v02 of the Vehicle structure, without using the new operator. Explain why this is possible. | Add the following to the method Main above:
`Vehicle v02;`
This is possible because a struct is a value type. |

5.	Modify the solution to exercise 4 above to print out the fields of v02 just as done for v01.	The code will not compile. For the object v01 its fields were automatically initialized to their default values because you used the new operator to create the struct. However, for v02, because you did not do so, no such initialization was done as would be done using new and therefore you yourself have to initialize the fields of v02 before using them. Note though that even without using new, v02 exists because it is a value type and you do not actually have to use new to instantiate a value type variable.
6.	Modify the Vehicle structure and set the following default value: `public ushort VehicleYear=2000;` then recompile and run the exercise above.	
	It will *not* compile. The reason is that you cannot initialize instance fields directly within a structure.	

7.	Add the constructor below to the code for the structure. Report the result of your attempt to compile the code.
	
	``csharp
	public Vehicle()
	{
	   VehicleYear = 2000;
	}
	``	

	The code will *not* compile, because a structure cannot have a parameterless constructor.	
8.	Add a public field named purchaseDate of type DateTime to the Vehicle structure. Print the value thereof out alongside the other fields for object v01.	

	``csharp
	using System;
	
	namespace practiceYourCSharp
	{
	  struct Vehicle
	  {
	    public string make;
	    public string regID;
	    public ushort VehicleYear;
	    public DateTime purchaseDate;
	  }
	
	  class Program
	  {
	    static void Main(string[] args)
	    {
	      Vehicle v01 = new Vehicle();
	      Console.WriteLine("The Vehicle info is: make={0} regID={1} year={2},purchaseDate={3}",
	                  v01.make, v01.regID, v01.VehicleYear, v01.purchaseDate);
	      Console.ReadKey();
	    }
	  }
	}
	``
	
	Output
	The output for the purchaseDate field will be 1/1/0001 12:00 AM. This happens because DateTime is a structure and so field purchaseDate is a structure and thus its default values will be printed out.	

9.	Write a constructor for the structure Vehicle. This constructor should accept values for each of the fields of the structure.	

	The constructor for the structure is as follows:
	
	``csharp
	public Vehicle(string make, string regID, ushort VehicleYear, DateTime purchaseDate)
	{
	   this.make = make;
	   this.regID = regID;
	   this.VehicleYear = VehicleYear;
	   this.purchaseDate = purchaseDate;
	}
	``	

| 10. | Given the following two structures:<br><br>```
struct Vehicle
{
  public string make;
  public string regID;
  public ushort VehicleYear;
}
```<br><br>*and*<br><br>```
struct Car
{
  public string make;
  public string regID;
  public ushort VehicleYear;
}
```<br><br>Rewrite the code above to make the struct `Car` inherit from the struct `Vehicle`. | A `struct` cannot inherit from a `struct`. Therefore what was requested is not possible. |
|---|---|---|
| 11. | What is wrong with this code?<br><br>```
struct Car
{
  protected string make;
  public string regID;
  public ushort VehicleYear;
}
``` | The members of a `struct` cannot be declared as `protected` for the reason that a struct cannot be inherited and therefore the concept of `protected` is meaningless in the context of a structure because `protected` would imply that the given structure member can be accessed by descendants and structures cannot have descendants. |
| 12. | What is wrong with this code?<br><br>```
struct Car
{
  public string make;
  public string regID;
  public ushort VehicleYear=2000;
}
``` | A field in a struct cannot be initialized, unless the field is declared as `const` or `static`. |
| 13. | Can a `struct` implement an interface? | Yes. |
| 14. | How do you define a `static` structure? | A structure cannot be defined as `static`. |

Chapter 27. Tuples

C# tuples are classes which are largely useful for returning sets of data from one method to another. In this chapter, exercises on the C# concept of tuples are presented.

The key class presented in this chapter is the class `Tuple`.

1.	What is a `tuple` and what is it useful for?
	A `tuple` is a built-in class that can support multiple fields. The `tuple` class also provides support for generics. It is useful for the tidy returning in a single variable of multiple pieces of data from one method to another without having to define your own structure or class, or having to use `out`/`ref` parameters for each returned field. The fields in a tuple have generic names, which is sometimes sufficient and convenient. Note however, that once you create a `tuple`, you cannot modify its fields, therefore, *its members must be initialized at its instantiation*.
2.	Create a static method named `exponentials` that returns n^7, n^5 and n^3 in a 3-tuple of type `double` for any given value *n*. Test the method by calling it from `Main` to compute the values for n=5. Print out the received results in `Main`.
	<pre>using System;
using System.Collections.Generic;

namespace PracticeYourCSharp
{
  class Program
  {
    public static Tuple<double, double, double> exponentials(double n)
    {
      double n_7= Math.Pow(n,7);
      double n_5= Math.Pow(n,5);
      double n_3= Math.Pow(n,3);

      Tuple<double,double,double> tuResults = new Tuple<double,double,double>(n_7, n_5, n_3);
      return(tuResults);
    }

    static void Main(string[] args)
    {
      Tuple<double, double, double> tu01 = exponentials(5);
      Console.WriteLine("The returned values are {0},{1} and {2}.",tu01.Item1, tu01.Item2,
                   tu01.Item3);
      Console.ReadKey();
    }
  }
}</pre> |
| 3. | Create a static method named `stats` which returns in a 2-tuple of nullable `double` the sum and the average of the data passed to it in a *parameter array* of `double` numbers. If an empty array is passed to it, it should return null values for the sum and the average. Test the method by calling it from `Main`. Have `Main` print out the results for the following input: *(1)* nothing passed, *(2)* the values 25, 30 and 35. |
| | <pre>using System;
using System.Collections.Generic;

namespace PracticeYourCSharp
{
  class Program
  {
    public static Tuple<double?, double?> stats(params float[] inputData)
    {</pre> |

```csharp
            if (inputData.Length <= 0)
            {
                Tuple<double?, double?> tu01 = new Tuple<double?, double?>(null, null);
                return (tu01);
            }
            double sum = 0;
            double average = 0;
            for (int count = 0; count < inputData.Length; count++)
            {
                sum += inputData[count];
            }
            average = sum / inputData.Length;
            Tuple<double?, double?> tuResults = new Tuple<double?, double?>(sum, average);
            return (tuResults);
        }

        static void Main(string[] args)
        {
            Tuple<double?, double?> tu01 = stats();
            Console.WriteLine("Sum={0},Average={1}.", tu01.Item1, tu01.Item2);

            Tuple<double?, double?> tu02 = stats(25.0f, 30.0f, 35.0f);
            Console.WriteLine("Sum={0},Average={1}.", tu02.Item1, tu02.Item2);
            Console.ReadKey();
        }
    }
}
```

E1	Write a method which receives an array of type `double` and returns the maximum, minimum, sum, average and mode of the numbers passed to it in a 5-tuple of type `double?`. If the array passed to it is empty, then it should set all the values in the tuple to null.
E2	*Further study:* Examine how to handle tuples which need to return more than 8 fields.

Chapter 28. Passing By Reference, Passing By Value

A proper understanding of the concepts of *passing by reference* and *passing by value* is necessary in C#. While indeed exercises on these topics have been presented to some degree in previous chapters (especially in Chapter 21 on *Methods*), there is a need for focused exercises on the topic. This chapter presents exercises with which to hone your understanding of these concepts.

1.	Describe the difference in passing *by value* from a method$_A$ to a method$_B$ (including what effect an attempt by method$_B$ to change the variable passed to it) a variable of each of the following types: • a value type • a reference type
	When you pass a <u>value type</u> *by value* from a method$_A$ to a method$_B$, you are in effect merely passing *a copy* of the data in the value type variable from method$_A$ to the method$_B$. That copy does not have anything to do with the original variable!
	However, when you pass <u>a reference type</u> *"by value"* to a method, given that a reference type is really the address of the data that it refers to, you are actually passing a *copy of an address* (as opposed to a value type where you were passing a copy of data; here you are passing a copy of the address where the data is). Think of it this way; I have someone's address written on paper and I am writing that address on a different piece of paper for you.
	The result of an attempt by method$_B$ to change the variable passed to it is: 1. *for a value type*: if method$_B$ changes the value of a <u>parameter</u> passed to it, it doesn't have any effect on the value of the <u>variable</u> in method$_A$ because you never really passed the variable in method$_A$ to it, you only told method$_B$ a value; method$_B$ knows nothing about the original variable that contained the value. 2. *for a reference type*: if method$_B$ changes the value in a parameter passed to it, it definitely has an effect on the value of the variable in method$_A$, because, using the address analogy, method$_B$ has been told where the data resides (an address was passed to method$_B$) and therefore method$_B$ can modify the contents of the address (have a look at the solution to exercise 6 in Chapter 23. Types, Boxing & Unboxing for a refresher on how data is accessed behind the scenes for a reference type). Note that this does not hold for strings which we have seen are an *immutable reference type*.
2.	What is the difference in passing *by reference* from a method$_A$ to a method$_B$ each of the following: • a value type • a reference type
	For *value types* passed by reference from a method$_A$ to a method$_B$ where method$_B$ modifies the value, the value is changed in method$_A$ as well because passing a value type by reference means, continuing with the writing an address on paper analogy, that you have passed to the called method the location where the contents of the value type are stored and thus the called method is free to change what is at that address. Therefore when you come back to method$_A$ the variable in question is what method$_B$ modified it to.
	When you pass a *reference type* by reference from a method$_A$ to a method$_B$, the value that the reference type points to can be modified by method$_B$ and so when you come back to method$_A$ the variable in question is what method$_B$ modified it to. So far this sounds exactly like passing the reference type by value, but there is one particular difference; extending the address on a piece of paper analogy given in the preceding solution, in this case method$_A$ is handing the very sheet on which it has the address of the variable off to method$_B$, not merely writing the address on a different piece of paper to give to method$_B$. If method$_B$ tears up that sheet, method$_A$ will not be able to access the data because it has handed off the sheet on which the address is written to method$_B$ which tore it up (tearing it up here would be the setting of the parameter to `null` in the called method).
3.	What keywords are used to effect passing by reference?
	The keywords **ref** and **out** are the keywords used to effect passing by reference.

4.	What is the difference in behavior between **ref** and **out**?
	ref requires that the *caller* initialize the variable in question before it is passed. The called method is free to change (or not) the value of the **ref** variable. **out** demands that the variable be assigned a value by the called method before it is sent back. **Note:** these keywords have previously been explained in *Chapter 21. Methods (Introduction)*.
| 5. | In the program below, we attempt to modify certain variables in a called method named `Modify`.<br>*Predict* the output of the program for the attempted modification of each of an **int**, an **int** passed by reference using the keyword **ref**, **int[]**, **string**, **string[]** and a **StringBuilder**.<br><br>```csharp
using System;
using System.Text;

namespace PracticeYourCSharp
{
  class Program
  {
    public static void Modify(int z1, ref int z2, int[] a, string str01, string[] sa01,
                                     StringBuilder sb01)
    {
      z1++; z2++;                    // Try to modify the integers
      str01 = str01 + "Modified!!";  // Try to modify the string
      sb01.Append("Modified!!");     // Try to modify the StringBuilder
      sa01[0] += " Modified!!";      // Try to modify the string in the array
      if (a.Length < 1) return;      // Try to modify the integers in the array
      for (int count = 0; count < a.Length; count++)
        a[count]++;
    }

    static void Main(string[] args)
    {
      int z1 = 500; int z2=221;
      int[] a = new int[] { 1, 2, 3, 4, 5 };
      string str01 = "Hello. ";
      string[] sArray01 = new String[] { "String element 0 " };
      StringBuilder sb01 = new StringBuilder("Hello. ");

      Modify(z1, ref z2, a, str01, sArray01, sb01);

      Console.WriteLine("1. Integer     : z1={0}, z2={1}", z1, z2);
      Console.WriteLine("2. Int Array   : The int array contents are: ");
      for (int count = 0; count < a.Length; count++)
        Console.WriteLine("\t{0}", a[count]);
      Console.WriteLine("3. String      : {0}", str01);
      Console.WriteLine("4. String Array : sArray[0]={0}", sArray01[0]);
      Console.WriteLine("5. StringBuilder: {0}", sb01);
      Console.ReadKey();
    }
  }
}
``` |

Results	Explanation
1. Integer : z1=500, z2=222;	1. The int z1 will not be modified as passed, because integers are value types. For a value type to be modified you have to pass it by reference (**ref** or **out**) as was done for z2. Observe that z2 was modified successfully.

2. Int Array   : The int array contents are:
    2
    3
    4
    5
    6
	2. An array is a reference type! Therefore when we pass an array to a method, we are passing the address of the array and <u>thus implicitly passing the address of each of its contents</u>. Therefore, even though the array is an array of integers which are a value type,

```

	`3. String       : Hello.`
	
	`4. String Array : sArray[0]=String element 0: Modified!!`
	`5. StringBuilder: Hello. Modified!!`
		the contents can be modified by a called method.
		3. The `string` was not modified. Strings, as discussed earlier, are immutable reference types and they can be seen as being passed to other methods the way value types are.
		4. An array is a reference type! Therefore the contents are changeable by a called method.
		5. A `StringBuilder` is a reference type and therefore its contents can be modified.

6. Explain why the `string str01` in the earlier example was not modifiable, but the string in the array element `sArray01[0]` was modifiable when passed to another method.

The `string` variable `str01` was not changed when it was passed to the method `Modify` because strings, as discussed earlier, are immutable reference types and they are passed to other methods like value types. (The immutability of a `string` has been discussed in the chapter on strings).

Now, why was the `string` that was in the array changeable? The reason is actually because an array of `string` like any other array is a reference type, therefore when it is passed, its address (and thus implicitly that of its contents) are passed as well, therefore when the target method modified the string being pointed to by an index in the array, since it really had the address of the target string, it was able to change what was contained at that address!

7. *Passing objects*

What is the expected output of this code?

```
using System;

namespace PracticeYourCSharp
{
  public class Person
  {
    public string firstName;
    public string lastName;
  }

  class Program
  {
    public static void Modify(Person y)
    {
      y.firstName = "Me";
      y.lastName = "Myself";
    }

    static void Main(string[] args)
    {
      Person p = new Person(); //see class Person defined above
      Modify(p);
      Console.WriteLine("The person is: {0} {1}", p.firstName, p.lastName);
      Console.ReadKey();
    }
  }
}
```

Output: `The person is: Me Myself`

What is being shown here is the fact that objects, being reference types, have their addresses passed and thus their values can be modified by the called method.

What happens exactly is that when the object is passed, the compiler in essence sets the parameter `y` in the method declaration of method `Modify` to the memory address of `person p` in `Main`. So now we have two variables (`y` in `Modify` and `p` in `Main`) pointing to the same object.

Think about it using this analogy; I have someone's address written on a piece of paper and I want to give the address to you. I can either give you my piece of paper, or copy the address to another piece of paper and keep my original piece of paper. In this case, I have copied the address to another piece of paper and given it to you.

8.	What is the difference if person p is passed using the **ref** option as shown in the following modifications **(shown in bold)** to the code of the preceding exercise?
| | ```csharp
public static void Modify(ref Person y)
{
   y.firstName = "Me";
   y.lastName  = "Myself";
}

static void Main(string[] args)
{
   Person p = new Person();
   Modify(ref p);
   Console.WriteLine("The person is: {0} {1}", p.firstName, p.lastName);
   Console.ReadKey();
}
``` |
| | There is no difference in output (as expected), however, what we have done in this case is that we have actually passed p in Main to the method Modify! Using the analogy from the preceding exercise, Main has actually given Modify the piece of paper on which it (Main) wrote the address of p. If Modify loses the piece of paper (done by setting y=null in the method Modify), then neither Main nor Modify would have the address anymore (i.e. any reference we had to the object would be lost and in effect the object itself would be lost in memory! In actuality, once the garbage collector sees that there are no references to the object, it destroys the object). |
| 9. | Predict the output of this code, where we set y = null in the earlier shown method Modify. |
| | ```csharp
public static void Modify(ref Person y)
{
   y.firstName = "Me";
   y.lastName  = "Myself";
   y = null;
}

static void Main(string[] args)
{
   Person p = new Person();
   Modify(ref p);
   Console.WriteLine("The person is: {0} {1}", p.firstName, p.lastName);
   Console.ReadKey();
}
``` |
| | When we attempt in Main to print out the values p.firstName and p.lastName, the exception System.NullReferenceException will occur. This is because, using our earlier analogy of passing the address on which we wrote the address to another method which then "shredded" the paper (by setting y=null), Main doesn't know where to find p anymore! It (Main) gave its own sheet of paper on which the address of p was written to Modify, which shredded the piece of paper and so Main doesn't know where p lives anymore! |
| 10. | Predict the output of this code.
(What we've done in this code is to no longer pass p by reference, yet set y = null in the method Modify). |
| | ```csharp
public static void Modify(Person y)
{
   y.firstName = "Me";
   y.lastName  = "Myself";
   y = null;
}

static void Main(string[] args)
{
   Person p = new Person();
   Modify(p);
   Console.WriteLine("The person is: {0} {1}", p.firstName, p.lastName);
   Console.ReadKey();
}
``` |
| | **Output:** The person is Me Myself |
```

	Setting y=null in this code had no negative effects in Main because when we passed p by value, all we did was, to use the address on a piece of paper analogy, to copy the address of p to another sheet of paper and hand it to the method Modify. Modify tore up its own copy of the sheet (by setting y=null;), but Main still has the address on its own original sheet of paper p.

11.	Predict the output of this code.
	
	``csharp
	using System;
	using System.Text;
	
	namespace PracticeYourCSharp
	{
	  struct Product
	  {
	    public string productName;
	    public decimal price;
	    public string[] ingredients;
	
	    public Product(string name, decimal price)
	    {
	      this.productName = name;
	      this.price = price;
	      ingredients = new String[3];
	    }
	  }
	
	  class Program
	  {
	    public static void Modify(Product prod01)
	    {
	      prod01.productName = "Rice Mix";
	      prod01.price = 25.00m;
	      prod01.ingredients[0] = "rice";
	      prod01.ingredients[1] = "salt";
	      prod01.ingredients[2] = "starch";
	    }
	
	    static void Main(string[] args)
	    {
	      Product product01 = new Product("Peas Mix",1.0m);
	      Modify(product01);
	      Console.WriteLine("Product Name = {0}", product01.productName);
	      Console.WriteLine("Price = {0}", product01.price);
	      Console.WriteLine("Ingredients are: {0} {1} {2}", product01.ingredients[0],
	                        product01.ingredients[1], product01.ingredients[2]);
	      Console.ReadKey();
	    }
	  }
	}
	``
	
	Output
	``
	Product Name = Peas Mix
	Price = 1.00
	Ingredients are: rice salt starch
	``
	
	The method Modify attempted to change the product name from *Peas Mix* to *Rice Mix* and the price from 1.00 to 25.00 but because a struct is a value type, its value type fields and immutable reference type subfields cannot be changed when the structure is passed by value.
	However, its reference type subfields can be changed, that is why the ingredient list, which is an array, was modifiable.

12.	What is the output if product01 is passed by reference from Main to Modify? Contrast the results with the results from passing the structure by value as done in the preceding exercise. **Output** ``` Structures: Product Name = Rice Mix ```

|    | ```
Price         = 25.00
Ingredients are: rice salt starch
``` **Notes:** The product name and price which are value types are now modifiable by a called method when the structure instance **prod01** was passed by reference. |
| E1 | **(6.0)** For exercise 9, rewrite the output line in **Main** to prevent an exception from even occuring when we attempt to print out the object fields.
Hint: null-propagating operator. |
```

Chapter 29. Operator Overloading

Operator overloading is an interesting concept which permits the redefinition of standard operators for your purposes. This chapter presents exercises with which to hone your skills in this topic.

1.	What does the term *operator overloading* mean?	
	Operator overloading is the name given to the functionality to within C# write equivalent methods for various operators (such as +, -, <, > among others). For example, if we have two matrices which we want to add, we would normally express the addition with a method we create and call in the following fashion: `matrix3=addMatrices(matrix1,matrix2)`. However, with operator overloading we can write a method to overload the plus(+) operator and be able to express the same computation more naturally as: `matrix3 = matrix1 + matrix2.`	

2.	Using the class `Square` defined in Chapter 24 on Classes, I want to be able to add two objects of class `Square` to produce another `Square` object such that the `length` of the side of the new `Square` is the `length` of the side of a square whose area is the sum of the area of the two `Square` objects being added.
	
	To wit, write code to overload the plus(+) operator for the class `Square` to support such functionality. This overloaded operator returns the `Square` object whose `length` is the computed side length.
	
	Test your code by adding two objects of class `Square` of side length 5 and 9 together. Print out the `length` field of the resulting `Square`.
		add this method to class Square
		```\npublic static Square operator +(Square sq1, Square sq2)\n{\n double area = sq1.Area() + sq2.Area();\n double length = Math.Sqrt(area);\n return new Square(length);\n}\n```
		usage
		```\nstatic void Main(string[] args)\n{\n Square sq01 = new Square(5);\n Square sq02 = new Square(9);\n Square square03 = sq01 + sq02; //the plus is "overloaded"\n Console.WriteLine("square03 has a side length of {0}",\n square03.GetSideLength());\n Console.ReadKey();\n}\n```

3.	Using the overloaded + operator, add three objects of class `Square` of `length` 5, 10 and 15 respectively. Print out the `length` field of the resulting `Square`.	*usage* ```\nstatic void Main(string[] args)\n{\n Square sq01 = new Square(5);\n Square sq02 = new Square(10);\n Square sq03 = new Square(15);\n\n Square square04 = sq01 + sq02 + sq03;\n Console.WriteLine("square04 has a side length of {0}",\n square04.GetSideLength());\n Console.ReadKey();\n}\n```
4.	Overload the > and < operators for the class `Square`. The methods should be passed two `Square` objects. In the case of the method for the overloaded > operator, if the 1st object is greater than the 2nd in length/area then return `True`, otherwise return `False`. For the overloaded method for the < operator which will be passed the same parameters, return the opposite. Test the method for the > operator by calling it from `Main`, using two `Square` objects of side length 5 and 9. If the 1st `Square` object is smaller in size than the 2nd, print this fact out. If it is greater in size than the 2nd, print this fact out.	
	(Add the following two methods to class `Square`)	

```
public static Boolean operator >(Square sq1, Square sq2)
{
   if (sq1.length > sq2.length)
     return (true);
   else
     return (false);
}

public static Boolean operator <(Square sq1, Square sq2)
{
   if (sq1.length < sq2.length)
     return (true);
   else
     return (false);
}
```
Usage
```
static void Main(string[] args)
{
   Square sq01 = new Square(5);
   Square sq02 = new Square(9);
   if (sq01 > sq02)
     Console.WriteLine("sq01 is bigger than sq02");
   else
     Console.WriteLine("sq01 is smaller than sq02");
   Console.ReadKey();
}
```

5.	Using the class Circle defined in exercise 57 of Chapter 24, I want to be able to add the area of two Circle objects together to produce another Circle object such that the radius of the new Circle is equal to the radius of a circle whose area is equal to the combined area of the two Circle objects being added.
	
	To wit, write code to overload the plus(+) operator for the class Circle to support such functionality. This overloaded operator returns a Circle object whose radius is the computed radius.
	
	Test it by adding two objects of class Circle of radius 12 and 8 together. Print out the radius of the resulting Circle.
		add this method to class Circle
		
		```public static Circle operator +(Circle c1, Circle c2)\n{\n double area = c1.Area() + c2.Area();\n\n double radius = Math.Sqrt(area / Math.PI);\n return new Circle(radius);\n}```
		
		Usage
		```static void Main(string[] args)\n{\n Circle c01 = new Circle(12);\n Circle c02 = new Circle(8);\n Circle c03 = c01 + c02; //the plus is "overloaded"\n Console.WriteLine("circle03 has a radius of {0}",\n c03.getRadius());\n Console.ReadKey();\n}```

E1	Overload the *equality operator (==)* for the class Circle to compare the radii of two Circle objects passed to it, returning true if they are of equal radius and false if their radii differ.	
E2	Overload the *minus operator* for the class Circle to return a Circle object whose radius is the radius of a circle whose area is determined by the *area of a circle object A – area of a circle object B*.	
E3	Overload the *multiplication operator* for the class Circle to return a Circle object whose radius is the radius of a circle whose area is determined by the *area of a circle object A multiplied by the area of a circle object B*.	

Chapter 30. Properties

Properties are a feature within C# with which to access object fields and computations related to given classes without giving direct access to the fields (i.e. not making them `public`), or using explicit methods, while presenting field-like syntax. This chapter presents exercises with which you can practice your skills in using properties.

1.	What is a property?	
	A property is special method called an *accessor* that is used to access the private fields of an object or computed values derived from the object's fields, or computations relevant to the class or class instance, without presenting a method to the calling method and without making the fields in question `public`. Due to their appearance, properties give the user of the properties the perception that a field is being directly accessed.	
2.	List some of the reasons for why you might use a property.	
	1. A property can be used to present a public interface with field-like syntax for setting/getting a private field. 2. Properties help hide implementation details by exposing the property rather than exposing the details of the supporting field(s) behind it, thus allowing for the modification of the details behind a property without forcing a change to the way the class data in question is accessed by non-class members. 3. Getting and setting individual fields (or computations based on field values) in an object is a common feature in a lot of programs. Without properties, you would have to explicitly write a public get method and a public set method for each computation/private field of interest. Properties allow for the accessing of the data in the same field without having to invoke a method but rather employ field-like syntax. In this sense, properties can be said to be "syntactic sugar".	
3.	In the context of properties, what is a getter accessor?	
	A getter accessor is the property method that returns the field/computation value that a given property represents. The getter method is always named `get`.	
4.	In the context of properties, what is a setter accessor?	
	A setter accessor is the property method that sets the field(s) that a given property represents. The setter method is always named `set`.	
5.	Explain the meaning of the keyword `value` in relation to properties.	
	The keyword `value` is used in the setter method of a property. It is used to represent the value that is being passed to the setter.	
6.	How are read-only properties implemented?	
	Read-only properties are implemented by the property only having a getter method but not a setter method.	
7.	Give examples of read-only properties that you have encountered in this book.	
	`<String>.Length`, `DateTime.Now` and `List<T>.Count`. `DateTime.Now` is an example of a static property. Also, its internals do not derive from any value in the class itself, rather it represents the determination on demand of the current time from the system clock by a call to a lower level function. This is an example of a property which does not return a field of its class/object, but rather performs a computation that is relevant to the class that it is in, as clearly, the determination of the current date and time fits in the `DateTime` class.	
8.	How are write-only properties implemented?	
	Write-only properties are **not** permitted in C#.	
9.	How are read/write properties implemented?	
	Read/Write properties are implemented by giving the property both a setter and a getter accessor.	
10.	What is a static property?	
	A static property is a property that is associated with a class, rather than an instance of the class. The property `DateTime.Now` is an example of a static property.	
11.	With respect to properties, what is the concept of a "backing store"?	

	When you have a property, the actual field that the property writes to/reads from is called the backing store. This often is a private field in the object in question.
12.	What is an automatic/auto-implemented property?
	An auto-implemented property is a property for which you the programmer do not perform any logic in your accessors (your getter and setter methods) and so are content to let the compiler implement a private backing store (whose name you don't know and don't care to know) for the property.
| 13. | Rewrite the following code using properties for the individual fields age, firstName and lastName:<br><br>```csharp
using System;

class Person
{
  private string firstName;
  private string lastName;
  private int age;

  public string getFirstName()                 { return (firstName); }
  public void setFirstName(string firstName)   { this.firstName = firstName; }
  public string getLastName()                  { return (lastName); }
  public void setLastName(string lastName)     { this.lastName = lastName; }
  public int getAge()                          { return (age); }
  public void setAge(int age)
  {
    if ((age >= 0) && (age <= 250))
      this.age = age;
  }
}

class Program
{
  static void Main(string[] args)
  {
    Person p01 = new Person();
    p01.setFirstName("John");
    p01.setLastName("Doe");
    p01.setAge(50);
    Console.WriteLine("My name is {0} {1} and I am {2} year(s) old.", p01.getFirstName(),
      p01.getLastName(), p01.getAge());
    Console.ReadKey();
  }
}
``` |
| | ```csharp
using System;

class Person
{
  private string firstName;
  private string lastName;
  private int age;

  public string FirstName
  {
    get { return (firstName); }
    set { firstName = value; }
  }
  public string LastName
  {
    get { return (lastName); }
    set { lastName = value; }
  }
  public int Age
  {
    get {
          return (age);
``` |

```
          }
       set {
           if((value >= 0)&&(value <=250))
              this.age = value;
           }
       }
    }
    class Program
    {
       static void Main(string[] args)
       {
          Person p01 = new Person();
          p01.FirstName= "John";
          p01.LastName= "Doe";
          p01.Age=50;
          Console.WriteLine(p01.Age);
          Console.WriteLine("My name is {0} {1} and I am {2} year(s) old.",p01.FirstName,
                       p01.LastName, p01.Age);
          Console.ReadKey();
       }
    }
```

14.	Rewrite the class **Person** above, using auto-properties where possible.
| | ```
using System;
class Person
{
   private int age;

   public string FirstName {set;get;}
   public string LastName {set;get;}
   public int Age
   {
      get {
          return (age);
         }
       set {
           if((value >= 0)&&(value <= 250))
              this.age = value;
           }
       }
    }
``` |
15.	**(6.0)** Looking at the method **Main** in exercise 13, rewrite the instantiation and initialization of the properties of object **p01** of class **Person** using property initializers.
	`Person p01 = new Person() { FirstName = "John", LastName = "Doe", Age = 50 };`
16.	Can properties be declared to be **virtual**, just like methods?
	Yes they can and therefore they can be overridden in descendant classes.
17.	I have the following class definition:
	``
class Human
{
   public virtual string Gender
   {
    get{
       return("unspecified");
       }
   }
}
```
Derive a class called **Male** from it and override the property **gender** to return a value of "male".
```
class Male:Human
{
   public override string Gender
``` |

	``
    {
      get{
          return("male");
         }
       }
    }
```
The objective of this exercise was to show that properties can be `virtual` and can be overridden in descendant classes. | |
| 18. | **(6.0)** Rewrite the exercise and the solution to the preceding exercise using an <u>auto-property initializer</u>. | |
| | ```
class Human
{
   public virtual string Gender {get;} ="unspecified";
}
class Male:Human
{
   public override string Gender  {get;} = "male";
}
``` | |
| 19. | **(6.0)** Rewrite the solution to the preceding exercise using expression bodied properties. | |
| | ```
class Human
{
   public virtual string Gender   => "unspecified";
}
class Male:Human
{
   public override string Gender  => "male";
}
``` | |
| 20. | Rewrite the code below using properties instead of methods. | |
| | ```
class Temperature
{
  // In this class we store the temperature in Fahrenheit, but we give the user the option
  // to set or retrieve it in Fahrenheit or Celsius.
  // Retrieving it in Celsius results in the code doing a conversion from Fahrenheit to Celsius.

   private float tempF;

   public Temperature(float temp)       { tempF = temp;}  // Input as fahrenheit to constructor
   public float getTempInF()            { return(tempF); }
   public void setTempInF(float t)      {  tempF=t;  }
   public float getTempInC()            {  return((tempF-32)*((float)5/(float)9));}
   public void setTempInC(float tempC)  { tempF = tempC * ((float)9/(float)5) - 32; }
}
``` | |
| | ```
class Temperature
{
   private float tempF;

   public Temperature(float temp)  {tempF = temp;} //constructor
   public float TempInF
   {
     get { return (tempF); }
     set { tempF = value; }
   }
   public float TempInC
   {
     get {return ((tempF - 32) * ((float)5 / (float)9)); }
     set { tempF = value * ((float)9 / (float)5) - 32; }
   }
}
``` | |
| 21. | Can properties be passed by value? If so, then why, if not, then why not? | Yes properties can be passed by value. The reason for this is that when a field/variable is passed by value, the value of what the field/variable being passed contains is what is passed, not the variable itself; so also for |
```

		properties.
22.	Why can't properties be passed by reference to a method just like object fields can?	Only variable references can be passed by reference; properties are actually methods and therefore cannot be passed by reference.
23.	When would you choose to use a method to access field data versus using getter/setter methods?	You would use a method when the access-time of the property is not deterministic. For example, if the data being accessed involved access to a remote database, this access clearly having greater latency than accessing a variable in memory, then it would be better to use a method, as a property is assumed by its appearance to be a field whose data is accessed directly.
24.	What is an abstract property?	
	An abstract property is one which does not implement the property accessors, leaving them for child classes to implement. Abstract properties appear only in abstract classes.	
E1	Rewrite the class Shape from the chapter on classes, using an abstract property for Area and override it in the child classes.	

Chapter 31. Delegates

The concept of delegates is an important one in C# as it facilitates the passing of methods as arguments to other methods, a capability that can increase the efficiency of code. Delegates also facilitate the chaining of methods.

The exercises in this chapter ensure that you have a clear understanding of this topic.

1.	What is a delegate? Give an example to aid in understanding the concept of what a delegate is and how it functions.
	In its simplest terms it is explained in this single line: **A delegate <u>is an object</u> which encapsulates method(s).**
	A delegate object is an instance of a programmer defined type called a *delegate type* that is based on the built-in `System.Delegate` class. A delegate type is defined with a declaration just like that of a method. Instances of a delegate type are objects (the delegate object) which <u>encapsulate methods</u>, thus giving you the ability to pass methods around like parameters and use them like parameters.
	Delegate objects also support method chaining, that is, a single delegate can be configured to encapsulate multiple methods (this achieved by the fact that the `System.Delegate` class has in effect overloaded the addition and subtraction operators), thus letting you trigger multiple methods in sequence simply by invoking the delegate.
	We elucidate by way of example as shown below.
	We have two methods, `printFactorial` and `printCubed` with the following method declarations:
| | ```
public void printFactorial(int x);
public void printCubed(int x);
``` |
| | Note that both of them have the same input parameter(s) (one `int`) and that both have the same return type (`void` in this case). We will apply these methods to a delegate shortly. |
| | **Step #1**: *Declaring a delegate type*
 We declare a *delegate type* as follows: |
| | ```
public delegate void delegateNumberFunctions(int);
``` |
| | This is just the "*delegate <u>type</u>*" definition. We named this particular delegate type `delegateNumberFunctions`. From the definition we can see that the delegate type can stand in for methods which take one `int` and return a `void`. |
| | **Step #2**: *Instantiate a delegate object/instance*
 Now that we have a delegate type, we "instantiate" a delegate as follows: |
| | ```
delegateNumberFunctions del01;
``` |
| | We now have a delegate object `del01` which is an instance of the delegate type `delegateNumberFunctions`. |
| | **Step #3**: *Assigning methods to delegates*
 We now assign methods to this delegate object. |
| | ```
del01 = printFactorial;   // we assign the method printFactorial to the delegate object
del01+= printCubed;       // we  assigned another method to del01, so it will run the methods
                          // printFactorial and printCubed in the order in which they were
                          // assigned to the delegate. Adding more than one method to a delegate
                          // instance is called delegate chaining.; the delegate object is then called a
                          // multi-cast delegate.
``` |
| | **Step #4**: *Usage/Running the delegate object* <br> If for example we run the following line of code: <br> ```
del01(3);
``` |

247
```

	What happens is that the methods `printFactorial(3)` and `printCubed(3)` that were assigned to the delegate object are invoked in order of their being assigned to `del01`. **Modifications to delegates: Removal of methods** If we run the following line of code: `del01 = del01 - printCubed;` it removes from `del01` the method `printCubed` that it would have run. If we then run the following line of code: `del01(3);` then only the method `printFactorial(3);` is called, because we have just removed `printCubed` from the list of methods that `del01` can run. **Note:** In our earlier example we stated that our delegate type could stand in for methods which take one `int` and return a `void`. However, through the feature of *covariance*, a delegate can stand in for return types that are child classes of the declared return type. Through the feature of *contravariance*, a delegate can stand in for parameter types that are parent classes of the defined parameters. Covariance and contravariance are beyond the scope of this book.
2.	Explain what is meant by the concept of *delegate chaining*.
	Delegate chaining is the functionality by which a delegate object can be assigned multiple methods. When the delegate object is invoked, the methods are run in the order in which they have been assigned to the delegate object. The means by which this chaining is done is simply by using the addition operator (+) (see the example in the preceding exercise). If it is desired that any method be removed from the chain, then the method in question is simply removed by using the subtraction operator (-) on the delegate object (see the example in the answer to the preceding exercise). When we chain methods for a delegate, the delegate is called a multi-cast delegate.
3.	When we have a delegate with a set of chained methods each of which returns a value, what is the value that is returned by the delegate when it is run?
	The return value of the last method run in the chain is what is returned by the delegate.
4.	Create a method with the declaration `float Add2Ints(int a, int b);` which returns a `float` that is the result of the addition of the two integers passed to it. This method should also print out the statement *"The sum is <result>"*. Invoke this method from `Main` for the values `9` and `10` by calling the method via a delegate. Print out the return value from the delegate.
	<pre>using System;

namespace practiceYourCSharp
{
  class Program
  {
    public static float Add2Ints(int a, int b)
    {
      Console.WriteLine("The sum is {0}", (a + b));
      return(a + b);
    }

    public delegate float delNumberOperations(int x, int y); // delegate type definition

    static void Main(string[] args)
    {
      delNumberOperations del01; // Declare the delegate object

      del01 = Program.Add2Ints; // Assign the method to the delegate

      // Now test it
      Console.WriteLine(del01(9, 10));
      Console.ReadKey();
    }
  }
}</pre> |

5.	Extend the solution to the preceding exercise to support the following two new methods: 1. `float Mult2Ints(int, int);` which multiples the numbers passed to it and then prints out the statement *"The multiplication is <result>"* and returns the result in a `float`. 2. `float div2ints(int, int);` which divides the first number passed to it by the second (floating point division), prints out the statement *"The division is <result>"* and returns the result of the calculation in a `float`. Using a single delegate object, call the three methods in series for the number pair *7 and 9* from the method `Main`. Have `Main` print out the value returned from the called delegate instance.
| | ```
using System;

namespace practiceYourCSharp
{
  class Program
  {
    public static float Add2Ints(int a, int b)
    {
      Console.WriteLine("The sum is {0}", (a + b));
      return (a + b);
    }
    public static float Mult2Ints(int a, int b)
    {
      Console.WriteLine("The multiplication is {0}", (a * b));
      return (a * b);
    }
    public static float Div2Ints(int a, int b)
    {
      Console.WriteLine("The division is {0}", ((float)a / (float)b));
      return (a / b);
    }

    public delegate float delNumberOperations(int x, int y);

    static void Main(string[] args)
    {
      delNumberOperations del01; // Declare the delegate object

      del01 = Program.Add2Ints; // chain the methods
      del01 += Program.Mult2Ints;
      del01 += Program.Div2Ints;

      // now test it out.
      Console.WriteLine(del01(7, 9));
      Console.ReadKey();
    }
  }
}
```<br>**Note:** Observe that the return value of the delegate itself is the return value of the last method that it called, `Div2Ints`. |
| 6. | We have the following class:<br><br>```
public class Person
{
  public string Name;

  public Person(string Name)        { this.Name=Name;}
  public static void Hotwater()     { Console.WriteLine(" hot water");}
  public static void Teabag()       { Console.WriteLine(" tea bag"); }
  public static void Sugar()        { Console.WriteLine(" sugar");}
  public static void Milk()         { Console.WriteLine(" milk");}

  public delegate void del01(); // This is the delegate type declaration
  public del01 teaMakingOrder;  // This is an instance of the delegate type in question
``` |

}

Note that the delegate type definition and the delegate type instance are members of the class.
Also note that the methods pertain to ingredients for making a cup of tea.

Write a program which will do the following in an infinite loop, using the class `Person` above:
1. Ask for the name(case insensitive) of a `Person`. Create an object for each `Person`. Store every `Person` object in a `List<Person>`.
2. If there is no such user already represented in the `List<Person>` (the `Name` field of the `Person` should be used as the search key), then present the user with a menu asking him to indicate, using the first letter of the ingredients (Hotwater, Teabag, Sugar and Milk), the order in which he puts in the ingredients into a cup to make his tea.
3. Assign to the delegate object `teaMakingOrder`, in order, the respective methods that pertain to the tea making ingredients in the order in which the person puts the ingredients into his cup (i.e. chain the methods in the object in the order in which the user puts the ingredients in his cup of tea).
4. If such a user is already represented in the `List<Person>`, output the statement "*<user> is already in here and their tea making order is:*"> and using the delegate, print out their tea making order.
5. Break out of the infinite loop when the user types **Q** or **Quit** (case-insensitive) when asked for a name.

```csharp
using System;
using System.Collections.Generic;

namespace practiceYourCSharp
{
  public class Person
  {
    public string Name;

    public Person(string Name) { this.Name = Name; }
    public static void Hotwater() { Console.WriteLine(" hot water"); }
    public static void Teabag()   { Console.WriteLine(" tea bag"); }
    public static void Sugar()    { Console.WriteLine(" sugar"); }
    public static void Milk()     { Console.WriteLine(" milk"); }

    public delegate void del01(); // This is the delegate type declaration
    public del01 teaMakingOrder;  // This is an instance of the delegate type in question
  }

  class Program
  {
    static void checkCustomerExist(List<Person> list01, string name,
                                   ref bool exists, ref Person p)
    {
      int count = 0;
      exists = false;
      if (list01.Count < 1) return;
      do
      {
        if (list01[count].Name.Equals(name))
        {
          exists = true;
          p = list01[count];
          break;
        }
        count++;
      }while (count < list01.Count);
    }

    static void Main(string[] args)
    {
      List<Person> personList = new List<Person>();
```

```csharp
            bool exitProgram = false;
            while (exitProgram != true)
            {
              Console.Write("\nWhat is your name please? ");
              string name = Console.ReadLine();
              name = name.ToLower();
              if ((name.Equals("q")) || (name.Equals("quit")))
              {
                return; // Exit the program
              }
              bool customerExists = false;
              Person currentPerson = null;
              checkCustomerExist(personList, name, ref customerExists, ref currentPerson);

              if (customerExists == true)
              {
                Console.WriteLine("You are already registered {0}. Here is your order of
                            ingredients in making your tea: ", name);
                currentPerson.teaMakingOrder();
              }
              else
              {
                Console.Write("What order do you make your tea? (Indicate in order by the first
                            character of each ingredient):   ");
                Console.Write("Hot Water(H)\nTea(T)\nSugar(S)\nMilk(M):");
                string teaOrder = Console.ReadLine();
                Person p1 = new Person(name);
                teaOrder = teaOrder.ToUpper();
                // Note, no great error checking here. Note the way the addition operator is
                // overloaded for delegates to support chaining the running of methods

                for (int k = 0; k < teaOrder.Length; k++)
                {
                  if (teaOrder[k] == 'H') p1.teaMakingOrder += Person.Hotwater;
                  if (teaOrder[k] == 'T') p1.teaMakingOrder += Person.Teabag;
                  if (teaOrder[k] == 'M') p1.teaMakingOrder += Person.Milk;
                  if (teaOrder[k] == 'S') p1.teaMakingOrder += Person.Sugar;
                }
                personList.Add(p1);
              }
            }
          }
        }
      }
}
```

7.	Is a delegate a reference type or a value type?
	A delegate is a reference type. Remember that it is an *object* that encapsulates a method.

Chapter 32. Exceptions

The concept of exceptions is a very important one in C# as it provides a means to gracefully handle abnormal situations that might occur during program execution. This chapter presents exercises which aid in understanding the concept of exceptions and also help in clarifying the appropriate and necessary placement of exception handling within C# programs.

1.	What is an *exception*?
	An exception is an alarm notification raised by the C# runtime engine, third party libraries, or even your own application code due to unacceptable situations/conditions in any of the C# runtime engine, the third party libraries, your application or even the computer itself. Such examples of unacceptable conditions include but are not limited to: attempted division by 0, attempted access beyond array bounds, attempted access of non-existent files/directories, as well as out of memory errors.
	Exceptions were designed to ensure that you the programmer handle aberrant situations gracefully.
	When such conditions arise, the running of the program will actually be aborted unless you the programmer have written code to "catch" the exception.
	In order to "catch" exceptions, the code that is liable to "throw" exceptions must be contained in a `try` block, as exceptions are only caught when you actually *try* to catch them.
2.	Why should you make sure that you catch every exception that might be thrown?
	1. One key reason for catching every exception is that the program stops running when an exception is thrown but not explicitly caught! Abnormal program termination is not acceptable to end users. 2. Catching exceptions ensures that the application has an opportunity to recover from errors gracefully, ensuring that the end user at worst suffers only minimal loss due to the exception condition(s).
3.	Run the program below and observe the exception that it will throw. ```\nusing System;\n\nclass Program\n{\n static void Main(string[] args)\n {\n int a = 5;\n int b = 0;\n Console.WriteLine(a / b);\n Console.WriteLine("After the calculation\\n");\n Console.ReadKey();\n }\n}\n```
	This will throw a `System.DivideByZeroException` exception. The program will not even get to the line which outputs the string *"After the calculation"*.
4.	Modify the program in the preceding exercise to catch the exception that was thrown. Your exception `catch` block should print out the statement *"I caught the exception!"*
	```\nusing System;\n\nclass Program\n{\n static void Main(string[] args)\n {\n int a = 5;\n int b = 0;\n try\n {\n Console.WriteLine("{0}/{1}={2}",a, b,(a/b));\n }\n```

| | ```
        catch (System.DivideByZeroException)
        {
            Console.WriteLine("I caught the exception!");
        }
        Console.WriteLine("After the calculation\n");
        Console.ReadKey();
    }
}
``` |
| 5. | What is the resulting exception from this code that is trying to access an uninitialized object reference?<br><br>```
using System;

class Program
{
    static void Main(string[] args)
    {
        string s = null;
        int length = s.Length;
        Console.ReadKey();
    }
}
```<br><br>The exception thrown is a `System.NullReferenceException` exception. |
| 6. | Modify the program in the preceding exercise to catch the exception thrown and also to print the message of the exception out. |
| | ```
using System;

class Program
{
    static void Main(string[] args)
    {
        string s = null;
        try
        {
            int length = s.Length;
        }
        catch (System.NullReferenceException x)
        {
            Console.WriteLine("Exception caught.");
            Console.WriteLine("{0}", x.Message);
        }
        Console.ReadKey();
    }
}
``` |
| 7. | State which exception is thrown by the code shown below.<br><br>```
using System;

class Program
{
    static void Main(string[] args)
    {
        int x1 = int.MaxValue;
        int x2 = int.MaxValue - 1000;
        int x3;

        checked
        {
            x3 = x1 + x2;
        }
    }
}
```<br><br>The exception thrown is a `System.OverflowException` exception. |
| 8. | Modify the program in the preceding exercise to catch the thrown exception and print out the text *"I caught the* |

	overflow exception!" in the exception handler.
|   | ```
using System;
class Program
{
  static void Main(string[] args)
  {
    int x1 = int.MaxValue; int x2 = int.MaxValue - 1000;
    int x3;

    try
    {
      checked
      {
        x3 = x1 + x2;
      }
    }
    catch (System.OverflowException)
    {
      Console.WriteLine("I caught the overflow exception");
    }
    Console.ReadKey();
  }
}
``` |
| 9. | What exception does the following code trying to access a non-existent file on the desktop throw?<br>```
using System;
using System.IO;

class Program
{
  static void Main(string[] args)
  {
    string fileName = "ThIsFiLeDoESntExIST.txt";
    string sTarget;

    sTarget = Environment.GetFolderPath(Environment.SpecialFolder.Desktop)
            + Path.DirectorySeparatorChar + fileName;
    FileInfo fInfo = new FileInfo(sTarget);
    fInfo.CopyTo(Environment.GetFolderPath(Environment.SpecialFolder.Desktop));
  }
}
``` |
| | The exception thrown is a `System.IO.FileNotFoundException` exception. |
| 10. | Modify the program in the preceding exercise to catch the thrown exception. When it is caught, print out the following statement:
"The file <filename> was not found". |
|   | ```
using System;
using System.IO;

class Program
{
  static void Main(string[] args)
  {
    string fileName = "ThIsFiLeDoESntExIST.txt";
    string sTarget;

    sTarget = Environment.GetFolderPath(Environment.SpecialFolder.Desktop)
            + Path.DirectorySeparatorChar + fileName;
    FileInfo fInfo = new FileInfo(sTarget);
    try
    {
      fInfo.CopyTo(Environment.GetFolderPath(Environment.SpecialFolder.Desktop));
    }
    catch (System.IO.FileNotFoundException)
``` |
```

| | ``` 
       {
          Console.WriteLine("The file {0} was not found.", sTarget);
       }
       Console.ReadKey();
    }
}
``` |
| 11. | What exception does the following code trying to access an out of bounds array index throw?<br><br>```
using System;
using System.IO;

class Program
{
   static void Main(string[] args)
   {
      int arrayIndex = 10;
      int[] iArray = new int[5];
      iArray[arrayIndex] = 1500;

      Console.WriteLine("After the array index access\n");
      Console.ReadKey();
   }
}
```<br><br>This will throw a `System.IndexOutOfRangeException` exception. |
| 12. | Modify the program in the preceding exercise to catch the thrown exception and print out the text *"I caught the exception!"* in the exception handler.<br><br>```
using System;

class Program
{
   static void Main(string[] args)
   {
      int arrayIndex = 10;
      int[] iArray = new int[5];

      try
      {
         iArray[arrayIndex] = 1500;
      }
      catch (System.IndexOutOfRangeException)
      {
         Console.WriteLine("I caught the exception!");
      }
      Console.WriteLine("After the array index access attempt\n");
      Console.ReadKey();
   }
}
``` |
| 13. | Modify the exception handler in the solution to the preceding exercise to print out the following information about the exception from the exception object:

1. Exception name
2. Exception description
3. Program name
4. Stack Trace at the point of the exception
5. The method in which the exception occurred. |
| | ```
using System;
using System.IO;

class Program
{
   static void Main(string[] args)
   {
      int arrayIndex = 10;
``` |

|   | ```
      int[] iArray = new int[5];
      try
      {
        iArray[arrayIndex] = 1500;
      }
      catch (System.IndexOutOfRangeException e)
      {
        Console.WriteLine("1. {0}", e.GetBaseException());
        // Exception name, exception description, fully resolved method name
        // (<namespace>.<class>.<method>), source file name, line number
        Console.WriteLine("2. {0}", e.Message);      // Exception description
        Console.WriteLine("3. {0}", e.Source);       // Program name
        Console.WriteLine("4. {0}", e.StackTrace);   // Exception location: fully
                                                     // resolved method, file location, line #
        Console.WriteLine("5. {0}", e.TargetSite);   // the method in which the exception occurred
      }
      Console.WriteLine("After the array index access attempt\n");
      Console.ReadKey();
    }
}
``` |
| 14. | Modify the solution to the preceding exercise to use the top level exception `System.Exception` instead of the `System.IndexOutOfRange` exception. |
| | ```
using System;
using System.IO;

class Program
{
  static void Main(string[] args)
  {
    int arrayIndex = 10;
    int[] iArray = new int[5];
    try
    {
      iArray[arrayIndex] = 1500;
    }
    catch (System.Exception e)
    {
      Console.WriteLine("1. {0}", e.GetBaseException());
      Console.WriteLine("2. {0}", e.Message);
      Console.WriteLine("3. {0}", e.Source);
      Console.WriteLine("4. {0}", e.StackTrace);
      Console.WriteLine("5. {0}", e.TargetSite);
    }
    Console.WriteLine("After the array index access\n");
    Console.ReadKey();
  }
}
```

Notes: `System.Exception` (also known as `Exception`, when you have <u>using System;</u> in your code) is the ancestor class for exceptions, that is why, through polymorphism, it is able to catch all other exceptions. The reader is advised to take care in handling `System.Exception` because it is the highest level exception handling class. |

| 15. | Explain the compilation error that results from the following code:<br><br>```
using System;

class Program
{
    static void Main(string[] args)
    {
        int arrayIndex = 10;
        int[] iArray = new int[5];
        try
        {
            iArray[arrayIndex] = 1500;
        }
        catch (System.Exception e)
        {
        }
        catch (System.IndexOutOfRangeException e)
        {
        }
        Console.WriteLine("After the array access\n");
        Console.ReadKey();
    }
}
``` |
	The compiler will let you know that the 2nd exception handler cannot be reached due to the fact that there is a preceding `catch` that is capable of handling what the 2nd exception handler can catch, thus making the 2nd exception catcher "unreachable code". This is the case because `System.Exception` is a parent exception to `System.IndexOutOfRangeException`.
16.	Exchange the position of the exception handlers above and explain the result of the compilation.
	The code compiles and runs without any problem. The reason for this is that no longer is the exception handler that handles the exception `System.IndexOutOfRangeException` unreachable code. Now, does this mean that the exception handler that handles the exception `System.Exception` is unreachable code? No, because at compile time the compiler does not know what exceptions might result from the `try{}` block and thus does not know whether the catch block that catches `System.IndexOutOfRangeException` will catch every exception that might result. And since the catch block that catches `System.IndexOutOfRangeException` will not cause the code block that catches `System.Exception` to be unreachable, the compiler has nothing to complain about. Also it can be seen from this example that multiple exception catchers for different possible exceptions can be applied to a single `try` block.
17.	Describe what a `finally{}` code block does with respect to exception handling.
	A `finally{}` block is a block of code which is run after a series of `try/catch` blocks, whether or not the contents of the `try/catch` blocks throw exceptions or not. The `finally` block is a good place to put resource cleanup code, for example, code for releasing file handles, code for releasing network connections and such like.
| 18. | Modify the code below by adding a `finally` block to it to print out the date/time at which the code was run.<br><br>```
using System;

class Program
{
    static void Main(string[] args)
    {
        int arrayIndex = 10;
        int[] iArray = new int[5];
        try
        {
            iArray[arrayIndex] = 1500;
        }
        catch (System.IndexOutOfRangeException)
``` |

|   | ```
      {
         Console.WriteLine("I caught the exception!");
      }
      Console.WriteLine("After the array index access violation\n");
      Console.ReadKey();
   }
}
``` |
|   | ```
using System;
class Program
{
   static void Main(string[] args)
   {
      int arrayIndex = 10;
      int[] iArray = new int[5];
      try
      {
         iArray[arrayIndex] = 1500;
      }
      catch (System.IndexOutOfRangeException)
      {
         Console.WriteLine("I caught the exception!");
      }
      finally
      {
         Console.WriteLine("Finally block:Code ran at {0} ", DateTime.Now);
      }
      Console.WriteLine("After the array index access violation\n");
      Console.ReadKey();
   }
}
``` |
| | **Note:** You can modify the array index to bring it within bounds and rerun the code to confirm that indeed the `finally` block is run whether or not the `try/catch` block was invoked. |
| 19. | *Deliberately throwing an exception*
Write a program which divides a given float value by another (hardcode the values for testing). Throw the exception `ApplicationException` when the divisor is divisible by 2. Also ensure that you catch the built-in `DivideByZeroException` exception.
The catch block for the `ApplicationException` should print out the message *"Divisor divisible by 2 exception"*. |
|   | ```
using System;
namespace PracticeYourCSharp
{
   class Program
   {
      static void Main(string[] args)
      {
         float a = 10, b = 2;
         float c;
         try
         {
            if ((b % 2) == 0)
            {
               throw new ApplicationException("Divisor divisible by 2 exception");
            }
            c = a / b;
            Console.WriteLine(c);
         }
         catch (ApplicationException e)
         {
            Console.WriteLine(e.Message);
``` |
```

	``
	}
	catch(DivideByZeroException e)
	{
	Console.WriteLine(e.Message);
	}
	Console.ReadKey();
	}
	}
	}
	``
20.	Predict and explain the output of the program below.
	``
	using System;
	namespace PracticeYourCSharp
	{
	class Program
	{
	public static void A()
	{
	int a = 10, b = 0;
	int result;
	try
	{
	result = a / b;
	}
	catch (DivideByZeroException)
	{
	Console.WriteLine("A divide by zero situation has occurred. Rethrowing this exception!");
	throw;
	}
	}
	static void Main(string[] args)
	{
	try
	{
	A();
	}
	catch (DivideByZeroException e)
	{
	Console.WriteLine("In main...exception caught.");
	}
	Console.ReadKey();
	}
	}
	}
	``
	Output
	``
	A divide by zero situation has occurred. Rethrowing this exception!
	In main...exception caught.
	``
	Observation/Explanation
	The method A(), called from Main(), has a try block in Main around it. When A() catches an exception and rethrows it using the keyword throw, the try block in Main recatches the same exception.
	From this exercise the following can be observed:
	1. try blocks that catch rethrown exceptions (or in fact non-rethrow exceptions, see next exercise) do not have to be local to the method in which the rethrow occurs.
	2. When designing a program, you can have a try block in your method Main that can serve as a catch-all for any exceptions not caught elsewhere in your program.
21.	Predict and explain the output of the program below.
	``
	using System;
	``

```
namespace PracticeYourCSharp
{
  class Program
  {
    public static void A()
    {
      int a = 10, b = 0;
      int result;

        result = a / b;
    }
    static void Main(string[] args)
    {
      try
      {
        A();
      }
      catch (DivideByZeroException e)
      {
        Console.WriteLine("In Main...exception caught.");
      }
      Console.ReadKey();
    }
  }
}
```

Output
```
In Main...exception caught.
```

Observation/Explanation
An exception condition was triggered in the method `A()`, but caught in another method, `Main()`, which had invoked `A()` from within a `try` block.

This scenario further emphasizes the fact as displayed in the preceding exercise that a calling method can actually catch uncaught exceptions in the methods that it calls.

22. *User-defined exceptions*

Write a program which divides a given `float` value by another (hardcode the values for testing). Create your own exception named `DivideBy2Exception` which you should throw when the divisor is divisible by 2.

Have the `catch` block for the exception print out the following:
   1. the `Message` field of the exception
   2. the phrase: *"Divisor divisible by 2 exception"*

```
using System;

namespace PracticeYourCSharp
{
  class DivideBy2Exception : Exception
  {
    //This simple class to define our new exception suffices for our exercise.
  }
  class Program
  {
    static void Main(string[] args)
    {
      float a = 10, b = 2;
      float c;
      try
      {
        if ((b % 2) == 0)
        {
          throw new DivideBy2Exception(); //Here we throwing the exception.
        }
```

```
          c = a / b;
          Console.WriteLine(c);
        }
        catch (DivideBy2Exception e)
        {
          Console.WriteLine(e.Message);
          Console.WriteLine("Divisor divisible by 2 exception");
        }
        Console.ReadKey();
      }
    }
}
```

23.	*Rethrowing exceptions*
	Predict the output of the program below, then run it and explain the reason for the output.
	
	``
	using System;
	
	namespace PracticeYourCSharp
	{
	  class Program
	  {
	    static void Main(string[] args)
	    {
	      try
	      {
	        int a = 10, b = 0;
	        int result;
	
	        try
	        {
	          result = a / b;
	        }
	        catch (DivideByZeroException)
	        {
	          Console.Write ("Divide by zero situation has occurred.");
	          Console.WriteLine("Rethrowing this exception.");
	          throw;
	        }
	      } // end of outer try block
	      catch (DivideByZeroException e)
	      {
	        Console.WriteLine("Outer try block...exception caught.");
	      }
	      Console.ReadKey();
	    }
	  }
	}
	``

	Output
	  Divide by zero situation has occurred. Rethrowing this exception!
	  Outer try block...exception caught.
	
	Explanation
	This code displays the concept of "rethrowing" an exception and how this works in conjunction with nested **try** blocks. The following points are noted in this code:
	1. The inner **try** block has a corresponding **catch** block that rethrows the caught exception simply by using the keyword **throw**.
	2. The outer **try** block, which catches the rethrown exception.

24.	Modify the catch for the outer **try** block in the exercise above to catch exceptions of class **Exception**. Run the modified code and explain the results.
	The output is the same as in the preceding solution. The reason for this is that **Exception** (also known as **System.Exception**) is the parent exception class and

	therefore its handler can act as a catch-all for whatever is not caught.
25.	Give a scenario in which you might want to implement the rethrowing and catching of an exception.
	A scenario where this might occur would be in a case where you have local handling for the exception, but then at a higher level you have more general handling for that exception wherever it occurs in the code.
26.	Give a reason/scenario where nested **try** blocks would be of value to your code.
	We might, for example, have inner **try** blocks in order to catch all exception scenarios, however perhaps not all exception scenarios have been foreseen. An outer **try** block that catches the parent exception **Exception** will help your application to handle any such failure gracefully.
27.	**(6.0)** Using exception filters, rewrite the code in question 19 to create two different **DivideBy2Exception** catch blocks, the first to handle the case when the divisor is >=10, the other for when the divisor < 10.
| | ```csharp
using System;

class DivideBy2Exception : Exception
{
  //This simple class to define our new exception suffices for our exercise.
}

class Program
{
  static void Main(string[] args)
  {
    float a = 10, b = 2; float c;
    try
    {
      if ((b % 2) == 0)
      {
        throw new DivideBy2Exception(); //Here we throwing the exception.
      }
      c = a / b;
      Console.WriteLine(c);
    }
    catch (DivideBy2Exception e) when (b >= 10)
    {
      Console.WriteLine(e.Message);
      Console.WriteLine("Divisor divisible by 2 exception handling when divisor >= 10");
    }
    catch (DivideBy2Exception e) when (b < 10)
    {
      Console.WriteLine(e.Message);
      Console.WriteLine("Divisor divisible by 2 exception handling when divisor < 10");
    }
    Console.ReadKey();
  }
}
``` |
```

Chapter 33. Character Encoding

The intent of this chapter is to ensure that you are conversant with the concept of character encoding. The concept of character encoding is an important one as it pertains to understanding the fact that there are different encoding schemes by which data can be represented and output for storage. In this chapter, exercises are presented on the concept of Unicode and its related encoding schemes. Exercises on the ASCII character encoding scheme and its relationship to UTF-8 are also presented in this chapter. We also look at the presentation of strings in different encodings and the concept of endianness as pertains to strings.

Classes utilized in this chapter include `StringInfo`, `Char`, `UnicodeEncoding`, `UTF8Encoding`, `UTF32Encoding` and `BitConverter`.

1.	What is Unicode?	Unicode is a standard for the representation and encoding of most of the known alphabets in the world. Each character is represented in Unicode by a hexadecimal value.
2.	In Unicode what is a "code point"?	For general intents and purposes, "code point" is the name given to the numerical value assigned to each Unicode character.
3.	What is the numerical range of the code points that Unicode supports?	`0000` to `10FFFF` *(Hex)* which is equivalent to `0` to `1114111` *(Decimal)*. This covers 1,114,112 characters.
4.	Describe a Unicode plane.	A Unicode code plane is a specific designated range of code points within the Unicode code point range. Each plane has space for 65536 code points. There are 17 code planes *(numbered 0 to 16 in decimal)* defined. As stated earlier, each code plane has space for 2^{16} characters. The Unicode code point range (`0000` to `10FFFF` as noted earlier) is split evenly and contiguously across the 17 code planes. Not all code points in all planes have been filled, for various reasons including: 1. they have not yet been assigned characters. 2. certain code points are left blank for use as "private code points" for private fonts. 3. they are used as mapping space for other code planes (to be seen later).
5.	How many code planes are there in Unicode?	17 planes, numbered `0` to `10` (Hex).
6.	In Unicode, what does "BMP" refer to?	BMP = **B**asic **M**ultilingual **P**lane. This is the 1st plane (code plane 0). The characters for most modern languages reside here.
7.	What are the planes other than BMP referred to as?	They are called Supplemental Planes. Not all code points in them are assigned at present.
8.	How many code points are there space for in each Unicode code plane?	2^{16} = 65536 possible code points; they would be numbered in hexadecimal from `0` to `FFFF`.
9.	What is the nomenclature for presenting Unicode characters?	U+<assigned code point, in hexadecimal> For example, the character 'A' is referred to as `U+0041` The character '5' is referred to as `U+0035` The character '€' is referred to as `U+20AC`
10.	What is the total number of characters that can possibly be represented in Unicode?	This value is given by *(number of code planes)* x *(number of code points per plane)* = 17 x 65536 = 1,114,112 In hexadecimal, these are represented by code points `0` to `10FFFF`

11.	What is a Unicode encoding scheme?	A Unicode encoding scheme *(called a Unicode Transformation Format or UTF for short)* is a standard scheme by which characters in the Unicode space are represented. There are a different number of schemes, each of which has a different emphasis; for example, UTF-8 is a scheme best used when you know you have a lot of data that is ASCII conformant because UTF-8 encodes these efficiently in one byte. However, UTF-8 is a variable byte scheme which might not be an optimal one for file-seeking purposes. UTF-16 is a fixed 2 or 4 byte scheme and if your application uses all BMP characters, then you have 2 bytes representing each character uniformly. UTF-32 is a fixed 4 byte scheme which uses 4 bytes for each number, however that might be considered a waste of space if you do not use characters in planes higher than BMP.
12.	Give the names of the current most common Unicode encoding schemes.	UTF-8, UTF-16, UTF-32
13.	How many assigned code points are there actually in the BMP?	There are actually only the following code point ranges pre-defined in BMP: `0000 – 0D7FF & E000 – FFFF` The gap between both ranges is <u>illegal</u> for use for characters that are represented by 2 bytes. Note also that within the 2nd range specified above, `E000` to `F8FF` are not pre-defined; these are "Private Use Areas" within the BMP.
14.	Why is there a gap in the BMP code point ranges?	The reason for this is in order for UTF-16 to have the ability to support the higher code planes than just BMP. The gap in the BMP code point numbering scheme corresponds to the range `D800 – DFFF`. Values in this range are used to indicate and also represent the fact that a character from a higher code plane than BMP is coming along in the data stream. Recall that UTF-16 uses either 2 or 4 bytes to represent each character. In a given UTF-16 data stream, if all 65536 characters were used to represent characters, how would we be able to know when we should be looking at 2 bytes or 4 bytes? Therefore we need a range of numbers within the `0 – FFFF` space that we will use as indicators to let whatever is interpreting the data stream know that it should assess 4 bytes to be interpreted as a character rather than just 2 bytes.
15.	What is the name given to the 1st 2 bytes of a 4 byte UTF-16 encoded character?	Lead surrogate (formerly known as <u>high surrogate</u>).
16.	What is the number range of the 1st pair of bytes of a *4 byte UTF-16* encoded character?	`0xD800 - 0xDBFF`
17.	What is the name given to the 2nd pair of bytes of a 4 byte UTF-16 encoded character?	Trail surrogate (formerly known as <u>low surrogate</u>).
18.	What, in hexadecimal, is the number range of the 2nd pair of bytes of a 4 byte UTF-16 encoded character?	`0xDC00 - 0xDFFF`
19.	Describe the ASCII encoding scheme.	ASCII is a character encoding scheme that predates Unicode. It is a 7 bit scheme, thus supporting only 0-127 = 128 characters.

20.	What is UTF-8 and how many bytes does UTF-8 use to encode a character?	UTF-8 is a variable-byte encoding scheme that uses an effective 1 to 4 bytes to encode characters.
21.	What is the relationship between UTF-8 and ASCII?	UTF-8 was designed to be backwards compatible with ASCII and thus ASCII is a subset of UTF-8. The ASCII character set characters are the characters that UTF-8 encodes in its values 0-127.
22.	How many bytes does a UTF-16 character occupy?	2 or 4. The basic characters represented by UTF-16 are represented in 16 bits (2 bytes) (this covers the characters in the BMP). Most languages characters are covered within the BMP; however if a character outside the BMP is used, it is then necessary to represent the character with 4 bytes. Note though that most characters that we use will be within the BMP and thus only require 2 bytes. Contrast this with UTF-8 which is a variable-byte encoding scheme.
23.	How many bytes does UTF-32 occupy?	A fixed 4-bytes per character.
24.	What is the character encoding used for the `char` type in C#?	UTF-16. That is, each character will be represented by 2 bytes if it is in the BMP (which most characters used are in) However, if you have characters beyond the BMP then C# will use 2 chars (4 bytes) to represent the character in question. **Note that in C#, the word "Unicode" is used to mean UTF-16.**
25.	How many bytes are used to represent a char in C#?	A `char` is defined as occupying 2 bytes. You can verify this by executing the following code: `Console.WriteLine(sizeof(char));` The `char` type has the same number range as a `ushort`, which has a range of `0000` to `FFFF` (Hex) and thus can fully represent each code point in the BMP.
26.	Since a `char` is set to a fixed size of 2 bytes in C#, how are characters that are beyond the BMP represented in C#?	C# will use as many chars as necessary to represent the character in question, therefore for anything above the BMP, it will use 2 chars (which is 4 bytes) to represent the character, one char for the lead surrogate and one char for the trail surrogate. Note that if you are assigning the value of a non-BMP plane character to a `char`, then you the programmer have to assign the lead surrogate to a `char` and the trail surrogate to the `char` adjoining the first (implies use of a `char` array).

		Character	ASCII	UTF-8	UTF-16	UTF-32
27.	Give the encoding *in hexadecimal*, in each of ASCII, UTF-8, UTF-16, UTF-32 of the following characters: 'A', '€', '7', '8', 'é' *Hint: look on the web for a converter, or look at www.unicode.org*	A	41	41	00 41	00 00 00 41
		€	Not in standard english ASCII range	E2 82 AC	20 AC	00 00 20 AC
		7	37	37	00 37	00 00 00 37
		8	38	38	00 38	00 00 00 38
		é	E9	C3 A9	00 E9	00 00 00 E9

28.	Looking at the ASCII table, what character does the value 36 (Decimal) refer to?	The dollar sign ($)
29.	What is the UTF-16 representation of the character $?	U+0024 0024(Hex) = 36 Decimal

30.	Write a code fragment that shows the assignment of the value 40 (decimal) to a `char c1` and prints the character out to the	`char c1 = (char)40;`
		`Console.WriteLine(c1);`
		what is printed out is the right bracket character.)

		console.

31.	*Mapping a non-BMP number to the BMP plane*
	
	We have the code point `U+20213`. Manually determine the lead and trail surrogates that this code point translates to.
	
	Also, write a code fragment which shows how to print out the character that corresponds to the code point (Since this is greater than `FFFF`, clearly this will need to be represented by 4 bytes (i.e. 2 chars)).
		First you note that the value `20213` is greater than `FFFF`, therefore this number is not in the BMP. As a result, you have to break it into its leading surrogate and trailing surrogate values (this implies that this character occupies 4 bytes = 2 `char`s). You can do this by manual calculation using the conversion formula, or locate a converter/calculator which will do the conversion for you.
		
		Manually the conversion is as follows:
		
		First determine the lead surrogate...
		20213 − **10000** = 10213
		Next: convert to binary: 00010000001000010011 (it must be 20 bits in length)
		Identify the top 10 bits: 0001000000
		Add these to D800: = **D840**. This is the lead surrogate
		
		Now, to calculate the trail surrogate...
		Identify the low 10 bits of the earlier binary number: 1000010011
		Add these to DC00: = **DF13**. This is the trail surrogate
		
		You see how these two numbers (the surrogates) have been mapped into the 16-bit range that is left blank in the BMP to indicate surrogates pairs.
		
		Now for the code fragment:
		`char[] cArray01 = new char[2];`
		`cArray01[0] = '\xD840';  // The leading surrogate`
		`cArray01[1] = '\xDF13';  // The trailing surrogate`
		`string s1 = new String(cArray01);`
		
		Note: The console at best directly supports only extended ASCII characters, therefore, instead of printing a recognizable character, it will use a "replacement character" to stand in for the characters that it cannot print. Therefore, while outside the scope of this book, if you are conversant with Windows Presentation Foundation programming, put this string into a `TextBox` and it will show you the actual character in question.

32.	What is the result of the following code applied to the string `s1` from the preceding exercise? `    Console.WriteLine(s1.Length);`	
	It returns an incorrect value of 2. The returned value is incorrect, because we only have one character in the string, however yes, it is represented by 2 chars. **Conclusion**: for non-BMP range characters, using the `Length` property of class `String` in question will not (at least not as of this version of C#) yield the correct result.	

33.	Using the class `StringInfo`, write the lines of code that will return the proper length of the string above.	The code fragment is as follows
		(ensure to include **using System.Globalization;**):
		
		`    StringInfo si01 = new StringInfo(s1);`
		`    Console.WriteLine(si01.LengthInTextElements);`
		
		This returns the proper length, which is **1**.
		
		Therefore, for proper calculation of the "number of characters" in a string, the way the characters would be counted by a human being, `StringInfo` is the correct class to use.

34.	Manually determine the leading and trail surrogates of the code point `U+11201`.	leading surrogate = `D804` trailing surrogate = `DE01`

35.	I have an array of `char` with the following UTF-16 values: 0023, D809, DE03, FEF0 and 0439 Write a program which loops through this array and prints out each element and whether it is a leading surrogate, trailing surrogate, or a BMP character. *Hint:* Char.IsHighSurrorgate, Char.IsLowSurrogate	
| | ```
using System;
namespace PracticeYourCSharp
{
  class Program
  {
    static void Main(string[] args)
    {
      char[] charArray01 = new char[]{'\x0023','\xD809','\xDE03','\xFEF0','\x0439'};
      for(int i=0; i< charArray01.Length;i++)
      {
        if(Char.IsHighSurrogate(charArray01[i])==true)
          Console.WriteLine("{0:X} hex is a high surrogate",(int)charArray01[i]);
        else if(Char.IsLowSurrogate(charArray01[i])==true)
          Console.WriteLine("{0:X} hex is a low surrogate", (int)charArray01[i]);
        else
          Console.WriteLine("{0:X} hex is in BMP", (int)charArray01[i]);
      }
      Console.ReadKey();
    }
  }
}
``` | |
| 36. | What is the default encoding scheme that the `StreamWriter` class uses for writing files to disk? | It uses UTF-8 encoding.<br>The following code fragment shows how you can confirm this:<br>```
StreamWriter sw = new StreamWriter(<give name of a new file>);
Console.WriteLine(sw.Encoding);
Console.ReadKey();
``` |
Converting strings between encoding types		
37.	*Endianness* What is Endianness? Describe also what is meant by little-endian and big-endian.	Endianness refers to the chosen convention used to interpret the byte order making up a word(2 bytes) when those bytes are stored in memory. We will use the example of the word CDF1. This value will take up two bytes in memory. For this example we will use memory locations [0] and [1]. A little-endian system will store the lower byte in the lower numbered memory location and the upper byte in the higher numbered memory location, so for this example, the values of the memory locations will be: [0] = F1 [1] = CD A big-endian system will store the most significant byte in the lower address (it is like writing from left to right in latin script). And this result in the word CDF1 being stored as: [0] = CD [1] = F1
38.	Manually write out, in decimal, the UTF-8, UTF-16 and UTF-32 encoding of the character 'H'.	UTF-8 : 72 UTF-16: 0 72 UTF-32: 0 0 0 72
39.	Manually write out, in decimal, the UTF-8, UTF-16 and UTF-32 encoding of the string "He".	UTF-8 : 72 101 UTF-16: 0 72 0 101 UTF-32: 0 0 0 72 0 0 0 101
| 40. | Using a `UnicodeEncoding` object and the `string` variables s01="H" and s02="He" and s03="€", write a program which prints out | ```
using System;
using System.Text;

namespace PracticeYourCSharp
{
``` |
```

	the following:
	1. how many bytes are used to represent each string *and*
	2. the actual bytes in hexadecimal that represent the string.
	Note: In C#, when the phrase "Unicode" is mentioned, it is referring to UTF-16 in particular.
		``cs
		class Program
		{
		  public static void PrintBytes(byte[] x)
		  {
		    if (x.Length == 0) return;
		    for (int i = 0; i < x.Length; i++)
		    {
		      Console.Write("{0:X} ", x[i]);
		    }
		    Console.WriteLine();
		  }
		
		  static void Main(string[] args)
		  {
		    UnicodeEncoding enc01 = new UnicodeEncoding();
		    string s01 = "H";
		    int byteCount = enc01.GetByteCount(s01);
		    Console.WriteLine("Byte count={0}", byteCount);
		    byte[] ba01 = enc01.GetBytes(s01);
		    PrintBytes(ba01);
		    Console.WriteLine();
		
		    string s02 = "He";
		    byteCount = enc01.GetByteCount(s02);
		    Console.WriteLine("Byte count={0}", byteCount);
		    byte[] ba02 = enc01.GetBytes(s02);
		    PrintBytes(ba02);
		    Console.WriteLine();
		
		    string s03 = "€";
		    byteCount = enc01.GetByteCount(s03);
		    Console.WriteLine("Byte count={0}", byteCount);
		    byte[] ba03 = enc01.GetBytes(s03);
		    PrintBytes(ba03);
		    Console.ReadKey();
		  }
		}
		``
		Output:
		Byte count=2
		48 0
		
		Byte count=4
		48 0 65 0
		
		Byte count=2
		AC 20

41.	Explain why in the answer above, using the variable `string01` as an example, the bytes were printed out as **48 0**, which is the reverse of the order in which they are supposed to be.	The reason the code outputs **48 0** (i.e. the bytes in the word were printed in reverse order) is because of the little-endian scheme that is employed in both C# and the x86 processor that the code is running on. As each character was assessed, its bytes were put into the byte array in little-endian order; therefore the lower order value was put into `[x]` and the higher order value was put into `[x+1]`. The solution to this is to be cognizant of endianness when accessing/printing out such data.

42.	Redo the solution to exercise 40, ensuring that the bytes of the input string are output in their proper order (i.e. taking endianness into account).	*Modify the `PrintBytes` method above as follows:*
		
		``cs
		public static void PrintBytes(byte[] x)
		{
		  if (x.Length == 0) return;
		  if(x.Length % 2==1)
		``

	Hint: Use `BitConverter.ToInt16`	```
    {
        int newLength = x.Length + 1;
        // Then extend the array and pad it with one byte
        // so that it has an even number of bytes
        // You see, since we are assessing the bytes in pairs
        // and UTF-8 might not give an even number of bytes
        Array.Resize(ref x, newLength);
        x[(newLength-1)] = 0;
    }
    string outStr = "";
    for (int i = 0; i < x.Length; i += 2)
    {
        short short01 = BitConverter.ToInt16(x, i);
        outStr += short01.ToString("X") + " ";
    }
    Console.WriteLine(outStr);
}
```
**Notes:** Here we see that `BitConverter.ToInt16` takes the endianness of the data into account, accessing the lower byte and the upper byte of the data and presenting it in the proper order of upper byte then lower byte. |
| 43. | For a given string s1="Hello", print out the following information for each of the following encodings UTF-16 (which in C# is referred to as "Unicode"), UTF-8 and UTF-32:<br>• The name of the encoding being applied<br>• The *Windows code page* that the encoding is regarded as being on<br>• The number of bytes used to encode the string in the given encoding scheme<br>• The actual bytes that the string is encoded as | *Note that we will still use our `PrintBytes` method from the solution to the preceding exercise.*<br>```
static void Main(string[] args)
{
    UnicodeEncoding enc01 = new UnicodeEncoding();
    Console.WriteLine(enc01.BodyName);
    Console.WriteLine(enc01.CodePage);
    string s01 = "Hello";
    int byteCount = enc01.GetByteCount(s01);
    Console.WriteLine("byte count={0}",byteCount);
    byte[] ba01 = enc01.GetBytes(s01);
    PrintBytes(ba01);
    Console.WriteLine();

    UTF8Encoding enc02 = new UTF8Encoding();
    Console.WriteLine(enc02.BodyName);
    Console.WriteLine(enc02.CodePage);
    byteCount = enc02.GetByteCount(s01);
    Console.WriteLine("byte count={0}",byteCount);
    ba01 = enc02.GetBytes(s01);
    PrintBytes(ba01);
    Console.WriteLine();

    UTF32Encoding enc03 = new UTF32Encoding ();
    Console.WriteLine(enc03.BodyName);
    Console.WriteLine(enc03.CodePage);
    byteCount = enc03.GetByteCount(s01);
    Console.WriteLine(byteCount);
    ba01 = enc03.GetBytes(s01);
    PrintBytes(ba01);
    Console.ReadKey();
}
``` |
| E1 | Write a converter which will convert BMP values to their leading surrogate and trailing surrogate values. | |

Chapter 34. File Streams I

The file stream functionality of C# facilitates fine control over file input and output. File streams support specific read/write modes on files, specific file access modes, specific file-sharing permissions and also, control over the encoding scheme used to write files.

This chapter exercises your skills on the above details as well as various file operations such as reading, writing, appending, seeking and modifying file contents. These exercises involve the use of FileStream, BinaryReader/Writer and StreamReader/Writer objects.

The exercises and answers in this chapter will help to solidify your understanding of file streams in C#.

In a previous chapter you have already done some work in writing and reading files from disk using a class layer that is above the file streams; however it is with file streams that you have far greater control over what and how you read and write from disk.

Note: While indeed streams in C# deal not only with disk systems, our focus in this book will be on reading from and writing to disk.

M	Manually create a folder named fstests on the *Desktop*. We will be using this folder as our primary folder for the coding exercises in this chapter.	
1.	What is the result if you initialize a FileStream with mode Append for a file that is *not* already existent?	The file in question will be created.
2.	What is the result if you initialize a FileStream with the mode Create on an already existing file?	The file will be overwritten.
3.	What is the result if you initialize a FileStream with the mode CreateNew on an already existing file?	An exception will be thrown.
4.	What is the result if you initialize a FileStream with file mode Open on a non-existent file?	An exception, System.IO.FileNotFoundException will be thrown.
5.	What is the result if you initialize a FileStream with the mode Truncate on a file?	The file will be truncated, i.e. the contents erased and thus the file size becomes 0.
6.	Initialize a FileStream on a file named test_file_01.txt in the earlier created directory fstests with the mode Create. Catch any potential resulting exceptions. Close the stream immediately after creating it.	

```
using System;
using System.IO;

namespace PracticeYourCSharp
{
  class Program
  {
    static void Main(string[] args)
    {
      string dirName01 = "fstests";
      string fileName01 = "test_file_01.txt";
      try
      {
        Environment.CurrentDirectory =
```

```
                    Environment.GetFolderPath(Environment.SpecialFolder.Desktop)
                    + Path.DirectorySeparatorChar + dirName01;
                // In effect, change directory to the directory fstests

                FileStream fs01 = new FileStream(fileName01, FileMode.Create);
                Console.WriteLine("File {0} created\n", fileName01);
                fs01.Close();
            }
            catch (Exception e)
            { Console.WriteLine(e.Message); }
            Console.ReadKey();
        }
    }
}
```

Notes: Note where the `try` block starts in this code.

Expected Results

If no exception was thrown, look inside the folder `fstests`; the file `test_file_01.txt` will have been created, with a size of 0.

M	Manually open the just created file `test_file_01.txt`. Type your name into it, then save and close it. Note the size of the file.	
7.	Re-run the code from exercise 6 above and explain the effects on the file `test_file_01.txt`.	**Expected result** The contents of the file are wiped out (i.e. the file has been truncated to a size of 0), because file mode `Create` overwrites already existing files.
8.	Attempt to create a `FileStream` on the file `test_file_01.txt` above, using the mode `CreateNew`.	Code: Modify the solution for exercise 6 to use `FileMode.CreateNew`. **Expected result** An exception, `SystemIO.IOException` will be thrown (and caught with this code), indicating that the file already exists, for `CreateNew` indeed will attempt to create a new file only if the file does not already exist.
9.	Explain what the following `FileAccess` members mean: 1. Read 2. Write 3. ReadWrite	1. **Read** – means that the `FileStream` which is used to access the file in question will only be used to read the file, not write it. If you try to write with it, an exception will result. 2. **Write** – means that the `FileStream` which is used to access the file in question will only be used to write the file, not read it. If you try to read with it, an exception will result. 3. **ReadWrite** – means that the `FileStream` which is used to access the file in question can be used to both read and write the file.

10.	What is the difference between:
	 `FileAccess.Read|FileAccess.Write`
	 and
	 `FileAccess.ReadWrite`	

	There is no difference. `FileAccess` is a bitwise enumeration, therefore in the 1st statement, we are "turning the read flag on and also the write flag on". The second statement is simply a shortcut for the first.	
M	Manually modify the permissions of the file `test_file_01.txt` to *read-only* by right clicking on the file and setting the permission appropriately in the presented window.	
11.	Write a program which attempts to open the previously created test file `test_file_01.txt` in `Append` mode, with `FileAccess` mode `Write`.	
	``using System;
using System.IO;

namespace PracticeYourCSharp
{
    class Program
    {
``` | |
```

|   | ```cs
static void Main(string[] args)
{
  string dirName01 = "fstests";
  string fileName01 = "test_file_01.txt";

  try
  {
    Environment.CurrentDirectory =
                    Environment.GetFolderPath(Environment.SpecialFolder.Desktop) +
                    Path.DirectorySeparatorChar + dirName01;
    // In effect, change directory to the directory fstests

    FileStream fs01 = new FileStream(fileName01, FileMode.Append, FileAccess.Write);
    fs01.Close();
  }
  catch (Exception e)
  { Console.WriteLine(e.Message); }
  Console.ReadKey();
}
``` |   |
	Expected Results An exception will occur due to the fact that we are trying to obtain Write access to a file which has been designated *read-only*.	
12.	Explain the concept of file-sharing permissions.	
	File-sharing permissions in this context means the mode in which you want other streams to be able to access a file that you currently have opened a stream on. For example, on opening a stream for writing, you might find it acceptable to allow other applications to open a stream on the same file for reading, but not for writing while you are writing to the stream. In other circumstances, you might not even want any other application to open a stream for reading or writing on that file at all and in yet other instances you might be content with other FileStreams writing and reading the file at the same time as you.	
13.	Explain each of the following file sharing enumeration options: • None • Read • ReadWrite • Write	• None – Once a FileStream is opened with this option, no other FileStream will be able to access the file concurrently for any purpose. • Read – When a FileStream is opened with this, other FileStreams are able to access the file in question for reading at the same time. • ReadWrite – When a FileStream is opened with this, other FileStreams can read and write to the open file at the same time. • Write – When a FileStream is opened with this, other FileStreams can write to the file at the same time, however they are not permitted to read the file. **Note:** Even if you set any of these options, specific behaviors of the other applications accessing the file might keep them from taking advantage of how your application has set the file sharing options; for example, the other application(s) may want exclusive access to a file.
M	Manually modify the permissions of the file test_file_01.txt to *remove the read-only permission* that it was previously set to. Also, type your name into the file again and save it.	
14.	Modify the solution to exercise 11 in the following manner: • Add the attribute FileShare.None. • Add the statement Console.ReadKey(); *before* the line where the FileStream is closed. Run the code; it will halt at the line Console.ReadKey(). *During that halt*, manually attempt to open the previously created file test_file_01.txt using Notepad and report the results.	
|   | ```cs
using System;
using System.IO;

namespace PracticeYourCSharp
``` |   |

```
{
  class Program
  {
    static void Main(string[] args)
    {
      string dirName01 = "fstests";
      string fileName01 = "test_file_01.txt";

      try
      {
        Environment.CurrentDirectory =
        Environment.GetFolderPath(Environment.SpecialFolder.Desktop) +
                        Path.DirectorySeparatorChar + dirName01;
        // In effect, change directory to the directory fstests

        FileStream fs01 = new FileStream(fileName01, FileMode.Append,
                                       FileAccess.Write,
                                       FileShare.None);
        Console.ReadKey(); // Hold it here while you open the file manually.
        fs01.Close();
      }
      catch (Exception e)
      {
        Console.WriteLine(e.Message);
      }
      Console.ReadKey();
    }
  }
}
```

Expected Results
On trying to open the file manually in Notepad, Notepad cannot do so due to the `FileShare.None` option placed on the file. Notepad gives a message similar to the following: *"The process cannot access the file because it is being used by another process"*.

15.	Change the `FileShare` mode in the solution to the preceding exercise to `FileShare.Read`. Rerun the experiment above, this time manually adding text to the file <u>when the program is paused</u> and then attempt to save it. Describe the results seen.	**Expected Results** On trying to open the file manually in Notepad, Notepad will open the file. Notepad does allow the typing of data into the file, however on attempting to save the data, Notepad states: *"The process cannot access the file because it is being used by another process"* and thus does not allow us to save our modifications.
16.	How can you determine whether an existing file is currently being accessed by another application?	The solution is to attempt to open the file in question with `FileMode.Open` and `FileAccess.Read` and `FileShare.None`. If it returns an exception, then you know that another application is accessing the file.
17.	Do the following: 1. Write a program to open the file `test_file_01.txt` using the options noted in the solution above *Do not run this program until step 3*. 2. Open the file using Microsoft Word. 3. Run the program written in step #1. State your observations.	
| | ```
using System;
using System.IO;

namespace PracticeYourCSharp
{
  class Program
  {
    static void Main(string[] args)
``` | |
```

| | ```
      {
        string dirName01 = "fstests";
        string fileName01 = "test_file_01.txt";

        try
        {
          Environment.CurrentDirectory =
          Environment.GetFolderPath(Environment.SpecialFolder.Desktop) +
                          Path.DirectorySeparatorChar + dirName01;
          // In effect, change directory to the directory fstests

          FileStream fs01 = new FileStream(fileName01, FileMode.Open,
                                                      FileAccess.Read,
                                                      FileShare.None);
          fs01.Close();
        }
        catch (Exception e)
        {
          Console.WriteLine(e.Message);
        }
        Console.ReadKey();
      }
    }
}
``` |
	Observations The code will throw an exception, because another program already has the file open. Our code was to check whether another application had this file already open; we implemented this check by attempting to get an exclusive lock on it. The text of the exception will be something like *"The process cannot access the file <file name> because it is being used by another process."* **Notes** We had to use Microsoft Word for this experiment due to the way in which Notepad handles files that it has opened; Notepad appears to not hold an open `FileStream` on a file that it has opened, choosing rather to reacquire the `FileStream` later when it needs to write to disk.
18.	In C#, how many bytes does a `char` occupy and why?
	A `char` occupies two bytes. A `char` is used to represent Unicode UTF-16 encoded characters and these occupy either 2 bytes (for each of the characters in the BMP) or 4 bytes each. If there is a need to support characters which require 4 bytes, then 2 chars (which take up a total of 4 bytes) will be used in such a case.
19.	Open a `FileStream` on the file `test_file_01.txt` and print out the size of the file. *(If it does not have any data in it, using Notepad, type your name into it and count the number of characters (including spaces) that you've put into the file).*
| | ```
using System;
using System.IO;

namespace PracticeYourCSharp
{
  class Program
  {
    static void Main(string[] args)
    {
      string dirName01 = "fstests";
      string fileName01 = "test_file_01.txt";
      long length = 0;

      try
      {
        Environment.CurrentDirectory =
                Environment.GetFolderPath(Environment.SpecialFolder.Desktop) +
``` |

	<pre> Path.DirectorySeparatorChar + dirName01;
            // In effect, change directory to the directory fstests

            FileStream fs01 = new FileStream(fileName01, FileMode.Open);

            length = fs01.Length;
            fs01.Close();
            Console.WriteLine("The length is {0}", length);
        }
        catch (Exception e)
        { Console.WriteLine(e.Message); }
        Console.ReadKey();
      }
    }
}</pre> **Expected Results**
The reported length of this text file should equal the number of characters that you typed in (if the characters that you typed are in the ASCII space for your code page). |
20.	Given the fact that as noted earlier a `char` in C# is represented by two bytes, why is the length of the stream exactly the number of characters in the file and not twice that number?
	The reason is clearly because this file was saved by Notepad in either ASCII or UTF-8 encoding; and for the characters entered, these all fit into the ASCII character set (or the first 127 character range of UTF-8) which only requires one byte per character for representation.
21.	What are the advantages and disadvantages of the ASCII character set?
	Advantages: The ASCII character set occupies less space. It only requires one byte per character. **Disadvantages**: It cannot support more than a limited diversity of characters and is therefore unsuitable for multi-lingual data sets. *The relevance of these encoding exercises regarding character sets and byte encoding will become apparent later in this chapter. It is needful for you to be comfortable with the concepts of the size of and relationship between ASCII characters, the char type, Unicode characters and C# string encoding in order to enjoy the exercises in this chapter.*
22.	What is the data type that the `FileStream` writes and reads in?
	`byte`. What this means is that `FileStream` natively "thinks" of the data passed to it as a stream of bytes, not as a stream of `char`, or any other type.
23.	*Copying the contents of one `FileStream` to another* Using the appropriate `FileStream` methods, copy the file `test_file_01.txt` to a new file named `test_file_02.txt` in the same directory. Visually verify the creation of the new file and its contents.
	<pre>using System;
using System.IO;

namespace PracticeYourCSharp
{
  class Program
  {
    static void Main(string[] args)
    {
      string dirName01 = "fstests";
      string fileName01 = "test_file_01.txt";
      string fileName02 = "test_file_02.txt";

      try
      {
        Environment.CurrentDirectory =
                Environment.GetFolderPath(Environment.SpecialFolder.Desktop) +
                                    Path.DirectorySeparatorChar + dirName01;
        // In effect, change directory to the directory fstests</pre> |

```
            FileStream fs01 = new FileStream(fileName01, FileMode.Open, FileAccess.Read);
            FileStream fs02 = new FileStream(fileName02, FileMode.Create, FileAccess.Write);
            fs01.CopyTo(fs02);
            Console.WriteLine("Copying done");
            fs01.Close();
            fs02.Close();
          }
          catch (Exception e)
          { Console.WriteLine(e.Message); }
          Console.ReadKey();
        }
      }
    }
```

24.	Use the FileStream.Write method to add the text "\nMary had a little lamb\n" to file test_file_01.txt Write these out as a stream of ASCII characters rather than the default UTF-16 that C# uses. Use Notepad to view the resulting file. *Hint:* Encoding.ASCII.GetBytes(<string>)

```
using System;
using System.IO;
using System.Text;

namespace PracticeYourCSharp
{
  class Program
  {
    static void Main(string[] args)
    {
      string dirName01 = "fstests";
      string fileName01 = "test_file_01.txt";
      string newline = Environment.NewLine;
      string string01 = newline + "Mary had a little lamb" + newline;

      // Convert the string to a byte Array with an encoding type of ASCII.
      byte[] byteArray01 = Encoding.ASCII.GetBytes(string01);
      try
      {
        Environment.CurrentDirectory =
                Environment.GetFolderPath(Environment.SpecialFolder.Desktop) +
                                    Path.DirectorySeparatorChar + dirName01;
        // In effect, change directory to the directory fstests

        FileStream fs01 = new FileStream(fileName01, FileMode.Append, FileAccess.Write);
        fs01.Write(byteArray01, 0, byteArray01.Length);
        fs01.Close();
      }
      catch (Exception e)
      { Console.WriteLine(e.Message); }
      Console.ReadKey();
    }
  }
}
```

25.	Read in all the contents of the file test_file_01.txt, convert them to a string and print them out.

```
using System;
using System.IO;
using System.Text;

namespace PracticeYourCSharp
{
  class Program
  {
    static void Main(string[] args)
    {
```

```
            string dirName01 = "fstests";
            string fileName01 = "test_file_01.txt";
            string string01; // To get the data from the file
            byte[] byteArray01;

            try
            {
              Environment.CurrentDirectory =
              Environment.GetFolderPath(Environment.SpecialFolder.Desktop) +
                             Path.DirectorySeparatorChar + dirName01;
              FileStream fs01 = new FileStream(fileName01, FileMode.Open,
                                          FileAccess.ReadWrite);
              byteArray01 = new byte[fs01.Length];
              fs01.Read(byteArray01, 0, (int)fs01.Length);
              //We wrote it out in ASCII so we now convert it from ASCII to a string
              string01 = Encoding.ASCII.GetString(byteArray01);

              Console.WriteLine("The file contents are:\n{0}", string01);
              fs01.Close();
            }
            catch (Exception e)
            {
              Console.WriteLine(e.Message);
            }
            Console.ReadKey();
          }
        }
    }
```

Note: with respect to the first highlighted line in the solution, it is because we know that this particular file that is being read occupies less space than an `int` (which is what `FileStream.Read` takes as parameter) and is quite a small file that we were able to cast the file length to an `int` and direct that the read be done in one go. Normally, you should read the file chunk by chunk in a loop until you read all of its contents. The reason for this chunk by chunk reading is that there is a risk that the disk might not necessarily return the whole file to you in one go and therefore you have to ask the disk (via `Read`) for what you want, check what you have been given and if they don't match, keep asking until you get everything requested.

| 26. | Rewrite the solution to the exercise above, this time however, reading the file in safely, chunk by chunk. Presume that the file size fits into an integer.
Hint: `<FileStream>.Read(byte[] array, int offset, int count)` |

```
using System;
using System.IO;
using System.Text;

namespace PracticeYourCSharp
{
  class Program
  {
    static void Main(string[] args)
    {
      string dirName01 = "fstests";
      string fileName01 = "test_file_01.txt";
      string string01; // To get the data from the file
      byte[] byteArray01;

      try
      {
        Environment.CurrentDirectory =
        Environment.GetFolderPath(Environment.SpecialFolder.Desktop) +
                       Path.DirectorySeparatorChar + dirName01;
        FileStream fs01 = new FileStream(fileName01, FileMode.Open,
                                    FileAccess.ReadWrite);

        byteArray01 = new byte[(int)fs01.Length];
```

```
                    int bytesReadSoFar=0;
                    int numBytesToRead=(int)fs01.Length;
                    int bytesReadThisTime=0;

                    while(numBytesToRead > 0)
                    {
                      bytesReadThisTime = fs01.Read(byteArray01, bytesReadSoFar, numBytesToRead);
                      bytesReadSoFar += bytesReadThisTime;
                      numBytesToRead = numBytesToRead - bytesReadSoFar;
                    }
                    //We wrote it out in ASCII so we now convert it from ASCII to a string
                    string01 = Encoding.ASCII.GetString(byteArray01);

                    Console.WriteLine("The file contents are:\n{0}", string01);
                    fs01.Close();
                }
                catch (Exception e)
                {
                    Console.WriteLine(e.Message);
                }
                Console.ReadKey();
            }
        }
    }
```

27. Write a program which uses the `FileStream.Write` method to write the text *"Mary had a little lamb"* to a new file `test_file_03.txt` in the directory `fstests` in the UTF-16 encoding format.

    Also, print the following out: (1) the length of the string and (2) the length of the resulting file. Explain any difference between these two lengths.

    Hint: `Encoding.Unicode.GetBytes(<string>)`

```
using System;
using System.IO;
using System.Text;

namespace PracticeYourCSharp
{
    class Program
    {
        static void Main(string[] args)
        {
            string dirName01 = "fstests";
            string fileName01 = "test_file_03.txt";
            string newline = Environment.NewLine;
            string string01 = "Mary had a little lamb";

            //Print out the string length
            Console.WriteLine("The length of the input string = {0}", string01.Length);
            //Now translate the string to a string of bytes for the FileStream to write
            //We are however writing a UTF-16 string.
            //Don't forget that C# calls UTF-16 Unicode!
            byte[] byteArray01 = Encoding.Unicode.GetBytes(string01);

            try
            {
                //Change directory to the directory fstests
                Environment.CurrentDirectory =
                        Environment.GetFolderPath(Environment.SpecialFolder.Desktop) +
                                        Path.DirectorySeparatorChar + dirName01;

                FileStream fs01 = new FileStream(fileName01, FileMode.Append, FileAccess.Write);
                fs01.Write(byteArray01, 0, byteArray01.Length);
                //Print out the file size
                Console.WriteLine("File size = {0}",fs01.Length);
                fs01.Close();
```

	``` } catch (Exception e) { Console.WriteLine(e.Message); } Console.ReadKey(); } } } ```
	Observation/Explanation The input string length is 22 characters and this yielded a file size of 44 characters. The reason for this is that UTF-16 occupies 2 bytes per character.
28.	What does the method `FileStream.Seek` do?
	When a stream is open, there is a 'cursor' with which the `FileStream` keeps track of where it is within the file. Any operations regarding the file are relative to where the cursor is. This cursor can be moved back and forth explicitly by using the method `FileStream.Seek`. This kind of back and forth movement is quite helpful because we often do not necessarily access the contents of a file sequentially all the time and therefore the ability to jump from location to location within a file is more efficient than having to going through each byte of the file if it is not necessary. One example of where we might employ the use of this method is in cases where we have data sets of known fixed size and therefore we can move the cursor in multiples of the fixed size of the data set in question to target the needed data set rather than going through every single byte of the file.
29.	Explain the meaning of each of the following three constants: 1. `System.IO.SeekOrigin.Begin` 2. `System.IO.SeekOrigin.Current` 3. `System.IO.SeekOrigin.End`
	1. `Begin` – this constant is used to perform seek operations relative to the beginning of the file. For example, `<FileStream>.Seek(10,System.IO.SeekOrigin.Begin);` means *seek 10 from the beginning of the file*. 2. `Current` – this constant is used to perform seek operations relative to the current position of the cursor. 3. `End` – this constant is used to perform seek operations relative to the end of the file; and since the relative number can be a negative number this can be used to walk backwards through a file.
M	Manually modify the contents of the file `test_file_01.txt` to *"Mary had a little lamb"*.
30.	Write a program to change the word *"Mary"* in the file `test_file_01.txt` to *"John"*. Recall that the file is in ASCII format. After this, read the contents of the file and print them to the console. Open the file in Notepad to confirm the contents after running the program.
	``` using System; using System.IO; using System.Text; namespace PracticeYourCSharp { class Program { static void Main(string[] args) { string dirName01 = "fstests"; string fileName01 = "test_file_01.txt"; string string01 = "John"; string sFileContents; byte[] byteArray01 = Encoding.ASCII.GetBytes(string01); //convert "John" to ASCII byte[] byteArray02; // We will use this to read the contents back try { Environment.CurrentDirectory = Environment.GetFolderPath(Environment.SpecialFolder.Desktop) + Path.DirectorySeparatorChar + dirName01; ```

```
                FileStream fs01 = new FileStream(fileName01, FileMode.Open, FileAccess.ReadWrite);
                // The 'cursor' starts at the beginning of the file when using this
                // particular file mode.

                // Write the 1st 4 bytes in byteArray01 to the current cursor
                // position of the file.
                fs01.Write(byteArray01, 0, 4);

                byteArray02 = new byte[fs01.Length]; // we are going to use this
                // to read the file contents
                // Now move the 'file cursor' to a position 0 bytes away from the
                // beginning, i.e., move to the start of the file.
                fs01.Seek(0, System.IO.SeekOrigin.Begin);

                fs01.Read(byteArray02, 0, (int)fs01.Length);

                sFileContents = Encoding.ASCII.GetString(byteArray02);
                // Conversion of the ASCII byte array to a string.
                Console.WriteLine("The file contents are now: {0}", sFileContents);
                fs01.Close();
            }
            catch (Exception e)
            { Console.WriteLine(e.Message); }

            Console.ReadKey();
        }
    }
}
```

Notes

Please note the comments in the solution well.

An experiment to try: you can comment out the line containing `fs01.Seek` line and observe the resulting output. (First reset the file to its original contents).

BinaryWriter, BinaryReader, StreamWriter, StreamReader

The `FileStream` class gives fine control on a byte by byte basis over the contents of a file. In our exercises so far in writing data out using a `FileStream` we converted the data to an array of bytes first. Sometimes though, we just want to write to file C# strings (which are in Unicode), integers, floats and such like to disk without any direct concern for happenings at the byte level. We now go up to a higher layer that facilitates this ease of reading/writing; the *BinaryWriter/BinaryReader* and the *StreamWriter/StreamReader*.

31.	Explain why you would choose a `BinaryWriter/Reader` over a `StreamWriter/Reader`.
	If your data contains binary data, for example, mpeg files, jpeg files, then you should choose a `BinaryWriter/Reader`. However if your data contains *only* "textual" data, such as strings and numbers then choose a `StreamWriter/Reader`, as this is primarily used for representation of textual data.
	Note that a `BinaryWriter/Reader` is a valid Writer/Reader for the things that a `StreamWriter/Reader` can do.
32.	Using a `BinaryWriter`, store the following values into the file `file01.bin` in the earlier used directory `fstests`; 55, 22, 44, 870.1, "hello!".
	(so we're writing data of type int32, int32, int32, float and then a string).
| | ```
using System;
using System.IO;

namespace PracticeYourCSharp
{
  class Program
  {
    static void Main(string[] args)
    {
      string dirName01 = "fstests";
      string fileName01 = "file_01.bin";

      try
``` |
```

|  | ```
        {
          Environment.CurrentDirectory =
                    Environment.GetFolderPath(Environment.SpecialFolder.Desktop) +
                    Path.DirectorySeparatorChar + dirName01;

          FileStream fs01 = new FileStream(fileName01, FileMode.OpenOrCreate,
                                                      FileAccess.ReadWrite);
          BinaryWriter bw01 = new BinaryWriter(fs01);

          bw01.Write(55); bw01.Write(22); bw01.Write(44); bw01.Write(870.1);
          bw01.Write("Hello");

          bw01.Close(); // Also closes the underlying stream
        }
        catch (Exception e)
        { Console.WriteLine(e.Message); }
        Console.ReadKey();
      }
    }
}
``` |
| 33. | Using a `BinaryReader`, read back the data written out in the preceding exercise and print it out to the console. |
| | ```
using System;
using System.IO;

namespace PracticeYourCSharp
{
  class Program
  {
    static void Main(string[] args)
    {
      string dirName01 = "fstests";
      string fileName01 = "file_01.bin";

      try
      {
        Environment.CurrentDirectory =
                  Environment.GetFolderPath(Environment.SpecialFolder.Desktop) +
                  Path.DirectorySeparatorChar + dirName01;

        FileStream fs01 = new FileStream(fileName01, FileMode.Open,
                                                    FileAccess.Read);
        BinaryReader br01 = new BinaryReader(fs01);

        // Since we know what we wrote, let's read & print
        Console.WriteLine(br01.ReadInt32());
        Console.WriteLine(br01.ReadInt32());
        Console.WriteLine(br01.ReadInt32());
        Console.WriteLine(br01.ReadDouble());
        Console.WriteLine(br01.ReadString());

        br01.Close(); // This also closes the underlying stream.
      }
      catch (Exception e)
      {   Console.WriteLine(e.Message); }
      Console.ReadKey();
      }
    }
}
```
**Note:** A `BinaryReader` requires that you know what kind of data you wrote to the file and in which order. For example, if you have data of a single type in a file it is straightforward to write a loop to read the data from a file. If you write mixed data to the file, your program has to know the kind and order of the data. |
| 34. | Using a `BinaryWriter`, write the integers from `1000` to `1115` to a file and then using a `BinaryReader`, read them back and print them out. |

```
using System;
using System.IO;

namespace PracticeYourCSharp
{
  class Program
  {
    static void Main(string[] args)
    {
      string dirName01 = "fstests";
      string fileName01 = "file_02.bin";

      try
      {
        Environment.CurrentDirectory =
                Environment.GetFolderPath(Environment.SpecialFolder.Desktop) +
                                Path.DirectorySeparatorChar + dirName01;

        FileStream fs01 = new FileStream(fileName01, FileMode.OpenOrCreate,
                                              FileAccess.ReadWrite);
        BinaryWriter bw01 = new BinaryWriter(fs01);
        for (int i = 1000; i <= 1115; i++)
          bw01.Write(i);

        // Alright, now read them back using a loop.
        Console.WriteLine("At the reader!");
        BinaryReader br01 = new BinaryReader(fs01);
        br01.BaseStream.Position = 0;
        // Says "set the underlying stream to the start"
        // We could also have written fs01.Seek(0, SeekOrigin.Begin);

        long length = fs01.Length;
        int iInput;
        for (long count = 0; count < fs01.Length; count += sizeof(Int32))
        {
          iInput = br01.ReadInt32();
          Console.WriteLine(iInput);
        }

        bw01.Close();// Also closes the underlying stream
        br01.Close();
      }
      catch (Exception e)
      { Console.WriteLine(e.Message); }
      Console.ReadKey();
    }
  }
}
```

35.	How does `BinaryWriter` store numbers?
	`BinaryWriter` stores numbers in the same format in which they are stored in memory. For example, an `int` occupies 4 bytes in memory; `BinaryWriter` will use only 4 bytes to store it in a file in the same format in which an `int` variable is represented in memory.
36.	What is the data that `BinaryWriter` prepends a stored string with and why?
	`BinaryWriter` prepends any string it writes out with the length of the string. The reason for why this prepending is done is so that a `BinaryReader` knows how many bytes it should read when it is directed to read a string from a file.
37.	For a `FileStream`, if we want to seek to a position, we use the `Seek` method. What is the equivalent `Seek` method for `BinaryReader/Writer`?
	`<BinaryReader/Writer>.BaseStream.Position = <int position>` Think of *BaseStream* as meaning *"underlying stream"*.

StreamWriter, StreamReader

38. Using a `StreamWriter`, write the following three line rhyme to a file named `rhyme.txt` in the directory `fstests`;

Mary had a little lamb
little lamb
Mary had a little lamb that was as white as snow.

```csharp
using System;
using System.IO;

namespace PracticeYourCSharp
{
  class Program
  {
    static void Main(string[] args)
    {
      string dirName01 = "fstests";
      string fileName01 = "rhyme.txt";

      try
      {
        Environment.CurrentDirectory =
        Environment.GetFolderPath(Environment.SpecialFolder.Desktop) +
        Path.DirectorySeparatorChar + dirName01;

        FileStream fs01 = new FileStream(fileName01, FileMode.OpenOrCreate,
                                         FileAccess.ReadWrite);
        StreamWriter sw01 = new StreamWriter(fs01);
        sw01.WriteLine("Mary had a little lamb");
        sw01.WriteLine("little lamb");
        sw01.WriteLine("Mary had a little lamb that was as white as snow");
        sw01.Close(); // Also closes the underlying stream
      }
      catch (Exception e)
      {
        Console.WriteLine(e.Message);
        Console.WriteLine(e.ToString());
      }
      Console.ReadKey();
    }
  }
}
```

39. Using a `StreamReader`, read the data back from the file `rhyme.txt` created earlier and output the data to the console.

```csharp
using System;
using System.IO;
using System.Text;

namespace PracticeYourCSharp
{
  class Program
  {
    static void Main(string[] args)
    {
      string dirName01 = "fstests";
      string fileName01 = "rhyme.txt";

      try
      {
        Environment.CurrentDirectory =
        Environment.GetFolderPath(Environment.SpecialFolder.Desktop) +
        Path.DirectorySeparatorChar + dirName01;

        FileStream fs01 = new FileStream(fileName01, FileMode.Open, FileAccess.ReadWrite);
        StreamReader sr01 = new StreamReader(fs01);
```

|  | ```
        while (sr01.Peek() != -1)
        {
          string s = sr01.ReadLine();
          Console.Write("{0}\n", s);
          //Note that we have to add \n to the end of our output so that its prints out properly
        }
        sr01.Close();
      }
      catch (Exception e)
      {
        Console.WriteLine(e.Message);
        Console.WriteLine(e.ToString());
      }
      Console.ReadKey();
    }
  }
}
``` |
| 40. | Using a `StreamWriter`, write the number 17 to a file called number.txt and then print out the file length. |
| | ```
using System;
using System.IO;

namespace PracticeYourCSharp
{
  class Program
  {
    static void Main(string[] args)
    {
      string dirName01 = "fstests";
      string fileName01 = "number.txt";

      try
      {
        Environment.CurrentDirectory =
        Environment.GetFolderPath(Environment.SpecialFolder.Desktop) +
        Path.DirectorySeparatorChar + dirName01;

        FileStream fs01 = new FileStream(fileName01, FileMode.Open, FileAccess.ReadWrite);
        StreamWriter sw01 = new StreamWriter(fs01);
        sw01.Write(17);
        Console.WriteLine("The file length = " + fs01.Length);
        sw01.Close(); // Also closes the underlying stream
      }
      catch (Exception e)
      {
        Console.WriteLine(e.Message);
        Console.WriteLine(e.ToString());
      }
      Console.ReadKey();
    }
  }
}
```
**Note:** Contrast this file size with the file size when such an integer value is written out using a `BinaryWriter`. |
| 41. | Using a `StreamReader`, read back the data written to the file in the preceding exercise and convert it back to an integer. |
|  | ```
using System;
using System.IO;

namespace PracticeYourCSharp
{
  class Program
  {
    static void Main(string[] args)
``` |
```

```csharp
      {
        string dirName01 = "fstests";
        string fileName01 = "number.txt";
        int i01;

        try
        {
          Environment.CurrentDirectory =
          Environment.GetFolderPath(Environment.SpecialFolder.Desktop) +
          Path.DirectorySeparatorChar + dirName01;

          FileStream fs01 = new FileStream(fileName01, FileMode.Open, FileAccess.ReadWrite);
          StreamReader sr01 = new StreamReader(fs01);
          while (sr01.Peek() != -1)
          {
            string s = sr01.ReadLine();
            if (Int32.TryParse(s, out i01))
            {
              Console.WriteLine("The recovered integer = {0}", i01);
            }
            Console.Write("{0}", s);
          }
          sr01.Close();
        }
        catch (Exception e)
        {
          Console.WriteLine(e.Message);
          Console.WriteLine(e.ToString());
        }
        Console.ReadKey();
      }
    }
  }
}
```

E1	Write a program which can read in the contents of a file whose length is greater than Int.MaxValue.
E2	Do a comparison of the file handling methods shown in this chapter with the file handling methods of class File as used in Chapter 16.

Chapter 35. File Streams II: A Finer Look at File I/O

This chapter is written with the intent to ensure that the reader has an even deeper understanding of exactly what is written to disk when files are written, taking encoding into account. This chapter builds on the immediately preceding chapter.

In order to understand and appreciate this chapter, the reader needs to have worked through Chapter 33. Character Encoding as well as Chapter 34. File Streams I.

Key classes utilized in this chapter include `FileStream`, `BinaryReader`, `BinaryWriter`, `StreamReader`, `StreamWriter` and `Encoding`.

1.	Write a program which will save the integer value 37 to a file using a `StreamWriter` and the default encoding of a `StreamWriter` (UTF-8). Use `FileMode.Create`. Read back the contents *into a byte array* using a **BinaryReader** and explain the contents. (A `BinaryReader` is being used because we want to look at the exact bytes written to disk, and `BinaryReader` is the correct class for such operations).
| | ```
using System;
using System.IO;

namespace PracticeYourCSharp
{
  class Program
  {
    static void Main(string[] args)
    {
      string dirName01 = "fstests";
       // directory for output on the desktop. Must already exist.
      string fileName01 = "file_03.bin";

      try
      {
        Environment.CurrentDirectory =
                    Environment.GetFolderPath(Environment.SpecialFolder.Desktop)
                    + Path.DirectorySeparatorChar + dirName01;
        FileStream fs01 = new FileStream(fileName01, FileMode.Create,
                                          FileAccess.ReadWrite);
        StreamWriter sw01 = new StreamWriter(fs01);
        sw01.Write(37);
        sw01.Flush(); // Make sure it writes it to disk before we go read it.

        BinaryReader br01 = new BinaryReader(fs01);
        br01.BaseStream.Seek(0, SeekOrigin.Begin); // back to the start of the stream
        // Now read it in as a string of bytes
        byte[] byteArray = br01.ReadBytes((int)fs01.Length);
        // We cast to int only because we know it is a short file

        Console.WriteLine("The number of bytes read = {0}", byteArray.Length);
        Console.WriteLine("The bytes are:");   // Now write the bytes out
        for (int x = 0; x < byteArray.Length; x++)
        {
          Console.Write(byteArray[x]);
          Console.Write(" ");
        }

        br01.Close(); // This also closes the underlying stream.
``` |
```

	``
            }
            catch (Exception e)
            { Console.WriteLine(e.Message); }
            Console.ReadKey();
        }
    }
}
```
**Output:** `51 55` *(it says that only 2 bytes are present in the file and these are their values)*
**Explanation/Analysis:** (As you know, the default encoding scheme for the `StreamWriter` is UTF-8, which for characters in the ASCII range is the same, therefore for items in that number range, you can look either at a UTF-8 table or an ASCII table).
We note that the output is `51 55`. We can look at either a UTF-8 conversion table or an ASCII table to convert these. We find that `51` and `55` correspond to the characters `3` and `7` respectively…and what did we write? `37`!
What this means is that the `StreamWriter` writes the string representation of whatever we given it. |
| 2. | Write a program, using a `StreamWriter`, to store the number `289.57` into a file using a `StreamWriter`. Read back the contents into a *byte array* using a `BinaryReader` and explain the contents. *(simply modify the solution code to the preceding exercise)* |
|   | **Output:** `50 56 57 46 53 55` *(it says that 6 bytes are present in the file and these are their values)*
**Explanation/Analysis:** Looking at an ASCII table or at a UTF-8 table, we convert these bytes as follows: `[2][8][9][.][5][7]` … in short the string representation of `289.57`.
Clearly it can be seen the value we gave was converted to a UTF-8 string and put into the file as in the preceding exercise. |
| 3. | Write a program, using a `StreamWriter`, to store the character '€' into a file using a `StreamWriter`. Read back the contents into a *byte array* using a `BinaryReader` and explain the contents. *(simply modify the code for the preceding exercise).* |
|   | **Output:** `226 130 172` *(there are 3 bytes are present in the file and these are their values).*
This converts to `E2 82 AC` (Hex).

**Explanation/Analysis:** A UTF-8 table has to be consulted to translate this sequence of characters (this is beyond the ASCII character range); the UTF-8 table will confirm that these 3 bytes are the UTF-8 representation of the character '€'.

This exercise simply confirms that the default output encoding for a `StreamWriter` is UTF-8. |
| 4. | Write a program which uses a `BinaryWriter` to write the number `37` to a file. Read back the contents into a *byte array* using a `BinaryReader` and explain the contents. |
|   | ```
using System;
using System.IO;

namespace PracticeYourCSharp
{
    class Program
    {
        static void Main(string[] args)
        {
            string dirName01 = "fstests";
            string fileName01 = "file_03.bin";

            try
            {
                Environment.CurrentDirectory =
                    Environment.GetFolderPath(Environment.SpecialFolder.Desktop) +
                    Path.DirectorySeparatorChar + dirName01;

                FileStream fs01 = new FileStream(fileName01, FileMode.Create, FileAccess.ReadWrite);

                BinaryWriter bw01 = new BinaryWriter(fs01);
                bw01.Write(37);
                bw01.Flush(); // Make sure it writes it.

                BinaryReader br01 = new BinaryReader(fs01);
``` |

```
          br01.BaseStream.Seek(0, SeekOrigin.Begin); // Back to the start of the stream
          // Now read it in as a string of bytes
          byte[] byteArray = br01.ReadBytes((int)fs01.Length);
          Console.WriteLine("The number of bytes read = {0}", byteArray.Length);
          // Now write the bytes out
          for (int x = 0; x < byteArray.Length; x++)
          {
            Console.Write(byteArray[x]);
            Console.Write(" ");
          }
          br01.Close(); // This also closes the underlying stream.
        }
        catch (Exception e)
        { Console.WriteLine(e.Message); }
        Console.ReadKey();
      }
    }
}
```

Output: 37 0 0 0 *(it says that only 4 bytes are present in the file and these are their values).*

Explanation/Analysis: The `BinaryWriter` writes numbers out in the form in which they are stored in memory. The number 37 is an `int` (which occupies 4 bytes in memory) and that is why we have four bytes returned in the file. The data is written out to the file in reverse byte order. The correct/natural byte order is 0 0 0 37. Converting this back to its decimal representation we get 37.

What this means is that the `BinaryWriter` writes the actual in-memory reprentation of numerical types.

5.	Repeat the same experiment using a value of 950.	
	Output: What is read back is: 182 3 0 0 (It is in reverse byte order, so we set the bytes aright as 0 0 3 182). Converting this back to its base 10 representation we get the original value $3*2^8 + 182 = 950$	
6.	Repeat the same experiment using a value of 65801.	
	Findings: The printed contents are 9 1 1 0, so we manually convert it to its correct/natural byte order which is 0 1 1 9. We convert it to base 10 as follows: $0*2^{32} + 1*2^{16} + 1*2^8 + 9 = 65801$	
7.	What main difference(s) do you observe between the way a `BinaryWriter` writes data versus the way a `StreamWriter` writes data out?	The `StreamWriter` converts what is being written out to a string and then encodes it in UTF-8 and writes it out. The `BinaryWriter` on the other hand takes the internal representation of the data and writes it out that way to the target file (with some prepended fields if necessary).
8.	Using a `BinaryWriter`, write the single-precision floating point number 289.57 to a file. Read back the contents into a `byte array` using a `BinaryReader` and explain the contents.	The resulting bytes, accounting for byte-order, are the following 4 bytes: 67 144 200 246 This corresponds to the IEEE format for storing single-precision floating point values. Contrast this with the way in which a `StreamWriter` stores the same data.
9.	Using a `StreamWriter`, store the character 'A' in a file. Read back the contents using a `BinaryReader` into a byte array and explain the contents.	**Output:** 65 This is the UTF-8 representation of the character A. Therefore, for single characters (non-numeric), the `BinaryWriter` simply writes out the UTF-8 representation of the character in question.
10.	Using a `BinaryWriter`, store the character '€' in a file. Read back the contents using a `BinaryReader` into a `byte` array and explain the contents.	**Output:** 226 130 172 *(decimal)* This is the UTF-8 representation of the character €. Therefore, for single non-numeric characters (non-numeric), the `BinaryWriter` simply writes out the UTF-8 representation of the character in question. This in this case is the same as for a `StreamWriter`.
11.	Using a `StreamWriter`, store the string "*Hello*" in a file. Read back the contents using a `BinaryReader` and explain the contents.	**Output:** 72 101 108 108 111 Looking at the UTF-8 table (the ASCII table will suffice for these characters) this corresponds to: [H] [e] [l] [l] [o]

12.	Using a `BinaryWriter`, store the string *"Hello"* in a file. Read back the contents using a `BinaryReader` and explain the contents.	5 72 101 108 108 111 We see the prefix 5, which indicates that a 5-character string follows. However, the rest of the string is exactly the same as in the `StreamWriter` case.
	Summary/Conclusions: `StreamWriters` always convert the data, whether `string`, `char` or number to a `string` which by default it encodes as UTF-8 and then writes them out. `BinaryWriters` however, for numbers, use the internal representation of a number as the format in which they write numbers out. The `BinaryWriter` writes `char` and `string` data out in UTF-8 representation; for strings the data is prepended by a prefix which indicates the length of the string.	

Chapter 36. Saving Your Objects to Disk: Serialization & Deserialization (Introduction)

There are times when it is desirable to save objects to disk for later retrieval. In our work so far in this book, we have not retained object state information. In this chapter, we present exercises that deal with converting objects to a storable form (serialization), saving them to disk and then reading the serialized objects back from disk and restoring them back to object form (deserialization).

Key classes used in this chapter include `Stream` and `BinaryFormatter`.

1.	Explain the concepts of *Serialization* and *Deserialization*.	Serialization is the means by which objects are converted to a form of choice (Binary, XML, SOAP) and stored in, or transmitted to a location of choice, which could include a flat file, a database, memory or across a network. Deserialization is the process of taking the serialized data and converting it back to the original object form.
2.	Why serialize objects?	Serialization is useful in the following scenarios (not limited to these): when you want to retain object state in-between program sessions (for example character states in games) and when you want to transmit an object to another system in a form that the target system can use to reconstruct the object.
3.	What are the types of serialization that exist in C#? Describe them briefly.	1. *Binary serialization* – this converts to and stores the object(s) as a stream of bytes. 2. *XML serialization* – this puts the fields of the object in question in the form of an XML stream according to a user-specified schema. 3. *SOAP serialization* – this is actually a variant of XML serialization which serializes objects into an XML stream that conforms to the SOAP specification.
4.	What key differences are there between binary and XML serialization?	Binary serialization can serialize all the fields of the type being serialized, whereas XML serialization serializes only public properties and fields; in short XML serialization does not preserve the full fidelity of the type being serialized.
5.	How do you make a class serializable?	Add the following *attribute*, (*brackets included*) just above the definition of the class that you want to serialize: `[Serializable]`
6.	Are structures serializable?	Yes. The same way as classes.
7.	If a given class is serializable, are its child classes automatically serializable?	No. The `[Serializable]` attribute has to be put just above each class that is intended to be serializable; child classes do not inherit the `[Serializable]` attribute from their parent classes.
8.	Will the constructor for an object be called when the object is deserialized?	No. This is a fact that one should be aware of if the constructor does more than initialize field values (field values are preserved in the serialization).

9.	Given the program below, write code to implement binary serialization and deserialization of the object `circle01`.
	
	To verify the correct functioning of your code, serialize the object `circle01` and then recover the serialized object of class `Circle` into a new `Circle` object `circle02` and print out the area, circumference and diameter thereof to prove that indeed the values of `circle02` do correspond to that of `circle01`.
	
	`[Serializable]`
	`public class Circle`
	`{`
	`    private float radius;`	

```csharp
    public Circle(float radius)
    {
      this.radius = radius;
    }

    public double area
    {
      get { return (Math.PI * radius * radius); }
    }
    public double circumference
    {
      get { return (Math.PI * 2 * radius); }
    }
    public double diameter
    {
      get { return (2 * radius); }
    }
    public float GetRadius()
    {
      return (radius);
    }
}

static void Main(string[] args)
{
  Circle circle01 = new Circle(12.53f);
}
```

```csharp
using System;
using System.Collections.Generic;
using System.Text;
using System.IO;
using System.Runtime.Serialization; // For serialization
using System.Runtime.Serialization.Formatters.Binary; // For serialization

namespace PracticeYourCSharp
{
  // Add the statement [Serializable] to the top of the circle class

  [Serializable]
  public class Circle
  {
      //Class Circle definition placed here
  }

  class Program
  {
    public static void SerializeCircle(Circle x, string serFile)
    {
      // -- Serialization method --
      BinaryFormatter formatter = new BinaryFormatter();
      Stream stream = new FileStream(serFile, FileMode.Create, FileAccess.Write,
                                                      FileShare.None);
      formatter.Serialize(stream, x);
      stream.Close();
    }

    public static Circle DeSerializeCircle(string serFile)
    {
      // -- Deserialization method --
      BinaryFormatter formatter = new BinaryFormatter();
      Stream stream = new FileStream(serFile, FileMode.Open, FileAccess.Read, FileShare.Read);
      Circle x = (Circle)formatter.Deserialize(stream);
      stream.Close();
```

```csharp
            return (x);
        }

        static void Main(string[] args)
        {
            Environment.CurrentDirectory =
                           Environment.GetFolderPath(Environment.SpecialFolder.Desktop);
            string serFile = "ser01.bin";
            // The file into which we will store the data on the desktop.

            Circle circle01 = new Circle(12.53f);
            Console.WriteLine("this type is {0}", circle01.GetType().Name);
            Console.WriteLine("radius = {0}", circle01. GetRadius());
            Console.WriteLine("Area = {0}", circle01.area);
            Console.WriteLine("Diameter = {0}", circle01.GetRadius(), circle01.diameter);
            Console.WriteLine("Circumference ={0}", circle01.GetRadius(), circle01.circumference);
            Console.WriteLine("Now going to serialize");
            SerializeCircle(circle01, serFile);

            Console.WriteLine("Now going to deserialize");

            Circle circle02 = DeSerializeCircle(serFile);
            // We've deserialized circle01 into circle02. Let's look at the values of circle01 to
            // indeed prove that we deserialized properly.
            Console.WriteLine("this type is {0}", circle02.GetType().Name);
            Console.WriteLine("radius = {0}", circle02.GetRadius());
            Console.WriteLine("Area = {0}", circle02.area);
            Console.WriteLine("Diameter = {0}", circle02.GetRadius(), circle01.diameter);
            Console.WriteLine("Circumference ={0}", circle02.GetRadius(), circle01.circumference);
            Console.ReadKey();
        }
    }
}
```

10. We have the following `Circle` objects which have been put into a `List<Circle>` as follows:

    ```csharp
    Circle circle_01 = new Circle(2.5F); Circle circle_02 = new Circle(3.5F);
    Circle circle_03 = new Circle(12F);  Circle circle_04 = new Circle(25F);
    List<Circle> circleList01 = new List<Circle>();
    circleList01.Add(circle_01); circleList01.Add(circle_02); circleList01.Add(circle_03);
    circleList01.Add(circle_04);
    ```

    Write a program which serializes and then deserializes this `List<Circle>`, printing out the radius of each of the `Circle` objects in the deserialized list.

    Add the following methods to the solution to the preceding exercise:

    ```csharp
    public static void SerializeCircleList(List<Circle> x, string serList)
    {
      // -- Serialization method --
      BinaryFormatter formatter = new BinaryFormatter();
      Stream stream = new FileStream(serList, FileMode.Create, FileAccess.Write, FileShare.None);
      formatter.Serialize(stream, x);
      stream.Close();
    }

    public static List<Circle> DeSerializeCircleList(string serList)
    {
      // -- Deserialization method --
      BinaryFormatter formatter = new BinaryFormatter();
      Stream stream = new FileStream(serList, FileMode.Open, FileAccess.Read, FileShare.Read);
      List<Circle> x = (List<Circle>)formatter.Deserialize(stream);
      stream.Close();
      return (x);
    }
    ```

```
static void Main(string[] args)
{
  Environment.CurrentDirectory = Environment.GetFolderPath(Environment.SpecialFolder.Desktop);
  string serFile = "ser01.bin"; // The file into which we will store the data on the desktop.

  Console.WriteLine("Going to serialize this circle list of circles of radius 2.5,
            3.5,12,25");
  Circle circle_01 = new Circle(2.5F); Circle circle_02 = new Circle(3.5F);
  Circle circle_03 = new Circle(12F);  Circle circle_04 = new Circle(25F);
  List<Circle> circleList01 = new List<Circle>();
  circleList01.Add(circle_01); circleList01.Add(circle_02); circleList01.Add(circle_03);
  circleList01.Add(circle_04);
  SerializeCircleList(circleList01, serFile);
  Console.WriteLine("Serialization of circle list done. Now going to deserialize it");

  List<Circle> circleList02 = DeSerializeCircleList(serFile);
  Console.WriteLine("The circle list has been deserialized");
  foreach (Circle cc in circleList02)
    {
      Console.WriteLine("The radius is {0}", cc.GetRadius());
    }
}
```

E1	In addition to the earlier defined class `Circle`, I also have a class `Square` defined as follows:
	``public class Square
{
  private float length;

  public Square(float length)
  {
    this.length = length;
  }

  public double area
  {
    get { return (length * length); }
  }
  public double perimeter
  {
    get { return (length * 4); }
  }
  public float GetLength()
  {
    return (length);
  }
}``` |
| | We have the following objects: an object of class `Circle` of radius 25 and an object of class `Square` of side length 15.
Write code to perform binary serialization and deserialization of the objects into/from a single file. |
| | **Hint:** To deserialize the objects, read each of the deserialized objects into a `List<object>` and then using the method `<object>.GetType()` determine the correct class of the deserialized object and assign it to an object of the correct class. |
| E2 | Do *XML* serialization and deserialization of the same example given above. |

Index

6.0 Features

autoproperty initializer, *244*
Exception filters, *263*
expression bodied methods, *178*, *202*
expression bodied properties, *244*
index initializer, *131*
null propagating operator, *162*, *238*
property initializer, *243*
string interpolation, *7*
`using static`, *3*

A

accessor
    Properties, *241*
Arrays, *73*
    multi-dimensional arrays, *79*
        Length, *79*
        Rank, *79*
Attributes
    [Serializable], *293*

B

Boolean, *45*
    value
        False, *45*
        True, *45*
Boxing/Unboxing, *18*, *186*

C

casting, *18*
    implicit, *19*
    objects, *18*
class
    inheritance, *194*
    inheritance(multiple), *194*
    member accessibility
        internal, *190*
        private, *190*
        protected, *190*, *196*
        protected internal, *190*
        public, *190*
    member modifier
        abstract, *203*
        new, *203*
        override, *203*
        sealed, *203*
        static, *203*
    member modifier
        virtual, *203*
    methods
        abstract, *205*
        expression bodied methods, *178*
        hiding(new), *203*, *210*
        method declaration, *173*
        method signature, *173*
        overloading, *173*
        passing by reference, *175*
        passing by value, *175*
        sealed, *208*
        static, *173*
        virtual, *210*
    static, *201*
    type, *200*
        abstract, *189*, *200*, *204*
        internal, *200*
        partial, *200*
        public, *190*
        sealed, *189*, *200*, *208*
        static, *200*
class (definition), *189*
class (members), *189*
Class Listing
    Collections
        Dictionary, *131*
        List, *127*
        SortedDictionary, *132*
    Encoding
        UnicodeEncoding, *271*
        UTF32Encoding, *271*
        UTF8Encoding, *271*
    Input/Output/File System
        BinaryReader, *283*
        BinaryWriter, *283*
        Directory, *141*
        DriveInfo, *135*
        File, *149*
        FileInfo, *149*
        StreamReader, *283*
        StreamWriter, *283*
    Misc
        ArrayList, *187*
        BinaryFormatter, *294*
        BitConverter, *270*
        Char, *108*
        Console, *5*
        Environment, *135*
        KeyValuePair, *133*
    String
        StringBuilder, *165*
        StringInfo, *268*
        `System.Object` (`object`), *186*
        Tuple, *231*
    Numerical
        BigInteger, *33*
        Complex, *31*
        Int32, *29*
        Math, *23*
    Time
        DateTime, *115*
        Stopwatch, *125*, *169*
        TimeSpan, *119*
Collections, *127*
    Dictionary, *131*
    List, *127*
    Queue, *127*
    SortedDictionary, *132*
    Stack, *127*
Comments
    /*...*/, *3*
    //, *3*
Conditional Operators, *67*
    else, *67*
    if, *67*
    if/else, *67*
    multiple conditions, *69*
    switch statement, *70*
        break, *70*
        case, *70*
        default, *70*
constants, *21*, *22*
    DateTime.MaxValue/MinValue, *120*
    Double.MaxValue, *15*
    Double.MinValue, *15*
    Float.MinValue, *14*
    Infinity(∞), *30*
    Math.E, *21*
    Math.PI, *21*
    NaN, *30*
    Negative Infinity(-∞), *30*
    Single.Epsilon, *15*
constructor, *191*
    calling parents', *191*, *195*
    default parameterless, *191*
    invoking from other constructor, *198*
    overloaded, *193*, *198*
    parameterless, *191*
control characters
    new line '\n', *5*

D

Delegate Type, 247
Delegates, 247
    chaining/multi-cast, 248
Deserialization, 293
Destructor, 194
Directive
    `using`, 1
    `using static`, 3
dynamic resolution, 221

E

Encoding schemes
    ASCII, 266
    Unicode
        UTF-16, 266
        UTF-32, 266
        UTF-8, 266
Endianness, 269
    big-endian, 269
    little endian, 269
enum, 181
    default value, 181
escape characters
    " \i, 6
    string
        @, 6
Exceptions, 253
    Example
        System.DivideByZeroException, 30, 253
        System.Exception, 257
        System.FileNotFoundException, 255
        System.IndexOutOfRangeException, 256
        System.NullReferenceException, 254
        System.OverflowException, 29, 254
    filters, 263
    finally, 258
    rethrowing, 262
    throwing, 259
    user defined, 261
expression bodied methods, 202

F

FileStream
    `FileAccess` modes, 274
    `FileMode`, 273
    `FileShare` mode, 275
Formatting
    tab '\t', 5
    style
        composite formatting, 8
        concatenation, 8
        string interpolation, 8
formatting(output)
    DateTime, 122
    method `String.Format`, 65
    numerical
        currency, 37
        exponential format E, 38
        format D, 37
        format G, 39
        format P, 40
        hexadecimal, 40, 41
        hexadecimal format (justified), 40, 41
        justification, 34
        output precision, 36, 38
        scientific notation, 37
    strings, 63
        left justification, 64
        right justification, 64

G

Generics, 127
getter *(see properties)*, 241

I

instance, 186
Interface, 225
    IComparer, 226
Iterations
    do while loop, 86
    for loop, 82
    foreach, 84
    infinite loops, 86
    keyword
        break, 90
        continue, 88
        goto, 88, 89
        label, 88
    nested loops, 87
    while loop, 81

K

keyword
    abstract, 189, 200
    abstract (member modifier), 203
    as, 220
    base, 194, 198, 222, 223
    bool, 45
    byte, 10
    catch, 253
    checked, 29
    class, 189
    const, 21
    decimal, 15
    default, 9
    delegate, 247
    do, 86
    double, 15
    dynamic, 221
    else, 67
    enum, 181
    false, 45
    finally, 258
    float, 14
    for, 82
    foreach, 84
    if, 67
    in, 84
    int, 9
    interface, 226
    internal, 200
    is, 219
    long, 12
    namespace, 1
    new, 73
    new (member modifier), 203
    null, 56
    object, 186
    operator, 239
    out, 175, 234
    override (member modifier), 203
    params, 176
    partial, 200
    private, 190
    protected, 190
    public, 190
    readonly, 223
    ref, 175, 234, 236
    return, 3, 203
    sbyte, 11
    sealed, 189, 200
    sealed (member modifier), 203
    short, 11
    sizeof, 267
    static, 200
    static (member modifier), 203
    static readonly, 224
    switch, 70
    this, 192, 199
    throw, 259
    true, 45
    try, 253
    typeof, 183
    uint, 9

Index

ulong, *13*
unchecked, *30*
ushort, *12*
using, *1*
value, *241*
var, *171*
virtual (member modifier), *203*
void, *2*
while, *81*

L

label, *88*

M

Math
  keyword
    checked, *29*
    overflow, *20*
Math operations
  integer overflow, *29*
  integer/integral overflow, *29*
Matrix/Matrices, *79*

N

named arguments, *177*
namespace (definition), *1*
Nullable Types, *159*
  null coalescing operator, *162*
Number Types
  BigInteger, *33*
  byte(**byte**), *10*
  Complex Numbers, *31*
  decimal, *16*
  decimal(**decimal**), *16*
  double(**double**), *15*
  float(**float**), *14*
  Hexadecimal numbers, *34*
  integer(**int**), *9*
  long integer(**long**), *12*
  short integer(**short**), *11*
  signed byte(**sbyte**), *11*
  suffixes/postfix, *17*
  unsigned integer(**uint**), *9*
  unsigned long integer(**ulong**), *13*
  unsigned short integer(**ushort**), *12*

O

object (definition), *186*
object instantiation, *186*
Operator overloading, *239*
operators
  as, *220*

Bitwise
  AND (&), *42*
  one's complement (~), *43*
  OR(|), *42*
  XOR (^), *42*
Boolean
  !=, *47*
  &, *48*
  ^, *50*
  |, *52*
  <, *46*
  <=, *46*
  ==, *45*
  >, *45*
  >=, *46*
  short-circuiting, *48*
  &&, *48*
  ||, *49*
default, *9*
is, *219*
lambda (=>), *178*
Math
  Addition(+), *22*
  Decrement(--), *31*
  Division(/), *28*
  Increment(++), *31*
  left-shift (<<), *43*
  multiplication (*), *20*
  Remainder(%), *22*
  right-shift (>>), *43*
  shorthand, *32*
    *=, *32*
    /=, *32*
    +=, *32*
    -=, *32*
  Subtraction(-), *22*
null coalescing operator, *162*
null-propagating
  ?., *162*
ternary operator ?:, *70*
optional arguments/default parameter values, *179*

P

parameter
  passing by reference, *175*
  passing by value, *175*
parameter array, *176*
passing by reference, *233*
passing by value, *233*
polymorphism, *18*, *203*
Properties, *241*
  abstract, *245*
  automatic/ auto-implemented, *242*
  autoproperty initializer, *244*

  backing store, *242*
  expression bodied, *244*
  getter, *241*
  initializers, *243*
  read/write, *241*
  read-only, *241*
  setter, *241*
  static, *241*
  virtual, *243*, *244*
  write-only, *241*

S

Serialization, *293*
  Binary, *293*
  SOAP, *293*
  XML, *293*
setter *(see properties)*, *241*
string
  immutability, *55*
  string/char relationship, *110*
structures (**struct**), *227*

T

Tuples, *231*
type, *185*
  char, *105*
  default value, *185*
  reference type, *185*
  reference type, passing, *233*
  value type, *185*
  var, *171*

U

Unicode, *105*, *265*
  Basic Multilingual Plane(BMP), *265*
  code plane, *265*
  code point, *265*
  encoding schemes, *266*
    UTF-16, *266*
    UTF-32, *266*
    UTF-8, *266*
  Mapping to BMP, *268*
  Supplemental Planes, *265*
  surrogate
    lead/high surrogate, *266*
    trail/low surrogate, *266*
unified type system, *186*

V

variable, *185*

Made in the USA
Middletown, DE
19 February 2021